Blood and Fire

A book in the series

Latin America Otherwise: Languages, Empires, Nations

Series editors: Walter D. Mignolo, Duke University

Irene Silverblatt, Duke University

Sonia Saldívar-Hull, University of California at Los Angeles

Blood and Fire

La Violencia in Antioquia, Colombia, 1946–1953

MARY ROLDÁN

Duke University Press   Durham and London 2002

© 2002 Duke University Press
Printed in the United States of
America on acid-free paper ∞
Designed by Rebecca Giménez
Typeset in Adobe Minion by
Tseng Information Systems, Inc.
Library of Congress Cataloging-
in-Publication Data appear on
the last printed page of this book.
Publication of this book was made
possible by a subvention granted
by the Hull Memorial Publication
Fund of Cornell University.

Frontispiece: Urrao, August 1953.
To heal the wounds of three years
of partisan strife, the parish priest
of Urrao organized a collective
Catholic burial of Liberal and
Conservative casualties of *la
Violencia*. The priest kept careful
notes in the parish registry of
deaths that were the direct result
of *la Violencia* and after the
military coup of June 13, 1953,
instructed his parishoners to
collect the remains of their dead
relatives scattered outside the town
limits. The coffins are child-sized.

About the Series

History and immigration are changing the principles and assumptions of Area Studies programs that were set up during the Cold War. Mary Roldán's superb study of hegemony and violence in Colombia is not just another study in which Latin America is the object observed from the United States. When Roldán explicitly states in the epilogue that "during two long stretches" of her investigation, between 1989 and 1992, "I lived in my parents' apartment in downtown Medellín in the heart of Medellín's commercial district," she brings to the foreground the phenomenological and existential dimension of her study. While Area Studies project the "objective" and "disembodied" perspectives of the social sciences, Roldán's investigation builds on the existential and phenomenological while using the scholarly tools of the social sciences. By enriching her analysis with her personal and emotional investment in the issues being explored, Roldán works to correct the shortcomings of Area Studies, particularly those that detach the researcher from the local history of his or her investigation.

Blood and Fire is an outstanding historical description and interpretation of a fundamental period in the history of Colombia and of Latin America (1946–1958). It is also a theoretical contribution to the understanding of the State beyond existing theories, mainly based on paradigmatic examples of the European State. State building in Latin America was simultaneous with state building in Europe during the nineteenth century, but while in Europe many states were imperial, in Latin America all the states were neo- or postcolonial. In Latin American state building, the notion of "internal colonialism" is essential, and Roldán makes good use of it. By so doing, she also inscribes her work in a Latin American tradition of critical social thought that goes back to the late 1960s. In this regard Roldán introduces a second significant change in relation to Area Studies. She builds upon the theoretical legacies of critical social thought to show that Latin America is not only a place for the cultivation of violence, but a place where critical thought can flourish.

About the Photographs

The inclusion of recent photographs of displacement and violence in a book about *la Violencia* — a phenomenon that took place some fifty years earlier — may seem like a peculiar choice to many readers and so requires some explanation on the part of the author. When my editor, Valerie Millholland, first approached me about providing photographs to accompany this text, I demurred. Most of the existing images of the period were ones used to fan partisan hatred by one group against another and were almost without exception lurid representations that exploited the victims and titillated the viewer but contributed little to a deeper understanding of the complexity and human sorrow of violence. On a research trip to Medellín in June of 2001, as this book was about to enter into production, I happened upon an exhibit of works by Jesús Abad Colorado in the recently renovated Museo de Antioquia. I was so moved by his photographs of the current conflict in Antioquia and by the fact that nearly all of them were taken of displacements and violence occurring in the very same towns most affected by violence during the period I study in this book, that I resolved then and there to approach the photographer about the possibility of using some of his photographs to accompany this text. Little did I know that in addition to being an extremely gifted visual storyteller, Jésus Abad Colorado wrote narratives to accompany his photographs that in their basic outlines mirrored almost exactly the stories I recount here. It is the hope of both the photographer and myself that the conscious association of these images of recent violence in Antioquia with a written narrative of events taking place half a century earlier will invite readers to draw connections between past and present violence. Perhaps the anguish of recurrence these images bring to mind may lead to a greater understanding of the historical roots of conflict in Colombia. That is certainly our wish and motivation. — *Mary Roldán*

Jesús Abad Colorado received his journalism degree from the University of Antioquia in Medellín, Colombia. Between 1992 and May of 2001 he worked as a photojournalist for the regional daily newspaper, *El Colombiano.* His work has appeared regularly in national magazines and social research books. He coauthored the book *Relatos e Imágenes, El desplazamiento Forzado en Colombia,* and his photographs have been exhibited both in Colombia and abroad.

Contents

Acknowledgments

Over the years, many individuals and institutions have contributed to and supported the research and writing of this manuscript. In Colombia I would like to thank the employees at the Archivo de la Gobernación de Antioquia for allowing me to consult the governor's correspondence and other regional government materials in 1986 and 1987; the Centro Jorge Eliécer Gaitán in Bogotá and its Director Gloria Gaitán; the Fundación Antioqueña de Estudios Sociales in Medellín; the library and newspaper collection at the Universidad de Antioquia, Medellín; the research collection at the Instituto de Estudios Regionales at the Universidad de Antioquia; the Salón Antioquia in the Bibliotéca Pública Piloto in Medellín; the Bibliotéca Luis Angel Arango in Bogotá; the Bibliotéca Nacional in Bogotá; the Archivo de la Alcaldía Municipal de Urrao and that town's Parish Registry and Casa de la Cultura; and Froilan Montoya Mazo's personal archive in Medellín. Dr. Montoya Mazo, who has since died, also very kindly introduced me to and obtained interviews for me with several *gaitanista* leaders of the *Violencia* period and with several Liberal ex-guerrillas. Colombian colleagues and friends too numerous to name have also provided hospitality, affection, and intellectual guidance, among them: Jorge Pérez, Maria Mercedes Botero, Alvaro Tirado Mejía, Jorge Orlando Melo, Victor Alvarez, Beatriz Patiño, Patricia Londoño, Constanza Toro, Ana Lucía Sánchez, Jesús María Alvarez, Maria Teresa Uribe de Hincapie, Gonzalo Sánchez, and Mauricio Romero. I could not have completed the research for this book without the assistance of several students from the Universidad de Antioquia, among them: Gloria Granda, Rodrigo Arango, and Mario Gaviria. Many thanks to Gustavo Ochoa for his excellent map-making skills and to Fernando Mejía for many hours of tedious data entry.

Several colleagues and institutions in the United States also supported my work since its initial emergence as a Ph.D. dissertation at Harvard University. The Tinker Foundation provided summer research support during three summers as did the Radcliffe President's Fund, the Committee on Iberian and Latin American Studies, the history department, and the Sheldon Kennedy Traveling Research Fund at Harvard University. Financial support was also provided by a Fulbright-Hays Doctoral Dissertation Grant. I could not have asked for a more intellectually demanding adviser or mentor than John Womack Jr. He was never satisfied with easy explanations, always prodded me to push my research and fine-tune my interpretations further, and, though I sometimes proved stubborn or resistant to his good advice, I recognize that he shaped the way I think about history in profound and intangible ways. As an assistant professor at Cornell University I received support from the Society for the Humanities Summer Research Fund, the John T. and Catherine D. MacArthur Foundation Peace Studies Research Fund, and the Latin American Studies Summer Faculty Research Fund.

My colleagues at Cornell have been unfailingly supportive. For good meals, helpful readings, critical thoughts, and kind words, I wish to thank: Tom Holloway, Walter LaFeber, Sandra Greene, Rachel Weil, Itsie Hull, Shirley Samuels, Billie Jean Isbell, Tom Volman, Lourdes Benería, Bill Goldsmith, Barbara Lynch, Debbie Castillo, and Mary Jo Dudley. I want to single out Tom Holloway for help above and beyond the call of duty. Tom read my dissertation when I arrived at Cornell, told me what he thought was good in it and what had to go, then looked me in the eye and asked, "Where's the blood?" It took me two years to figure out how to face the "blood" of Colombian violence and then some more years to get to the middle of it, but I am very grateful to Tom for forcing me to face my inner demons. When Tom read the completely revised manuscript in its entirety and emitted a gruff, "great stuff," I went off and cried from sheer relief. I particularly want to thank Catherine LeGrand who has been the kindest of friends and the most generous of colleagues. She has given me unfailing intellectual encouragement, provided gently critical but probing comments of my work, and, whenever I lost faith, applied cleverly flattering remarks so I would press on. I also wish to thank Lisa Dundon, Richard Stoller, Jim Brennan, and Jeff Rubin. Michael Jiménez died before this book went to press. I wish to acknowledge here what a special being he was and the great honor it was to have been his friend. Several graduate students have provided a fertile environment for the discussion of thorny theoretical issues and comparative problems over the years, among them are Estelle Tarica, Brett Troyan, Leslie Horowitz, Anne Brophy, Angela Wilson, and Michelle Bigenho.

The writing of this manuscript was made possible by the generosity of COLCIENCIAS and their program "Movilidad de Investigadores," the Centro de Estudios Regionales Cafeteros y Empresariales (CRECE) in Manizales and its Director, Dr. Cesar Vallejo Mejía, and Planeación Nacional in Bogotá. These three institutions provided the financial support and time away from teaching necessary to the completion of this book. Thank you. Valerie Millholland was a patient, encouraging, and wonderful editor. This book might never have reached the publication stage without her prodding, and the enormously helpful criticisms of Duke University Press's anonymous readers. Whatever errors and omissions remain are solely my responsibility.

Finally, I wish to thank my dear friend, Margarita Crocker, for unflagging moral support over many years and my husband, Christopher London, who is my best intellectual partner and the person who always sees the point of what I do even when I lose faith. Bearing and raising children has given me a new perspective on violence and work. I hope Lucas and Sophia will forgive their mother for remaining glued to a computer for nearly two years and not infrequently declining to go outside and play.

Blood and Fire

Peque, July 2001. When
a guerrilla commander
told her to flee in the
wake of a paramilitary
attack, the elderly woman
in this portrait refused,
commenting, "I've been
running since 1950."

Introduction

For many people violence and Colombia are synonymous. Colombia
(map 1), after all, produces the bulk of the coca processed into cocaine
and shipped to the world's largest consumer of drugs, the United States,
and suffers the crime and corruption that result from this illicit trade.
Colombia is also home to the oldest guerrilla insurgency in the Western
Hemisphere; the country that accounted for half of the world's kidnappings in 2000; the place where paramilitaries inscribe bloody messages
on the bodies of their largely peasant victims; a land the U.S. media likes
to refer to as "twice the size of France"; a land over which the central state
exerts little authority; and a formal democracy where a handful of elite
families are thought to monopolize control of the media, politics, and
the nation's (licit) economy. Until recently, the Colombian city considered to represent the apex of lawlessness was Medellín, the capital of the
northwestern province of Antioquia and, for the better part of two decades, the financial center of a global narcotics enterprise known as the
"Medellín cartel."[1]

This book is not directly about narcotics or Colombia's contemporary
crisis. Instead, it examines the experience of the department of Antioquia
(see map 2) during the first seven years (1946–1953) of a civil war that was
spurred by a struggle for power between members of the Conservative
and Liberal parties and that has come to be known simply as *la Violencia*
or "the Violence."[2] Initially, I did not intend to draw parallels between
the period of *la Violencia* and contemporary Colombia, but I came to
see that recent and past periods of violence are inextricably intertwined.
I can pinpoint the day I ceased to regard *la Violencia* as something entirely distinct from current, daily, lived Colombian reality. I was sitting
in my office preparing the last lecture of the spring semester for my survey course on modern Latin America. In a moment of procrastination I
checked my email. There was a message from a friend in Bogotá—a fellow *violentólogo* at the National University[3]—telling me that a colleague
from the University of Antioquia in Medellín had just been assassinated
at point-blank range by three hooded individuals who carried guns with

Map 1. Colombia. (Source: Charles Bergquist, *Labor in Latin America: Comparative Essays on Chile, Argentina, Venezuela, and Colombia* [Stanford University Press, 1986])

silencers. My friend had omitted the name of the murdered professor, but I knew the moment I read the message, with a certainty I cannot explain, that it was Hernán Henao, a man with whom I had collaborated for several months on an interdisciplinary seminar devoted to analyzing violence in Medellín and thinking about peaceful ways to end it.

This was not the first time someone I knew had been killed. During one particularly horrible period in the early 1990s, it seemed as if there was a funeral every week, sometimes more, of a professor, journalist, student, or human rights advocate. People called each other frequently to tell their loved ones that they were on their way home, had just arrived at the office, or were leaving to run an errand because otherwise ordinary delays were cause for mortal fear. Despite this familiarity with violence, Hernán's death plunged me into a deep depression from which it took months to recover. I wandered the halls of my building that day howling with pain. I replayed over and over again in my imagination the sight of Hernán agonizing in a pool of blood in the campus office of the Instituto de Estudios Regionales (INER), every inch of which was as familiar to me as my own house. I remember feeling anger, fear, numbness, disbelief. I couldn't think why anyone would kill Hernán, an academic whose life had been devoted to discussing and anguishing over a way to negotiate a space for tolerance, mutual respect, and plurality in an increasingly polarized society, but who had never himself advocated violence or taken part in violent activities. Neither Hernán nor any of the other professors affiliated with INER believed that the massacres, forcible displacements, or persistent violations of human rights that take place daily in Colombia were attributable to a single cause. Hernán and others had reached out to the victims of violence of the right and left, regardless of ideology, and offered them solace, education, and programs to help rebuild their lives. His murder seemed utterly senseless.

In the midst of feeling betrayed and vulnerable, I suddenly realized the point of terror and how it worked. I mean that I realized it in every fiber of my body, not as an intellectual abstraction. I had just finished a preliminary version of this manuscript and felt that I simply couldn't face thinking about violence any longer. I fantasized about setting it aside, as if by doing so I could set aside the reality of violence, too. And then the realization struck me. I knew that even if I could never absolutely establish the trajectory by which violence had occurred or the exact motivations behind it, even if I could not swear to the existence of an objective "truth"

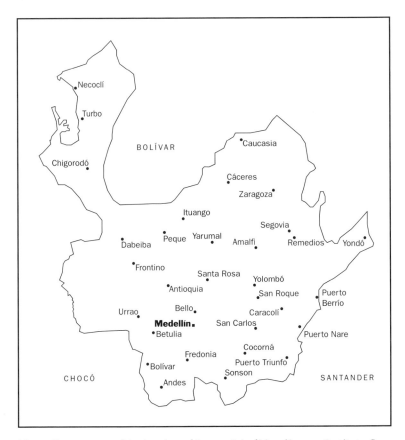

Map 2. Department of Antioquia and its municipalities. (Source: Instituto Geográfico Augustín Codazzi)

about historical events, I nonetheless had to try to trace, with the greatest precision I could muster, the complicated, murky, sometimes contradictory, and seemingly unrelated events that led to violence. The only way to overcome my own terror was to refuse to be silenced.

This book is the result of that realization; it is the outcome of a conviction that what has happened in the past is crucial to understanding what is happening today and that refusing to accept that most violence is inchoate, random, or inexplicable is a moral obligation. It is also a small tribute to the people whose insistence on uncovering unwelcome truths in the face of extreme threat has been a cause of constant inspiration to me. My awareness of links between past and present conflict, however, should not be understood as a belief that violence in Colombia is somehow inherent, unique, inevitable, or static. On the contrary, if the case of *la Violencia* in Antioquia is at all representative of Colombian violence as a whole, then what is significant about this study is the discovery of how selective and concentrated supposedly generalized violence has been, and to what degree factors such as ethnicity and race, cultural differences, class, and geography have shaped the evolution, trajectory, direction, and incidence of violence in Colombia over time. The historical act of glossing *la Violencia* as a generalized phenomenon gives short shrift to the memories of those who refused to take part in violence and to the memories of its true victims, the thousands of unnamed rural folk who died and whose voices have been silenced or forgotten. Hernán Henao dedicated himself to elucidating the causes of violence and the identity of its victims, and in its own way this book tries to carry that legacy forward.

La Violencia in Antioquia

Two hundred thousand Colombians are estimated to have died as a result of violence between 1946 and 1966. Over two million others migrated or were forcibly displaced from their homes and towns, the majority were never to return. The impact of *la Violencia* was so great that it provoked Colombia's only twentieth-century military coup and led later to an unprecedented agreement between the leaders of the Liberal and Conservative parties to alternate control of the presidency and share political power for nearly twenty years.

Of the Colombian regions hardest hit by violence, Antioquia ranked third in the total number of violent deaths registered nationally between 1946 and 1957, as approximately 26,000 of the province's inhabitants are estimated to have died as a result of the Violence. In 1951 nearly 14 percent or 1,570,000 of Colombia's total population of 11,500,000 lived in Antioquia. Thus, there was a regional, per capita casualty rate of nearly 1.7 percent over the time period.[4] In other words, many deaths occurred in Antioquia, but because the overall regional populations of other severely affected provinces were much smaller than Antioquia's, the impact of casualties in these other provinces was even more pronounced.[5] Antioquia also registered the eighth highest number of migrations as a result of violence in Colombia (117,000 or 6 percent of the national total of migrations caused by violence). But, again, in regional terms, the seven provinces that led the nation in total migrations as a result of violence

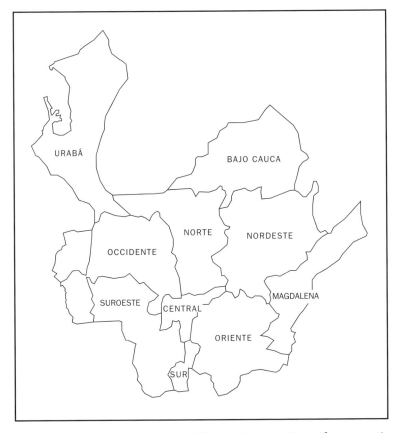

Map 3. Administrative subregions. (Source: Instituto Geográfico Augustín Codazzi)

had populations significantly smaller than Antioquia's and therefore experienced a much higher proportional displacement of their population.[6] What makes the case of Antioquia during *la Violencia* significant is not the number of casualties or migrations that occurred as a result of violence, but rather where violence took place in the province and why.

In this book I draw on previously untapped sources such as regional and municipal government archives, judicial testimony, parish death records, and interviews to tell a story that echoes the findings of researchers tracing the trajectory of violence in other Colombian regions between 1946 and 1953 and also challenges them. Despite ranking third as the department most severely affected by violence, Antioquia was not beset by widespread violence nor was the violence most pronounced or concen-

Map 4. Peripheral municipalities. (Source: Instituto Geográfico Augustín Codazzi)

trated in the coffee-producing municipalities of the southwest as has historically been thought.[7] Instead, violence proved most severe in Antioquia's geographically peripheral zones where land tenure, production, labor, and the state's authority were markedly different from the dominant paradigm in Antioquia's centrally settled municipalities. In Antioquia, the earliest stage of *la Violencia* (1948–1953) affected in indelible ways those areas situated in the department's geographic periphery such as the tropical lowlands of Urabá, the Bajo Cauca (lower Cauca Valley), and Northeast and Magdalena Medio (middle Magdalena Valley), but not Antioquia's coffee sector or centrally located municipalities. (See maps 3 and 4.)

Violence-related death statistics provide a crude index of the spatial and temporal dimensions of Antioqueño violence. The total number of officially registered deaths in Antioquia during the years of *la Violencia* varied only slightly between a low of 22,210 (1948) and a high of 25,125 (1951).[8] But deaths in three categories: "homicide," "unspecified or ill defined," and "other violent deaths" rose significantly between 1948 and 1951, and then declined until 1959. In 1951 the cumulative total of deaths encompassed by these three categories peaked at 10,212, accounting for nearly 41 percent of all the deaths registered in that year.[9]

Death statistics collected by Antioquia's governor's office (for internal purposes, not public dissemination) give a more precise picture of regional violence.[10] Before 1949, the regional government did not keep a separate statistical record of deaths specifically related to violence, but government records and interviews with survivors suggest that violence was largely sporadic between 1946 and 1949 and concentrated in centrally located towns where the total number of violence-related deaths was low.[11] Three quarters (twelve of sixteen) of the officially registered deaths specifically listed as the direct consequence of violence by the governor's office in 1949, for instance, occurred in centrally located towns. By 1950, however, the pattern of sporadic, centrally concentrated deaths shifted. Deaths explicitly deemed the result of violence numbered in the hundreds by 1950 and were concentrated in Antioqueño towns located in the furthest southwest (Urrao),[12] western Antioquia, and in the far eastern portions of the department (the Northeast, Bajo Cauca, and Magdalena Medio). Core area towns such as Medellín, the industrial towns near Medellín (such as Bello or Envigado), the coffee-producing south and southwest, the near east (*oriente*) and the immediate north-central subregions, in contrast, reported very few violence-related casualties between 1950 and 1953.[13] In fact, half of the more than four thousand violence-related regional deaths officially registered between 1949 and May 1953 took place in just five municipalities (Dabeiba, Puerto Berrío, Urrao, Cañasgordas, and Remedios), all of them located on Antioquia's periphery (map 5; also see appendix A.1, A.2.)

Of all the violence-related deaths tallied by the regional government, 43 percent occurred in western Antioquia and Urabá, 20 percent occurred in the southwest, 14 percent in the Magdalena Medio region, and 13 percent in the northeastern section of Antioquia. With the exception of the highly populated southwest, all of the areas with the highest percentage of casualties were also the least populated in Antioquia. Also, of all

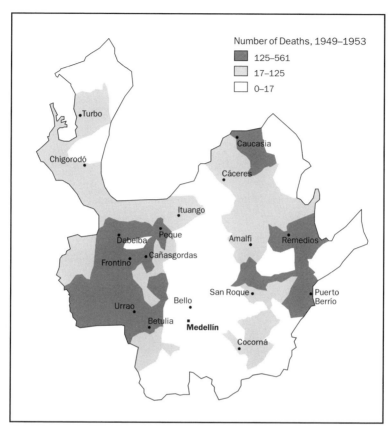

Map 5. Deaths due to violence, 1949–1953. (Source: Instituto Geográfico Augustín Codazzi and Archivo Privado del Señor Gobernador de Antiquia, 1953, vol. 9, "Informe sobre la acción del bandolerismo de 1949 a mayo de 1953," Medellín, May 1953)

the officially registered deaths from violence occurring between 1949 and 1953, half occurred in a single year, 1952. Just one town, Puerto Berrío, accounted for nearly a quarter of these. The selective and concentrated nature of violence is even more striking when deaths related to violence are measured as a percentage of local population. Based on the census of 1951, only one quarter of 1 percent of Antioquia's population suffered violence-related deaths between 1949 and 1953, but Puerto Berrío in the Magdalena Medio lost 6 percent of its population to violence while Caucasia in the Bajo Cauca lost nearly 4 percent of its inhabitants. Western towns such as Urrao, Dabeiba, and Cañasgordas, moreover, lost be-

tween 2 and 3 percent of their populations to violence during a three-year
period.

The "official story" of violence represents it as a widespread, generi-
cally partisan phenomenon waged indiscriminately between Liberal and
Conservative rural folk, but the official record uncovers a violence re-
markably limited in scope and far more varied in impulse. How are we to
account for the geographic and temporal specificity of violence-related
deaths in Antioquia? Why were towns located on the margins of the department the sites of most severe and prolonged violence? Why were the
majority of towns in the coffee heartland (the southwest), which were
equally Liberal and where it has always been supposed that the violence in
Antioquia was centered, so much less violent than towns on the periphery? Is it possible that factors in addition to partisan differences influenced the severity of violence and shaped a more pronounced concentration in specific geo-cultural areas? Did the objectives of violence shift
over time and were they dependent upon factors peculiar to local rather
than generalized national circumstances? If so, how would we have to rethink our conceptualization of the relationship between partisan politics
and violence in Colombia?

Antioquia was Colombia's most populated, Conservative, and economically influential department at mid-century. The province was also
—and had been for some decades—one of Colombia's largest regional
producers of coffee for export, the nation's main producer of gold, and the
national leader in industry, commerce, and finance. Antioqueños were
sometimes less likely to occupy national political office than the inhabitants of other Colombian provinces, but Antioquia's voters were numerous and the province's men of capital dominated powerful private producer associations such as the National Federation of Coffee Growers
(FEDECAFE), the National Federation of Merchants (FENALCO), and the
National Association of Industrialists (ANDI), entities instrumental in
shaping Colombian economic and social policy.

In a country where Liberal and Conservative differences were thought
to define individual identity and to have caused the majority of Colombia's violent struggles since the nineteenth century, moreover, Antioquia
was perceived as both a political maverick and as reluctant to take up
arms in the name of politics. Indeed, there was little in Antioquia's past
to suggest that it should have become an area hard hit by partisan violence during *la Violencia.* Neither the province of which Medellín is the

capital nor Medellín itself was associated with violence in the Colombian imaginary. A stereotype existed of Antioquia and its inhabitants, but it was one that characterized *paisas*[14] as the nation's sharpest businessmen and pragmatic technocrats, a region of aggressive colonizers who were also fiercely Catholic. A prolific lot, Antioqueños figured in the national imagination as the people who opened and peopled Colombia's southwestern frontier, who came to embody coffee cultivation and culture in the early twentieth century, and who gave rise to a society characterized by a sense of strong regional identity, large families, and small property holders. Many a joke was made targeting regional inhabitants as too obsessed with making money to spare the time to take part in politics. When forced to choose between going to war over political differences and arriving at a negotiated solution that would preclude social unrest and allow business to continue unimpeded, the region's inhabitants were perceived as usually opting for the latter. What happened then by mid-century to make Antioquia an important locus of violence?

To those familiar only with the recent history of Colombia or Antioquia, the association of violence with both the country and the region might seem self-evident. As David Bushnell ruefully notes in the introduction to his recent synthesis of Colombian history, "Colombia is today the least studied of the major Latin American countries, and probably the least understood."[15] In contrast to many of its neighbors, Colombia has rarely suffered from dictatorships, boasted no powerful military, managed its finances conservatively, and displayed no conflict based on ethnic differences. Moreover, except for the brief appeal of Liberal populist leader Jorge Eliécer Gaitán in the 1940s and the military government of General Gustavo Rojas Pinilla in the mid-1950s, Colombia rarely fell victim to the sway of populist or authoritarian politics. By the mid-twentieth century, the persistence of identification with the same parties that had oriented individual political affiliation since the nineteenth century at the expense of supposedly more modern forms of political expression reinforced the idea that Colombia was somehow unique and that there existed no common frame of reference with which to compare events in Colombia to those in the rest of Latin America. This has relegated the phenomenon of *la Violencia* to a kind of historical limbo much written and obsessed about by Colombian specialists but regarded by other Latin Americanists as an aberration peculiar only to Colombia.

At first glance *la Violencia* does appear as a throwback to an earlier age of caudillo civil wars and peasant atavism that confirms the notion of Colombia as out of step with other "modernizing" nations in the region. The bulk of the killing during *la Violencia* took place in rural areas, and peasants constituted the majority of casualties. Victims were often tortured, dismembered, and sexually mutilated, and women were frequently raped in front of their families. These conditions alone, however, are insufficient to distinguish conflict in Colombia from that typical of the rest of Latin America. But, while national political struggles, personal feuds, agrarian unrest, and clientelist competition informed conflicts in other Latin American societies, these had either taken place in the nineteenth or early twentieth centuries, involved war with another nation, or occurred in the context of suppressing an indigenous population.[16] Alternatively, violence occurring in Latin America in the post-*Violencia* years was explained as leftist insurgency or anticommunist state terrorism waged in defense of national security and democracy.[17] There seemed to be no Latin American precedent for a conflict in which those killing each other were citizens of the same state who attacked one another because of partisan differences and who did so with a savagery rarely seen outside the context of racially or ideologically motivated wars.[18] In other words, what distinguished the Colombian *Violencia* from twentieth-century violence occurring elsewhere in Latin America was that it was fought in terms of mid-nineteenth-century political partisanship not modern political or social objectives. There were of course comparably brutal and complex cases of civil conflict in other parts of the world to which *la Violencia* might be compared, but this required attributing the same symbolic and innate power to Colombian partisan differences as that attributed to religious and ethnic and racial differences present elsewhere.[19]

But cultural, religious, and ethnic and racial differences did exist in Antioquia and were fundamental features of how violence unfolded in the region. Indeed, it is the argument of this study that *la Violencia* in Antioquia can only be understood against the backdrop of profoundly perceived differences between geo-cultural areas internal to the province, and that these differences were often as critical as, or more so, than partisan factors in determining the intensity, incidence, and trajectory of violence in the region. To make clear how the Antioqueño experience of *la Violencia* differs from historical interpretations of the phenomenon, and the significance of these differences for the study of violence

in Colombia more generally, I have divided the remainder of this introduction into three parts. First, I provide a brief overview of Colombian
politics and society in the decades preceding *la Violencia*. I then summarize the various interpretations and regional case studies that form
the core of *Violencia* studies from the 1970s to the present in order to
provide a comparative basis for a consideration of the issues raised by
the Antioqueño experience of the Violence. Lastly, I lay out a theoretical framework for thinking about the relationship between geography,
politics, ethnicity and race, class, and violence and explore the reasons
why these issues, rather than partisan identity alone, shaped the course
of mid-century conflict in Antioquia.

Politics and Society in the Decades before *la Violencia*

Initial attempts to make sense of *la Violencia* sought an explanation in the
peculiarities of Colombian political history. Like Liberals and Conservatives elsewhere in nineteenth-century Latin America, Colombian political parties were divided into opposing camps of protectionists and free
traders, centralists and federalists, and pro- and anti-clerical feeling. The
significance of specific issues to the determination of individual political understanding and comportment differed to some degree from region to region, depending on the availability of resources, the structure
of land tenure and production, kinship relations, accidents of history,
and myriad other intangibles. An Antioqueño Conservative of moderate
stripe, for instance, might simultaneously embrace both free trade and
federalism (positions more typically associated with the Liberal party)
and yet strongly support the Catholic Church (a position more typical
of pro-clerical Conservatives). What set Colombia's parties apart from
Liberal and Conservative parties in other Latin American countries, however, was the Colombian system's ability to foster a deep identification
between the parties and the vast majority of its citizens.[20] The Colombian
parties attracted individuals of all classes, regions, and racial and ethnic
origin and, in the absence of a well-developed sense of national identity, scholars have argued, party affiliation shaped the average Colombian's sense of self and belief from the nineteenth through the twentieth
centuries.[21] Identification with one of the two parties also persisted in
Colombia long after Liberal and Conservative parties elsewhere in Latin
America disappeared or gave way to multiparty systems.

Policy and ideological differences between Liberals and Conservatives fueled most of the repeated nineteenth-century civil wars for which Colombia became famous, although the majority of the so-called civil wars occurring in Colombia before the War of the Thousand Days (1899–1902) might more accurately be described as skirmishes. The ostensible catalysts of such "wars" were not insignificant—the suppression of convents, the abolition of slavery, the empowerment of artisans, struggles to seize control of the central government, and so on—but they rarely engaged more than a small percentage of Colombians in actual physical combat. Civil war casualties were for the most part also relatively few, although the destruction and confiscation of property affecting a particular individual, clan, or interest group could become the basis of long-standing resentment that cemented partisan identity. In the end, however, despite a reputation for chronic disorder, nineteenth-century Colombia does not appear to have been noticeably more violent than other Latin American countries of the time.[22]

In 1880 Liberal Rafael Nuñez won control of Colombia's presidency and, with the support of the Conservative party revoked many of the political and social reforms passed during several decades of Liberal political domination. The revised Constitution of 1886 replaced state autonomy with strict centralism, converted previously elected offices into a hierarchically determined system of government appointments, established literacy requirements for male suffrage in national elections, and restored the preeminence of the Roman Catholic Church in matters such as public education.[23] A severe downturn in the export price of coffee during the second half of the 1890s as well as growing discontent among Liberals over their political exclusion eventually sparked the outbreak of the War of the Thousand Days, the last and greatest of Colombia's nineteenth-century civil conflicts.[24] In contrast to the limited engagements characteristic of earlier struggles, the war produced more than 100,000 casualties, a large number of maimed and displaced people, and the irrevocable loss of Panama.[25]

There were fears that, if the war were allowed to continue, further territorial dismemberment (beyond the already dramatic loss of Panama) would occur and Colombia's economic future would be compromised at the very moment when coffee seemed to promise a way out of economic stagnation. Ultimately, these fears converged to bring fighting to an end. General Rafael Reyes, Colombia's first twentieth-century military

ruler and the man behind the elimination of the most exclusionary policies associated with the Regeneración (as the Nuñez regime was known),
came to power in 1904. Reyes enjoyed the overt support of the moderate faction of the Conservative party known as the Historical Conservatives—many of whom were Antioqueño capitalists—and the tacit support of many Liberals.[26] Reyes institutionalized minority representation
in Colombia's various legislative bodies and promoted policy initiatives
that proved crucial to the support of domestic industry and the export
economy, especially the coffee sector. Although a combination of factors
led to Reyes's quick fall from grace, he laid the basis for a period of economic expansion within a climate of relative bipartisan cooperation that
characterized what has sometimes been called the *pax conservadora* of
1904 to 1930.[27]

Several aspects of coffee production helped it to emerge as a focus
around which members of both parties and numerous regional interests
could cooperate to set aside the partisan antagonisms that had undermined national political stability during Colombia's first century of independent existence. First, by the 1920s significant sectors of the population
of both historically Liberal and Conservative regions were associated with
coffee production or its commercialization. Second, coffee was grown
by both large landowners in the eastern and central regions as well as
by small and medium-sized property holders in the central cordillera
(among them Antioquia and the regions its inhabitants colonized to
the south). Charles Bergquist has argued persuasively that these circumstances ensured that "a large proportion of the Colombian body politic
identified with the political economy of the export-import interests in
control of the government after 1910" and that smallholders "fully endorsed the liberal political ideology, social conservatism, and pro-export
economic policies of the new order."[28]

Despite continued differences between Liberals and Conservatives,
consensus emerged between businessmen and coffee growers from 1910
to 1930 regarding the importance of and need for state investment in
infrastructure and economic development. During these years many of
the elite leaders of both parties intermarried, attended the same schools,
and dominated regional and national politics.[29] The 1920s in particular
witnessed unprecedented private and public expenditure on an ambitious program of public works and education. But investment and economic growth did not benefit all Colombians during the heady years

that came to be known as the Dance of the Millions. The Conservative coalition of coffee growers, export merchants, and industrialists that had dominated Colombian political fortunes for more than two decades toppled in 1930 amid rumors of fiscal mismanagement and accusations that they sacrificed the lives of Colombian workers to U.S. interests during the 1928 United Fruit strike in Santa Marta.[30]

During the presidential election of 1930, the Conservative party split and lost to the Liberal opposition. The change from one political administration to another in Colombia typically meant the substitution of one party's members for those of the other in patronage jobs and government positions. When Liberal Enrique Olaya Herrera was elected president (1930–1934), violence broke out in several regions of Colombia where Liberals unleashed their long-suppressed resentment on the Conservative opposition. Indeed, while many scholars consider the assassination of Liberal populist, Jorge Eliécer Gaitán, on April 9, 1948, as the seminal event that catalyzed *la Violencia,* the factors that led up to the Liberal leader's death and the emergence of severe unrest in its aftermath can in part be traced to the changes occurring in Colombia during the 1930s and 1940s.

Industrial employment and unprecedented public works investment had begun to transform Colombia from a predominantly rural to an increasingly urban country in the early decades of the twentieth century. In 1925 a third of Colombia's population was classified as urban whereas by 1951 nearly half of the nation's inhabitants lived in urban areas. Rural migration to cities was only temporarily interrupted by the contraction of employment during the period of economic recession between 1928 and 1932.[31] The effects of urban growth—pressure on public services, the increased cost of living, and the emergence of an increasingly vocal underclass—were felt in cities such as Bogotá, Medellín, Cali, and Barranquilla.[32] Urbanization thus coincided with both the shift to a period of Liberal government after nearly fifty years of Conservative rule in 1930 and the emergence of popular demands for expanded political recognition and participation. These profound national changes were reflected in the administration of Liberal Alfonso López Pumarejo who allied with sectors of his party to shift Liberal policy in a more progessive and socially inclusive direction in 1934.

Alfonso López Pumarejo's Revolution on the March (1934–1938) was a more modest version of the Cárdenas administration that came to power

in the same year in Mexico and the progressive Popular Front governments that sprang up in other parts of Latin America during the 1930s.
López initiated social legislation, abolished literacy requirements for suffrage, and extended legal recognition and rights to workers and peasants.[33] As he expanded the functions of the state, López also centralized
its power, elevating the state into a mediator between conflicting social
and economic interest groups.[34]

Agrarian unrest had become acute in several Colombian regions in
the years immediately preceding López's rise to power.[35] In some areas,
colonists hoping to escape the effects of economic downturns in the
1920s migrated in search of regions with supposedly abundant public
lands only to find that these had been swallowed up by recently established large-scale commercial agriculture and cattle ranches. Conflicts
in these areas emerged between landless folk competing with each other
and with powerful capitalist landowners. In other areas, previously un-
organized rural workers mobilized to protest changes in tenancy laws,
dismissals, and poor wages on plantations.[36] To resolve the problem of
growing agrarian unrest and to preclude economic disruption in regions
where struggles over land were most severe, López initiated Law 200 of
1936. The law declared that property had a social function and sought to
mediate competing claims to public lands while providing titles to those
petitioners who could prove they had resided on and made improvements to the land. López did not intend to undermine the principle of
private property in Colombia nor was it his intent to do away with large
landowning.[37] Although agrarian unrest diminished after Law 200's passage, the land reform law confirmed only a limited number of squatter
claims, making the validity of petitions not initiated before 1934 much
more difficult to prove.[38] Reaction to the law, in any case, rested less upon
its actual impact than upon the elite's perception of its threat.

When taken in conjunction with López's recognition and legalization
of labor organizations such as the Confederation of Colombian Workers
(CTC), and his introduction of organized labor into the once restricted
arena of elite politics, his social policies fueled resentment among men
of capital like those in Antioquia.[39] In addition, López's toleration of
Communist leaders—many of whom headed important labor unions
(affiliated with the newly created CTC) in strategic sectors such as oil,
transportation, and mining—led the more reactionary members of both
parties to repudiate the López administration as dangerously radical.[40]

The nearly hysterical alarm evinced by the nation's entrepreneurs and industrialists over López's championing of working-class interests and his extension of state authority between 1934 and 1938 formed a critical backdrop to the vituperative red-baiting that helped incite partisan violence in the forties and is only understandable when set against the background of growing capitalist investment and economic expansion taking place in the decade preceding the outbreak of *la Violencia*. Colombian industry, for instance, embarked upon a period of expansion that led it to grow in real terms at an unprecedented rate of 10 percent per year between 1932 and 1940. Nowhere was the impact of industrial growth more clearly felt than in Antioquia, especially in the industrial hub around Medellín where textile mills and other light industries formed the core of the local economy.[41]

At the end of López's term, the Liberal party sought out a candidate who might halt the momentum of López's revolution and reassure elite interests. They found their champion in Eduardo Santos, a prominent businessman and the patriarch of Colombia's family-owned, largest circulation daily newspaper, the Bogotá-based *El Tiempo*. During his presidency (1938–1942) Santos muzzled labor unrest, put down strikes, and deflected popular demands so as to curtail the movement of labor his predecessor had nurtured and encouraged.[42] Despite the distrust he generated among members of the elite, however, Alfonso López remained a charismatic political leader and he returned to power in 1942 with the support of the very groups whose interests he had defended during his first presidency. But López's second term in office proved a disappointment to his more progressive supporters. Disagreement within the Liberal party, increasingly fierce Conservative opposition, and the intensification of rural partisan conflict culminated in 1944 with a failed military coup led by disgruntled army officers.[43] When López was finally forced from office in 1945 and Liberal Alberto Lleras Camargo assumed the presidency in May, the conservative social trend already apparent in the later years of Liberal government became more pronounced. One of Lleras Camargo's first acts as president was the dissolution of a long and bitter strike led by the Magdalena Transport Workers (FEDENAL), perhaps Colombia's strongest and most militant union, and the only one with a closed shop.[44] Lleras Camargo also implemented Law 6 of 1945 regulating collective bargaining agreements in Colombia. While the law confirmed the social services and benefits labor had won under Alfonso

López Pumarejo's Revolution on the March, it also marked a critical shift in the relationship that had been established between labor, the Liberal party, and the state in the mid-thirties. The law strictly defined the criteria for a legal strike, outlawing strikes in the *sector público,* that is, for workers employed in public works, transportation, communication, and municipal and state government (the source of most patronage hiring). These were precisely those sectors of the workforce that were most vocal and most dependent upon an alliance with the Liberal state for their well-being.[45] Failure to comply strictly with the labor code's criteria for a strike became the basis for dismissing workers' demands, however well intentioned or legitimate they might have been. Popular and working-class interests, already battered by declining real wages, unemployment, and harassment, were further weakened by the loss of state advocacy on their behalf.[46]

In addition to the growth of the urban population, industrialization, and the incipient political empowerment of an organized working class, an emergent middle sector of professional politicians of non-elite origin had also gradually come to demand greater political participation in the national political arena during the 1930s and 1940s. Some of these professional politicians identified with the program embraced by the parties' traditional elite leadership, but others used populist appeals and criticism of bipartisan elite rule to expand their electoral support and confirm their political participation in party directorates and the national government. The divide between the political culture of *convivialismo* (as elite bipartisan political rule was called) and the new politics of mass inclusion was embodied in the figure of Liberal populist Jorge Eliécer Gaitán. A dark-skinned man of humble birth, Gaitán symbolized not only the rise of a growing nonwhite, urban popular core in Colombian society, but also the rise of non-elite politicians emboldened by the extension of education and suffrage that had taken place during the previous two decades.[47] The urban lower class and the aspirants to political power among the provincial middle-class or petit bourgeois sectors linked their fortunes together to press for an opening of the political sphere. The clash between the popular forces represented by young, up-and-coming politicians of both parties and an elite concerned with reasserting the exclusionary, paternalistic rule of pre-1930 Colombia came to a critical climax in the presidential campaign of 1946.

The Liberal party split over the candidacies of Gabriel Turbay Ayala (the party's official candidate) and the dissident, Jorge Eliécer Gaitán, and lost the election to the moderate elite Conservative, Mariano Ospina Pérez. Partisan conflicts like those experienced in the early thirties, when power changed from Conservative to Liberal hands, once more emerged at the municipal level. Conservatives excluded from participation in government patronage and elected offices during the previous sixteen years of Liberal hegemony celebrated the defeat of the Liberal opposition with acts of intimidation and physical harassment in a number of Colombian departments. Although Ospina himself campaigned on a bipartisan political platform that promised the inclusion of Liberals in his cabinet, gubernatorial offices, and municipal government positions, his stance encountered considerable opposition from extremists within the Conservative party and the Liberal followers of Gaitán. When the Liberal party won the congressional elections of 1947, the basis of Ospina's National Union compromise dissolved.[48] Tensions between the Conservative government and the opposition escalated steadily from that point on, reaching a climax with the assassination of Gaitán by a mentally disturbed gunman in Bogotá on April 9, 1948.

The Bogotazo, as the popular uprising in response to Gaitán's assassination came to be known, left the nation's capital a smoldering mass of ruins; churches and public buildings were transformed into heaps of rubble; trolley cars were derailed and burned; stores looted; the city's sidewalks overflowed with the debris of broken glass and ruined merchandise. Meanwhile, decomposing corpses hurriedly thrown in piles in Bogotá's central cemetery seemed to give material testimony to the existence of an anonymous, dangerous crowd that had captured the elite imagination and provoked increasing anxiety of an impending attack upon elite privilege by a ragged, bloodthirsty army of the nation's excluded.[49] Surrounded by a burning and looted city and unsure of just how many troops or individuals might come to his defense, Ospina nonetheless resisted Liberal demands that he hand over power.[50] Instead, the president purged the police of Liberals (many of whom had turned against the government and collaborated with the rioters), reshuffled the cabinet and once more attempted to establish a bipartisan government. The administration also implemented modest reforms of the social security system, established price controls on basic food items, and sponsored a U.S. economic mission to examine the nation's development policies and make recommendations on how best to maximize the state's efficiency.[51] But Ospina's attempt to shift attention away from partisan issues to less controversial technocratic matters proved unsuccessful. The Conservative party leader, Laureano Gómez, and his followers (known as *laureanistas*) led a violent bid for the presidency during 1949 that further ignited already combustible partisan animosities in Colombia's countryside. In the wake of growing incidents of partisan unrest, Ospina Pérez declared a State of Siege, and in November 1949 the president closed the congress indefinitely.[52] Congress would remain inactive for the next nine years.

A surreal quality enveloped Colombia between 1950 and 1953. As violence raged in rural areas and multiple groups under local and regional leadership terrorized the countryside, in Bogotá, Laureano Gómez ruled seemingly removed from the din and clamor of widespread strife.[53] In urban areas such as Medellín, moreover, business went on as usual; business, in fact, boomed. In 1950 the president of the National Association of Industrialists could coolly declare that Colombia's economy had never been better, repeating his assertion on the eve of the military coup in 1953.[54] Insisting that violence was in check, denying its severity, and blaming its existence upon isolated, depraved bandits, the national government seemed oblivious to its inability to assert its authority outside Bogotá and the nation's principal cities. By 1952 tentative attempts at bipartisan dialogue between the more moderate members of the parties, many of them representatives of prominent economic interests, were under way. Several months later a military coup—Colombia's first and last during the twentieth century—backed by significant civilian and elite support put an end to Laureano Gómez's presidency on June 13, 1953.

The military dictatorship that came to power under the leadership of General Gustavo Rojas Pinilla in 1953 and which ruled Colombia until 1957 initially succeeded in reducing partisan tensions in Colombia.[55] The government pardoned Liberal guerrilla groups and removed some of the more hated Conservative local leaders who had been in charge of mobilizing paramilitary groups against the Liberal opposition in rural areas. After a brief respite, however, partisan-motivated violence gave way to common criminal delinquency, social banditry, and incipient, radical peasant leagues. Rojas Pinilla's growing ambition, moreover, frightened the very civilian elite forces that had initially supported the general's military coup. In 1958 power reverted once more to civilian rule and, in an unprecedented attempt to simultaneously put an end to violence and preclude future military intervention, leaders of the Liberal and Conservative parties agreed on a power-sharing arrangement known as the National Front. What had begun as partisan conflict in the countryside took on a distinctly social and economic cast by the later years of the 1950s, giving rise in some areas to the nucleus of what would constitute insurgent, leftist guerrilla groups in the 1960s. It appeared that *la Violencia* had not ended, but simply evolved.

Interpreting *la Violencia*

In the 1960s social scientists took up the challenge of understanding *la Violencia* and devised numerous theories to explain it. These alternatively attributed violence in Colombia to conflicts provoked by the transition from a "premodern" to a "modern" society, to exaggerated aggression fueled by status deprivation, or to rivalries between patron-client systems in which peasants blindly followed the dictates of an elite leadership or party boss.[56] While the patron-client analysis offered clues to the seemingly national scope of violence, it failed to explain why, if disputes originating among an elite leadership in Bogotá could incite the most distant citizen to take up arms, significant areas within Colombia remained untouched by *la Violencia*. Other than through some vague "quasi-religious" appeal, how were ideology and party allegiance actually disseminated and understood?

New scholarship in the 1970s shifted the focus of work on *la Violencia* in other directions. The power of the state, the expansion of the political arena, the rise of new political actors and leaders such as Jorge Eliécer Gaitán in the decades preceding *la Violencia,* and the quest for alternative forms of economic and political mobility were issues increasingly singled out as playing important roles in the development of the violence.[57] As scholars grounded their research in region-specific studies, moreover, it became apparent that while partisan conflict provided the initial catalyst to violence, and perhaps even a seemingly logical framework in which to understand the intensity of the conflict, reliance on the notion of inherited party hatreds was insufficient to account for the divergence and specificity of violence. *La Violencia* resembled the Mexican Revolution in the way that historians might agree that the latter phenomenon was set off by Porfirio Díaz's decision not to seek reelection, but they might not agree on the composition of those fighting, their exact objectives once violence got under way, or the long-term implications of the revolution. *La Violencia* has similarly proven to be an extraordinarily heterogeneous and complex phenomenon.[58]

Indeed, recent studies of *la Violencia* raise as many questions as they answer. They reveal, for instance, how little is actually known about the workings of Colombian politics at the local, regional, or national levels or about the internal organization of the parties themselves. Were the parties monolithic?[59] How did understandings of partisan affiliation differ among individuals belonging to different classes, regions, or ethnic and racial groups?[60] Was it really true that partisan affiliation took precedence over any other kind of identity in Colombia?[61] If not, what shaped people's beliefs, actions, and sense of identity? Even less was known about the nature of the Colombian state, how strong or weak it was or whether a central state existed at all. Was power centralized in the state to such a degree, as some researchers argue, that competition between the parties for its control could set off national unrest of the scope of *la Violencia*?[62] Or was the problem just the opposite? Perhaps no central state existed or it had so tenuous a presence in most areas of the national territory that it proved helpless to control conflict between omnipresent political parties when it broke out?[63]

Then there were the social and economic implications of *la Violencia*. Was violence the response of a frightened elite to the mid-twentieth-century expansion of the Colombian electorate and the rise of middle-sector politicians?[64] Had the rise of Jorge Eliécer Gaitán and his political movement introduced class struggle in Colombia? Did *gaitanismo* represent a threat to the exercise and workings of traditional politics in Colombia?[65] Did the spread of popular uprisings in the aftermath of Gaitán's assassination and their subsequent repression constitute the seeds of a failed social revolution?[66] Was violence waged under traditional party banners to deflect attention away from or to justify crushing other latent sources of conflict such as struggles over land, declining opportunities for social mobility, and growing worker unrest?[67]

Two very influential analyses of the violence posited that *la Violencia* was the result of excessive partisan clientelism and the growing competition between two monolithic parties to control access to the central state. Paul Oquist argued that as the central state grew in the 1930s competition between Conservative and Liberal leaders to monopolize access to the state's largesse and influence became increasingly urgent. According to Oquist, the struggle to achieve "hegemonic" control of the Colombian state unleashed violence that led to its partial "breakdown."[68] French sociologist Daniel Pécaut, on the other hand, argued that the state's power to build a sense of national identity or act as a suprapartisan arbiter of conflict between different sectors of Colombian society had been eclipsed by the persistence of two "subcultures."[69] These subcultures were defined by individual identification with either the Liberal or Conservative party. Since only partisan affiliation could guarantee individual material needs and physical survival, any conflict between the parties inevitably resulted in widespread conflict. The use of force, over which the Colombian state had never achieved complete monopoly, in turn, Pécaut suggested, became more dispersed among competing corporate interests as partisan competition to control the state intensified.

Various scholars gave greater empirical precision to the hypotheses of violence put forth by Oquist and Pécaut. Herbert Braun, for instance, focused on the urban rather than the rural manifestations of violence, more specifically, on the prelude to and aftermath of Gaitán's assassination in Bogotá on April 9, 1948. In much greater detail than Pécaut, Braun laid bare the insular, aristocratic, aloof character of political exchange in pre-Gaitán Colombia. Braun argued that elite members of both parties coincided in their social views and interests, and political decision-making took place not in congress, but over shots of whiskey at Bogotá's exclusive gun or jockey clubs.[70] The critical question always present in the minds of Colombia's elite, and roused to hysterical urgency by Gaitán's persona, Braun argued, revolved not around ideological differences but rather around the issue of how to deal with the lower classes.[71] Gaitán challenged the insularity of gentlemen's politics precisely by reveling in his plebeian and mixed-race origins and by manipulating his identification with and appeal to the popular classes into a major political movement.[72] Braun did not believe, however, that the basis of violence was the insurrectionary or revolutionary content of Gaitán's message to the poor. On the contrary, in Braun's estimation, Gaitán had a fundamentally petit bourgeois attitude toward the masses, admonishing them to bathe and act responsibly and to overcome their socioeconomic condition through hard work and education, not class struggle.[73] Braun suggested that the overreaction of a dominant class terrified by its own prejudices against a lower class it had long demonized and its misconception of Gaitán's political message led it to dangerously raise the stakes of political exchange. The divisive and vituperative rhetoric employed by the elite had the unintended effect of promoting and legitimizing violence among the parties' nonelite membership rather than reasserting the political system as it had existed before Gaitán's mobilization of the popular classes. While Braun noted that Liberal and Conservative elites were equally opposed to Gaitán, he blamed Conservatives more than the Liberals for the inception of violence. Braun argued that Conservative efforts to shore up an eroding electoral position led the party to unleash violence in order to recuperate the loyalty of the popular classes, and he implied that Conservatives embraced Christian Socialist rhetoric when addressing workers only as a political ploy to undermine Gaitán's movement. While the effort to substitute Liberals in office was certainly a critical factor in fomenting violence, Braun may have been too cynical in assuming that the adoption by some Conservatives of a kind of Christian Socialist position vis-à-vis workers was nothing more than posturing.[74]

Braun's theses were quite compelling, but he limited his study to Bogotá, leaving unanswered the question of whether or not and in what manner Gaitán and the reaction he elicited among Bogotá's politicians affected the emergence and nature of violence outside the capital. Meanwhile, Gonzalo Sánchez, Carlos Ortíz, and scholars such as Jaime Arocha, James Henderson, and Darío Fajardo gave specificity and concrete meaning to the abstraction of battles waged in the capital by examining the day-to-day patterns of violence in several Colombian regions.[75] In looking at political culture from the "bottom" up, these scholars also reintroduced the relationship between socioeconomic conditions and violence that had faded from the discussion of la Violencia since the early allusions to such a link in the days of patron-client analysis.

Gonzalo Sánchez argued that an analysis of Gaitán and his movement was the necessary starting point for understanding la Violencia. Like Braun, Sánchez also believed that the issue of lower-class mobilization or political incorporation was at the very heart of la Violencia. In sharp contradiction to Braun, however, Sánchez insisted that Gaitán had introduced the question of class into the Colombian arena, and that Gaitán's movement constituted a first attempt at a revolutionary challenge to the established Colombian economic and political system. For Sánchez, April 9 marked a critical turning point in Colombian history. Answering the question left in suspense by Braun, Sánchez insisted that Gaitán's movement had profoundly affected Colombian society at all levels, constituting "a national insurrection, which, particularly outside Bogotá, laid bare the enormous creative capacity of the masses for revolutionary action."[76] Although the "revolution" failed because it lacked coordination and because Colombia's elite cohered against it, everyone now had a glimpse of what class war might be like. Sánchez argued that the aftermath of Gaitán's assassination triggered a violent reaction and retrenchment by Colombia's elite, first against Gaitán's followers and then, as Conservatives gained power, by Conservatives against Liberals, unions, agrarian leagues, and any other group that might represent a threat to the status quo.

According to Sánchez, once the threat of social revolution from below was suppressed by elite coercion, what followed, at least during the first phase of *la Violencia* from 1948 to 1953, was a period of violence characteristic of that experienced during Colombia's nineteenth-century civil wars. The ultimate impact of this period of *la Violencia* was to reinforce old party identities and the strength of *gamonales* — the local bosses or power brokers — within the parties.[77] The tenor of violence changed, however, when in 1952 armed popular groups in the cattle frontier of the Llanos split into those led by Liberals and those under Communist direction. By the end of the first phase of *la Violencia,* Sánchez argued, partisan violence had given way to violence that had little to do with disputes between Colombia's Liberal and Conservative parties.[78] Some former Liberal guerrillas, in turn, became the nucleus for Colombia's contemporary leftist guerrillas.

Gonzalo Sánchez recognized (along with other scholars) that the objectives and nature of violence could vary from region to region depending on the economic conditions and social arrangements in each. Fajardo, Arrocha, and Sánchez theorized that violence in cattle frontiers such as the Llanos, for instance, was most likely to shift away from traditional to more radical objectives. Coffee-producing towns, in contrast, evinced partisan but not revolutionary violence because, unlike cattle frontiers, coffee towns were nationally integrated through commercial, political, and social networks. Both Sánchez and Fajardo drew a further conclusion that violence coincided with the emergence of large agribusiness haciendas.[79]

Regional examinations of the course of violence suggested important differences in the day-to-day workings of politics outside the capital and the factors that influenced variations in the experience and trajectory of *la Violencia.* By the 1980s, the notion of a single, blanket interpretation of violence gave way to the acknowledgment that violence had many manifestations and meanings. Local conditions appeared to be the most significant factor in determining the nature of violence and its objectives. In the most thorough regional study to date, Carlos Ortíz Sarmiento focused precisely on local issues in his examination of the development of violence in Quindío.[80] Like Sánchez, Pécaut, and Oquist, Ortíz acknowledged the importance of party identity in shaping the course of violence, but he also noted the influence of an individual's place of birth, kinship relations, municipal loyalty, and cross-party relationships.[81] While Ortíz acknowledged the weak presence of the state, he disagreed with Oquist who assumed that the absence of the state necessarily provoked a vacuum of authority. Instead, Ortíz showed how local political arrangements and beliefs were not automatically affected by national developments.[82] Ortíz laid bare the nexus of local political understandings and behavior that operated at the regional level, arguing that faraway disputes between vaguely recognized national leaders were unimportant unless they coincided with local struggles over revenues, boundaries, and patronage. Ortíz also focused his attention on determining exactly who held power and how they used it at the *vereda* and *municipio* levels.[83] Rather than assuming that patron-client relations worked from the top down, he demonstrated convincingly how these were also constantly renegotiated from the bottom up. Bogotá and the *municipio* were connected through intricate, dynamic links between *gamonales* and national politicians. The currency of political adhesion was patronage and votes.

Although introduced by Pécaut, Sánchez, and Braun, the concept of the professional politician who gained power and challenged the elite in the mid-twentieth century was brought down to local terms by Ortíz. Gaitán, for instance, after an initially lukewarm reception, gradually attracted Liberal support in Quindío, but in the aftermath of his assassination had faded from the region's politics.[84] *La Violencia* emerged around the intrusion of "outsiders" with ambitions to become local power brokers—policemen and mayors appointed to *municipios* by the central and regional government in 1949 whose presence disturbed webs of local power—rather than as a result of Gaitán's death.

In exploring the alliances and confrontations that emerged in the 1940s and 1950s, Ortíz also traced the complexities of individual allegiances, while rooting these within a framework of economic and political changes in the region and the nation. Such changes spawned tensions not only between classes or individuals but also between villages, towns, regions, and the national government.⁸⁵ Ortíz concluded that violence was due less to an umbilical relationship between dominant national politicians and their obedient followers in the localities, and more to the presence of specific social actors operating within a particular context who might or might not choose to capitalize upon national ideologies and movements to achieve local objectives and satisfy local aspirations.⁸⁶

Where then does the case of Antioquia fit within the broader framework of regional studies of violence? In what ways does the experience of Antioquia during *la Violencia* confirm or challenge the findings of studies of violence for Colombia as a whole?

One of the central premises of this book is that violence in Antioquia was intimately linked to struggles waged between the regional and the central states and between the regional state and its peripheral inhabitants over the right to determine political, social, economic, and cultural practices. Mid-century violence, moreover, was built on latent, unresolved conflicts in the areas where it was most intense and cannot be understood outside the context of broader structural issues and transformations affecting Colombia as a whole. While no single analytical framework can adequately capture the multiplicity of reasons why violence did or did not occur in specific localities, a close reading of individual incidents of violence in Antioquia can bring to the surface multiple, lived realities that are crucial to a reconstruction of violence and its motivations and that continue to shape the geo-specific incidence of violence in contemporary Colombia. A regional study of the heterogeneous experience of local violence thus enables us to explore how the meanings of concepts such as the state, partisan affiliation, clientelism, regional identity, and citizenship were contested and redefined in historically contingent ways by different sectors of society at different times and in different places.

La Violencia was—and violence in Colombia continues to be—about state formation and reformation. The process of state formation occurred and was fought out at multiple sites among diverse, dynamic sectors and produced varying outcomes. How local and regional participants experienced the effects of state formation and how they responded to these varied in relation to specific and subjective individual and collective positionings within the region and the nation. The emergence of violence in

Antioquia was therefore not the result of a monolithic, coherent, top-down dissemination of inherited party hatreds or the result of central strategy or mandate. Rather, the escalation of partisan conflict between Colombia's two parties provided the catalyst for latent regional and local conflicts to come to the fore in the 1940s and created unprecedented opportunities for previously marginalized sectors to pursue divergent struggles in their pursuit of power. Not all Antioqueños experienced their relationship to the state or the parties in the same way. Indeed, multiple realities coexisted in Antioquia. How individual Antioqueños negotiated the complexities and challenges of mid-century change and why these negotiations were expressed most violently in peripheral areas form an essential aspect of the individual stories that make up the larger narrative of regional violence in this book. In short, for the areas most severely affected, *la Violencia* did not represent the culmination or apex of a history of partisan hatreds so much as it marked a critical stage in an evolving history of regional state and identity formation. In the peripheral areas that formed the central locus of conflict, *la Violencia* represented a fundamental struggle — and ultimate failure — to impose a hegemonic regional project of rule predicated on notions of cultural, ethnic, and racial difference.

A Theoretical Framework for Thinking about the State and Clientelism

In a recent anthology examining the impact of the Mexican Revolution and the formation of the Mexican state, Derek Sayer and Phillip Corrigan suggest that the state may either be conceptualized as a "thing," a tangible, fixed entity where power is believed to reside or, more dynamically, as a "*claim.*" In the latter instance, the state represents an attempt to "give unity, coherence, structure, and intentionality to what are in practice frequently disunited, fragmented attempts at domination."[87] For Sayer and Corrigan that which we call "the state" is subject to constant change and renegotiation. To study it requires abandoning the notion that there exists an already defined, fully operational apparatus in which power is centered. Instead, Sayer and Corrigan suggest, the study of the state is the study of how ruling practices are developed and exercised over time. The central issue of inquiry thus becomes how political power is constructed and naturalized, the effects of this naturalization, and the ways in which those that the state supposedly dominates also shape the practice of politics. "Performances," Sayer and Corrigan argue, constitute a crucial dimension of the power that represents itself as "the state" and us as members of the "body politic": "it is the exercise of power pure and simple that itself authorizes and legitimates; and it does this less by the manipulation of beliefs than by defining the boundaries of the possible."[88]

Thus, the mundane rituals of obtaining a driver's license, observing the speed limit, and paying taxes are what construct power and, over time, legitimize it. Sayer identifies the institutionalization of such rituals as the coercive aspect of the organized exercise of power. But coercive practices may also enable power. People may seize upon the obligations or forms imposed by the state to do things that were not envisioned by the framers of those forms. The state, moreover, also "incorporate[s] elements of counter-hegemonic cultures" in the interests of advancing some other agenda or as a mechanism of achieving "legitimacy." Indeed, "the hegemony of the state is also exactly what is most fragile about the state, precisely because it does depend on people living what they much of the time know to be a lie."[89]

How does a theoretical formulation of the state as a dynamic and contested process help us to understand the relationship between the state and violence in Colombia? First, by treating the state as a claim that is constantly being constructed and negotiated rather than as an immutable, ahistorical thing, it is possible to consider the existence of competing claims or states and the role such competition may have played in the development of violence. A struggle between two competing state claims, or two hegemonic projects, if you will, is precisely what I argue occurred in Antioquia in mid-century. There existed, on the one hand, a regional claim whose ruling practices—constructed over the course of the late-nineteenth and early-twentieth centuries—were characterized by a suprapartisan, pragmatic, technocratic rule, and an emphasis on material development at the expense of rigid partisan ideology.[90] It was an elite-led, paternalistic form of rule in which popular participation was limited, but it promised some social protection, education, employment, mobility, public investment, and development at a time when the central state was not yet in a position to guarantee these. In return, the regional state demanded of its citizens conformity (or the illusion of it, the "performance" to which Sayer alludes) to a specific set of values such as Catholic ritual observance, marriage, work discipline, capitalism, and political moderation. A bargain emerged in Antioquia that guaranteed a modicum of order and regularity of rule, but it operated only where the values the regional state claimed to embody found material form, that is, where access to property ownership or mobility was possible, an extensive nuclear family structure existed, and a strong sense of Catholicism operated. The linchpin of "order" was the prioritization of regional and economic interests over partisan differences and the containment of the expression of partisan differences within boundaries that would not challenge the regional status quo.

The strength of the regional state claim precluded the emergence or viability of a central state claim in Antioquia until the 1930s. One could even argue that the politics of *convivialismo,* based on the alliance of coffee producers and merchants that characterized the period from 1910 to 1930, represented a moment in which conflict between the central and regional state projects was minimized because these were one and the same. The period between 1910 and 1930—one of the few periods in Colombian history when Antioqueño politicians occupied the presidency and played a visible role in national politics—may be read as a moment in which Antioqueño elites attempted (but failed) to remake Colombia in their own idealized image. Changes in Colombia's suffrage law, the rise of the Liberal party to national power, and the expansion of what until then had been a weak and largely ineffective central state, however, brought into competition and conflict the regional and national projects of rule. Indeed, one of the most important effects of this competition between distinct state claims was that partisan clientelism threatened to eclipse a suprapartisan or bipartisan regional model of the state. The regional state model of rule mediated inclusion in the state through patron-client relations embedded in economic associations (the Federation of Coffee Growers, for instance), kinship relations, shared local origin, and the appearance of satisfaction of an idealized regional regime of cultural conformity, but not necessarily, or only secondarily, through either the Liberal or Conservative parties.[91]

The limited significance of partisan clientelism in Antioquia before the 1930s was due mainly to the availability of economic avenues of mobility whose access was not primarily or exclusively dependent upon partisan affiliation (such as coffee production, mining, and commerce). It was due as well to the persistence of a regional vision of government as technical management rather than what elite Antioqueños disdainfully referred to as *politiquería,* or politicking. This was not altruism on the elite's part per se, but rather the result of fearing class conflict more than privileging partisan loyalty. The dominance of private over public investment or, rather, the complexly intertwined nature of public and private spheres in Antioquia limited the mobilization and integration of regional clientalist networks through the central state.[92] Antioqueños who relied on state employment were obviously part of partisan patron-client machines (teachers, municipal employees, and public works personnel), but these were often regulated by regional rather than national dictates, and patronage positions constituted a small percentage of overall employment in the region before 1930.

A regional tradition of not overly privileging partisan affiliation in the distribution of even state-determined employment was so strong, moreover, that it could still be found operating even in the midst of *la Violencia* when partisan competition over patronage distribution became most acute. Antioqueño Conservatives reminded their Conservative governor in 1953 of an implicit agreement not to "take political reprisals against workers and lower-ranking employees since the individuals [Liberals] who are detrimental to the government's party are those that hold high ranking positions."[93] Even those most sympathetic to Conservative exclusionary rule insisted to the governor that he "use all the means at [his] disposal to ensure that men who fulfill their social obligations not be deprived of work or thrown into the street just because they oppose our political creed, since most of these men are fathers."[94] At the apex of *la Violencia,* the maintenance of a gendered social system of family-based capitalist integration took precedence over partisan concerns in Antioquia. In areas of the economy (agriculture, ranching, and mining) where capitalists belonged to different parties but shared economic interests, moreover, hiring was neither contingent upon partisan affiliation nor upon voting for a particular party.[95] Indeed, the apparent indifference with which the average Antioqueño approached the question of partisan politics was significant enough to prompt acute concern among politicians anxious to replace the regional model of suprapartisan rule with that of partisan clientelism during *la Violencia.* They despaired publicly of "the excessive insistence of our working people on simply economic affairs" and lamented that "Antioquia's human groups play so small a role in the struggle between the parties."[96] This tendency in Antioquia contrasted with that of other Colombian departments where employment and survival had been dependent upon public or state patronage hiring and was indexed to patron-client networks mediated through the parties since the nineteenth century, long before the emergence of an identifiably important central state.

The claim of the central state contrasted sharply with that of the regional state. The central state project was not predicated upon conformity to a specific set of cultural, economic, or social values in the way that the regional state model of rule was. Participation in the central state was technically open to any adult male simply by virtue of having been born on Colombian territory. Despite the more inclusive nature of the central state ruling project, however, the state's inability to consistently enforce its presence at either the regional or municipal level diminished its appeal among Antioqueños. While the central state's promise of labor and social legislation, land reform, and expanded political participation was certainly embraced by regional inhabitants, the central state's inability to make good on its promises undermined its potential base of support. Reluctance to identify with the project of the central state was particularly pronounced among Antioqueños residing in centrally located areas where the regional state exerted a strong presence and responded with reasonable agility to local demands and needs. For, while the regional state ruling project was predicated on conservative notions of "respectability" and "social conformity," Antioquia's political leaders were in some respects economically and socially progressive. They could be tiresomely paternalistic, but they were aggressive builders of schools, factories, health facilities, and roads. Access to the benefits of paternalistic rule, moreover, was not predicated primarily on shared partisan affiliation. Discipline and a willingness to work were held in far higher esteem than partisanship, while access to individual mobility (though not inclusion in the elite) was based on the appearance of cultural conformity and merit. Antioquia's elite was not egalitarian nor did the hegemonic bargain implied by an exchange of education, employment, and limited political access in return for apparent compliance represent an equal exchange between regional inhabitants and their leaders. But, the "bargain" struck between central core inhabitants and Medellín's elite did represent an exchange, one that typically had a better chance of being partially fulfilled than did comparable exchanges between the central state and local citizens. Such an attitude contrasted sharply with the governing style of other Colombian regions or even the central state. In centrally settled areas, moreover, conformity to regional state ruling practices and values guaranteed the enabling power that Sayer notes is the flip side of coercion. Inhabitants in core municipalities could parlay their conformity to regional ruling practices into demands that the regional state take their calls for political recognition and inclusion seriously. Further, they could demand—and expect—that the regional state prevent violence from jeopardizing local economic prosperity or the status quo regardless (in most cases) of their partisan affiliation.

The national state model of rule, in contrast, was most appealing to those sectors of Antioqueño society who in the 1930s benefited from the central state's expanded control of patronage and recently achieved regulatory functions. The growth of the central state coincided with the Liberal party's rise to power. Thus, members of the Liberal lower-class and emergent middle-class politicians in Antioquia were initially integrated into the central state's ruling project through the expansion of state employment and the recognition and co-optation of organized labor.[97] The central state project also appealed to Antioqueños left out of the regional state model of political rule, that is, the majority of the inhabitants residing in the region's periphery, including important sectors of unionized labor employed in foreign-owned industries such as mining and oil production. These sectors, in addition to identifying with the Liberal Party or parties friendly to the left wing of the Liberal party (such as the Communist or Socialist parties) defied or failed to conform to the cultural values which underpinned the regional state ruling project. The failure to reproduce the values associated with Antioqueñidad barred peripheral inhabitants from participation in the hegemonic bargain that governed relations between central core inhabitants and the regional authorities. Peripheral areas, moreover, were ones where the regional state was either absent, weak, or present only as a repressive force.

In sum, clientelism and the competition over the state did indeed play central roles in the definition of violence in Antioquia as they did elsewhere in Colombia during *la Violencia*, but the reasons why they did are specific to Antioquia and must be understood at the regional level. In the areas where the regional state was strong and enjoyed legitimacy, partisan violence never threatened the status quo and was largely avoided or was mediated in nonviolent ways. In the areas where the regional state's relationship with the local citizenry was hostile and intermittent, partisan-based clientelist networks and a central state project clashed with suprapartisan clientelism and a regional ruling project, provoking a violent conflagration that precluded the possibility of mediation. It was in geographically peripheral areas where the regional and central state claims and their respective clientelist networks came into severe competition and formed a significant catalyst to violence.

Ethnicity, Culture, and Core and Periphery Violence

In her work on frontiers and peasant protest, Catherine LeGrand suggested a close connection between the areas where *la Violencia* was most severe in the 1950s and those experiencing land conflicts in the 1920s and 1930s. Regional studies of *la Violencia* confirmed that a relationship existed between land issues and violence, but the coincidence between conflicts over land and partisan violence was considered to have occurred primarily in coffee-producing areas.[98] A very clear correlation exists between the areas experiencing the most severe violence and those where land struggles had occurred in the 1920s and 1930s in Antioquia.[99] However, the incidence of land and labor restructuring did not typically occur in Antioquia's coffee towns.

One explanation for the apparent discrepancy in experience between Antioquia and other regions in Colombia may have to do with the location of frontiers and regional migration patterns. While coffee frontiers were still open and recent migration from a variety of departments characterized provinces where violence was also severe such as Valle del Cauca, Tolima, and Viejo Caldas (the contemporary departments of Caldas, Quindío, and Risaralda), in the thirties and forties, the coffee frontier in Antioquia had effectively closed by the early part of the twentieth century. The market for land in Antioquia's traditional coffee belt was relatively static, while coffee lands in places like northern Valle, Tolima, Quindío, and Caldas were still volatile. Another factor that shaped the different geographic focus of otherwise similar conflicts in Antioquia and other departments identified as coffee producers had to do with ethnic and cultural differences between the different groups colonizing areas where violence was most pronounced.[100]

The peripheral areas experiencing the most acute violence in Antioquia shared several features which distinguished them in important ways from the settlement and dominant production and land-tenure patterns evident in the central or core zones of Antioquia. All peripheral areas bordered on departments perceived to be ethnically and culturally quite different from Antioquia or at least from an "imagined" Antioqueño ideal. Urrao bordered on the Chocó, the Pacific-lowland province with the greatest Colombian population of African descent. Bajo Cauca bordered on what was then the province of Bolívar (today Bolívar, Sucre, and Córdoba), an area connected to the Afro-Caribbean coast. Urabá bordered on both the Chocó and Panama and opened out to the Caribbean Sea, while the northeast and Magdalena Medio towns bordered on the Magdalena River and the provinces of Santander, Cundinamarca, and Boyacá. (The latter two departments being important areas of indigenous settlement.) Ironically, since Antioquia was known for its colonizing vigor, all of these areas (with the exception of Urrao) were colonized in large part by non-Antioqueño migrants from the Afro-Caribbean coast, Chocó, Bolívar, and Santander.

Before the 1930s, Antioquia's peripheral zones (all but Urrao's tropical, lowland areas) had held little attraction for Antioqueño settlers from the mountain valleys and highlands of centrally settled municipios. Regional myth attributed the reluctance of Antioqueños to venture into the northwestern and northeastern areas of their department to fears of the insalubrious climate and the presence of "wild" inhabitants in outlying areas.[101] The myth that such places were empty but for a few scattered barbarians and intrepid miners had long dominated the regional imagination. Or, as former president Carlos E. Restrepo bluntly put it when explaining why the Bajo Cauca and Urabá were unappealing sites for colonists from the central region, "Antioqueños, like the Swedes and the British, can only work where they establish their homes [hogar] [and] home cannot flourish where malaria exists."[102] Even before Carlos E. Restrepo penned these lines in 1927, however, Antioqueños shifted their colonization route away from the traditional southern coffee belt and toward distant western and eastern sections of their homeland and the lower Cauca Valley.[103] Colonists from centrally settled municipios arrived in peripheral areas as squatters hoping to work what they assumed were nearly unlimited public lands, or as cowboys, miners, and public works personnel on the railroad and newly begun, state-financed road projects. When it became apparent that many so-called tierras baldias were actually claimed by large capitalist concerns, conflicts between squatters, colonists, mining companies, and large landowners ensued.[104]

Unlike the inhabitants of centrally settled towns, the majority of non-Antioqueño residents in peripheral zones were unwilling to behave in ways that made reciprocity between the regional state and the people of the core municipalities possible. The regional state's historic absence or intermittent presence only as a punitive force in such areas also meant that none of the infrastructure, public investment, and institutional presence that integrated peoples in the central zone to the regional state was present. The construction of a relationship of hostility and distrust between the regional authorities and the periphery was intimately related to the historically colonial relationship forged between core and periphery. Local inhabitants of peripheral areas viewed Medellín and migrants from core municipios as arrogant interlopers who considered themselves both "whiter" and more civilized than non-Antioqueño migrants, while the authorities and inhabitants of Antioquia's traditionally settled areas dismissed the inhabitants of the periphery as everything they perceived themselves not to be: lazy, unruly, promiscuous, irreligious, and shifty. The periphery was linked to disorder in the minds of the regional authorities and centrally settled inhabitants and was thought to be in need of morality and control (by force if necessary). In contrast, the center was perceived as absolutist and exclusionary by peripheral inhabitants, and responsive only to demonstrations of local defiance and violent threat. But mutual distrust and antipathy between the core and periphery in Antioquia existed long before the advent of *la Violencia* and alone would have been insufficient to catalyze intense violence in peripheral areas. However, the construction of stereotypes of cultural difference gained new importance when peripheral areas emerged as Antioquia's most economically dynamic and valuable in the decades of *la Violencia*. On the one hand, the stereotype of the periphery as a site of chronic misrule became a justification for the regional state's refusal to engage in the politics of negotiation and compromise characteristic of the state's interactions with residents of central areas. On the other hand, local perceptions of the regional state as a colonial and repressive force legitimized the use of defiance by inhabitants of the periphery to counter regional attempts to impose partisan hegemonic control.

To understand the nature of violence in peripheral regions within Antioquia during *la Violencia,* then, one must acknowledge the inequalities of power embedded in colonialism.[105] Like colonies and imperial metropoles everywhere, this relationship was steeped in fantasies of extractive wealth, political domination, and cultural subordination. The latter were expressed and rooted in a regional discourse historically based upon hierarchies of cultural difference that segregated Antioquia into centrally located areas perceived to conform to a regional value system and peripheral areas perceived to deviate from it. In this study I define "centrally based municipios" as those located in the southwestern coffee region—the embodiment of Antioqueño values and comportment—the north as far as Yarumal, the south to Abejorral, and the east as far as Santo Domingo. A town such as Urrao on the border between the southwestern coffee district and the western towns of Dabeiba, Frontino, and the region of Urabá, would occupy an intermediate position, a buffer zone between the values of Antioqueñidad and external threats to the integrity of regional identity and order. The Magdalena River Valley, the lower Cauca Valley, the mining regions of the northwest and the southeastern areas of Antioquia (San Luis, Cocorná), in contrast, formed part of the unstable zone I refer to as the "periphery."

Labels such as non-Antioqueño, "*costeño*," "*negro*," and "*cosmopolita*," that is, nonwhite, were used to legitimize marginalization or exclusion and were coded to a series of attributes or patterns of behavior that might or might not characterize peripheral inhabitants but which had come to constitute a frame of reference that Antioquia's core inhabitants, authorities, and elite used to describe the "other."[106] These behaviors typically included sexual partnerships that took the form of free union (rather than Catholic marriage), physical impermanence (seasonal migration, transience, vagabondage), collective cultivation (rather than privately owned plots), a tendency to embrace dissident political movements, and the practice of folk rather than institutionalized religion.[107] These were attributes believed to contradict and endanger the ideals associated with regional identity or Antioqueñidad.

In most instances, difference was conflated with deviance, criminality, and corruption: the "other" threatened the stability of Antioqueño identity, authority, and prosperity. "Cultural competence," or the satisfaction of norms of "respectability," was in turn linked to "cultural milieu," the idea that "racial and national essences could be secured or altered by the physical, psychological, climatic, and moral surroundings in which one lived."[108] In spatial and ideological terms, Medellín and the centrally located towns over which it governed met the criteria of Antioqueñidad. These were areas defined in official discourse as being peopled by "individuals of noble race, strong, healthy, valiant and hardworking, the birthplace of liberators and heroes."[109] Peripheral or frontier towns located in the northwest (Urabá), Bajo Cauca (Caucasia), and Magdalena Medio (Puerto Berrío, Maceo) were, in contrast, tropical lowland areas of African, Indian, or non-Antioqueño migration and settlement (see appendix A.3). The inhabitants of these areas were imagined by centrally based Antioqueños as "sickly," "full of indolence," and full of "a passionate nature and inconstancy, superstitious in spirit, [and] predisposed to fetishism and anarchy."[110] More importantly, peripheral areas were not characterized by the presence of a smallholder landowning tradition, a strong local church that could broker local interests, a resident elite linked to powerful producer associations, or political representatives integrated into the bipartisan networks of Antioqueño rule.

The regional state project of hegemony, constructed and deployed by Antioquia's men of capital and political leaders, was based on the maintenance of hierarchies of difference.[111] The appeal of such norms extended beyond the elite. Tropes of supposed cultural difference could be deployed, as they were during *la Violencia,* by the central zone peoples of lower-class origin to justify homicide, usurpation of property, and rape against the "coastal peoples" (*costeños*) and "revolutionaries" (*revolucionarios*) of a similar social level. The existence of an "other" was also used to construct and reinforce the central zone inhabitant's sense of positive identity ("I am *this* because I am not *that*") and deployed as a mechanism of negotiation when bargaining for recognition or political inclusion with the regional elite. The ruling forms embedded in the regional hegemonic project thus enabled non-elites to legitimize violence in the name of protecting regional values or Antioqueñidad.

In suggesting the existence of a regional hegemonic project, and the use of stereotypes of cultural difference to further it, I am not arguing that there really existed any distinction between peripheral and central areas and their values, or that even where observable differences of production, organization, and belief were present, that these were static or inherent. Rather, I am marking the construction and manipulation of dynamic, profound, and widespread preconceptions of difference and identity and signaling their political and social repercussions. The geographer James Parsons once noted that "contemporary Antioquia was shaped out of an initial mixing of Spaniards, Indians and Black slaves," and yet Antioqueños embraced "an ethnological heresy by which the inhabitants refer to themselves as the Antioqueño race [*la raza Antioqueña*]."[112] Belief in themselves as members of a separate race (defined by the norms of respectability I have already mentioned) was "firmly rooted in popular consciousness," Parsons argued, even though by the 1940s, when he conducted his study of Antioqueño colonization, regional censuses showed that "the preponderance of mixed blood . . . stood in flagrant contradiction of the assertion that Antioquia is a province of whites."[113]

Among the core municipalities of Antioquia there emerged over time a sense of region and regional identity comparable to what Benedict Anderson has dubbed the "imagined community" that he argues enabled the emergence of nations and national identity.[114] In Antioquia, however, cultural distinctions were constructed and deployed to characterize particular areas within the region and imbue them with symbolic meaning as part of a larger process of constructing regional identity and power against both peripheral populations and the larger Colombian nation. Communities create boundaries and oppositions against which their identity may form and be marked. For Antioquia's elite and political authorities, the limits of a regional community were drawn around spaces that were long-held objects of desire. These were areas of strategic importance, characterized by natural resources and economic potential to enrich and extend Antioqueño power, but which, for various reasons, had historically proven difficult to control or resistant to Antioqueño cultural, political, and economic domination.[115] Peripheral areas were the sites in which the parameters of regional identity and authority were fought over and shaped and where violence became endemic and widespread.[116]

An adequate understanding of *la Violencia* in Antioquia thus requires the exploration of characteristics and conditions that transcend partisan considerations. What was the ethnicity of the people in conflict? What cultural patterns and expectations ruled their behavior? For how long had the zone been occupied, and where did the settlers come from? Where was the village located in relation to the older core of the department? What were relations between Liberals and Conservatives in the area before the emergence of *la Violencia*? What state institutions operated in the area, through what agents, and to what effect? What were the predominant economic activities in the area, and how were local inhabitants connected to them? What relative degree of Antioqueñidad can be ascribed to the groups in conflict? An examination of these and other elements, their interaction, and their evolution through time, occupies the body of this work.

The Book's Organization

In the first chapter I trace the attempts, from 1946 to 1949, by emergent Conservative middle-sector politicians to conservatize Liberal municipalities and to replace Liberal workers in state employment positions with Conservative followers.[117] I also examine why public works employment and competition to control patronage positions in Antioquia became so critical to the consolidation of electoral fortunes in the 1940s. When conservatization efforts met with limited success, sectors of the regional state who were followers of Conservative leader Laureano Gómez created paramilitary forces (*contrachusmas*) and deployed them into peripheral areas where the state had little support but where state-determined patronage posts were most concentrated. The official use of systematic violence provoked a rupture within the regional Conservative party that surfaced in the conflict between a regional suprapartisan political tradition and the new politics of national, state-sponsored, partisan hegemony. Chapters 2, 3, and 4 are, respectively, detailed analyses of the evolution and impact of violence in three peripheral zones: Urabá and western Antioquia; Urrao and the Southwest; and eastern Antioquia (the Bajo Cauca, Magdalena River Valley, and the Northeast). These were areas where armed Liberal guerrillas emerged to resist the Conservative national government between late 1949 and 1953. I examine how the regional and national states responded to violence in each of these areas, where the state's monopoly over force was transferred to paramilitary organizations, the reasons why this happened, and the long-term implications of such a course of action. I also explore the differences between different guerrilla groups from region to region, how partisan conflict intersected with latent tensions over land, labor, and resources in some areas, and explore the factors that impeded the possible mediation of violence. I argue that violence in peripheral areas was largely the product of concerted and systematic harassment waged by selected regional authorities rather than the "natural" outgrowth of partisan conflicts among local residents. In other words, the regional state and its forces were the primary instigators of violence on the periphery, and their object was not just the establishment of partisan hegemony but the forcible imposition of Antioqueñidad. Local resistance to the regional state was thus waged not only along partisan lines but also involved struggles over the right to cultural self-determination and the articulation of alternative conceptions of citizenship and identity. The epilogue concludes with a reflection on the relationship between current states of "disorder" in Antioquia and *la Violencia,* in particular the consolidation of private and paramilitary forms of terror in contemporary Colombia.

Pavarando, municipality of Murindo,
Urabá. April 1998. Government officers
visit this displaced persons' camp.

1. Medellín and Core Municipalities

Violence in Antioquia developed in two major stages over a seven-year period. The first stage began in 1946 and ended in 1949, the second began in 1950 and lasted until the military toppled the Conservative government of Laureano Gómez on June 13, 1953. During the first phase, violence revolved around three central objectives: achieving Conservative electoral domination in municipal, regional, and national elections; replacing Liberals in state-determined patronage or administrative positions; and crushing organized labor affiliated with the Confederation of Colombian Workers (CTC).

Violence during the first stage was selective and sporadic; it was aimed primarily at Liberals employed by the state and at towns where the level of integration between the municipal and regional government suggested that officially executed harassment, fraud, and intimidation were likely to win an electoral advantage for the Conservative party. The towns most severely affected by electoral violence were thus concentrated in centrally settled or core municipalities where the Conservative party was well represented, local government was linked through a variety of offices and mechanisms to regional administrative power structures, and local residents reproduced most closely the values associated with Antioqueñidad. This early phase of violence initially differed very little from the age-old struggles over offices and votes typical of Colombian political competition since the nineteenth century. Two issues, however, shifted the course of partisan violence and considerably intensified its potential reverberations: the assassination of Liberal populist Jorge Eliécer Gaitán in April 1948 and the creation of state-endorsed Conservative civilian police forces (*contrachusmas*) in the aftermath of the murder. Further, when official intimidation failed to wrest electoral victories or jobs away from the opposition in early 1949, the measures adopted by selective sectors of the regional government and the Conservative party in their quest for political domination became more extreme. The escalation of partisan violence provoked severe dissension within the regional Conservative and Liberal parties and revealed the existence of a threshold or boundary beyond which many Antioqueños were unwilling to go in the pursuit of partisan objectives. The intensification of state-directed violence also exacerbated tensions between municipal and regional authorities over issues of prerogative and jurisdiction and, ultimately, prompted Liberals in peripheral areas to take up arms against the state.

This chapter lays out the complicated and, at various points, contested path by which partisan conflict evolved into armed confrontation between the state and the opposition and attempts to uncover the ways in which nonpartisan issues were implicated in Liberal/Conservative conflict. *La Violencia* intersected with and magnified a series of latent and unresolved struggles concerning the power of the state, economic development, and class relations in Antioquia. As familiar partisan tensions threatened to develop in directions that challenged the social, economic, and political status quo, a still-influential elite sector intervened to mediate the consequences of violence in core municipalities. By 1949 it became evident, however, that violence waged over elections and appointments had evolved in focus and location and transcended the parameters of traditional partisan conflict.

Conservative Clientelism and Electoral Violence

On August 7, 1946, moderate Conservative, Mariano Ospina Pérez was sworn in as Colombia's president after an intensely contested electoral battle. Two Liberal candidates, Liberal populist Jorge Eliécer Gaitán and the official Liberal party candidate, Gabriel Turbay, split Colombia's Liberal majority and brought to an end sixteen years of uninterrupted Liberal control of the presidency. In his native state of Antioquia where Conservative voters still slightly outnumbered Liberals, Ospina proved a popular candidate among the region's businessmen, coffee growers, and industrialists who formed the core of the region's elite. Local capitalists hoped that Ospina's victory might signal a return to the politics of bipartisan compromise, a restoration of the pre-1930 elite alliance that many remembered nostalgically as an era of social peace unmarred by the political demands of the lower classes or emergent professional politicians. Antioquia was a province where career politicians were viewed with suspicion and where elite Liberals and Conservatives had constructed and promoted an image of themselves as selfless statesmen whose political participation was motivated by civic duty, not vile ambition.[1] Ospina's lack of direct experience in electoral politics, his impeccable business credentials, and his ideological moderation appealed to a regional bourgeoisie that had grown wary of what they perceived as increasingly extreme tendencies in both parties and the rising influence of parvenu political ambitions.

Among other Colombian Conservatives, however, Ospina Pérez was less popular. Indeed, his candidacy had been the result of reluctant compromise within the national party leadership, many of whose followers would have preferred to have made the brilliant but controversial national party chief, Laureano Gómez, their official candidate. Gómez had made a name for himself as a fierce nationalist, an outspoken admirer of Franco's Spain and a critic of Communism, an unabashed defender of Hispanic values, and a corporatist for whom the increasing secularization of modern society and mass participation in politics were anathema. The Conservative party chief was also a master orator, an ideological incendiary whose followers revered him with an intensity that bordered on religious fervor, but his intransigence elicited strong reactions from Antioquia's Conservatives as well as the Liberal opposition. Gómez's often mystical and violent rhetoric particularly frightened Antioquia's Conservative moderates who feared the repercussions of pursuing the hegemonic partisan objectives the party leader and his followers embraced. Temporarily thwarted from the presidency by moderates in his party, Gómez resigned himself to ensuring that those loyal to him would exert instead a powerful presence in local and regional politics during Mariano Ospina Pérez's administration.

In contrast to members of the regional elite, Antioqueño non-elite politicians, many of whom formed part of an incipient middle sector of first-generation professionals who had never previously held office, repudiated moderation.[2] The middle sector believed bipartisan or suprapartisan arrangements concentrated power in the hands of a small, wealthy minority and relegated ideological differences between the parties to a secondary plane in the interests of promoting common economic objectives. Many middle-sector Conservatives considered Gómez a powerful ally in their ploy to undermine the region's bipartisan approach to politics. The Conservative leader had publicly attacked *convivialismo,* the system of elite bipartisan cooperation that shaped Colombian politics from 1910 to 1930 and in which Antioquia's elite had played a central role. Indeed, Gómez implicitly blamed the Conservative party's fall from national power in 1930 on the willingness of Antioquia's elite to sacrifice ideology in the interests of economic modernization. When members of Antioquia's Conservative party collaborated with the Liberal government of Eduardo Santos (1938–1942), for instance, Laureano Gómez excoriated them mercilessly as mercenaries interested only in defending their economic interests at the expense of both party doctrine and non-elite party members.[3] Antioquia's middle-sector Conservatives, who sought to distinguish themselves from the elite, adeptly invoked Gómez's inflammatory anti-Liberal and anti-Communist rhetoric, took up the banners of militant Catholicism, and equated the politics of compromise with a utilitarian conception of society and a lack of party fervor. Ideological differences were then deployed to justify wresting control of public patronage positions away from the opposition and the reins of regional power away from moderates in both parties.

Three significant changes took place during the period of Liberal rule between 1930 and 1946 that sharpened distinctions between elite and emergent political forces within the parties and made competition for control of state patronage after 1946 an unprecedented component of electoral victories in Antioquia. First, the restructuring of capital and production following the 1929 stock market crash and the ensuing Great Depression prompted migration from coffee-producing and traditional agricultural areas such as those located immediately to the south and east of Medellín toward the provincial capital and new areas of colonization on Antioquia's periphery. The specter of social conflict arose in newly colonized areas as squatters, recent migrants, foreign-owned companies, and regional capitalists competed for control in areas where political mechanisms of expression and infrastructure were weak or nonexistent. Simultaneously, young, provincial aspirants to power migrated to Medellín in search of educational, economic, and political opportunities in unprecedented numbers. These developments were not necessarily or directly a consequence of the rise of the Liberal party to power, but the temporal coincidence of the Conservative Party's political decline and an increase in social and economic dislocation within Antioquia produced the appearance of a causal relationship, particularly in the eyes of a nervous elite worried about populist and radical threats to their political control.

Second, when Liberal Alfonso López Pumarejo's first administration (1934–1938) passed legislation expanding the size of Colombia's electorate

and recognizing and institutionalizing the political importance of organized labor, the tenor of regional political debate changed. Before the implementation of López's legislative changes, class-based appeals directed
specifically at the needs or interests of the lower and especially the urban
working class had simply not constituted an important component of
political discourse in Antioquia. The newly enhanced presence of Communist and left Liberal leadership in labor unions, and the dissemination
of political programs directed specifically at workers and the disenfran-
chised poor, based on their identity as members of a distinct class rather
than on their regional identity as suprapartisan Antioqueños, brought
into sharp relief the distinctions between "right" and "left."[4] The acrimo-
nious character of political debate between members of the two parties
increased, as did divisions within the parties between an elite alarmed by
López's reforms irrespective of their partisan affiliation and middle- and
lower-class sectors in both parties, some of whom viewed ideologically-
based partisan differences as an opportunity to press for political inclusion.

Finally, the central state's power and attributions grew under López
Pumarejo. As the state's power expanded, the Liberal party worked to
create links between the party and the state that would enable Liberal
brokers to control the distribution of public patronage jobs, access to
government intercession, and public monies. As new ministries such as
Labor (*trabajo*) emerged, and as individuals organized into labor unions
affiliated with the Confederation of Colombian Workers, the importance
of brokers who could control lower-class voters, especially urban voters,
increased dramatically.[5] The expansion of public works and patronage
jobs that accompanied the electoral and political changes introduced by
López prompted excluded regional Conservatives to associate partisan-
determined patronage hiring as a policy identified with — and crucial to
the maintenance of — Liberal domination. By the eve of the Conservative
party's return to power in 1946, control of the central state's largesse and
the monopoly of patronage distribution thus emerged to a previously unprecedented degree as crucial preconditions of political success in Antioquia. This phenomenon drove a sizable wedge between middle-sector
politicians anxious to build a political machine like that constructed by
their Liberal counterparts and a regional Conservative party elite anxious
to restore the status quo of the pre-1930 era.

The generation of men who had governed Antioquia's political fortunes from the turn of the twentieth century to 1930 was not primarily or exclusively dependent upon political careers for its place in society or political influence. Instead, these men combined political leadership with their roles as captains of industry, financiers, and coffee exporters and growers. They relied on familial connections and reputations as nonpartisan "statesmen" committed to technocratic and development-oriented policy-making to cement their political claims. Antioquia's elite was more concerned with keeping social unrest at bay than in monopolizing government positions; they attended the same schools, shared the same professions, and married into one another's families across party lines. Despite differences in partisan affiliation (which were often the result of arbitrary or serendipitous family traditions dating back to the independence era and the nineteenth century) many members of Antioquia's elite shared a worldview. This worldview was shaped by a shared education under the Jesuits at schools such as San Ignacio in Medellín or at the public Universidad de Antioquia and the regional School of Mines. The shared experience of studying under the Jesuits may also partially account for the frequency of anti-Communist discourse, as well as the invocation of the ideals of social justice, as promulgated in papal encyclicals such as Leo XIII's *Rerum Novarum,* among Antioquia's elite political leaders of both affiliations.[6]

The existence of a relatively cohesive regional approach to politics among Antioquia's elite leaders born before 1910 ensured that no definite line divided the public from the private sector while the regional bourgeoisie ruled the department. In moments of crisis a governor such as Camilo C. Restrepo (Liberal) might appeal to other members of the elite from both sides of the partisan divide, for instance, to bail out the departmental treasury and avoid a rebellion by unpaid public-sector workers, without putting up any other collateral than his word as a gentleman — an action largely inconceivable in any other Colombian department. Although Antioquia's elite belonged to both parties and had philosophical differences, Liberal and Conservative elites shared an understanding of government as a technocratic endeavor, and their central concern was maintaining the status quo. Furthering economic development and maintaining social stability defined the regional political agenda.

In contrast to the bipartisan elite, emergent middle-sector politicians were neither wealthy nor well connected. Nor was the emergent middle sector inscribed in networks of familial, business, educational, professional, or social associations with the opposition to the same degree that the elite was. The only means open to the middle sector in its quest for political power, moreover, was to generate votes, preferably among a newly enfranchised, lower-class population of urban voters. Bipartisanship was of course antithetical to such an enterprise. Unlike the regional elite who once depended on deference, paternalism, and kin- or geographically-based clientelist networks to attract voters, emergent, middle-sector politicians had to exaggerate, not underplay, partisan differences in order to distinguish themselves from politicians of comparable social extraction in the opposition. In the thirties and forties, as never before in Antioquia, politics revolved around the struggle to amass voter support and to exchange this for patronage positions and subsidies provided by an expanding central state.

The coincidence of demographic change and the suffrage reforms instituted under López thus made political competition more acute after 1935. Medellín's population quintupled between 1912 and 1951, rising from 72,000 inhabitants in 1912 to 168,000 in 1938, and on to 358,000 in 1951.[7] By 1951, Antioquia's urban areas were growing at a far quicker rate than the region's rural areas. While the province's number of urban inhabitants grew 77 percent between 1938 and 1951, the number of rural residents increased by only 13 percent during the same period.[8] As Medellín grew, so did the number of potential voters and provincial migrants in search of education and a chance to break into regional politics.[9] The sudden growth in voters, the demographic shift to the city from the countryside, the expansion of the role and influence of the central state, and the passage of favorable laws under the Liberal administration of Alfonso López Pumarejo all conspired to up the ante (and the possibility of conflict) in the Antioqueño political arena by 1946.

It would be misleading, however, to suggest that naked ambition and opportunism alone shaped the urgency with which Conservative middle-sector politicians tackled the problem of public patronage positions and electoral contests in Antioquia after 1946. Real ideological differences existed between some Liberals and Conservatives, and the Conservative preoccupation with the moral and political impact of radical, materialist ideologies on Colombian politics and society also influenced the zealousness with which the extremists attacked the Liberal opposition. Industrialization and the birth of an identifiably urban working class were recent phenomena in Medellín. The repeated booms and busts of the 1913 to

1929 period and the social and economic dislocations to which these gave rise formed the backdrop of most emergent politicians' political coming of age. Although in real terms the Communist party posed little real threat in Antioquia (or Colombia), the presence of real social discontent and the rapid economic transformation over the previous decade enabled right-leaning Conservatives to capitalize on inchoate anxieties present in Colombian society. Some of these Conservatives (men such as Belisario Betancur or José Mejía y Mejía) sympathized with working people and advocated socially progressive measures based in Catholic social teachings even though they repudiated class struggle. Others (such as Dionisio Arango Ferrer) considered the "popular classes" inherently unruly and believed that only educated men were fit to determine the destiny of the nation. For this group of Conservatives any measure that might undermine "tradition" was automatically characterized as radical agitation and the prelude to social revolution. The threat of a Communist-led revolution could be conveniently used to discredit both the Liberal opposition and their own party's bipartisan elite. "Communism" and "Communist" became catch-all terms that could be trotted out against anything or anyone who appeared to challenge the status quo, including working women in short skirts, the demand for a wage increase, or modernist overtones in regional painting.

The young men who came to form the middle sector were drawn into and shaped by public debates concerning the future of capitalism, the appeal of radical ideas among discontented workers, and the "breakdown" of traditional values and morality produced by modernity. In the 1930s, Medellín's universities and newspapers became ideological battlefields, and public demonstrations led by workers, populists, and fascist gangs competed for the city's space and the loyalties of the young. The educational reforms introduced under Liberal president Alfonso López in 1935, moreover, contributed to the growing ideological and social divide between Liberal and Conservative youth in the region. Unlike their elite leaders, Conservative and Liberal middle-sector politicians did not attend the same secondary schools or universities. When López Pumarejo redefined the national educational curriculum and incorporated Antioquia's School of Mines, where engineers—the epitome in regional elite eyes of the ideal profession for the region's leaders—had traditionally studied, into the National University system, he alienated many Antioqueño Liberals and Conservatives. Moderates from both parties resented the subordination of a regional educational establishment to a national system and the central state's effort to dictate educational policy without regional input, but more importantly they rejected the insinuation of partisan concerns in public institutions. López meant to make public schools and universities the sites of a Liberal and "modern" ethic, and he hired Liberals to further his objective. The consciously partisan nature of López's reforms spurred an exodus of Conservative students toward explicitly Catholic or Conservative educational institutions after 1935. The establishment of the Catholic Universidad Pontificia Bolivariana in Medellín and the Javeriana in Bogotá in 1936 by prominent advocates of Acción Católica and anti-Communists in the wake of the Spanish Civil War attracted middle-sector Conservatives who in another era would have attended Antioquia's public universities. López's conscious effort to purge the public schools of Conservative teachers, and his use of education as a medium of patronage through which he might advance the fortunes of his popular adherents, moreover, marked a conscious break with the politics of convivialismo embraced not only by his predecessor, Liberal Enrique Olaya Herrera, but by moderate Conservative administrations associated with Antioqueño leadership between 1910 and 1930. As such, López's educational reforms were explicitly intended to end the elite monopoly on education which through cooperation "had neutralized the opposition and excluded the *pueblo* [masses] from politics."[10]

López's reforms had a paradoxical effect on Antioqueño Conservatives. On the one hand, the region's bourgeoisie interpreted López's repudiation of the old convivialismo agreement not to meddle in education as a betrayal of gentlemen's politics.[11] Up-and-coming Conservatives from non-elite backgrounds, on the other hand, tended to agree that education, like any other aspect of government patronage, was fraught with political meaning and, as such, should be shaped by partisan ideals. The shift of these young people away from public schools became symbolic of their belief that if they remained in public schools dominated by Liberal ideas, they would forfeit their identity as Conservatives and any future claim to represent the ideological vanguard of the party. The attitude of middle-sector youth was also influenced by efforts at the municipal level of Acción Católica, the lay and religious organization devoted to sparking a reawakening of Catholic piety and countering the noxious effects of growing secularization brought on by modernity. Acción Católica vociferously called for a return to Catholic education and morals, thundered against coeducational establishments, and condemned López's reforms.[12]

The shift away from Antioquia's public secondary and university establishments by non-elite Conservatives also represented the middle sector's explicit rejection of the bourgeois ethic of technical education. Like López, young, non-elite, Conservative aspirants to power effectively understood that the regional elite's privileging of technical skill over partisan considerations exluded non-elites from access to political power.[13] By skillfully manipulating the terms of political "loyalty" and "legitimacy," mavericks could discredit suprapolitical bourgeois educational ideals as treason against the party and even as a threat to morality, social order, and the defense of religion. In the context of economic recession, popular mobilization, and global unease over Communism, such an attack amassed considerable force. In a sense, López's reforms gave middle-sector Conservative youth an incomparable justification for the more critical aspects of their rebellion against the technocratic ideal of bipartisan bourgeois leadership.

Conservative provincials who were excluded from the genteel dining rooms of the Club Unión or the editor's office of the region's elite-led daily newspaper, *El Colombiano,* took over the hallways and classrooms of local universities to air their grievances publicly and to hone their skills as orators and leaders during the sixteen-year period of Liberal rule. They forged relationships with non-elite members of their own party and joined alternative newspapers (*El 9 de Abril, La Defensa*), militant Catholic associations (La Cruz de Malta, Haz Godo Masculino, Alianza Para La Fé), and informal drinking circles where politics, ethics, and the nation's destiny were parsed and reshaped amid late-night tangos and *aguardiente* (liquor) in the bars and cafés of Medellín's bohemian sector, Guayaquil.[14] These experiences forged a sense of partisan and generational identity and left an indelible mark on the participants, many of whom rose to occupy positions of political power by the mid-1940s.[15]

Moreover, by 1945, stark disparities between social sectors were evident in Medellín. The elite, whose profits and production were expanding, and who could afford to celebrate their wealth by building elaborate art deco dwellings in upscale residential neighborhoods such as Prado, contrasted sharply with an urban working class that found it increasingly difficult to make ends meet. By the late 1940s, one-tenth of 1 percent of Colombia's population controlled 44 percent of all the profits created by what one contemporary observer termed "the highest earning period in the history of the [Colombian] economy."[16] At the same time, the worst salary years for workers in Antioquia occurred between 1939 and 1945, while the average growth of employment dropped from 1.9 percent between 1935 and 1940 to 1.4 percent between 1945 and 1950.[17] From the late 1930s through 1953, 64 percent of an Antioqueño worker's salary went to pay for food.[18] A study of railroad workers, a relatively privileged sector of Antioqueño labor, discovered in 1940 that the majority of workers' families suffered from chronic malnutrition, and in 1946 only 11 percent of Medellín's workers received wages above subsistence.[19]

Widespread misery does not by itself necessarily provoke social unrest nor threaten the status quo, but it does make those in power nervous, especially those who have only recently achieved it. The politicians who came to office in 1946 were men who balanced on a tightrope between their current professional "respectability" and a not-too-distant past as provincial, petit bourgeois supplicants who were providentially saved from rustic destinies by party-provided scholarships and support. As they surveyed their surroundings, the middle-sector politicians projected their fears of economic and social unrest onto potential rabble-rousers and "Communist" elements that they supposed were poised to infiltrate and subvert Antioquia's masses.

The impression that a radical uprising was imminent was confirmed for Antioqueño Conservatives and some elite Liberals when the dissident Liberal leader, Jorge Eliécer Gaitán, gained the electoral support of miners, port, and oil workers in peripheral towns such as Zaragoza, Caucasia, and Puerto Berrío in the 1946 presidential election. Three of the CTC's most militant unions (the oil, mining, and dock and river transport unions) were based in towns where Gaitán won between 32 percent and 59 percent of the vote.[20] The areas of Gaitán's support coincided with those hardest hit by the economic changes of the previous decade. Mining employment declined nearly 50 percent between 1938 and 1951, and over 200,000 agricultural jobs disappeared during the same years in Antioquia.[21] Conflicts between *colonos* (squatters) and landowners that had resulted in the violent expulsion of thousands of peasants in the 1930s and early 1940s, moreover, occurred precisely in the municipalities where dissident or radical political movements enjoyed the greatest support.

The implications of an intersection between mobilized workers and squatters, on the one hand, and a vibrant, dissident political leader in a moment of historical uncertainty and change, on the other, were not lost on anxious Conservative observers. Gaitán's supporters along the Magdalena River were far more militant and organized than were industrial workers based in Medellín and, as such, were not necessarily reliable indicators of the presence of a subversive substrata within Antioquia's working class. But the defiance of workers in peripheral regions in the 1940s served to give a tangible focus to Laureano Gómez's dire warnings of an imminent threat from the Left. While some levelheaded regional Conservatives recognized the difficult economic conditions that characterized the lives of rural and urban workers in the region and responded to unrest with proposals for reform, for the majority of recent political appointees, repression and red-baiting proved more expedient political options. The latter exploited local anxieties of further economic decline, pitted "responsible" urban industrial workers—many of whom were affiliated with the Jesuit-led Union of Antioqueño Workers (Unión de Trabajadores Antioqueños, or UTRAN)—against their "revolutionary" CTC-affiliated counterparts and invoked the need to defend God and nation against revolution. These visceral appeals were in turn used to justify the deployment of coercion against recalcitrant Liberal voters and the harassment and dismissal of members of the opposition from state patronage positions.

The Rise of the Middle Sector to Positions of Power

Governors and their administrative subordinates played an extraordinarily important role in the promotion of partisan violence in Antioquia between 1946 and 1949. Their powers of appointment over municipal mayors, departmental policemen, regional public works boards, contractors, inspectors, and supervisors ensured that the regional chief and his cronies could severely disrupt the conduct of municipal government through the calculated appointment of selected loyalists to local offices. Mariano Ospina Pérez appointed two kinds of Conservatives as Antioquia's governors between 1946 and 1950: moderates such as Fernando Gómez Martínez and more intransigent Conservatives either overtly affiliated with Gómez or sympathetic to him such as José María Bernal, Eduardo Berrío González, and Dionisio Arango Ferrer. The character and political sympathies of these men marked provincial politics and the development of la Violencia in important ways.

José María Bernal was Ospina's first appointee to the office of governor and served from August 1946 to November 1947. An engineer and businessman, Bernal occupied a kind of intermediate position between Antioquia's traditional bourgeois leadership and an emergent Conservative professional political class. He was an ardent Catholic and a right-leaning Conservative but did not explicitly define himself as a follower of Laureano Gómez, or *laureanista.* Bernal and Eduardo Berrío, the governor's hand-picked secretary, were products of San Ignacio, Medellín's Jesuit-run boys school, had participated in Acción Católica, contributed to the newspaper *La Defensa,* and worked together at various times in the private sector.[22] The two men shared an interest in consolidating their political careers, restoring the regional Conservative party's electoral strength, and capturing the patronage and electoral opportunities lost to the Liberal opposition over the previous sixteen years.

The governor used the months between Ospina's inauguration and the regional and municipal elections scheduled for March and October 1947 to register voters, appoint trusted Conservatives to key regional offices, and gradually rearrange the distribution of employment in Antioquia's most easily dominated *municipios.*[23] The towns experiencing the earliest incidents of partisan violence were thus those in which Conservative voters predominated or where politics were competitive (that is, divided between nearly equal numbers of Liberal and Conservative constituents). These towns were concentrated in the coffee zone, the industrial belt around Medellín, and in predominantly Conservative towns in the north, east, and west.[24] (See map 6.) Numerous factors influenced the choice of municipalities slated for conservatization by the regional governor and his supporters. Those likeliest to be targeted were densely populated and, in comparison with other parts of Antioquia, possessed of considerable wealth. After Medellín, these municipalities accounted for the largest percentage of regional budget expenses, national subsidies, and loans.[25] Affluence or economic potential was manifested through lucrative public works contracts to build roads, sewage systems, aqueducts, schools, and hospitals and constituted an important source of patronage-determined hiring (see Appendix B.1). These towns were also well integrated into the party system through municipal committees and the presence of state representatives such as mayors, police inspectors, and judges. Unlike peripheral municipalities where the regional state's presence was weak and the level of integration between local and regional

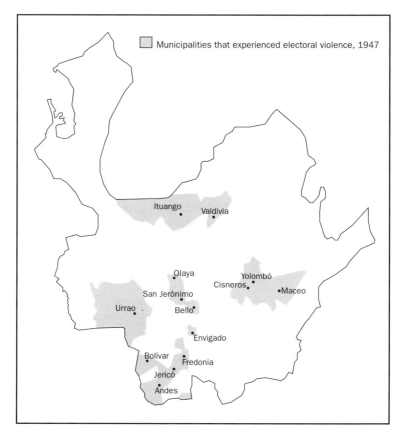

Map 6. Electoral Violence, 1947. (Source: Instituto Geográfico Augustín Codazzi and Colombia, Departamento Administrativo Nacional de Estadística)

government was tenuous, the centrality of core municipalities guaranteed that structures were already in place through which political influence could be exercised. Finally, regional hard-liners chose areas where the Conservative party already had a significant presence as their targets for electoral intimidation. Partisan numerical advantage was then used to effectively pressure into submission nearby towns with Liberal majorities where the number of Conservative voters would have been insufficient to turn the electoral tide alone (see table 1).

Direct attempts to reduce the electoral power of the opposition in overwhelmingly Liberal towns such as Santa Bárbara, Amagá, Venecia, or Angelópolis in the southwestern coffee zone were avoided. Instead, the regional authorities concentrated on converting towns around these

Table 1. Political tendencies of towns with electoral violence, Assembly Elections of March 16, 1947

Municipio	Region	Political tendency*	Liberals	Dissident Liberals	Conservatives
Santo Domingo	Oriente	Conservative	353	166	1,428
Jericó	Suroeste	Conservative	327	185	1,918
Ituango	Norte	Conservative	203	585	2,112
Amagá	Suroeste	Liberal	1,080	278	738
Yolombó	Nordeste	Liberal	876	694	1,551
Segovia	Nordeste	Liberal	514	468	339
Pueblorrico	Suroeste	Liberal	403	439	760
Ebejico	Central	Liberal	242	982	314
Olaya	Occidente	Liberal	32	132	170
Itagüí	Central	Competitive	1,132	47	753
Bello	Central	Competitive	1,382	134	1,240
Fredonia	Suroeste	Competitive	1,728	403	1,649
Envigado	Central	Competitive	1,383	538	1,762
Sopetran	Occidente	Competitive	566	329	852
Valdivia	Norte	Competitive	487	474	936
Maceo	Magdalena	Competitive	238	426	607
Bolívar	Suroeste	Competitive	510	1,162	1,594
Andes	Suroeste	Competitive	643	1,676	2,567
Caramanta	Sur	Competitive	34	747	863

(Source: Colombia, DANE, Anuario Estadístico de Antioquia, Años 1947, 1948, 1949, Apéndice 2/4 "Estadística Electoral")

*based on voting patterns prior to 1946

Liberal bastions through a strategy of intermittent cross-municipal harassment.[26] Policemen and mayors typically stripped individuals of their *cédulas,* or national identity cards, without which they were ineligible to vote; physically barred citizens from approaching the registration tables set up in the months immediately preceding elections; and harassed the opposition with verbal and physical abuse. Once towns such as Caramanta—disadvantageously bordered by solidly Conservative towns such as Támesis and Jardín—or Pueblorrico—caught between Conservative-leaning Andes and Jericó—were brought into the orbit of Conservative influence, political pressure was exerted against towns where Liberals represented a majority such as Tarso and Amagá. The towns closest to areas of solid Liberal domination that were gradually conservatized between 1947 and 1949, were, in turn, later used to extend the radius of Conservative control between 1950 and 1953.[27]

The carefully calculated use of scare tactics by public employees and members of the regional Conservative party in towns where the party already had some base of support initially failed to achieve an overwhelming victory for local Conservatives. Of the nineteen towns that reported electoral violence during 1947, six were (or had been until 1946) solidly Liberal, ten were (or had been until 1946) competitive and three were solidly Conservative. Six of the nineteen towns cast a significant percentage of their votes for Gaitán in the legislative assembly (*asamblea*) elections of March 1947 despite repeated harassment from government officers, while two towns that had not voted for Gaitán in March voted for local *gaitanistas* (followers of Gaitán) in the municipal council (*concejo*) elections of October 1947.[28] Miners and road workers, who constituted an important presence wherever support for Gaitán was statistically significant, formed the vanguard of Liberal resistance to Conservative electoral intimidation in many of these towns. Voting for Gaitán was also far greater in towns where Liberals were heavily outnumbered by Conservatives than in the rest of Antioquia's *municipios,* including those where Liberals predominated.[29] In fact, wherever Conservatives were a clear majority, Liberals relegated to the minority position voted in droves for Gaitán in what amounted to a clear act of protest and resistance against the regional government and, in some cases, against the elite-dominated Liberal party directorate and its mandates. In Abejorral, for instance, where Conservatives had historically dominated local elections and where electoral pressure did little to increase an already consolidated Conservative advantage, Liberals nonetheless delivered 88 percent of their votes for Gaitán in the Assembly election of March 1947, while 92 percent of the Liberal votes in equally Conservative Cocorná were also cast for Gaitán. The Liberal inhabitants of Toledo in the north who made up only 21 percent of the town's electorate cast all their votes for Gaitán (see table 2).

The results of the March 1947 elections proved disappointing to Conservative hard-liners. Conservatives handily won majorities in the southernmost corner of Antioquia from Andes up through Jericó, Támesis, Pueblorrico, and Amagá, areas where many inhabitants already belonged to the party, but they absolutely failed to destroy Liberal control over most historically Liberal towns. Only four towns where Liberals were

Table 2. Conservative towns with heavy Liberal-dissident voting, Assembly Elections, March 16, 1947

Municipality	Region	Liberals		Gaitanistas		Conservatives		Gaitanistas as Percentage of Liberal Total
		Number	%	Number	%	Number	%	
Cocorná	Oriente	11	1	121	6	1,810	93	92
Guatapé	Oriente	2	0	40	8	465	92	95
Angostura	Norte	21	2	96	7	1,244	91	82
Nariño	Sur	2	0	255	14	1,615	86	99
Peñol	Oriente	19	1	177	14	1,113	85	90
Campamento	Norte	30	3	136	13	851	84	82
Yarumal	Norte	55	1	610	16	3,185	83	92
Toledo	Norte	0	0	123	18	577	82	100
Liborina	Occidente	35	2	293	21	1,087	77	89
Ituango	Norte	203	7	585	20	2,112	73	74
Abejorral	Sur	125	4	878	27	2,212	69	88
Anorí	Nordeste	24	2	359	32	741	66	94

(Source: Colombia, DANE, Anuario Estadístico de Antioquia, Años 1947, 1948, 1949, Apéndice 2/4, "Estadística Electoral")

or had been an important presence before 1946—Olaya, Pueblorrico, Tarso, and Yolombó—were completely conservatized, although harassment lowered Liberal returns throughout the region.[30]

Although regional Conservative attempts to use official forces in the quest to achieve electoral domination produced unremarkable results, individuals such as José María Bernal and Eduardo Berrío González continued to deploy public forces for partisan purposes. Indeed, the first instances of local violence in Antioquia emerged as a direct consequence of state-directed harassment rather than from internal divisions between local members of the two parties. The Liberal party committee in the southern coffee town of Caramanta (which had boasted a slight Liberal majority before the Conservative party came to power in 1946) was the first Antioqueño town to accuse the regional authorities of instigating local partisan violence. The governor had replaced Caramanta's native-born mayor with a Conservative appointee from another part of Antioquia and used him to ensure an electoral victory for the government's party. When confronted with Caramanta's complaint, the governor retorted that his replacement of the native-born Liberal mayor by a nonnative Conservative had been guided by "purely administrative" concerns, and he scathingly reminded local Liberals that in the determination of appointments "there existed no Conservatives or Liberals, but only citizens."[31] Yet, as quickly became apparent, the right to control state patronage and shape local appointments was heavily influenced by partisan and personal considerations as was the response of the regional government when faced with municipal complaints regarding violence promoted by public employees or official regional policies.

For instance, wealthy Liberals in another coffee town, Titiribí, where some of the region's largest coffee haciendas were located, repeatedly complained to the governor of disputes arising from the municipal council election of 1947.[32] They warned the regional authorities in Medellín that if partisan tensions were allowed to proceed unchecked, they might provoke a violent reaction that could have serious economic consequences in the region as a whole. When Governor Bernal ignored Titiribí's complaints, members of the local elite simply bypassed the governor and went straight to the president instead. They appealed to Ospina Pérez as an elite, Antioqueño native son, a former businessman like themselves who could appreciate the dangerous economic consequences of using the state's officers to pursue a partisan policy. Alarmed as they hoped he would be, the president pressured Antioquia's governor to stop harassing Titiribí's Liberal constituents.[33]

Local reactions to officially sanctioned electoral intimidation and the regional government's response to local grievances increasingly intersected with older tensions between municipal and regional inhabitants regarding the centralization and usurpation of power by the regional state. The way in which regional and central governments chose to respond to complaints of violence such as those made by Titiribí's Liberal property holders also brought to the surface latent tensions within Antioquia's parties. In the case of Titiribí, for instance, the president shared the same preconceptions as local Liberal coffee growers. Like them, he balked at the use of partisan-motivated violence that might affect elite fortunes or jeopardize a critical sector of the regional economy. The governor, in contrast, had little in common with the town's elite and placed the possible economic repercussions of partisan-motivated policies considerably below his priority as a middle-sector party loyalist to ensure Conservative electoral victories. The case of Titiribí illustrates the inherent differences that emerged during *la Violencia* between a regional-elite political tradition that privileged economic development above partisan issues and the ideologically inspired politics of middle-sector regional Conservatives. But Titiribí's experience also laid bare the uneasy relationship between the president and his regional middle-sector subordinates. While the president's direct intercession ensured that Titiribí's grievances were redressed, the recalcitrant governor whose authority the president overrode remained firmly ensconced in office.

In Antioquia, 1947 was not a particularly violent year, but it was a year in which municipalities increasingly gave voice to and repudiated regional policies intended to shape local electoral politics and the determination of appointments to local offices. Two cases involving local complaints of partisan-motivated violence during the year illustrate the character of clashes between municipalities and the regional government and the variety of official responses to incidents of municipal unrest. Two months after Liberals in Titiribí filed their complaint, disgruntled townspeople in the sparsely populated, predominantly black frontier town of Cáceres in the Bajo Cauca region also reported incidents of partisan-motivated violence, but they were ignored by both the regional and central governments. Cáceres, like Titiribí, was an overwhelmingly Liberal town, but unlike Titiribí or other Liberal southwestern coffee towns, the inhabitants of Cáceres possessed little leverage with which to influence either the regional or national government. The town's voters were few, poorly organized, and historically had displayed a high rate of electoral abstention.[34] Cáceres also lacked brokers (such as elite coffee producers) who might have influenced the central government, through the mediation of a private producer association, to force a regional intervention on its behalf. Thus, when Governor Bernal's appointment of a Conservative mayor in Cáceres provoked local outrage as it had in Caramanta and Titiribí, it won Bernal a mild rebuke from the central government but effected no change in regional policy. Governor Bernal could and did defend his refusal to replace the offending town mayor by shifting blame away from the issue of partisan discrimination and toward the town's peripheral geographic location and general poverty: "I am not bent on maintaining ignorant elements in the office of municipal mayor," Bernal caustically responded to a central government reprimand, "the reality is that for those areas, climates, and salaries, one cannot obtain terribly competent elements. The governor's office would like to send a whole mayor [*todo un alcalde*], but can only send 180 pesos worth of a mayor [that is, a second-rate mayor]."[35]

Violence in economically important towns where Conservatives were numerous, in turn, elicited yet a different response from the central and regional governments.[36] The southwestern town of Fredonia was the largest volume producer of coffee in Antioquia. The regional railroad ran an expensive trunk line between Medellín and the town only to service coffee and cattle haciendas owned by members of the regional bourgeoisie. Evenly divided between Liberal and Conservative voters, Fredonia tended to give a slight local majority to whatever party happened to be in power in Bogotá.[37] In 1947, however, Liberals dominated the town council. They voted the salaries and controlled the appointment of several local government officers and the town's police. When Governor Bernal appointed a Conservative mayor to ensure Fredonia's shift back to a Conservative majority in the 1947 elections, the town council refused to cooperate with him. In fact, the local police hired by the council resisted the mayor's attempt to usurp the council's authority and shot a local Conservative leader when he interceded on the mayor's behalf.

Members of a locally influential Conservative political family and other highly placed regional politicians mobilized immediately to impress upon the governor the severity of the threat to public order in the town.[38] Governor Bernal rapidly deployed ten departmental guards and a police lieutenant to reestablish peace in the municipality, but when the departmental police interceded, a confrontation ensued, leaving seven individuals gravely injured and a member of Antioquia's Conservative party directorate dead. A flurry of preoccupied telegrams was exchanged between the governor, the president of Colombia and Fredonia's municipal officials. Both Bogotá's Conservative and Liberal dailies, *El Siglo* and *El Tiempo,* reported extensively on the happenings in Fredonia, and, in response to criticisms of gubernatorial mishandling made by both Liberals and Conservatives, the governor offered the president his resignation.

Violence in Fredonia elicited a response from both the governor and the president in a way that partisan violence affecting elite Liberal interests in Titiribí and Caramanta had not. The otherwise defiant Conservative governor's willingness to step down when violence in Fredonia was determined to be at least partially his responsibility, moreover, attests to the superior influence exerted by Conservative elite interests on both the regional and national governments. But these cases also point to the significance of well-established institutional mechanisms for ensuring

Medellín and Core Municipalities 63

the smooth functioning of accountability and power between municipal and regional authorities. Despite differences in their partisan make-up, both Fredonia's and Titiribí's experiences were typical of the trajectory of partisan violence within sectors of core or traditional settlement such as Antioquia's coffee zone. The combined effect of strategic economic interests and established networks of political influence enabled citizens to pressure either the regional or central government into taking their concerns seriously regardless of their political affiliation. In contrast, both the regional and central governments ignored local complaints of partisan violence waged in Cáceres. In addition to being overwhelmingly Liberal, Cáceres had no way of mobilizing a collective protest against the state in a way that would guarantee a receptive audience. It was economically valuable, but its wealth was in the hands of absentee landlords and foreign-owned mining concerns, while those who inhabited the town lacked the institutional intermediaries and political infrastructure to make their grievances count.

Decisions made to resolve incidents of violence in Antioquia's *municipios* were thus based at least in part on factors that transcended the partisan composition of a particular municipal electorate. More than whether a town was Liberal or Conservative, the location and composition (both ethnic and partisan) and the presence of powerful brokers whose interests either the regional or central government could not afford to ignore determined official responses to local incidents of violence. Such considerations become an important factor in determining why partisan violence in towns with Liberal majorities could evolve in fundamentally distinct ways.

Violence by Other Means:
The Substitution of Liberals on Public Boards

The effort to achieve electoral victories for the Conservative party in 1947 was accompanied by a concerted attempt to dislodge the Liberal opposition from its dominant position in public sector employment. Middle-sector Conservatives also sought to alter the composition of crucial municipal advisory bodies and regional boards that regulated public works bidding, hiring, and investment. What was at stake was control of an increasingly lucrative and electorally significant chunk of state-determined patronage.

Conservative municipal committees in towns such as Bello, a densely populated, industrial, working-class town within Medellín's metropolitan hub, were among the first to attempt to use the rise of their party to positions of regional authority to gain control of public patronage. Bello's local Conservative committee members demanded that the regional governor intercede and manage the election of the Concejo de la Cooperativa de Municipalidades (Municipal Cooperatives Board) in order to guarantee a majority of Conservative representatives. Majority control of the board would finally enable local Conservative politicians to usurp and build upon state-sponsored jobs and contracts long dominated by members of the opposition. A year later, in 1948, local Conservatives congratulated the governor for "eliminating . . . the evil cabal [*rosca*] that . . . used its power [on the board] to pursue hateful and exclusionary policies, engaging in abuses with the membership's dues."[39] The governor's behind-the-scenes manipulation of elections to the cooperative's board in Envigado, another important industrial town with a Liberal majority, also succeeded in guaranteeing local Conservatives an edge over the opposition. The newly elected board members promptly cut off funds and interrupted important public works contracts that were already in process and would have benefited Liberal political brokers and workers.[40]

Governors also intervened during *la Violencia* to rearrange the composition of administrative boards governing the railroad, customs, public roads, and the Social Security Institute, although this meddling that targeted elite members of the opposition sometimes proved difficult to accomplish. Only a cataclysmic event such as the death of Gaitán enabled Governor Dionisio Arango Ferrer to finally rid himself of the presence of Captain Julián Uribe Gaviria, Antioquia's Liberal party leader, a former governor of the department, and the president of the regional committee of the Federation of Coffee Growers who sat on Antioquia's powerful Junta de Rentas, or Customs Revenue Board.[41] Even so, Uribe Gaviria was not removed without a struggle. Within days of his dismissal the minister of government, Darío Echandía, formally complained that such unwarranted substitutions were unlawful and demanded Uribe Gaviria's reinstatement. But Antioquia's governor defended his actions by invoking Law 60 of 1930 which held that departmental officers of which the board members of the Junta de Rentas formed a part, could not simultaneously hold party offices, and that, in any case, Liberals continued to be represented on the Junta.[42] The governor's action stuck and the central government was forced to back down in the first of what would be many show-downs between regional and national authorities over appointments and administrative powers.

If some modicum of protection was exercised to prevent the subor-dination of regional material progress to the vagaries of partisan com-petition and to limit wholesale dismissals of members of the elite from influential regional boards during *la Violencia,* very little protection was extended to workers. Indeed, organized labor, especially that employed by the state, was one of the earliest sectors of Antioquia's population to feel the effect of regional, state-directed, partisan violence. In addition to wishing to replace Liberal workers with Conservative ones, Conservative hard-liners also targeted public sector workers for harassment in order to crush particular unions, specifically those affiliated with the CTC such as Antioquia's municipal employees, miners, road, railroad, public utilities, oil, and port workers.[43]

Conservative attacks on the Communist and *gaitanista* leadership and rank and file that made up the CTC initially met with little resistance from Antioquia's men of capital, including those professing a loyalty to the Liberal party. The regional bourgeoisie had made explicit their lack of sympathy for organized labor in general, but particularly for so-called "agitators" and "Communists" since the days of Alfonso López Puma-rejo's first presidential administration (1934–1938). In fact, when interim Liberal President Alberto Lleras cracked down on the Communist-led Magadalena Port Workers Union (FEDENAL) in 1945 and replaced 1,080 union members with scab labor, Liberal Antioqueño businessmen ap-plauded.[44] The most serious opposition to López's pro-labor measures within Colombia's Liberal ranks came, in fact, from Antioquia's business-men and industrialists. Thus, when Conservative Maríano Ospina Pérez struck at the CTC's influence by granting legal recognition to a compet-ing national labor federation, the Catholic-inspired Union of Colombian Workers (UTC), his actions elicited little opposition from Antioquia's em-ployers, regardless of their partisan affiliation. It was in Antioquia, the nation's leading industrial and mining center after all, where dissident Liberal leader Gaitán's regional followers had long lamented, "the weight of oligarchic strength [was] strongest" in Colombia.[45] Antioquia's bour-geoisie even opposed modest attempts to require employers to increase their already low contribution to the Social Security Institute (Instituto de Seguro Social) insisting that any expansion in state bureaucratic power constituted an unconstitutional attempt to diminish or wrest power of determination over social policy from private and regional hands.

The most militant sectors of labor in Antioquia thus anticipated that the rise of Ospina and his supporters to positions of power would intensify the state's reactions to labor unrest. They would be right. Shortly after the president's inauguration and his announcement of José María Bernal's appointment as governor, regional unions initiated a wave of strikes to protest conditions in foreign-owned mining companies and the rising cost of living. Rank-and-file petroleum workers in Remedios, Antioquia, and Barrancabermeja, Santander, employed by Shell and Tropical Oil and affiliated with the Colombian Petroleum Workers Union struck in October and November of 1946, while the Federation of Antioqueño Workers (FEDETA) to which municipal employees, teachers, and public road workers belonged, threatened to produce a list of demands if the petitions of the region's slaughterhouse workers were not met. As a form of political protest against the elite leadership of the Liberal party, moreover, miners, oil workers, and road workers in Antioquia voted overwhelmingly for *gaitanista* candidates in towns such as Betulia, Caucasia, Dabeiba, Ebéjico, Péque, Remedios, Turbo, Segovia, Zaragoza, Titiribí, and Puerto Berrío in the March 1947 elections.[46]

Gaitán threatened to call a general strike shortly after the March elections if Liberal victories in Asamblea and congressional elections were not respected by the central government.[47] In April the CTC voted to make Gaitán's threat a reality and struck to protest the unlawful dismissal of union members and the use of police surveillance and repression against workers. But Medellín's industrialists (of both parties) and the region's Catholic-inspired Union of Antioqueño Workers (UTRAN) refused to back the general strike, and Gaitán himself, after having issued the call for a strike, refused to openly support the CTC.[48] When in May Antioquia's railroad workers participated in the general strike to protest the growing use of official violence against workers, declining pay, and deteriorating social conditions, the regional government declared the strike illegal and seized the opportunity to dismiss railroad workers it deemed "inconvenient."[49]

Members of the CTC were clearly among the earliest objects of Conservative attack, but the only workers to consistently be made targets of Conservative harassment and dismissals were railroad and municipal workers, that is, individuals who held positions dependent upon political patronage and whose employer was the state. It was these workers whom Conservatives in the regional administration blamed for the party's inability to wrest control of strategic town councils during the 1947 elections. In contrast, the regional government was far more cautious when dealing with oil workers and miners who were not part of the state's patronage rolls. The governor's reaction to labor unrest at Shell Oil's Casabe camp in Remedios is a case in point. In August 1947 Shell's management telegraphed the governor urgently requesting twenty departmental policemen to protect the company from a labor uprising that threatened to take over the camp, but the regional government refused, insisting that it would be unseemly to defend a foreign company against Colombian workers.[50] Taking a nationalist line, Secretary of Government (lieutenant governor) Eduardo Berrío suggested the company hire off-duty policemen as other foreign-owned companies did rather than expect the regional government to underwrite Shell Oil's security needs.[51]

The governor's response to Shell's management did not emanate from any sort of personal empathy for oil workers. Indeed, the governor had more than once derided them as revolutionaries and Communists. Instead, Berrío was concerned that it might appear as if the regional government were kowtowing to the company by deploying departmental policemen to repress workers, and he did not want to risk being blamed for possible fuel shortages that might result from worker protests. Oil production in Antioquia had tripled between 1945 and 1947, and the revenue generated by an obligatory tax on it was used to pay for regional public works projects.[52] Oil was thus too strategic and lucrative a commodity for the regional government to risk jeopardizing its production even when ideological principles were involved. In refusing Shell's request for departmental aid the governor was slyly angling to force Shell Oil's hand, to convince the company's management of the wisdom of opening employment in the camp to Conservative workers and Conservative political influence while avoiding the impression that the government was interfering to benefit a foreign-owned enterprise.

The Casabe labor uprising spurred considerable anxiety among Antioquia's regional authorities, who increasingly worried about the presence of "provocateurs" among the ranks of Antioquia's labor force by late 1947. But regional authorities channeled such concerns toward public sector workers, not the miners or oil workers who were the likeliest sources of agitation. Consequently, the regional and central governments embarked upon a series of measures intended to restrict the mobility of labor in Medellín and other areas boasting a heavy presence of state employees.[53] Among other tactics, the authorities commissioned inquiries to measure the partisan composition and sympathies of workers in the railroad, road construction, and the municipal public works programs while simultaneously increasing the number of guards patrolling railroad dormitories. The regional authorities also enforced curfews and authorized searches of workers suspected to be carrying arms or engaged in "subversive" activities. The departmental police under the direct authority of the regional government emerged as the preferred medium of state repression directed at public sector workers. It was the departmental police, for instance, who were used to crush the railroad strike in May of 1947.

The routine use of policemen to repress and harass labor was not a phenomenon introduced during *la Violencia* nor a tactic exclusive to Conservative authorities in Antioquia, but it undoubtedly escalated and provoked greater resistance than had ever been true during earlier administrations. Regardless of partisan affiliation, for instance, earlier regional authorities had made a habit of deploying police agents to break up strikes and protect private property against the interests of labor since around 1910. This had fed a widespread sense of hostility between workers and policemen that went back several decades. But when animosity between workers and police took on partisan overtones, the tensions between these two groups rose to new heights. Finally, the assassination of Gaitán in April 1948 marked a new low in police and labor relations in Antioquia as the rate of attacks led by *laureanistas* in the regional government against public sector workers rose dramatically and as private forms of violence were introduced to complement the repressive activities of the police against public sector and industrial workers.

The Failure of Conservatization and the Escalation of Violence

Despite the use of officially sanctioned harassment against selective Liberal workers and towns during the first two years of Conservative rule in Antioquia, surprisingly few incidents of local violence actually took place in the region. Fewer still were reported in either the press or to the governor's office during the months between the October 1947 elections and the assassination of the Liberal leader, Jorge Eliécer Gaitán, in Bogotá on

April 9, 1948. The department's relative calm was shattered, however, by Gaitán's murder.

Gaitán had not been particularly popular in Antioquia before his death. In contrast to cities such as Cali or Bogotá where support for Gaitán had been significant (up to 50 percent of the urban vote, for instance), less than 5 percent of Medellín or Antioquia's electorate had voted for him in the 1946 presidential election. Antioqueño support for the Liberal dissident leader had begun to pick up by the congressional and regional assembly elections of March 1947, however, and a number of Gaitán's local followers won seats on Medellín's town council in the October 1947 election. Still, Gaitán's limited and selective popularity in Antioquia as a whole probably explains why Medellín and most of Antioquia escaped the more destructive effects of popular protest in the wake of his death. The primary target of armed popular violence in Medellín was the Conservative newspaper, *La Defensa*. The newspaper's offices were set afire to punish it for being the headquarters of right-wing Catholic and *laureanista* Conservatives who were blamed by popular sectors of the Liberal party for both Gaitán's death and the general escalation of partisan violence in Colombia. When compared with the effect of popular rage in Bogotá, where nearly half of the urban center was destroyed in less than twenty-four hours, however, the extent of damage inflicted in Medellín appears almost slight. Not so the reaction of the regional authorities.

A prominent labor lawyer in Medellín remembers that after Gaitán's assassination, "labor activists and leaders" and those "who sympathized with the left" were "indiscriminately imprisoned."[54] When the city's jail cells were filled to capacity, the authorities comandeered public schools and, having exhausted the available space in those as well, constructed a makeshift prison camp in the municipal bull ring. The majority of those held were "railroad workers, particularly those who worked the line between Medellín and Puerto Berrío."[55] The authorities chose to detain those from areas of Antioquia where violent demonstrations followed Gaitán's assassination and where, in some cases, revolutionary juntas had taken control of municipal governments. These were towns in which miners, oil, road, and port workers constituted a significant demographic and political presence. Most, although not all, of the sites of popular violence were located on Antioquia's periphery. The railroad workers employed on the line between Medellín and Puerto Berrío emerged as the conduits between provincial and urban rebellion.

Gaitán's assassination was felt most strongly in the port town of Puerto Berrío, the oil camps in Yondó, Remedios, southwestern towns such as Andes, Bolívar, Anzá, and Urrao, and in western towns such as Buriticá, Peque, and Turbo.[56] All of these were towns where public works projects employing road and railroad workers were present, and these workers played important roles in leading popular protests. Arson and the looting of commercial establishments and government offices such as the courthouse, mayor's office, and customhouse took place in Puerto Berrío, around the train station in Bolombolo, Venecia, and in the Shell Oil camp in Casabe. Acts of sedition were attempted in Dabeiba, Cáceres, Cisneros, Peque, Titiribí, Venecia, Fredonia, Concepción, Envigado, and Santo Domingo. Six of these towns were located in the southwest and near east, not the periphery, but all were characterized by the strong presence of organized labor, especially road workers, railroad personnel, and miners.[57] All of these were also towns in which a significant sector of the local Liberal electorate had voted for the *gaitanista* slate in the regional assembly and national congressional elections of October 1947.

The southwestern town of Bolívar emerged as a focal point of violence. A narrow Liberal majority had characterized it until 1945, but the town was conservatized between the election for town council in October 1945 and the presidential election of 1946. One of the first measures proposed by Bolívar's mayor in the wake of Gaitán's assassination was the right to substitute three Conservative workers for three CTC members from the local road working crew who were deemed to be "subversives." Local Conservatives then volunteered their services to the government with arms and vehicles to meet the challenges posed to state authority by workers up in arms.[58] The presence of ready and willing local Conservative volunteers and Bolívar's strategic location — it's proximity to both the department of Chocó and public sector workers in nearby southwestern towns — made it an ideal site for counterrevolutionary Conservative organization. These organizations, incorporating both local police and Conservative civilian volunteers (contrachusma) were deployed to quell Liberal uprisings in other areas. Bolombolo, a village in Venecia, where Liberals were powerful and where a large concentration of truck drivers, road crews, and railroad personnel worked and resided, for example, became the immediate target of Conservative posses from Bolívar in the wake of Gaitán's death.[59] When road workers from Quibdó and Carmen del Atrato in the Chocó rose up in arms in reaction to Gaitán's assassination, seized Antioqueño citizens, destroyed telegraph lines, and substituted their own supporters in public works jobs, moreover, it was counterrevolutionary forces based in Bolívar who were sent to put these disturbances down.[60] Although Governor Arango Ferrer authorized the creation of civilian police corps and handed out official arms to selectively recruited Conservative volunteers elsewhere in the department, Bolívar seems to have been one of the first testing grounds in Antioquia for the emergent contrachusma.[61]

The aftershocks of Gaitán's death were also acutely felt in areas where militant workers not employed by the state were present. Indeed, these workers appear to have been emboldened by the brief period of revolutionary takeovers of some town governments and the general chaos caused by Gaitán's assassination. Striking oil workers at the Shell Oil Casabe camp used the excuse of public disorder as a bargaining chip to demand the right to determine the political affiliation of candidates for the offices of inspector and judge as a condition of putting down their arms.[62] Demands such as these that were accompanied by the actual use or threat of violence fed a growing paranoia in the Conservative government. Regional and national authorities suspected conspiratorial plots to overthrow Conservative office holders everywhere and suspected organized labor of spearheading them. Hence the confidential warning secretly telegraphed by the governor admonishing his subordinates to keep an eye on explosives, transport, communications systems, radio stations, airports, munitions warehouses, aqueducts, electrical plants, fuel reserves, telephones, and oil pipelines.[63] Months after Gaitán's assassination, President Ospina Pérez continued to urge all governors to remain alert to the possibility of future subversive movements or orders for strikes to be carried out by CTC affiliates. He also exhorted governors to maintain a close level of coordination with local military commanders in order to have troops stationed in a timely fashion in the principal provincial cities.[64]

While few workers in Medellín and its industrial hub ultimately mobilized to protest the slain political leader's demise, the regional authorities capitalized on the incidence of revolutionary protest in other crucial Antioqueño towns to justify the general harassment and dismissal of state employees and workers everywhere. Conservative authorities pointed to popular insurrections in certain towns as incontrovertible evidence of a long-predicted Communist plot to seize control of Colombia. The force of this argument resonated with some members of the region's Liberal elite, who in subsequent years referred to popular outbursts of rage in the wake of Gaitán's death as a "copious criminal hemorrage" that justified the use of repression.[65] Members of Medellín's Liberal oligarchy such as Carlos Uribe Echeverri, for instance, threw their support behind Laureano Gómez after Gaitán's assassination, lamenting publicly that little effort to combat Communism could be expected from his own party.[66] While elite Liberals did not endorse the use of partisan policies to discriminate against fellow party members, state-directed repression against organized labor, especially that perceived to be under Communist leadership, certainly enjoyed the tacit endorsement of many members of the Liberal bourgeoisie in Antioquia.

Ospina Pérez understood the essentially conservative nature of his regional compatriots in both parties and the deep anxiety that popular mobilizations of any sort awakened in them, although he may have misjudged the choleric temper of the man he chose to restore order in his native department. To preempt the spread of popular insurrection in Antioquia, Mariano Ospina Pérez roused Dionisio Arango Ferrer out of bed at two in the morning the day after Gaitán's assassination and named him Antioquia's governor.[67] Part of the crowd of Jesuit-trained, middle-sector politicians, Arango Ferrer gradually forged a reputation as the Conservative party's troubleshooter. He was the man the party relied upon when public order matters reached critical proportions. Arango, like other members of the middle sector, opposed bipartisanship and was not reluctant to use force to maintain order. Where he differed from the younger, middle-sector politicians who surrounded him in the regional bureaucracy not only during his 1948 term as governor but later in 1952 and 1953 when he resumed the post, was his clear antagonism to populism. Arango believed that only the "intelligent" men of the party could keep insubordination at bay, and he was extremely distrustful of the *pueblo*.

An hour after the president's summons, Dionisio Arango Ferrer strode into the crowd milling around the Parque de Berrío to reclaim the governor's seat from what he disdainfully referred to as "the mob" and immediately called a meeting of "notable" Conservatives.[68] Convinced that the turmoil surrounding Gaitán's death was a prelude to a "Communist" takeover, the group agreed not to recognize any self-imposed revolutionary junta that might claim to have deposed Maríano Ospina Pérez in Bogotá.[69] Arango Ferrer did two more things during the morning of April 10: he called Eduardo Berrío González in the town of Santa Rosa and reappointed him departmental secretary, and he called up Conservative reserve officers from the southern town of Sonsón to protect Medellín.[70]

The governor's first actions had special significance. Eduardo Berrío González had been instrumental in the appointment of Conservative loyalists as mayors throughout Antioquia during his recent stint as departmental secretary. He had also played a seminal role in establishing the legal basis for the organization of armed rural civilian patrols during the same period (1946–1947). The mobilization of Sonsón's reserve officers, moreover, was significant because the town's inhabitants were known for their doctrinaire Catholicism and entrenched Conservatism. Arango Ferrer thus called upon partisan loyalists to defend Medellín and the governor's palace, rather than the departmental police, army, or national police which contained Liberal agents and non-Antioqueños. Under Arango Ferrer's administration, the rabid xenophobia that became a distinctive feature of Antioquia's administrative policies throughout the period of *la Violencia,* and which contributed in no small fashion to the intensification of local resentment against the regional government, received its first boost.

The eight months of Arango Ferrer's term as Antioquia's governor (April 10–December 4, 1948) were spent eradicating supposed centers of insurrection in the region. In July 1948, he empowered the customs revenue agents to foment the creation of permanent, auxiliary, civilian police forces at the municipal level.[71] This action made it evident why removing Liberal Captain Julian Uribe Gaviria from the customs board had been imperative and gave teeth to the paper tiger created by Governor Bernal in 1947 when he fought for the legal right of civilians to bear arms and organize rural patrol groups. The auxiliary civilian police were to be paid either through additional funds voted by local town councils or, wherever the town council refused to cooperate, by customs monies and the tax on the regional liquor monopoly.[72] The right to allocate funds for the creation of what amounted to a paramilitary organization that circumvented the veto power of legitimately elected municipal councils made customs officers into one of the most feared and powerful of the regional government's forces and marked an important watershed in the evolution of partisan conflict in Antioquia.

Along with the national police, customs revenue agents were among the public functionaries against whom the greatest number of complaints were registered.[73] When it became apparent how dangerous the autonomous armed groups bankrolled by custom agents could be to even Conservative interests, regional attempts (by *visitadores administrativos,* in particular) to curb them, were met with defiance and threats of violence.[74] A year after Gaitán's assassination, Conservatives in the southwestern town of Jardín complained of contrachusmas from the department of Caldas who had arrived sometime after Gaitán's assassination and began "sowing terror" in the region.[75] Contrachusma forces indiscriminately harassed both Liberals and Conservatives who repudiated their violent methods. They also routinely subverted the lines of authority that bound the regional and local government together. Regional detectives posted to oversee matters in Jardín, for instance, reported that when they appealed to the customs agents to help them capture the armed men from Caldas and protect the townspeople, the revenue agents rebuffed them: "We asked the administrator of the departmental customs revenues . . . to help us conduct a sweep against [the armed men from Caldas]," the local detectives complained to their superior and the governor, "but the administrator himself told us that when he instructed one of the revenue agents to help us, the agent replied that he'd rather be fired because he wasn't against those people, and we shouldn't think he was going to help us out." When the regional detectives threatened the customs agents with dismissal, they smugly retorted "that they were connected with certain political elements who would back them up and come to their aid if [the detectives] were to proceed against them."[76]

The dissemination of violence and the role of specific sectors within the regional state bureaucracy in promoting it, particularly in the aftermath of Gaitán's death, further fractured an already disunited regional Conservative party. While the majority of Antioquia's Conservatives might agree about the need to recapture offices and power from the opposition, no agreement existed among Conservatives regarding the means used to advance these objectives. When the "*reconquista*" began to have wider reverberations—affecting Conservatives as well as Liberals, compromising the realization of regional public works projects, threatening production, and spurring latent socioeconomic conflicts unrelated to partisan issues—dissension within the Conservative party became severe. Alarmed by the high-handedness of the individual to whom he had entrusted his native region's political fortunes, President Ospina Pérez dismissed Governor Arango Ferrer in late 1948 and named a conciliatory Conservative in his place.

An Interlude in the Escalation of Violence

Violence was never constant in Antioquia between 1946 and 1949, not even during the tenure of especially extremist political appointees or after the demise of such an important opposition leader as Jorge Eliécer Gaitán. Partisan unrest was cyclical and concentrated, most marked during periods of electoral competition or in the immediate aftermath of a devastating event such as the murder of Gaitán. In fact, reports of violence waged by public employees against the Liberal opposition in Antioquia receded during the last months of 1948. Then in early 1949 a long-simmering feud in Medellín's Liberal-dominated *concejo* once more brought partisan dissension to the forefront of regional concerns.

Council members were locked in a battle over the city's unresolved financial difficulties and the possibility that these might lead to bankruptcy. The newly appointed governor, Fernando Gómez Martínez (December 1948–July 1949) attempted to reason with recalcitrant Conservative council members and entreated them to negotiate with the *gaitanista* opposition who controlled several seats in the *concejo*. He insisted on calling together members of the Liberal and Conservative parties and enjoined them to cooperate to govern the city and resolve its financial problems without resort to violence.[77] The stubborn refusal of some *laureanistas* to have any dealings with those they pejoratively dismissed as "*nueve abrileños*," however, moved the governor to issue a manifesto exhorting Antioquia's citizens to respect differences of political opinion.[78]

The struggle between the governor and members of his own party assumed the character of a public debate regarding the meaning of politics and the appropriate way they should be conducted in Colombia. During a radio interview with the newly appointed secretary of education in Antioquia, Gómez Martínez seized the opportunity to launch an educational campaign to teach Colombians how to participate peacefully in politics. In Colombia, Gómez Martínez lamented,

> The period preceding the election is full of violent agitation, of insults against the opponent. . . . This mistaken understanding of what politics and parties are about is exactly what I would like to see changed

in the minds of Antioquia's children, [and this can be done] through the good offices of the secretary of education . . . . Politics is the art of governing not in the name of a party but in the interests of the general citizenry. . . . I would like to impress upon children's very soul the notion that it is savage to fight and hate one another over politics.[79]

The indiscriminate use of violent rhetoric and incessant wrangling over jobs and patronage distribution in the *concejo* also drew the ire of the regional executive committee of the National Federation of Merchants (FENALCO). After the heated council dispute between *laureanistas* and Liberals in February 1949, Medellín's FENALCO chapter wrote an open letter in which it reminded the governor of the region's historic commitment to technocracy, merit-based hiring, and economic growth. The federation insisted it was entirely "removed from partisan political issues" and acted "solely in its capacity as a social force interested in the progress of Medellín." But it also pointedly reminded the governor that as the "representative of the commercial sector" it "was the main contributor to municipal revenues" and thus entitled to express an opinion regarding "the lamentable state of bankruptcy in which the municipality finds itself."[80]

The city's fiscal situation had deteriorated since once-marginal, Conservative, middle-sector politicians had begun to compete with Liberal bosses over control of the city's patronage hiring and public works budget. The unprecedented struggle over public revenue had given rise, lamented FENALCO, "to the most insane policy ever seen in the city's history. The [regional] administration is in a state of constant flux: mayors and executives of public entities are removed because they fail to satisfy the electoral interests of one or another party, or are obliged to resign because they fail to meet with the cooperation necessary to develop an urgent administrative task."[81] The *concejo* had become little more than a boxing ring in which members of each party sparred to monopolize appointments in the public sector and control of the city's 45-million-peso budget and several thousand employees. FENALCO complained that deficits were remedied by overtaxing the city's citizens and businesses in an "illegal and antitechnical" manner; employees and workers were no longer paid on time; urgent "works of progress" were "paralyzed"; and the city had stopped investing in the modernization of working-class neighborhoods. The merchant's association asked unions and businesses to join it in an act of solidarity to demand that the regional government "place the public interest above partisan interests." In desperation, the association also called upon its affiliates to refuse to pay their taxes until the regional government assumed responsibility for mismanaging the city's affairs.

The unfortunate recipient of this missive was the only governor of the four Conservatives to serve in that office since 1946 who had explicitly not engaged in partisan hiring. Indeed, Gómez Martínez had had to withstand the excoriation of hard-liners within his party who berated him for refusing to dismiss faculty members at the University of Antioquia simply because they were Liberal. He had also refused to give in to Conservative criticism regarding his appointment of members of the opposition who he considered to be the best qualified as contractors and supervising engineers on the region's public works.[82] But FENALCO's point was well taken. For decades Antioquia had taken pride in not participating in "Bogotá's political train" and had considered itself a national leader in "administrative honesty and true political liberty."[83] The region's native son, Mariano Ospina Rodríguez had coined the phrase "to govern is to manage [gobernar es administrar] while Tulio Ospina Pérez and Alejandro López (a Conservative and Liberal, respectively), two of the region's best-known statesmen, had consistently argued that public service positions would be more efficiently run if they were not part and parcel of political patronage.[84] All three believed that the nation's ministerial positions should be filled with "engineers who are men of ministerial quality who can inspire confidence in the public" rather than professional politicians.[85] It was this tradition of suprapartisan technocratic management that FENALCO mourned had been sacrificed in the name of electoral interests.

The governor's speech on the need for political civility and FENALCO's letter warning that continued partisan conflict held back regional development prompted a derisive response from middle-sector politicians such as those connected with the newspaper La Defensa. These politicians made it clear that they were indifferent to comments that attempted to shame them into negotiating with their adversaries.[86] When several days later the governor wrote an editorial exhorting politicians to limit the use of hate speech, former regional secretary Eduardo Berrío González retorted by denouncing the existence of a Liberal Communist conspiracy against the nation.[87] In response, the governor warned fellow Conservatives not to manipulate the fear of Communist revolution to block or interfere with Liberal campaign meetings. He recommended Conservatives stay home to avoid possible clashes, and he prohibited the public use of "*abajos*" (down with) and "*mueras*" (death to) against the opposition. Gómez Martínez's attempts to reduce the escalation of partisan antagonism could not compete, however, with Eduardo Berrío's red-baiting. In such a climate, the governor's insistence that "Conservatives . . . should respect and accept the free exercise of the right [of free speech] by Liberals" fell on deaf ears, as did his warning to municipal mayors to be strictly impartial in the upcoming June elections.[88]

The governor's explicit denunciation of violence as a legitimate political tool and his refusal to countenance the idea that any means were legitimate in the pursuit of electoral victories marked a turning point in regional politics and in the development of *la Violencia*.[89] Officeholders and politicians, who were the standard-bearers of a hegemonic approach to politics, increasingly eclipsed Conservatives who defended and promoted the rights of the opposition to take part in political office and debate. Politicians such as Eduardo Berrío González embraced a no-holds-barred approach to campaigning, one that relied extensively on appeals to past sacrifices and perceived wounds received at the hands of the opposition. He and other extremists whipped up popular Conservative sentiment to discredit and upstage moderates. In the lexicon of the day, Gómez Martínez and moderates like him were dismissed as "notables" and "oligarchs," men whose aloof approach to politics deliberately excluded all but the members of the regional economic elite from real political participation and decision-making. These accusations were largely valid. Individuals such as Gómez Martínez did represent a paternalistic, top-down approach to politics, one that typically assumed that the popular classes were in need of civilizing and elite leaders who could govern for them. However, it was a poor bargain for regional voters to have to choose between populists who did not shy away from deploying physical coercion to achieve their political goals and an elite who deplored violence but could not bring itself to expand the parameters of the political arena to include others.

By April the break between the governor and his party directorate and, in a broader sense, between a regional bipartisan political tradition and the new politics of violent hegemony was complete. On April 21, Antioquia's Conservative directorate openly disobeyed the governor's call for a dialogue between Conservatives and *gaitanistas* in the still-simmering municipal council dispute. In a last ditch effort to restore a modicum of civility to the conduct of regional politics, the governor turned once more to the editorial pages of *El Colombiano,* this time to denounce recent attacks by the contrachusma against Liberal directorates and voters. "Our party," he warned, "does not accept services of that sort. . . . We are a collectivity of ideas not ferocious instincts, and we operate with reason or by reason. . . . Consequently, conservatism not only does not endorse attitudes of that nature, but rather publicly rejects and condemns them."[90] The governor's party, however, was now in the hands of extremists for whom electoral enforcers who terrorized the countryside and who dismissed anyone who disagreed or stood in their way as "traitors" were legitimate political allies. Fernando Gómez Martínez's dismay that violence had become an accepted strategy for members of his party was poignantly apparent in one of his last attempts to repudiate its use for electoral purposes: "We the directors of the parties unreservedly condemn the use of [violence] and ask all party members to also condemn it, whatever camp from which it may emerge, since it would be unfair to repudiate its use when one's own party is the victim while stimulating its exercise against the adversary."[91]

The governor's plea for a return to civility bore little fruit. Elections perceived to be critical to the future of the Conservative party were just around the corner; the first for municipal council, the regional assembly, and congress in June, and then in November the most important electoral contest of all, that for president. Having failed to consolidate their power in local and regional representative bodies during the 1947 elections, *laureanistas* perceived the need to win the 1949 elections with even greater urgency. The governor's public commitment to nonviolence and moderation was thus interpreted by middle-sector politicians as the principal impediment to the satisfaction of their ambitions. In such a context, the actions that won Fernando Gómez Martínez a modicum of Liberal trust could only guarantee him the enmity of ambitious and ideologically extremist members of his own party. José Corréa, Antioquia's Conservative party whip, in fact publicly derided Gómez Martínez as "a small intellectual and *mamatoco*" and accused him of governing "in fear of Emilio Jaramillo [the editor of the Liberal *El Diario*]."[92]

As the pressure to ensure a Conservative victory grew, the active participation in partisan attacks by official forces such as policemen and mayors became more frequent. Of twenty-three reports of violence or abuse sent to the governor's office between January 1949 and June 1949, eleven specifically attributed violence to the actions of a mayor. Seven reports also mentioned that the police took part in or refused to intercede on behalf of a victim being harassed by members of the opposition party. Indeed, as Eduardo Berrío González made clear to Governor Fernando Gómez Martínez in 1949, mayors who simply belonged to the party but who failed to use their position to aggressively promote the party's electoral interests were little better than "partisan functionar[ies], traitors [entreguistas], and as such a social menace."[93] Berrío recommended replacing such "elements" to avoid electoral defeat. The actions of "loyal" mayors like those endorsed by Berrío, however, prompted an escalation of local complaints regarding abuses of authority. Fights broke out in numerous municipalities over who should be allowed to register to vote; Liberals complained that their right to suffrage was inadequately protected, and local inhabitants in general protested the lack of reliable police agents or army troops able to respond to outbreaks of public disorder in Antioquia.[94]

The police were the most frequent accomplices of mayoral abuse, and unionized workers were usually the main target. In April the police were accused of mistreating Liberals in the towns of Cisneros and Itagüí where numerous railroad and industrial workers were based.[95] Itagüí's mayor, party whip, and police engaged in what the local Liberal directorate called "cannibal-like excesses" against the town's Liberals. This incident was followed the next month by partisan-motivated skirmishes in which several Liberals were wounded or killed.[96] Violence in the largely working-class town escalated so dramatically that the minister of government himself interceded to demand that the governor appoint a military mayor in the civilian mayor's place.[97]

Indeed, the initiation of the 1949 electoral season revived tensions between workers and the regional authorities that had seemingly dissipated in the months following Gaitán's assassination. In January, the police mounted a train carrying railroad union officers on their way to deliver a report to the union's annual meeting in Puerto Berrío and pushed these passengers off. The union promptly accused the government of engaging in "a new crime against the right to unionize."[98] In March the Frontino Gold Mines Union in Segovia complained that the mayor appointed by the governor was "an ANGLOPHILE" who defended the company instead of being "a safeguard for the people [*pueblo*]."[99] On April 23, road workers in the same town struck to protest the fact that they had long gone unpaid and that local merchants were refusing to extend them any more credit. Rather than negotiate, the governor sent a squad of police, exacerbating the strikers' defiance. The road workers threatened to take violent action and to commandeer government warehouses if in two weeks they were not paid their salaries that were four months overdue.[100] On April 30, when matters between the governor and the road workers reached a stalemate, the minister of public works in Bogotá expressed his concern that if the dispute with militant road workers in Antioquia were not resolved, it would give rise to "complications with tremendous repercussions in the country's other labor camps."[101] To make matters worse, shortly after this, the mayor of Medellín, Julio Arias Roldán, dismissed 450 municipal public works employees with between five and twenty years of seniority after first inquiring as to their political affiliation.[102]

In a resolution issued during their eighth annual union meeting in May 1949, the Federation of Antioqueño Workers (FEDETA), a CTC affiliate, publicly denounced the state's systematic use of violence against state workers. The union complained that public road workers in San Andres, Ituango, and Segovia "have ignominiously been harassed by both the civilian and eccleasiastic authorities" without the government lifting a finger in the workers' defense. Indeed, mayors appointed by the regional authorities in San Andrés and Ituango led the attack on workers, prompting FEDETA to warn both its affiliates and regional workers not affiliated with a union "not to allow themselves to be provoked or tricked by imposters and humbugs." In the same resolution, FEDETA also accused Segovia's mayor and the labor inspector, who were appointed by the governor, of using their positions to abuse workers at the Frontino Gold Mines Company.[103] Jobs as much as votes appear to have been at stake in the growing conflict between workers and the regional authorities. This became clear from a complaint made by the Conservative committee in Yarumal (near Ituango and San Andrés) in which members accused the road workers' supervisor of threatening to dismiss Conservative workers if they voted in the upcoming elections.[104]

Despite abundant evidence that the source of conflict in most Antioqueño municipalities was the result of public employee and departmental or national police abuse, the regional government insisted local conflicts were the work of labor agitators and excessive intemperance. In late April

1949 the national government passed a general prohibition of all union and party-related demonstrations regardless of the participants' affiliation. It prohibited as well the sale of liquor in the period immediately prior to the elections.[105] Attempts by the regional Liberal party to hold meetings with their followers without violating the central government's prohibition of public political demonstrations, however, only served to infuriate the local Conservatives and to further incite them into acts of violence. When Liberal leader Captain Julián Uribe Gaviria held a private conference with his followers in Andes that had the explicit prior approval of the governor, for instance, the mayor and police chief broke it up violently.[106] On the same day, the municipal Conservative committee in Bolívar telegraphed the governor to complain that Liberals from various southwestern towns had gathered en masse in Bolombolo to await the train bearing the Liberal leader. Campaign stops, like those which had taken place since time immemorial during election season in Colombia, were twisted by local extremists into conspiracies in which the ultimate aim of meetings held by the opposition was to "take over the southwest starting with Bolívar." The police and mayor then justified their attack against Liberals as an act of self-defense intended to restrain a "violent Liberal uprising" in the making.[107]

Even when the police did not actively intervene to abuse Liberal voters, they often refused to restrain public employees who did. Liberals in Yarumal complained that the town secretary (the mayor's right-hand man) had insulted another resident from a tavern, pulled out a gun and challenged the victim, yelling "down with those who accused the mayor, down with the son-of-a-bitch Reds, up with the Conservative party. . . . I've only got this gun and six bullets, but I'll pump them into you. We're in control, down with the Liberal party." The police, privy to the entire incident, stood by idly.[108]

Indeed, while many citizens attributed the escalation of violence to the absence of official forces, these forces were so often the perpetrators of violence between 1946 and 1949 that one wonders why anyone bothered to suggest that the presence of the authorities could have been much help. And yet citizens repeatedly requested that the regional government send forces to defend them. Liberals in San Roque and Caracolí in eastern Antioquia complained, for instance, that the police, Conservative civilians, and public employees had made them live "terrifying hours . . . endangering our lives, our homes, and our families," and then added that they "lacked any authorities."[109] In a broader sense, of course, citizen complaints that the state failed to protect them and that its forces were inadequately deployed throughout the region were intended as an explicit indictment of the regional state's policies. Antioqueños were expressing a profound sense of outrage that the regional state had violated its citizens' trust. By reminding Antioquia's regional authorities of their obligation to defend citizens' rights regardless of partisan affiliation, citizens (many of them Liberal) gave evidence that the use of violence by public employees for partisan purposes had transgressed the region's political traditions and expectations.

Persistent citizen complaints of official abuse that were addressed to the governor also underscored the existence of two competing mandates within Antioquia's regional administration. While Gómez Martínez defended the right of the opposition to take part in elections and hold offices, his subordinates followed other orders. Widespread insubordination within the regional government was apparent in a complaint filed with the governor's secretary protesting a local mayor's use of police and contrachusma forces to intimidate Liberal voters during the elections of June 1949. The petitioner described the terror unleashed in the once-Liberal town of Olaya where laureanista Conservatives were in the process of forcibly conservatizing the town's electorate. When confronted with complaints of partisan abuse and the threat that these actions would be brought to the attention of the governor, the mayor "mumbled under his breath that the upcoming elections would be won by the Conservative party by 'FIRE AND BLOOD' and that he didn't fear the governor of Antioquia [Fernando Gómez Martínez] or his secretary of government so long as [a certain individual] held the office of assistant secretary of government and [a certain individual] were in the administrative visitor's office, since the latter had expressly appointed him to the municipality to ensure the party's triumph." The petitioner pointed out that this attitude directly contradicted the governor's public declaration "of not tolerating the presence of politically belligerent individuals in the office of municipal mayor."[110] Indeed, when a bipartisan committee of Liberal and Conservative leaders in Jardín filed a similar complaint, they also emphasized the dichotomy between the governor's stated opposition to the participation of public employees in partisan affairs and the local reality.

In their town, for instance, those deploying the police and contrachusma against members of the opposition simply laughed when asked by a bipartisan commission to put an end to such abuses and scoffed that they had the full support of members of the regional government. They defiantly declared "that they are Conservatives and that they are connected to certain political elements who support them and would take up their defense were we to proceed against them."[111]

No monolithic party structure existed to ensure coordination between the various levels of party organization nor was the state sufficiently integrated to enable the governor to demand the loyalty of his subordinates. Power was a complicated thing negotiated at seemingly obscure levels of authority within the regional administration. Conservative loyalists who controlled the day-to-day workings of the regional bureaucracy in what appeared to be unimportant secondary posts knew that they could defy the governor because they enjoyed the protection and endorsement of political bosses such as Eduardo Berrío González (the party whip) or Manuel Chavarriaga (the superintendent of customs agents). Thus, by May 1949 when Gómez Martínez's policy of equitably distributing political posts among members of the opposition and Conservatives (otherwise known as *cruce*)—in keeping with Mariano Ospina Pérez's national policy—was attacked by local extremists, neither the governor nor the president were able to respond effectively. Extremists consistently complained that *cruce* enabled members of the opposition to hold political offices without having to commit themselves to any of the governing party's policies and also that the policy deprived local Conservatives of positions they regarded as their political due for having brought the party to power. To circumvent *cruce,* hard-liners had simply gone behind the governor's back and ignored or undermined the authority of Liberals who were appointed by the governor to local office.

Despite consistent disobedience from his subordinates in the regional administration, Gómez Martínez's efforts to defend the rights of all Antioqueños to take part in politics do appear to have made some small difference. Liberals who had held political office during Gómez Martínez's administration wrote the governor to reassure him that he had offered them "complete support [*plenas garantías*]." Only the breakup of the "national union" accord between Liberals and Conservatives in May 1949 had forced them to resign from the "government your lordship so ably directs."[112] The governor's commitment to the politics of civility also prompted prominent Liberals to intercede on the behalf of particular towns to request a military mayor even though they knew that every military appointment to a civilian office represented one less patronage post in the Conservatives' hands. Ricardo Moreno assured Gómez Martínez that "I have always admired you from my Liberal trench. Today as I read your public address I admire you more as a government leader," and he insisted that it was precisely because he believed "in the sincerity of your words" that he dared request a change of mayor for the overwhelmingly Liberal town of Remedios.[113]

But on May 24, 1949, assurances of loyalty and support for a bipartisan elite political tradition such as that rendered by Ricardo Moreno to Fernando Gómez Martínez became moot. Liberal governors resigned and the ministries of war, government, and justice were assigned to military officers. In a final, desperate gesture toward bipartisan accommodation, Governor Gómez Martínez offered those Liberal mayors in Antioquia who wished to do so the possibility of remaining in office, but it was already too late.[114] Divisions between the governor and his subordinates and between different sectors of the regional bureaucracy had reached critical proportions. In such circumstances no Liberal in his right mind was willing to risk his life or political future to support the governor.

Chaos reigned within the regional bureaucracy. *Rentas* officers and soldiers in Puerto Berrío knocked down the doors of the state-run liquor monopoly, looted the stocks, wounded employees, and came to blows with local state monopoly and tax officers [*Resguardo* agents].[115] In Caracolí on the eastern railroad line and in Conservative San Rafael to the southeast, Liberals requested that the municipal police be confined to their barracks on election day because they distrusted their ability to remain neutral or guarantee public order. Local Liberals demanded instead the presence of departmental police agents who were not the minions of local Conservative politicians.[116] In Titiribí, in contrast, the mayor requested that the military be left to keep order in the town until after the elections, because the municipal police were all Liberal and were likely to celebrate their electoral victory by leading violent attacks against local Conservatives.[117]

By late June it seemed as if any remaining will to restrain the escalation of conflict in Antioquia had dissolved. Both regional parties were internally divided and the chain of command between the governor and his subordinates had broken down. A free-for-all, played out mainly at the municipal level, ensued.

The Outcome of Electoral Violence

Three days after the June 9 elections, the regional newspaper, *El Colombiano,* publicly accused *laureanistas* of having waged Antioquia's electoral campaign against Governor Fernando Gómez Martínez and the daily.[118] What the newspaper's editors meant was that moderate Conservatives and the region's bipartisan tradition were the real losers in the June elections. Indeed, the irony of the June elections was that while the pronounced use of official intimidation irrevocably split regional Conservatives, repression had once more failed to change the partisan composition of most Antioqueño towns.[119] Liberal municipalities continued to retain their majorities and few competitive towns tilted in the Conservatives' favor.

Of the forty-four towns in which 60 percent or more of the votes cast in the legislative assembly elections of 1945 had been Liberal, twenty-four continued to be predominantly Liberal in 1949, nine still boasted a narrow Liberal majority (50 to 60 percent of total votes), and eleven shifted to a Conservative majority. Of seventeen historically competitive towns (45 to 55 percent of votes being either Liberal or Conservative), seven shifted over to a Conservative majority in the 1949 elections. While Conservatives were able to win a majority in the regional assembly (twenty to fifteen) and in the house of representatives (ten to seven), Medellín's town council remained solidly in Liberal hands (with a majority of nine to six).[120]

Thus, several towns that had always delivered a Liberal majority continued to do so despite the use of official force against Liberal voters. In some towns Liberals actually increased the number of votes cast for their party: nine towns increased their percentage of Liberal votes between 2 and 10 percent between the 1945 and 1949 Assembly elections. Liberals also won control of municipal councils in nearly all of the towns where they had historically constituted a significant majority of the electorate (see map 7).[121] In municipalities with a strong presence of public road workers and miners, moreover, a significant number of votes continued to be cast for candidates identified as *gaitanistas* (see table 3).

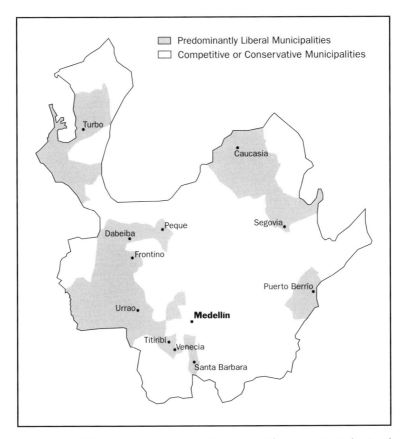

Map 7. Sites of Liberal power. (Source: Instituto Geográfico Augustín Codazzi and Colombia, Departamento Administrativo Nacional de Estadística)

Like the results of the 1947 elections, the towns in which electoral change as a result of the threat or use of violence was most pronounced tended to be historically competitive towns or towns where Liberals outnumbered Conservatives but could not be said to constitute an overwhelming majority (see table 4). There were also towns where an uncharacteristic surge in Conservative voters narrowed but failed to eliminate Liberal majorities between 1945 and 1949 (see table 5).

Several possible factors account for the reduced ability of these towns to withstand Conservative pressure when contrasted with the successful resistance of other towns in which organized labor had an important presence, such as those of the northeast, Magdalena Medio, west, and Urabá. Workers in centrally located towns tended to be industrial

Table 3. Percent total *concejo* votes for *gaitanistas,* 1949,
concejo elections, June 9, 1949

Region	Municipio	Percentage *gaitanista*
Occidente	Dabeiba	52
Urabá	Turbo	43
Bajo Cauca	Zaragoza	32
Occidente	San Jerónimo	32
Nordeste	Segovia	30
Central	Ebejico	26
Bajo Cauca	Cáceres	23
Occidente	Frontino	16
Oriente	Retiro	14
Urabá	Chigorodó	14

(Source: Colombia, DANE, Anuario Estadístico de Antioquia, Años 1947, 1948, 1949, Apéndice 2/4, "Estadística Electoral")

workers affiliated with Catholic trade unions. Moreover, unlike the towns in which the weight of organized labor was most strongly felt (Magdalena Medio, Urabá, the Bajo Cauca, and so on) Envigado, Itagüí, and Amagá had a significant number of Conservative residents. It generally proved impossible to conservatize towns such as those in eastern or western Antioquia where local Conservatives were few in number and where the surrounding municipalities boasted Liberal majorities.

The existence of "islands of liberalism" was acknowledged by regional *laureanistas* and essentially left alone. The *laureanistas* perceived the entire area north of the western town of Cañasgordas, the eastern half of Antioquia, the Bajo Cauca, and the Magdalena Medio (that is, the periphery) to be impervious to Conservative proselytizing, no matter how intimidating and severe.[122] Given these limitations and the fact that no consensus existed within the regional party regarding the use of force to achieve electoral victories, *laureanistas* focused their electoral efforts in 1949 as they had in 1947: on towns situated near monolithically or overwhelmingly Conservative municipalities. The strategy of mobilizing Conservatives from one town to attack Liberals in another helps explain why individuals who were interviewed about their memory of the emergence of violence associated it with an invasion led by outsider, or *forastero,* Conservatives.[123] Such outsider efforts could, of course, only

Table 4. Competitive and Liberal towns that were conservatized,
Assembly elections, 1945–1949

Electoral type	Municipio	Region	% Liberal		% decline of Liberals
			1945	1949	1945–1949
Competitive	Anorí	Nordeste	48	28	20
Competitive	Caramanta	Sur	54	40	14
Competitive	Valparaiso	Sur	56	44	12
Competitive	Andes	Suroeste	56	45	11
Competitive	Bolívar	Suroeste	53	42	11
Liberal	Tarso	Suroeste	94	36	58
Liberal	Pueblorrico	Suroeste	71	18	53
Liberal	Campamento	Occidente	61	11	50
Liberal	Olaya	Occidente	80	33	47
Liberal	Yolombó	Nordeste	91	47	44
Liberal	Concepción	Oriente	70	36	34
Liberal	San Roque	Nordeste	63	32	31
Liberal	Bello	Central	69	43	26
Liberal	Montebello	Sur	59	34	25
Liberal	Barbosa	Central	61	45	16

(Source: Colombia, DANE, Anuario Estadístico de Antioquia, Años 1947, 1948, 1949, Apéndice 2/4, "Estadística Electoral")

succeed where they resonated and found local support. Conversely, in solidly Conservative towns where Liberal voters had historically been a small minority, Liberals simply abstained from voting in *concejo* elections without any violence necessarily occurring.[124]

The results of the June 1949 elections suggest that towns susceptible to conservatization had already shifted their dominant affiliation from Liberal to Conservative between 1945 and 1947, that is, during Governor José María Bernal's administration. Very little if anything was thus accomplished by increasing the level of intimidation or force used to extend these electoral gains in 1949. Indeed, perhaps surprisingly, the use of violence as a tactic of political conversion proved rather ineffective in Antioquia, perhaps because to be successful local conservatization campaigns required considerable and consistent support from the regional administration. When hard-liners such as José María Bernal and Eduardo Berrío González, who endorsed the use of partisan aggression to achieve electoral victories, were in office as governors, local conservatizing efforts could succeed. But when the regional administration was internally di-

Table 5. Liberal towns that withstood conservatization,
Assembly elections, 1945–1949

Municipio	Percentage Liberal		Percentage decline of Liberals
	1945	1949	1945–1949
Betania	87	55	−33
Antioquia Vieja	79	60	−19
Cisneros	71	52	−19
Angelópolis	72	56	−16
Amagá	71	55	−15
Envigado	65	50	−14
Itagüí	63	53	−11

(Source: Colombia, DANE, Anuario Estadístico de Antioquia, Años 1947, 1948, 1949, Apéndice 2/4, "Estadística Electoral")

vided or the governor actively opposed such efforts, forcible conservatization largely failed. In this sense *laureanista* accusations leveled against Fernando Gómez Martínez were ironically accurate, his repudiation of violence probably did contribute to his party's inability to forcibly extend its electoral control in Antioquia.

Violence, in other words, was not inevitable and could not succeed when it was embraced or pursued by either a handful of local leaders or the regional government alone. This impression is particularly reinforced by the frequency with which local citizens of both parties attributed the evolution of violence into all-out partisan warfare to the point at which public employees and policemen appointed by the regional government intersected with the presence of local extremists. Thus, the towns where electoral violence had the greatest effect were precisely those where *laureanistas* enjoyed at least some local support and where structures such as party committees, the Catholic Church, and economic integration were strongest. Hence, the majority of the towns conservatized between 1945 and 1947 were located in the coffee-producing south and southwest and in the industrialized center (see map 8).[125] The success of official violence was therefore shaped by the presence of strong linkages between local society, the regional government, national institutions, and the existence of positions susceptible to patronage control.

Paradoxically, however, these very same towns were also those where it was easiest to put a stop to electoral or state-endorsed partisan violence when it threatened economic interests or deviated away from strictly par-

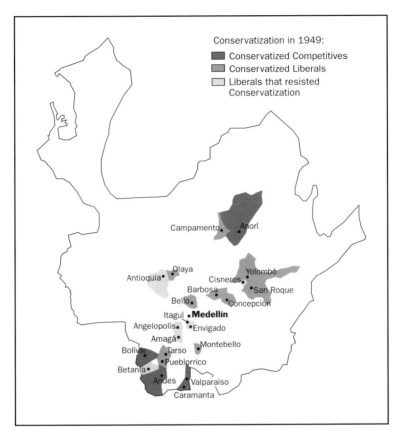

Map 8. Conservatization in 1949. (Source: Instituto Geográfico Augustín Codazzi and Colombia, Departamento Administrativo Nacional de Estadística)

tisan concerns. Since the success of electoral violence hinged on local and regional coordination and the active promotion of violence by public employees, the absence of structural linkages meant that there were no mechanisms through which to channel intimidation nor any structural basis on which to build a strategy of violence. If there were no mayor or police, who could act as the regional state's vanguard? And if there were no patronage posts to distribute, how could one construct a clientelist electoral machine?

The importance of linkages through which to channel violence as well as mediate conflict also partially explains why *laureanistas* avoided waging electoral battles outside centrally settled areas. Although the overwhelmingly Liberal affiliation of towns on the periphery was a natural

deterrent to conservatizing efforts, the absence of municipal Conservative party committees or a nearby area of solid Conservative support and
reliable means of communication were more significant impediments.
It proved logistically impossible to wage a conservatizing campaign or
exert physical intimidation through the presence of police officers or the
contrachusma where institutional supports were lacking.

It is also striking that the dominant partisan affiliation of a particular town was not an accurate indicator of the likely incidence of violence or of its success. A Liberal town such as Caucasia, where militant
road workers and miners were an important presence and where one
might have expected the government or the ambitious right-wing sector of the Conservative party to use partisan force to deal a deadly blow
to CTC affiliates, nearly quadrupled its Liberal electorate. A similar phenomenon occurred in Puerto Berrío where Liberals not only doubled
their votes but also voted in significant numbers for *gaitanista* candidates
in the local municipal council election. Ironically, while identification
as members of a militant labor organization made particular individuals the likeliest targets for Conservative violence, this same characteristic
proved the most effective deterrent to Conservative efforts to change the
electoral composition and autonomy of peripheral towns with a Liberal
majority.

Electoral Violence after June 1949

The discouraging outcome of the June 1949 elections taught Conservative hard-liners in Antioquia a very important lesson. *Laureanistas* now
knew that intimidation and the appointment of sympathetic public employees as local mayors were strategies insufficient to radically alter the
partisan composition of most municipalities in the province. This did
not lead them to question the efficacy of the use of coercion for electoral purposes. Instead, they concluded—as in fact the electoral results
also showed—that without a coordinated regional policy disseminated
through an internally unified regional bureaucracy manned by *laureanista* sympathizers, efforts to conservatize Antioquia would not succeed.
Hard-liners therefore lobbied to increase their presence in the regional
Conservative directorate and to remove from office any Conservatives
(including the governor) who might impede or disagree with their political objectives or tactics. While these strategies were being implemented,
laureanistas also promoted and bankrolled the creation of more extra-

official forces such as the contrachusma who had first emerged in response to the insufficiency of Conservative police officers to put down Liberal unrest after Gaitán's assassination.

The failure to win a mandate in the June elections spurred an intensification of Conservative-led violence throughout Antioquia. Indeed, widespread acts of violence only become commonplace in Antioquia in the second half of 1949, as hard-liners adopted an increasingly all or nothing (*a sangre y fuego*) attitude toward the pursuit of political power.[126] The first casualties of stepped-up violence in the immediate postelectoral period were the Liberal inhabitants of towns such as Andes, Pueblorrico, Betania, and San Carlos, who were forced to migrate by contrachusma forces.[127] Armed confrontation between Liberals and Conservatives in the pay of competing landlords or political brokers began to emerge during this period as well. Two such gangs paralyzed downtown Bolívar for several hours during a barroom brawl in July.[128] The next day a Conservative citizen was killed, ostensibly in retaliation for the assassination of a Liberal in June.[129] By August conditions in Bolívar had deteriorated to the point where the minister of government pointedly asked Antioquia's governor whether the appointment of a military mayor to the town might not be in order.[130] The governor ignored the minister's request, hell-bent on achieving Conservative domination of the southwestern town whatever the cost.

Cantinas emerged as the most frequent sites at which exchanges of insults and physical confrontations between members of the two parties took place. Townspeople and their drunken mayor shot a man in a cantina in Santa Barbara on the same day as the confrontation in Bolívar. A day later the mayor of Santuario in eastern Antioquia reported that two drunken peasants had shouted "*viva* the Conservative party" at the electoral registrar and other men who were also drunk. Santuario's Conservative mayor insisted to the governor that a fight had been averted by the timely intercession of the police, but several witnesses swore — in what became a commonplace occurrence — that the police had stood by and refused to intervene as the participants came to blows.[131]

The escalation of municipal violence prompted the national and regional governments to belatedly create bipartisan, *Pro Paz,* or pro-peace, committees. Liberal and Conservative representatives of major commercial, industrial, financial, and agricultural associations made up the membership of these. Members of the regional elite, for instance, dominated Antioquia's peace committee.[132] The viability of bipartisan compromise or mediation was undercut, however, by the removal from office of the region's most vocal advocate of bipartisan cooperation. In July, Fernando Gómez Martínez was relieved of his post as governor as part of a strategy to remove from office not only members of the opposition but anyone critical of any aspect of the regime or of *laureanistas* prior to the November elections.

As any possibility of retaining a middle ground faded, towns where there had previously been no indication of unrest began to complain of sudden outbreaks of violence between July and October of 1949. As was true of violence between 1947 and the first half of 1949, moreover, nearly all the complaints of persecution, extortion, or physical abuse forwarded to either the governor or the minister of government in the second half of 1949 involved public employees such as mayors, police inspectors, and policemen. The appointment of mayors with criminal records or who were named in cases of homicide and assault that were as-yet untried became common. Medellín's third circuit judge, for example, was forced to request that the governor remove the mayors of La Ceja and La Estrella (where governor Eduardo Berrío González had an important following) because of outstanding indictments against them for homicide and assault and battery.[133] Accused mayors often retained their posts or were merely transferred elsewhere. Thus, in some cases, mayors who had been sent previously to pacify a town, and who had earned a reputation for terrorizing the community and committing crimes, would be reappointed when local matters once more required an iron hand. Such was the unfortunate case of Puerto Berrío where the president of the town council denounced the recent appointment of a mayor he referred to as "a scourge in the memory of the citizens of this municipality."[134] The continued presence of such appointees in local offices, even when their criminal pasts became widely known, destroyed what little public confidence might have existed regarding the propriety or protective guarantees offered to citizens by the state's representatives.

The months leading up to the presidential election of November 1949 also proved unusually tense as Conservative extremists redoubled their attacks against organized labor. On October 11, Antioquia's Railroad Union denounced the murder of Providencia's railroad station-master and the wounding of a railroad employee at the hands of a drunken police inspector in nearby San José between Yolombó and Maceo in eastern Antioquia. On the same day at the opposite end of Antioquia in the south-

western village of Bolombolo in Venecia, the station-master and municipal police — yelling *vivas* to their party — attacked railroad workers enjoy-
ing lunch. The union insisted that the spate of attacks was not haphazard
nor simply the product of spontaneous partisan outbursts. Rather, it
blamed the state and its representatives (either in the form of policemen
or public employees), and their hostility toward organized labor for the
rising tide of violence against workers.

The regional authorities apparently hoped that by empowering Conservative civilians to lead attacks against public-sector workers such incidents would be dismissed as the product of unruly elements over whom
the regional government wielded no direct authority, thereby distanc-
ing the state from the appearance of being an instigator of violence. But
union officials saw through such a ploy. "Those attacks" they insisted,
"are not all the product of private citizens in an exalted state of partisan fervor, the majority are led, in collusion with individuals of low instincts, by the very public employees and agents charged with protecting the tranquility, honor, life, and goods of the union's membership."[135]
Police hostility toward "the railroad personnel," union representatives
insisted, "had been noticeable for some time" although the union felt it
had recently gotten worse, forcing workers to choose between "on the
one hand . . . a natural instinct of self preservation and, on the other, the
interests of the Antioqueño economy." The "frankly hostile" attitude assumed by the police against the railroad workers convinced the union
that the police were concerned by their responsibility to "protect private
factories," not the lives or rights of workers.[136]

Two months after the railroad union's complaint of police abuse
against railroad workers, the military personnel stationed in Venecia reported that a public road worker had been stabbed to death by civilians
while having a drink with his girlfriend at a local cantina. The incident
had taken place directly in front of the mayor's office and "with policemen less than twenty feet away and only two or three minutes after having
conducted a weapons search." But the routine search for arms, the military officer suggested, was unlikely to deter assassins for when it came to
searches of "certain individuals," these were done "in an entirely staged
fashion." Indeed, in this particular instance "the two assassins having
committed their crime left to hide their arms in the cantina of a Conservative boss . . . suspected of instigating the [contra]chusma to eliminate the Liberals in this town." A few days later neither the mayor nor

the cantina owner bothered to hide their links to the contrachusma. "All the contrachusma and part of those drunken Conservative men armed with a *peinilla* [small machete] and revolver [and] boasting of their power and official support" sallied forth into the town and terrorized with impunity. Attempts to stop the informally organized paramilitary forces were largely futile, the army officer lamented, because the police colluded with the leaders and "because the honorable mayor personally informs the contrachusma when it is safe to arm themselves."[137]

The Presidential Election

Reports of municipal violence received in the governor's office before October 1949 had almost all involved violence waged against Liberals, but in October the governor's office received reports of Liberal violence directed against members of the ruling party. These incidents did not involve Liberal guerrilla forces such as those that would soon organize in peripheral towns, but they did represent the first instances of Liberal resistance in Antioquia. Liberal retaliation against Conservative public employees and citizens was first reported in La Estrella, Montebello, Amagá, and Concordia, all towns that were affected by state-initiated electoral violence during the previous three years: a Conservative mayor was wounded in La Estrella, two Conservatives were wounded in Montebello, while Amagá and Concordia in the southwest reported a Conservative killed in each.[138] Meanwhile, a statue of the Virgin of Fátima, the patron of reactionary Conservatives and a symbol of their anti-Communist agenda arrived in Antioquia on a plane from Girardot, Cundinamarca. Townspeople throughout the southwest dated the beginning of *la Violencia* to the intrusion of processions honoring the Virgin of Fátima during the month of October.

The first inkling that unchecked partisan unrest might have economic repercussions emerged in October as well. To protect against rumored Liberal assault, the president of the FEDECAFE suggested that soldiers be deployed in southwestern areas where a heavy coffee harvest was expected.[139] Coffee growers were alarmed by reports that government agents such as a police sergeant by the name of Bedoya were forcing prominent hacienda owners in Fredonia—including the president of the regional Liberal party—to "abandon their haciendas . . . in the midst of the coffee harvest."[140] Growers were especially perturbed by reports

that Governor Berrío refused to intercede on behalf of the threatened hacienda owners or to send soldiers, even after the minister of government
in Bogotá had ordered him to do so. Repeated complaints had reached
the minister's office that violence led by government agents was threatening the coffee harvest and cattle and molasses (*panela*) production in
the southwest and was forcing the involuntary migration of many inhabitants. Like the members of the Federation of Coffee Growers, the minister
suggested that the governor deploy soldiers to patrol the area between
Andes and Fredonia to protect farmers and round up "troublemakers
[*maleantes*]" operating in the zone. He also insisted, however, that "to
pacify in harmony" it was necessary that any policy adopted to protect
coffee municipios be determined through bipartisan dialogue and cooperation.[141] The insistence on the use of negotiation and bipartisan participation in the resolution of conflict were features that distinguished the
state's approach to violence in core municipalities from that employed
in peripheral towns where repression was the more common official response to unrest.

The fate of the southwestern coffee towns where Conservatives had
concentrated all their efforts to achieve electoral victories in 1947 and
1949, and where the deployment of reactionary mayors, partisan policemen, and armed Conservative civilians had been greatest, for instance,
became a matter of obsessive preoccupation to the central government. In
part this concern was prompted by a desire to protect Antioquia's coffee
sector, the nation's second largest exporter of Colombia's primary source
of foreign exchange. But it also partly reflected the president and the minister of government's growing concern regarding the possible use of violence against members of the elite, regardless of their political affiliation,
and disagreements between the national the regional government over
how best to maintain public order. This became apparent in the remon-
strative and impatient telegrams with which Minister of Government Luis
Andrade and the president himself bombarded Eduardo Berrío González
in the aftermath of the forced exile of Liberal leader Julián Uribe Gaviria
from his properties.

When Governor Eduardo Berrío refused to collaborate with the opposition to put a stop to the disruption of the coffee harvest, the minister
was compelled to write the governor a second, more strongly worded
warning. He reminded Berrío of the serious impact violence could have
on Antioquia's cattle and commercial agriculture and impressed upon

the governor the damage such incidents inflicted on Colombia's image abroad. The individuals responsible for the flight of families and the threat to the coffee harvest should be pursued, Luis Andrade insisted, "without any considerations . . . [and] without regard to partisan labels." In case there should be any doubt in the governor's mind about the meaning of the minister's words, the minister reiterated that he explicitly meant that "assassins, [those engaged in] armed assault and incendiaries may not feel protected [by claiming to operate] under the banners of the traditional parties."[142] Again, he repeated, the solution would have to be a bipartisan one. When still the governor made no move to punish the government forces involved in perpetuating violence in the southwest, the minister admonished the governor once more, "we reiterate the [national] government's preoccupation that the criminal doings committed in the territory under your jurisdiction be severely and rapidly investigated so as to determine the delinquents responsible [for these acts] including possible government agents who, exceeding their mandate, may prove to be implicated." Punishment of those found guilty of promoting violence, the minister added, should take place "without partisan, social, or economic discrimination."[143]

Eduardo Berrío González must have known that President Ospina Pérez and his minister were in not in a position to demand the governor's resignation and that power had shifted definitively to the *laureanista* camp, for from this moment on the governor persistently defied the central government's demands and never moved to restrain the local shock troops crucial to his and other extremists' electoral ambitions. In coffee-producing towns where the Federation of Coffee Growers played an enormously influential role, the governor's indifference to partisan violence had less severe repercussions; the private producer association could and did appeal to the national government and the military to step in and shunt aside the governor's minions when the actions of these threatened the town's economy or carefully negotiated bipartisan relations. But in towns where a powerful mediating organization such as FEDECAFE did not exist, migration or armed resistance proved the only viable responses to intensified state-endorsed violence. When it became apparent that not even the president himself could stop the governor or his henchmen from promoting violence, prominent Liberal businessmen in towns such as Yarumal and Rionegro, for instance, simply closed up their businesses and left or good.[144]

The escalation of partisan conflict between October and November of 1949 had widespread repercussions. National Liberal party leader, Alfonso López Pumarejo, ordered fellow Liberals to abstain from participating in the presidential elections while Liberal leader Darío Echandía begged President Ospina Pérez to postpone elections and form a bipartisan government.[145] The offer of Liberal support came too late however. Ospina had already concluded that Laureano Gómez's sway over Conservatives and the party was too great to resist, and the president became increasingly isolated and coercively minded. Purged of its moderate members, Antioquia's newly reorganized Conservative directorate categorically rejected any collaboration with the Liberal party and declared itself fully in support of Laureano Gómez.[146] By October 29 any negotiations between Liberals and Conservatives were moot; Liberal leader Carlos Lleras Restrepo broke off talks, declared an insurrection, and ordered Liberal abstention across the board. In a powerful symbolic act, moreover, he forbade relations between Liberals and Conservatives.[147]

The national government responded to these actions and to Liberal threats of retaliation by stepping up the presence of the army throughout Colombia, especially in areas perceived to be economically and politically strategic, such as the coffee zone in Antioquia, the industrial hub around Medellín, and the region's ports. By November 9, Mariano Ospina Pérez put an end to democratic government and declared the nation to be in a state of siege. Decree 3518 closed the congress, the regional assemblies, and all of Colombia's town councils.[148] The response from investors and capitalists to these measures was immediate: stocks rose on the eleventh and cattle prices shot up nationwide as the government's prohibition of work slowdowns or solidarity strikes helped spur investor confidence in the propitious prospects of dictatorial power for capitalist development.[149] Coupled with July's executive decree nationalizing the police, the interruption of democratic forums ensured that anyone dissatisfied by the increasingly coercive nature of internal rule would have no nonviolent means through which to register their discontent.[150]

La Violencia Enters Its Second Phase

Shortly after President Ospina's declaration of a state of siege, Laureano Gómez ran and won the presidential election in an unopposed, but re-markably violent contest in late November. Troops were in such great demand to maintain public order in towns such as Santa Barbara, La Estrella, Ebéjico, Yarumal, Salgar, and Betulia that the regional government was unable to respond to the overwhelming number of municipal requests for government forces.[151] Towns where Liberal delegates were present reported that the police, with the tacit support and knowledge of the mayor, mercilessly harassed them. In some towns, moreover, Liberals were forced to vote for Laureano Gómez on pain of injury, prompting many citizens to flee to the surrounding hills to wait out the electoral period in the hope of escaping persecution by the opposition.[152] For instance, when Liberals in towns such as Tarso (which had been forcibly conservatized between 1945 and 1947) asked the mayor to protect them from contrachusmas who stripped them of their *cédulas,* the mayor refused and coldly suggested the victims leave town instead.[153]

Laureano Gómez's election marked other shifts in the development of regional violence as well. An armed Liberal guerrilla movement within Antioquia emerged in response to the escalation of official violence. Armed Liberal groups burned, looted, and led insurrections in Ebéjico, Betulia, and San Juan de Urabá to protest Gómez's election.[154] The inhabitants of San Juan de Urabá shot the police inspector and other members of the armed forces, then sought cover in the hills when Conservative authorities detonated a bomb in San Juan de Urabá to punish their refusal to acknowledge Gómez's victory or accept the imposition of regional appointees. The parish priest, acting as the town's intermediary, urged the regional government to deploy soldiers to reestablish public order. But he warned the governor not to send the police, for it was precisely their deployment during past electoral contests and their repressive acts that had catalyzed the organization of local resistance in the first place.[155]

The outbreak of rebellion throughout Antioquia's periphery in the wake of Laureano Gómez's electoral victory marked the end of episodic conflict in the region and the beginning of prolonged insurrection. Public sector workers—the primary targets of official harassment between 1946 and 1949—increasingly took up arms against the state or colluded with and protected armed Liberal groups operating in their geographic vicinity. Railroad workers on the trunk road Tulio Ospina-Anzá, for instance, expressed their repudiation of state policies by "blocking the search for Liberal bandits" and denying "the presence of the bandits to successive police teams deployed to different spots in that sector."[156]

Had the army—as the Pacific Railroad Union demanded in November 1949—been sent to patrol the Anzá and Urrao area and to defend railroad interests, perhaps railroad personnel might have felt less willing to cover for the newly created Liberal guerrilla groups.[157] Instead, state-employed workers flaunted their reputation for violent unruliness by threatening to stop work on important public works projects unless the state removed its repressive forces.

State-directed partisan violence involving paramilitary groups and the state's own employees provoked a full-blown struggle between local, regional, and national authorities over the monopoly of force and the jurisdictional rights of specific government sectors in Antioquia. These sources of contention shaped in determinant ways the escalation and outcome of conflict in the region from 1950 to 1953. Indeed, the use of the police to harass public-sector workers became so egregious that it prompted Colonel Carlos Bejarano, the general director in charge of the national police in Bogotá, to complain directly to Governor Eduardo Berrío González in January 1950. Colonel Bejarano argued that co-optation of the police by local party officials and bureaucrats and the use of the police in matters other than the maintenance of public order were contributing to the escalation of regional unrest.[158] The minister of government seconded the police director's concerns, warning the governor that the president was worried about the same issue. The minister specifically alluded to the persistent police and contrachusma persecution of road workers and employees in the area of Bolombolo, Venecia, and the regional and local authorities' seeming indifference to such abuses. The minister reminded the governor of the president's interest in seeing the road (connecting Bolombolo to the coffee municipalities and Medellín) completed and urged the governor to speak to his local subordinates—the mayor and police chief in Bolombolo—so that they would cease to harass Liberal road workers and their Liberal engineer supervisors.[159]

The commander of the military's Fourth Brigade in Medellín, Colonel Villamil, also warned the governor against using the contrachusma in public order matters. He pointed out the danger of allowing local mayors to expand the size and operation of the "civilian police" (contrachusma) in areas where public sector workers were present and where there were already sufficient numbers of police and soldiers to guarantee the maintenance of public order.[160] The minister of government had already warned Governor Berrío that his persistent, partisan use of the police did not enjoy the support of the central government. Yet, less than a day after receiving the minister's most recent rebuke, Berrío was busy conspiring with the governor of the Chocó, Guillermo Valencia Ibañez, about an envoy of 150 police agents and arms from Antioquia to be used to put local Liberals in their place in the Pacific lowlands department.[161] Berrio's insistence on deploying the police as partisan shock troops finally prompted the commander of the Fourth Brigade to write directly to the minister of government to complain about the Antioqueño governor's behavior. Colonel Eduardo Villamil informed the minister that he had contacted Eduardo Berrío several times regarding persistent civilian "complaints against the abusive behavior of the police," but each time his complaints had been ignored. The governor, the army commander insisted, retained in their posts insubordinate police officers such as Major Arturo Velásquez who was responsible for firing upon soldiers and being the commanding officer of "the agents responsible for abuses" against citizens in Bolombolo. The inhabitants of Bolombolo had been "forced to migrate" when it was the duty of the regional government to protect them and see to it that "they should return."[162]

Liberal citizens stopped bothering to complain about the police to the regional government shortly before the November presidential elections, and gradually so did regional Conservatives. The latter concluded that it was pointless to request that the governor do something about the police or the contrachusma so long as the man in charge of the region's fortunes was Eduardo Berrío González or someone of his ilk. Instead, well-off Conservatives who witnessed the exercise of police and contrachusma abuses directed their complaints to the president, perhaps driven by the vain hope that Ospina Pérez still represented some modicum of civility.

The crisis of legitimacy prompted by public employees who used violence to pursue partisan objectives was rendered poignantly evident in a letter written to the president by a Conservative Medellín businessman in 1950. The writer registered the growing sense of alienation and horror experienced by members of the regional elite who suddenly found themselves living in a police state. The businessman, unaccustomed to being a target of the police brutality that was common to lower-class Colombian life, was appalled by the police's sudden sense of self-importance and seemingly unlimited power. "Excellent Sir," his missive to the president began,

In my character as a Colombian, a Conservative, and a professional, I cannot but appeal to the First Magistrate to ardently plead for your intervention on behalf of fellow citizens who are being made the unfortunate victims of a merciless persecution before the complacent gaze, not of the highest authorities, but of certain police agents who . . . allow to occur before their very eyes outrages that daily increase the sediment of bitterness in those who with or without motive, are victims of the irresponsibility and cruelty of an infuriated and aggressive rabble.[163]

On a weekend drive back from his estate on the outskirts of Medellín, this businessman recounted how he had witnessed "fifteen completely inebriated individuals" who detained cars along the road into the city while shouting "*vivas* to the Conservative party." Meanwhile, "the police agent demanded [the writer's] driver's license and Conservative party identity card." While "the agent examined these documents, the occupants of the vehicle were forced to suffer the filthy and shameful vocabulary of extremists [the contrachusma]." Incredibly, "they did not limit themselves to assaulting us with their words, their machetes tested their hardiness against the car's windows, bumpers, and doors, the sparks produced by their bullets contrasted with the gunmen's metallic pallor, and all of this, I repeat, was done before the complacent gaze of three or four policemen." "Providence," the author said, "was kind to us" since he happened to be carrying his party identity card. The occupants of the house where he had been stopped along the road, however, proved less fortunate. To the sound of shouts of "long live the Pope and down with the Reds," the men who had stopped smashing his car once assured he was a Conservative, had begun to break down the dwelling's door. He had still, he assured the president, not recovered from the shock or shame of this dreadful experience.

Indeed, it was clear from the author's ensuing remarks that his encounter with the contrachusma and the police had marked a turning point in his moral and political development. "My ideals have been transformed overnight; the dream of a great Colombia, which always made me love her more, seems close to becoming a chimera, because it seems that peace and harmony are exotic plants in our midst." He went on to assure the president that he did not blame him personally for what was happening in Colombia. He felt current conditions had deeper historical roots and were not "born of the current administration, the previous regime sowed winds and now we have the unhappy task of harvesting tempests, all Colombians are victims of a state of uncontrollable events." His point in writing to the president had been to bear witness, to express the desire of "the man on the street . . . who aspires to live in peace with God and his fellow men . . . to live respecting and being respected by others."

A cautious man, the author stored his letter in the drawer of his office desk, thinking ruefully that it was hardly worth bothering the president with a complaint of events which "could easily be controlled by the authorities of this department." But in the interim in his position as an executive at the Banco Industrial Colombiano he had the opportunity to speak to "people of all kinds, from different towns and all the political parties." They had confided that "*la Violencia* has once again become in Antioquia the primary source of unrest." He listed all the towns where violence was present—Caldas, Itagüí, Envigado, Andes, Concordia, La Ceja, Amagá, Bolívar, Bolombolo, and Titiribí, and he noted that "the lives and goods of" Conservatives who dared to complain to the authorities or to the departmental party committee "are implacably persecuted." This had created a problem of political refugees made up "not of Liberals, but of Conservatives pursued by local political bosses," and this problem, coupled with "the rainy season and the high cost of living," was making life in Medellín increasingly difficult. So much injustice and the seeming absence of any regional recourse for redress had inspired him to send his missive after all. He begged the president to "enforce your authority" so that the regional authorities would order town mayors to stop promoting "treason [*manzanillaje*]" and so that they would punish those who wished to create further problems "using violent means."[164]

Once Laureano Gómez won the presidency, however, any possibility of a negotiated settlement to violence or even of a show of civil authority like that pled for by the Medellín banker who wrote in dismay to Mariano Ospina Pérez disappeared. Disagreements between moderates and *laureanistas* in Antioquia's Conservative party developed into an open rift after Laureano Gómez's election. In the corridors of regional power and in private salons, talk centered on the impending shake-up of appointees in the regional and municipal bureaucracies as Laureano Gómez's presidential inauguration drew closer and on the proliferation and influence of armed privately organized conservative forces in the countryside. It became evident, notwithstanding the insistence of Fernando Gómez Martínez and other *El Colombiano* columnists, that "harmony" did not and could not reign between Antioquia's *ospinista* and *laureanista* camps.[165]

For Antioqueño *laureanistas* such as José Mejía y Mejía and Belisario Betancur, who were journalists and idealists far removed from the bloody realities of rural partisan conflict, Laureano Gómez was a principled leader motivated by ideological convictions not materialism. They could explain away the proliferation of groups of poor, armed extremists as transient anomalies or as unauthorized fringe groups who were unrepresentative of *laureanismo*'s political objectives. Other *laureanista* sympathizers such as Dionisio Arango Ferrer and Eduardo Berrío González, in contrast, reconciled the existence of partisan armed groups as a necessary short-term measure that would disappear once society had been "cleansed" of Communists and radical Liberals. Indeed, they often dismissed reports that armed Conservatives were organizing throughout the countryside to eliminate the Liberal opposition as baseless rumors spread by the opposition to destabilize the Conservative government. To middle-sector Conservatives, Ospina and his bourgeois, Antioqueño supporters represented a different but far more sinister threat than did the *contrachusma*. The president and his supporters embodied the aloof, elite politician guided by technocratic considerations and pragmatism rather than political ideals or partisan ideology. *Laureanistas* such as Mejía y Mejía, Vallejo Alvarez, and Betancur detected a profound indifference to the plight and concerns of the "little person" under the *ospinistas*' studied neutrality and pacifism. For these Conservatives, *ospinistas* practiced a different kind of violence, the violence of exclusion, marginality, and condescension.

Thus, the August 1950 appointment as governor of Braulio Henao Mejía, a reticent former dean of the University of Antioquia's medical college and an in-law of one of the most powerful Conservative elite clans, came as a considerable shock to Laureano Gómez's Antioqueño followers.[166] Some loyalists assuaged their own initial sense of betrayal by insisting that Gómez's decision had been politically calculated to appease Antioquia's bourgeoisie, the party's wealthiest and strategically most important group of national supporters. Conservatives who had viewed Gómez with distaste but who were apolitical used the appointment of a bourgeois governor as confirmation that Gómez's Falangist rhetoric had always been part of an elaborate facade and that once in power the president would naturally seek to assuage powerful capitalists and privilege economic development. Many Liberals, however, and eventually the Conservative president's own local loyalists concluded (rightly) that Gómez could well afford to make the seemingly magnanimous gesture of appointing a non-*laureanista* to office in Antioquia, because he knew that throughout the regional bureaucracy and in the regional Conservative directorate, where it counted, his minions were in total control. Whatever Gómez's real motives, it became quickly apparent that Governor Henao Mejía did not have the president's ear and that his appointment was at least partly intended as a rebuke to a region and an elite that had always proved notoriously independent and undisciplined.

When they recuperated from their initial sense of disappointment, regional *laureanistas* realized they could bypass their newly named but dispensable bourgeois governor. They celebrated their sainted chief's long-awaited rise to power and took their Conservative crusade toward the last remaining unconverted partisan territory of Antioquia's periphery. Thus began the next and far bloodier phase of *la Violencia*.

Conclusions

By 1949 it was apparent that Antioquia, like Colombia, was a house divided. There was no one who could "enforce the state's authority": not the president, not the governor, not municipal leaders, not disgruntled party members. Real power was organized behind closed doors by political bosses and their local cronies and in the backroom discussions of certain regional appointees. The widespread expression of violence made manifest not the "breakdown of the State" as Paul Oquist suggested, but its morally weak and organizationally dispersed nature.[167] In such a context, the state could not exercise a "monopoly of force" nor could it fulfill its role as the defender of the well-being and rights of the citizenry as a whole. Instead, the very forces that should have represented the principle of order were nothing more than one among a competing array of armed groups, all of whom ultimately answered to private and particular interests and not to the interests of the public.

The use of the police to pursue partisan objectives until they ultimately grew into a force that not even the president could control represented not a departure but merely the logical fruition of a series of poorly thought-out civilian policies regarding Colombia's public order forces.

Fear underpinned these civilian policies. Unsure of their legitimacy or strength, Liberal and Conservative party leaders had historically proven unwilling to create viable forces of public order for fear that these might challenge or usurp civilian authority. Such public order forces consequently fulfilled the state's repressive functions but were never allowed to grow into sufficiently coherent entities bound by a code of ethics or professional identity. Poor pay, lack of discipline, and the subordination of public order to the interests of private parties and the shifting winds of political influence ensured that the armed forces would never compete for moral or physical parity with civilian rulers. This approach may have maintained intact the civilian leaders' monopoly of power in the short term, but it also guaranteed in the long term the impossibility of establishing a relationship of respect or trust between the armed forces and their civilian rulers. The police recognized themselves as the pawns of those who paid them—"*la rosca*" as one police agent put it—rather than the neutral guarantors of the general public's well-being.[168]

As the state found itself under attack from multiple sources during *la Violencia,* it relied more and more upon the repressive force of agencies such as the police to remain in power. This situation increased the autonomy of the police, while the state's authority over them lessened in proportion to its dependence and growing lack of legitimacy. To make matters worse, when faced with an escalation in violence and its own inability to control or direct the police, the regional government opted to further fracture the already splintered principle of a monopoly of force. It empowered paramilitary groups to do the work for which it could no longer rely upon the police—because they were unable—or the army—because it was unwilling—to do. Ironically, the regional state created and armed the very groups that would later most seriously challenge its authority and control over the regional territory.

Machuca, Segovia. October 1998. This man's
wife was among the sixty-six casualties of
an oil pipeline explosion caused by an Ejercito
de Liberación Nacional (ELN) attack.

2. Bajo Cauca, Magdalena Medio, and the Northeast

The geographic focus of violence and its character and organization fundamentally shifted after the presidential election of November 1949. The areas of Antioquia most affected by violence by early 1950 were located in the northwest and west (Urabá, Dabeiba, Cañasgordas, Frontino), extreme southwest (Urrao, Betulia, Salgar), northeast (Amalfi, Remedios, Zaragoza) and lower Cauca Valley (Caucasia, Cáceres), and Middle Magdalena Valley (Puerto Berrío, Puerto Nare, Puerto Triunfo). Partisan disputes over appointments and patronage such as those evident in centrally settled areas before 1949 also characterized the expression of conflict between Liberals and Conservatives in peripheral areas, but on the periphery these conflicts evolved into armed confrontation between organized groups. Liberal guerrilla groups developed and operated only in peripheral towns, and it was in these towns and not the core municipalities of traditional settlement where the greatest number of regional casualties and forcible displacements occurred from 1950 to 1953. Partisan violence in peripheral areas intersected with preexisting ethnic, cultural, or economic tensions, moreover, to produce a far more complex and multifaceted struggle than that of the exclusively electoral and patronage-based conflicts that were characteristic of violence in centrally settled towns during the first three years of *la Violencia*.

All of the peripheral towns experiencing violence after 1950 shared certain traits. They were overwhelmingly Liberal — many had supported the dissident leader Gaitán and his movement in local, regional, and national elections — and nearly all were areas of recent intense colonization efforts and extractive production. But the evolution of violence in the periphery also differed from area to area. Paramilitary organizations that were financed and tacitly or overtly endorsed by the regional and central governments emerged as the primary form of official public order maintenance in some towns, while in other towns paramilitary organizations were fleeting or nonexistent. In some peripheral municipalities, peculiarities of development, identity, and collective resistance determined that the army or the police contributed most to the intensification of conflict. In still other towns, violence began as a partisan struggle over power between Liberal guerrilla groups and the Conservative authorities and remained essentially so until 1953; while in other places partisan disputes gave way to incipient social demands that transcended partisan differences or to social and economic banditry and generalized criminality. In short, the story of *la Violencia* in Antioquia lies in the details of local history, and it is the attempt to explore and underscore these differences and similarities and to deduce the political and economic implications of *la Violencia*'s trajectory that shapes the geographically specific narratives that follow.

Geography and Violence:
The Bajo Cauca, Magdalena Medio, and Northeast

Three parallel chains of the Andes traverse Colombia from north to south and come together in a rumpled mass at the border of Ecuador in the *macizo central.* Two of these mountain chains—the western and central cordilleras—run through Antioquia. Coffee towns perch along steep mountain slopes in the southwestern part of the department, while in the core—to the immediate north, east, and south of Medellín—the department is characterized by a series of hills and valleys where the climate varies from *tierra templada* (3,000–6,500 feet above sea level) to pockets of *tierra fria* (6,500–10,000 feet). At the edges of the department, however, the mountain terrain drops dramatically, giving way in the northwest, far east, and northeast to tropical lowlands (1,000–3,000 feet above sea level) where the land is far less broken and the climate is hot.[1] To the east and northeast of Antioquia's Aburra Valley and Medellín lie major grasslands, rich lodes of ore, and a powerful river—the Magdalena—that constitutes the artery that connects Antioquia to the rest of Colombia. The towns cradled by the Cauca, Magdalena, Porce, and Nechí rivers and their numerous small tributaries are largely made up of flat, tropical lowlands characterized by extensive ranching, and gold and petroleum extraction (see map 9). The air is humid and heavy, awash in the muffled drone of cicadas and other insects. Gentle hills alternate with deep forests and flat plains. In the northeast, craterlike forms create islands of arid devastation amid the lush vegetation; these craters are the result of centuries of relentless gold mining. To the southeast and extreme east, grasslands extend to the horizon and drop off into the wide expanse of the

Map 9. Eastern Antioquia. (Source: Instituto Geográfico Augustín Codazzi)

Magdalena River. Already in the 1940s the rivers in this region ran a tur-
bid color, contaminated by silt, mercury, and human and animal waste.

Human populations in the northeast, Bajo Cauca, and Magdalena
River regions have historically been transient and sparse. In 1951, the
largest towns — Yolombó, Puerto Berrío, Amalfi, and Remedios — ranged
in population from 11,000 to 26,000 inhabitants. In contrast, municipalities such as Caucasia, Cáceres, Zaragoza, Segovia, and Maceo boasted few
inhabitants — even though their physical size was considerable — scarcely
those needed to herd cattle or man scattered mining operations. Although the northeast, Bajo Cauca, and Magdalena regions covered a third
of Antioquia's territory (22,000 square kilometers), they were home to
only 10 percent of the department's inhabitants. Because of the links between guerrilla groups operating over this territory, the ethnic and racial

composition of the local population, and the logistical peculiarities of local settlement and production, I have decided to treat these three distinct administrative units as a single geographical area for the purposes of this study. The mines and haciendas established in these areas and affected by violence often straddled more than one municipality, and the workers who labored for them and who became *la Violencia*'s primary victims circulated seasonally from the lower Cauca River Valley through the northeastern mining towns and the port of Puerto Berrío in search of permanent work and lands to colonize. Violence followed the circuits traced by such seasonal migration and consequently rendered largely insignificant the administrative boundaries that treat them as self-contained or discrete entities.[2]

The Beginning of Conflict

The first clashes between local inhabitants and the regional authorities in the Bajo Cauca, Magdalena Medio, and northeast (hereafter collectively referred to as eastern Antioquia) initially arose as they did in other parts of Antioquia because of disputes regarding the partisan affiliation of public employees and the right to appoint and control them. Shortly after the Conservative party took national power, Antioquia's regional party directorate wrote the governor to insist that the continued presence of Liberals as mayors and customs agents in towns such as Puerto Berrío, Remedios, Caucasia, Cáceres, and Amalfi constituted "a real danger to the government."[3] The Conservative directorate demanded that these Liberals be dismissed and replaced with Conservative loyalists. However, the fear that such actions would spark labor disturbances and general protests in areas of strategic economic importance, where the government had few supporters and only a weak institutional presence, kept even extremist governors from heeding the directorate's demands during most of the period from 1946 to mid-1948.

But when revolutionary "*juntas*" seized control of towns such as Puerto Berrío and labor uprisings broke out in many of the area's mining camps following Jorge Eliécer Gaitán's assassination in April 1948, the regional authorities were forced to reconsider their policy of restraint. Local disturbances in the area proved so severe and difficult to put down that Medellín's Conservative authorities became convinced that there were plans afoot to overthrow the regional government. To reassure himself, Governor Dionisio Arango Ferrer appointed a *visitador administrativo* to conduct a formal survey of the Magdalena Medio, Bajo Cauca, and northeast. The *visitador* was charged with measuring the amount of local Conservative support in the area and the population's attitude toward the regional government. After closely surveying Segovia, Remedios, Amalfi, and Zaragoza, the government's agent concluded that only a few of the inhabitants of El Bagre (a mining settlement in Zaragoza) could be considered "friends of the government" and that none of the towns he visited possessed the counterrevolutionary guidelines issued by the regional government to prevent "popular uprisings." Local Conservatives were so removed from access to the regional government and the party directorate that they were even unaware that a recent decree enabled them to create Conservative civilian police forces should they suspect the local municipal police of weakening loyalty or need help putting down future insurrections.[4] The *visitador* gave his regional superiors little hope that Conservatives or the regional authorities would soon overcome decades of official alienation and neglect in the area. In most far eastern towns, the general absence of infrastructure and the weakness of the regional state's presence, he ruefully reported, guaranteed that these towns operated in a semiautonomous fashion as even radical changes in the region's public order policy were never received or could essentially be ignored.

Many of the towns in eastern Antioquia were what might be called "company towns." These were places where a large percentage of the economically active population was employed in the same activity (mining or oil extraction) and by a single (usually foreign) employer in an industry considered crucial to the economic interests of both the regional economy and the central state. The town of Segovia was a case in point. In 1939, 40 percent of the town's seven thousand inhabitants were estimated to work for the Frontino Gold Mines Company, and the majority were members of the Frontino Gold Mines Union affiliated with the CTC. The town was also Antioquia's principal producer of gold in 1941.[5] When local union members took a stand or mobilized to protest the activities of the state or its public officials, they were supported by the united sentiment of nearly all the town's inhabitants. The same tended to be true of miners in Zaragoza and oil workers in Remedios. This gave the inhabitants of towns like Segovia, Zaragoza, and Remedios a leveraging power vis-à-vis both the regional and central authorities that was not easily reproduced in other peripheral or predominantly Liberal areas of Antioquia. Additionally, the power to effectively protest government policies was reinforced in the mining zone by the local presence of public sector workers such as road construction crews and railroad workers who, like the miners, were also affiliated with the CTC and shared many of the miners' concerns. At crucial moments, miners and public sector workers joined forces and mounted a coordinated offensive against both the state and their employers. In early 1949, for instance, Segovia's miners organized to protest the government's recent restriction of labor rights.[6] Two weeks later miners employed by Zaragoza's Pato Gold Mining Company allied with miners in Segovia and also announced a strike, in this case to protest the company's noncompliance with the collective-bargaining agreement signed by workers and management in the aftermath of Gaitán's assassination. Railroad workers on the Antioquia railroad and the departmental public employees union followed suit. The three groups jointly submitted petitions demanding a raise in salaries and improved social benefits.[7] Faced with a possible work stoppage by miners, public employees, and railroad workers in an area of the department where it enjoyed only a tenuous presence, the regional government had little recourse but to negotiate eastern workers' demands.

Coordinated union and political activity also enabled the inhabitants of eastern mining towns to deter attempts to intensify partisan intimidation during the campaign period preceding the June elections of 1949. Even when they failed to foil official measures absolutely, organized labor nonetheless effectively forced the governor to rescind the partisan policies implemented by local appointees. For instance, two weeks before the first anniversary of the death of the Liberal leader Jorge Eliécer Gaitán, *gaitanistas* in Caucasia complained directly to the governor that the mayor had taken away their copies of the musical record "They Killed Gaitán." The mayor had also prohibited local jukeboxes from playing the song. This seemingly insignificant act was construed by workers as political censorship and as a violation of their right to free speech. Workers threatened to retaliate violently if the governor did not restrain the mayor. The Conservative *visitador* sent to report on and arbitrate the dispute suggested that the municipal government was "infiltrated" by *gaitanista* sympathizers and that the town clerk (*personero*) and several other local public officials were also followers of the fallen leader. The complete absence of any local Conservative support forced the *visitador* to conclude that it would be prudent, given the local population's militancy, to insist that the mayor return the seized records and lift the prohibition against publicly playing the song.[8]

Although the *visitador*'s solution to the conflict in Caucasia was conciliatory on the surface, he had ulterior motives for suggesting that the government capitulate in its dealings with the townspeople. The *visitador* used his general report to drive home his perception of the inherently unruly and culturally inferior nature of Caucasia's inhabitants and to justify the future implementation of discriminatory policies against them. He made much, for instance, of the "*costeño*" (Caribbean coastal) element he found dominated the area and spared no effort to warn the regional authorities of the imminent danger that this Afro-Caribbean population posed to Antioquia's general state of public order. The area's townspeople, "especially those in Nechí and Colorado," he lamented, "were people accustomed to living without God or the Law. The number of marriages may be counted on the fingers of a single hand, the others live in public and scandalous concubinage for that is what is common there. Since no one respects an oath, crimes remain unpunished, besides which it is impossible to advance an investigation because it is for the most part, a cosmopolitan town." Locals were promiscuous, possessed no moral sense of right and wrong, and were bent on rising up against the regional government. "Authority is not respected," the *visitador* insisted, "the agents [of the government] are attacked, they are wounded in the back, their arms are stolen, and there is made against them, in sum, an open war if they attempt to fulfill their duty."[9] The term "cosmopolitan" was used as a code word to describe towns perceived to be dominated by the "other," where the values and patterns of organization and belief associated with the ideal of Antioqueñidad held little sway. Despite his diatribe, however, the *visitador* was sufficiently realistic to concede that it was beyond the power of the regional government to fundamentally alter the "nature" of such areas overnight. As an interim solution, he suggested that the offending mayor be switched with the mayor of nearby Cáceres where no tensions had been reported between the Conservative appointee and the local Liberal population.[10]

Local inhabitants in eastern towns further defied the regional authorities by using commemorations of Gaitán's death to rally public opinion against the Conservative government and its campaign of partisan intimidation. Some towns insisted on flying red flags at half-mast, others led public protests, and still others commandeered loudspeakers to publicly denounce past government abuses.[11] In Zaragoza, moreover, Liberals applied the same discriminatory and intimidating policies used against them to marginalize local Conservatives. El Bagre's Conservative minority complained that they felt too intimidated by Liberal public employees to attend political meetings or to vote and that the Liberal mayor, mayor's secretary, and municipal police had conspired to dismiss the few Conservative workers employed by the Pato Consolidated Mining Company.[12] Complaints of partisan discrimination from Yolombó also came from Conservative and not Liberal citizens. Conservatives insisted that the town's Liberal voting officials (*registradores electorales*) denied poor, rural Conservatives, who took time off from their agricultural duties to register to vote, the possibility of doing so.[13] Caucasia, however, remained the town where Liberal threats against the regional authorities' control were most severe. There, the town clerk, public school director, and president and vice president of the town council publicly incited the citizens to attack the departmental police troops stationed in the town. They then made it clear to the regional authorities that Conservative officials who dared to meddle in local matters would pay a heavy price.[14]

The Aftermath of the June Elections and the Evolution of Violence

The outcome of the June 1949 elections vindicated the importance of local Liberal resistance in eastern Antioquia. The number of Conservatives elected to municipal town council positions in towns such as Remedios, Caucasia, Zaragoza, Segovia, and Puerto Berrío dwindled to no more than one or two. Before the elections, Conservatives had avoided direct attempts to remove Liberals from office. Instead, they had worked to counter Liberal influence by dismissing public sector workers and appointing Conservatives as police inspectors, work inspectors, and mayors. The regional authorities had also been relatively circumspect about deploying Conservative policemen or sponsoring armed civilian forces to harass eastern towns, especially mining and port towns. This meant that the area's municipal police forces were still overwhelmingly Liberal and that Liberals still dominated local municipal councils and the majority of public offices even as late as mid-1949. However, when the number of Liberal voters in the June elections actually increased, the regional authorities decided that local defiance had gone too far and that it was time to replace all Liberal public employees, not just those employed in public works. The regional authorities also began to deploy additional police troops to eastern Antioqueño towns and to encourage the organization of Conservative contrachusma forces to assault or even kill workers.

At first, regional Conservative violence was directed against workers employed by the state, not the Liberal population as a whole. But given the nature of employment patterns in the region, violence against organized labor inevitably spilled over to affect even those inhabitants unconnected to public patronage positions. In the aftermath of the June elections, the unprecedented presence of departmental police agents in eastern Antioquia and, in particular, their broader mandate to intervene in public order matters exacerbated tensions between Conservatives and Liberals and between the foreign-owned mining companies, the police, and organized workers. In Segovia in August 1949, a row broke out in the *barrio de tolerancia* (red light district) between an off-duty policeman and an English mining company manager. The manager accused the policeman and his cronies of impeding the extraction of gold from company mines and insulted the officer by calling him an "ass-kisser" and a "flunky" (*lambón*). The policeman responded by pointing his gun at the manager. Brought up on charges of assault by the company's executives, the policeman defended his actions to the regional government, although he admitted that "I have a lot of enemies in the municipality of Segovia as a result of having had to proceed against them in the course of exercising my powers as an authority." The officer insisted the company was only persecuting him because he was a proven nationalist who had refused to allow the company's British managers to smuggle gold out of Colombia to avoid paying taxes. The mining company, Officer O'Brien argued, regarded the police as a private security force whose primary loyalty was to the company rather than to the nation. This was reflected in management's "lack of support for the commanders and guards who have lent their services in this area."[15]

What the dispute between Police Officer O'Brien and the Frontino Gold Mines Company's management actually appeared to be about was something else. In Colombia, the mining companies and foreign-owned companies in general (United Fruit, Tropical Oil, and so on) had long been accustomed to having regional governments underwrite the cost of security at their respective work camps. In return, preferential hiring for the governing party's sympathizers was arranged through the *vigi-*

lantes de seguridad (watchmen or security officers), *inspectores de tra-bajo* (labor inspectors), and *médicos oficiales* (doctors appointed and paid locally who doubled as the companies' security forces and health care providers). Since the mining companies had done much of their hiring during the previous sixteen years of Liberal rule and since most of the workers drawn to the camps were migrants from the Caribbean coast or the departments of Santander and Norte de Santander, the workers who filtered through this clientelist system in eastern Antioquia were almost exclusively Liberal and non-Antioqueño.[16] The advent of Conservative rule, however, suddenly put pressure on the companies to hire Antio-queños and Conservatives. One way in which this pressure was exerted was through the assignment of policemen such as Officer O'Brien as pub-lic order forces and security guards at the camps. The overtly partisan and repressive agenda of many such officers, however, elicited considerable hostility among the Liberal majority who felt victimized by the regional authorities' representatives of order. Policemen were accused of insulting and arbitrarily restricting workers' physical mobility and of perpetuating the notion that workers were continually disorderly or revolutionary in order to justify official repression. Foreign managers, for their part, were ambivalent about the presence of regionally appointed police agents in the camp, despite their role in curbing labor unrest. The companies par-ticularly worried about the effect that worker hostility toward the con-servatized departmental police might have on production and labor and management relations. Newly appointed policemen who were the benefi-ciaries of extremist patrons, moreover, felt entitled to give free expression to nationalist, antiforeign, and anti-Protestant sentiments that annoyed the British and Canadian managers who were typically in charge of min-ing operations in the region.

If Officer O'Brien perceived the foreign companies' efforts to limit the departmental police's authority in the camps as a transgression of national sovereignty, workers were no less ready to invoke the issues of sovereignty and national identity when discussing or justifying their ac-tions and grievances to the regional state. Miners accused the regional government of colluding with foreign companies in ways that funda-mentally violated their rights as citizens of the nation. The regional gov-ernment allowed the companies to limit worker mobility (restricting their and other civilians' access to the camps) and to use Colombian police troops to restrain and abuse Colombian workers on Colombian soil. These issues predated the Conservative rise to national and regional power but became more urgent and immediate once partisan politics became a more central aspect of the police's agenda. A year earlier, miners affiliated with the Pato Consolidated Gold Dredging Company in Zaragoza had made a point of protesting "the acute campaign of persecution currently advanced by the secretary of security [*vigilancia*] and the health inspector's office [*inspectoria de sanidad*]" in the Pato mining camp. Union officials charged the inspectors with having "decre[ed] disrespectful and authoritarian measures . . . against the company's workers." The measures included foisting decisions on the company's workers using "threats and coercive attitudes" and submitting workers to "unjustified searches and imprisonment."[17] The language in which the miners' union couched its complaints drew on a discourse of citizenship that emphasized universal rights and obligations. Workers appealed to the state first and foremost as citizens and only secondarily as individuals whose rights were protected and regulated by sector-specific limitations (such as a labor code). Indeed, workers portrayed the foreign-owned company's mistreatment of them as an action that, beyond violating the labor code, "conflict[ed] with the democratic tradition of our homeland [*patria*]," and they demanded that the regional government "impede the continued assaults against Colombian citizens who live and travel through this piece of national territory."[18] In their invocation of citizenship as a right conferred by birth on Colombian territory (not regional birth or identity), workers contested the regional government's notion of citizenship as a privilege predicated on the satisfaction of a series of social norms and codes of conduct.[19] By accusing the government of allying with the company against workers, moreover, labor turned the tables on the government, implicitly suggesting that it was the government's regional insularity, not the militant workers, who compromised Colombian sovereignty.

The Emergence of Armed Liberal Violence

The unprecedented intervention of newly appointed Conservative officers against mining camp workers and public sector workers, and the abuse unleashed on the local Liberal population by national policemen and Conservative public employees after June 1949, prompted the emergence of an armed Liberal reaction in eastern Antioquia. At first such groups were not based in Antioquia but rather recruited and organized in the department of Santander. After the assassination of Gaitán, they initially made their presence known by sporadically crossing the Magdalena River and assaulting Antioqueño properties and government offices. These armed Liberal bands were made up of individuals—many of them followers of Gaitán—who fled police and civilian Conservative abuse in Boyacá and Santander. They settled in the hills opposite Antioqueño port towns such as Puerto Triunfo, Puerto Boyacá, Puerto Nare, Puerto Perales, and Remedios where few state authorities operated or where they were badly armed and weak.

The first reported victim of this externally-based guerrilla violence was the port town of Puerto Perales in the municipality of San Luis where individuals from the department of Santander (Santandereanos) were blamed for destroying 120 houses and causing damages estimated at 150,000 pesos in September 1948.[20] Santander-based guerrillas next struck two months later in Zambito (located on the Santander side of the Magdalena River between Puerto Nare and Puerto Berrío but a settlement informally under Antioquia's jurisdiction). The Antioqueño *hacendados* (estate owners) and *colonos* (settlers) who dominated the area complained that they and their properties were the frequent targets of "escaped criminals [*prófugos*]" who capitalized on the absence of any government representative to infest the area.[21]

After these first two assaults, a six-month lull followed in which further unrest was absent, but nonetheless the threat of imminent guerrilla invasion was invoked by terrified Conservative propertyholders to extort the deployment of police troops and government protection. Local property owners insisted that the guerrillas were interlopers with no visible local following, yet earlier Conservative complaints suggested something different. During the elections of June 1949, for instance, Puerto Nare's Liberal municipal police searched Conservative party headquarters, arrested the local Conservative committee president, and tore down Conservative campaign posters. Members of the committee insisted that the municipal police were *gaitanistas* who had taken part in the violent upheavals that took place in the wake of Gaitán's assassination and who now sympathized and colluded with the guerrillas from Santander.[22] A month later the town's Society of Public Improvements, which was made up of the area's wealthiest and most prominent citizens, complained to the governor that the local police inspector and his secretary were in cahoots with "bandits" (that is, Liberal guerrillas). They spared no effort to persuade the regional authorities that such conduct was "clearly reprehensible and injurious to the tranquility and interests of local inhabitants" and that the local authorities (who like the municipal police were still Liberal) were "totally untrustworthy."[23] Members of the Society of Public Improvements pointed to the cases of a *bandido* who wounded a businessman and was allowed to go free only ten days later; the municipal police agent who levied a 300-peso fee for returning a citizen's stolen property; and the police inspector's practice of charging citizens for freeing them from arbitrary imprisonment. By September, Puerto Nare's Conservative president was requesting reinforcement troops from the governor to stem what he called the "Communist threat" represented by both the town's public employees and the guerrillas camped on the shores opposite the port.[24]

A year later the only officially reported guerrilla-related deaths in eastern Antioquia had occurred in two Magdalena River port towns: nine deaths in Puerto Perales in the municipality of San Luis and three in Puerto Triunfo in the municipality of Cocorná.[25] Conservative complaints of the threat posed by armed Liberals were thus not without substance, although there was little evidence of collusion between local Liberals and the guerrillas from Santander. What is crucial about these spatially circumscribed guerrilla attacks, however, is that they enabled both local Conservative extremists and the regional government to justify a widespread repressive campaign against all of eastern Antioquia's Liberal inhabitants. This campaign extended to areas where no violence had been reported or where violence was neither the result of Liberal guerrilla attacks nor of local Liberal "insubordination."

In September 1949, in keeping with the newly established policy of rearranging appointments in towns where the government enjoyed little or no support, Antioquia's governor finally adopted the regional Conservative directorate's suggestion that only "doctrinaire" Conservatives be appointed as mayors in historically Liberal towns such as Puerto Berrío. But the governor's appointee immediately prompted the Liberal president of the municipal council to accuse the mayor of provoking local unrest where there had previously been none. The new mayor had proceeded to usurp the authority of Puerto Berrío's municipal police (who enjoyed the support of the majority of the town's inhabitants) and had replaced them with Conservative departmental policemen. Next, the mayor and the departmental police worked to dismiss all of the town's Liberal municipal employees, shut down the taverns (a gross violation in a town of hard-drinking miners, stevedores, and sailors!), and prohibit the consumption of alcohol. The town had already had a taste of the mayor's repressive measures, moreover, for he appears to have briefly served in the immediate aftermath of Gaitán's assassination.[26]

The actions of Puerto Berrío's Conservative mayor were part of a broader regional Conservative strategy to marginalize the authority of Liberal municipal police forces in eastern towns where the police were perceived to be closely allied to sectors of organized labor in control of municipal council seats. Conservatives in both Puerto Berrío and Puerto Nare had persistently complained to the regional government that local police forces were overwhelmingly Liberal and "revolutionary" and urged the government to replace or circumvent their power. Indeed, a week after Puerto Berrío filed a complaint against the Conservative mayor, the regional authorities announced new rules to determine the selection of policemen assigned to patrol the mining camps of Providencia, Bagre, Pato, and Santa Margarita in the towns of San Roque, Zaragoza, and Amalfi. Forty agents were to be chosen from areas other than those in which they were to provide service to "avoid the grave inconvenience posed by police recruitment from among the local inhabitants."[27] The choice of men, however, was left in the hands of the regional national police commander and not the companies. This shift in the criteria for selection of policemen in the mining camps was matched by an increased deployment of Conservative national policemen to areas where public sector and unionized workers were concentrated. The number of reports of violent clashes between workers and policemen in eastern Antioquia rose accordingly.

In October the railroad workers' union complained that the trains and their personnel were the constant targets of abusive police activities all along the line between Medellín and Puerto Berrío. National policemen were aided, union officials added, by "individuals of low instincts," that is, by Conservative contrachusmas who migrated up from nearby southeastern towns or were recruited from among Conservatives in towns such as Maceo and San Roque, which bordered the rail line.[28] Violence involving railroad workers and police agents broke out again in November when well-armed policemen disguised as "*bandoleros*" (bandits) boarded the train operating between Medellín and Puerto Berrío. Policemen with machetes and guns also attacked Liberal workers in San José de Providencia (one of the mining camps to which national police agents had recently been assigned).[29]

The sudden increase in police violence directed against union members sparked widespread hostility in towns such as Puerto Berrío. Indeed, a few months after their arrival, national police agents were forced to seek refuge in the mayor's office for fear of the threat of violent retaliation by the army and civilians.[30] When the national government decreed a state of siege in November 1949, for instance, local inhabitants in the railroad town of Cisneros organized a demonstration in which they killed one policeman and wounded another.[31] The local army commander implicitly condoned the attacks on the police when he attributed them to popular frustration with the "mayor, judge, police, and customs agents." These officials, he insisted, had "used their official positions" to lead "a wave of violence in which they were accused of [committing] all kinds of crimes" against Cisneros's civilian population. Abuses were so severe that civilians had to flee to the "[military] barracks in search of protection."[32] Clashes between inhabitants and the police and between the police and public employees also occurred in the nearby railroad town of San José de Providencia in the municipality of San Roque and in the gold mining town of Zaragoza.[33]

Thus, in early 1950, when oil workers at Shell Oil's Casabe camp heard rumors that the governor planned to replace the local police inspector, they correctly surmised that this meant the introduction of a repressive policy directed against them that would be similar to the one already under way against railroad workers in the area around Puerto Berrío and Cisneros and against miners in the northeast. Their union mobilized to plead with the governor to keep the current inspector in his post, arguing that the camp had been "calm" since his appointment.[34] The governor ignored the union's request, however, prompting Shell Oil's legal representative to file a complaint on behalf of the company less than six months later protesting the conduct of national policemen and the police inspector assigned to oversee public order in the Casabe camp. The lawyer asserted that the inspector had "introduced a climate of discord among the personnel" which he ominously warned, "may give rise to a serious incident." Shell's legal counsel was quick to reassure the governor that it was not the company's intention "to interfere in any way in the actions of the departmental authorities in the Casabe camp." The company's actions were prompted "by the fear of future incidents which could have a very negative effect [on the company] and which could also create serious problems for the governor's office."[35] A veiled warning, but a warning nonetheless to a governor whom the Shell Oil management knew was a self-avowed nationalist who was critical of the foreign company's power and a political extremist who was the major force behind the deployment of partisan public employees and policemen in the area. The message appears to have struck home because, two weeks after Shell's complaint, local Conservatives wrote to Governor Eduardo Berrío González begging him to revoke his decision to remove the national police from the Casabe camp.[36]

The repressive presence of national police troops and the aggressive imposition of Conservative officials in eastern Antioquia eventually prompted a large-scale Liberal guerrilla attack against the regional government and its representatives. On August 4, 1950, guerrillas made up of men from both Antioquia and Bolívar converged on the hamlet of Guarumo in Cáceres and on the town of Caucasia in what appears to have been a coordinated operation that included guerrilla attacks in Urrao and Urabá (western Antioquia) on the same day.[37] The guerrillas burned buildings and killed local Conservatives in Guarumo before continuing on to the town of Caucasia. The town's telegraphist, who had managed to escape to Magangué in the department of Bolívar just prior to the guerrillas' arrival, urgently asked the governor to airlift army troops to the town to respond to the presence of three hundred armed men.[38] During the three-hour siege guerrillas sacked and looted the local stores. They also attacked the customs offices, mayor's office, local treasury and civil registry office, and killed the captain of the coast guard, the civil registry officer, two municipal policemen, a local merchant, and a national police agent.[39] It took the authorities several hours to reestablish control, but they claimed to have captured one hundred guerrillas and recaptured the majority of the police arms stolen by the guerrillas during the attack.[40]

It was no coincidence that the attacks on Guarumo and Caucasia occurred just before and immediately after Conservative Laureano Gómez's inauguration as Colombia's new president on August 7. What was surprising was how unprepared the regional government was to confront the possibility of an armed Liberal attack when it occurred. The regional government had been circulating rumors of an armed plot and had justified police repression during the previous months supposedly because such an event was imminent. Indeed, less than a month before the attack in the Bajo Cauca, the governor had received reports from three different sources warning him of possible insurrectionary activity on the San Jorge Road linking Antioquia to the Caribbean coast through Caucasia. The police inspector was the first to inform the governor that the authorities had seized several powerful bombs that had been stolen by criminals from the public road works in operation between Caucasia, Antioquia, and Montelibano, Bolívar. He warned the governor that the San Jorge Road was largely unpatrolled and that few workers were present because of constant "threats against the public order."[41] Two days later the governor of Bolívar confirmed the inspector's report when he complained that Antioquia exercised no control over the San Jorge Road and accused the road crew of helping local "leaders of the revolt." Bolívar's governor begged his counterpart in Antioquia not to send the road workers any more dynamite because the workers were only interested in "perturbing the public order."[42] Finally, on August 13, Major Arturo González Arcila, commander of the Division Colombia Police, informed the director of the national police in Bogotá that the guerrillas were led by an ex-army sergeant and former policeman (not an unusual feature of guerrilla commanders) named Ortíz. The guerrillas, the police major insisted, had publicly announced their intention to target the police (but not the army), and he confirmed that the attack was timed to coincide with an uprising by guerrillas in the Llanos that was designed to prevent Laureano Gómez from taking office.[43]

These reports should have prompted Antioquia's governor to reinforce the area troops against an essentially foregone assault, but throughout Antioquia the number of anticipated incidents protesting Laureano Gómez's rise to power proved too great for the meager public order forces at the regional government's disposal. Indeed, the attacks on El Guarumo and Caucasia were but the first of many armed Liberal actions. The attack exposed the nearly complete absence of regional authorities in strategically important portions of Antioquia, undermining any claim that the government might have made regarding its legitimacy and effective control over public order affairs. It soon became evident that while the regional government possessed sufficient men to harass and abuse the local opposition on an intermittent basis, it did not possess the necessary forces to confront the consequences of such a policy. In any case, it was easier for the incidence of public unrest in the Bajo

Cauca, to scapegoat the local road crew, agent provocateurs from the department of Bolívar, and the area's supposed history of rebellion than to consider the local effect of the state's recently appointed repressive forces. It was not fortuitous that the main objects of guerrilla attack were policemen and government offices, yet the local Conservative party committee blamed violence on the local chief engineer in charge of hiring the road crew. The engineer had precipitated violence by being "condescending to *paisas* (i.e., to Antioqueños)" and failing to "give priority in hiring decisions to local Conservatives."[44] Regional and partisan identity were conflated and the problem of partisan conflict was represented as a problem of cultural as well as political differences. If the public workers on the San Jorge Road had only been replaced with Conservative Antioqueños, the committee insinuated, armed assault could have been avoided.

Caucasia was calm for a brief, three-month period after the devastating attack in August, and no Liberal guerrilla activity occurred elsewhere in the northeast during that time either. But in November the national finance administrator informed the governor of a telegram he had received from a customs agent in the town who warned of rumors regarding a second guerrilla attack.[45] Again, the regional government did nothing to prepare the town, and, again, despite advance warning the town was caught off-guard by guerrillas penetrating from the department of Bolívar. Like the earlier attack on Caucasia in August, the one in December also appears to have been part of a coordinated assault on several Antioqueño fronts. On the same day that guerrillas struck in Caucasia, attacks occurred in Urabá and Urrao in western Antioquia and in Puerto Perales south of Puerto Berrío on the shores of the Magdalena River.[46] The guerrillas cut the telegraph line that linked Caucasia to Medellín and prevented any direct communication between the town and the regional capital for three months.[47] While the government failed to send troops to confront the guerrillas during the assault, Caucasia's electoral registrar reported that less than a month later the national police were informally conducting *aplanchamientos* against Liberal civilians in retaliation for the guerrillas' activities.[48] When the registrar publicly denounced the presence of three Conservative contrachusma members who aided the police in their assaults, the police attempted to assassinate the registrar and intimidated and threatened the mayor for jailing them.[49] Meanwhile detectives in the pay of the regional security department (*Departmento de Seguridad*) insisted—as the Conservative directorate three months earlier had—that the enemy in Caucasia was "within." The departmental detectives accused the road workers of being guerrillas and the contractors in charge of the road (all of whom were Liberal) of lending the guerrillas revolvers, trucks, and dynamite to attack the Conservative government and its local representatives.[50]

Public road workers, miners, and armed Liberal groups in the Bajo Cauca and northeastern regions did collude with one another, but it was only after a long period of government-directed dismissals, harassment, and police abuse against railroad and state road workers that they mobilized in openly insubordinate behavior. A letter written by a Conservative hacienda owner who lived in the hamlet of Colorado in Caucasia during the entire period of *la Violencia* corroborates the impression that local violence was not an organic development but the result of repeated provocations by the regional authorities. His account, which covers events in the region from 1949 through early 1952, provides a devastating chronicle of the role played by policemen and contrachusmas in the spread of violence and of the reluctance with which local Liberals and Conservatives greeted the emergence of armed Liberal resistance.

The author of the letter referred to himself simply as "Arturo."[51] He considered himself unusual among regional men of his class and generation for he had refused to "climb aboard the bourgeois train like a good Antioqueño." Instead, he had buried himself in the Bajo Cauca to work the land amid "the sometimes monotonous but often soothing sea of green." Arturo confided to "José," the intended recipient of his letter, that he and his neighbors in the Bajo Cauca and the department of Bolívar were waiting tensely to "fall into the hands of that den of assassins known as the police." He and other locals had already been forced to "witness the worst crimes imaginable, the very memory of which produces nausea." These experiences had prompted him to "write a book which is currently buried for fear of the uniformed killers." Although he feared the Conservative police, Arturo was no apologist for the Liberal guerrillas, who, he believed, had vowed to "fight until the last of them was alive and had vowed to kill every policeman or Conservative they happened upon."

To indicate this thirst for vengeance that motivated the guerrillas who operated in the area, Arturo cited the example of one group of twenty-two adult men and an eleven-year-old boy who were led by a young woman known as La Cucaracha (the cockroach). This guerrilla group had

vowed "not to shoot soldiers except as a last resort." When they "capture
[soldiers], they release them if they are alive, and if they should happen
to have killed them in combat, they leave their bodies undisturbed without even removing their guns." But, just as Major Arturo Velasquez had
earlier warned his superior in Bogotá, the guerrillas offered the police no
quarter. La Cucaracha and her men had repeatedly eluded the authorities
despite the "two hundred policemen and soldiers" sent to capture them.
Instead, the guerrillas proved adept at ambushing the police. They decapitated policemen in an elaborate and macabre ritual and then "played
soccer" with "the heads of the police . . . as if this were part of the program." La Cucaracha would dictate sentences of mutilation that corre-
sponded to the aggression and loss of family members that she herself
had suffered at the hands of the police and Conservative civilians: " 'Since
they killed my father,' she says, and they land a tremendous machete
blow to his neck. 'Since they killed my brother,' another blow is struck
against the throat. Then the head hangs precariously suspended by the
skin on either side of the neck. 'Since they killed my mother,' she adds,
and the last blow is dealt to the abdomen. In addition to this treatment,
when policemen are the victims, they are sliced into strips." Arturo acknowledged that the armed Liberal bands that roamed the region killing
Conservative civilians on a daily basis were heartless and bloodthirsty.
This he repudiated and abhorred. But he also felt that while the actions
of the guerrillas were execrable, they were also understandable. While
some guerrillas were undoubtedly "innate assassins or fanatical criminals
for a cause" many were also individuals crazed by the violence wrought
upon them. As he put it, "they are avengers of abuses that weigh them
down. . . . All are starved for vengeance against the government's people
who earlier assassinated their fathers, their sisters, and their brothers."

Arturo also noted that despite the region's overwhelmingly Liberal
population, the guerrillas initially enjoyed little support from the local
inhabitants. Indeed, the earliest response of Liberal and Conservative
peoples alike to the appearance of the guerrillas had been to mobilize "in
an open crusade against the rabble [chusmeros] in sincere and disinter-
ested support of the authorities." The local citizenry had been willing to
risk their lives to eliminate the Liberal armed bands, "even the very Liberals who constitute an overwhelming majority of the local population
(and who had nothing to fear from the guerrillas) in order to see peace
restored to the region." And peace, the author dryly noted, "arrived with

the police." Forty policemen from the department of Bolívar, under the command of police Lieutenant Muñoz, "made their triumphal entrance through the region of Sapo, burning the settlers' homesteads, shamelessly stealing the money from their pockets and the rice from their barns. No one to the present day has been able to know with certainty how many men died imprisoned by the flames of their own homes; any conjecture would be dangerous and audacious." The police "attacked, looted, and burned Villa Uribe"—a predominantly Liberal settlement that bordered the predominantly Conservative settlement of Regencia that had earlier been devastated by the Liberal "guerrillas [*chusma*] . . . after first assassinating many of its inhabitants." One unfortunate peasant had mistaken the police for guerrillas and identified himself as a Liberal. Lieutenant Muñoz "had his agents hang the peasant from a tree, they poked his eyes out with the point of a bayonet, and then Muñoz ordered him killed. The corpse of this poor Conservative was left there for the terrible crime of having said he was a Liberal." In another instance, the local police inspector stood idly by while a worker for Arturo's cousin was publicly "martyred" through the streets of the town for two days. And the guerrillas left him deaf "after cutting off his ears and making him eat them." The trauma also left him permanently speechless.

The police engaged in outright theft, cattle-rustling, and extortion, and their behavior enabled local individuals to justify killing Liberal neighbors in the name of the Conservative party when the real motive, Arturo implied, was mere greed, jealousy, or long-standing family feuds. But Arturo reserved his worst accusation for last, including at one point the shooting of a public tow truck driver and his assistant for the mere enjoyment of it and then the delivery of the bodies in a casket to the local mayor with a note attached that alleged the victims had been "killed in an encounter with the guerrillas." As if all these police activities were not bad enough, the police were not even capable of doing what they had supposedly been sent to the region to do: defeat and eradicate the Liberal "*chusma*" (Liberal guerrillas). Instead, Arturo insisted, "the police flee the *chusma,* they refuse to confront them, they are scared of them. [The police] only appear to pursue them to sow terror, finishing off what the guerrillas leave behind." And he concluded, presciently, as it would turn out:

> There can be no peace while elements of the government compete in criminality with the bandits and exceed them in delinquency [*ratería*].

There can be no peace while men, honest rural workers, withhold their trust from a government that has completely forfeited its legitimacy. The government has committed errors of such a magnitude that we are on the verge of a revolution, a revolution of hatred and vengeance because in each wounded heart lies the latent germ of a future avenger. May God prove me wrong, but in this area, in the fields and mountains, one can feel the truth pulsing with the force of immanent events. . . . If things continue as they are, we shall have no recourse but to seek the support of the guerrillas.

One can only speculate what impact this letter had when it was captured by the police in March 1952, handed over to the Minister of War, José María Bernal (Antioquia's former governor), and then forwarded to Governor Braulio Henao Mejía in Medellín. Its content, however, could not have come as a surprise to the regional authorities. Antioqueño Conservative criticism of the behavior of extremist public employees, fellow Conservative civilians, and the police was not new. On many separate occasions citizens had indicated that the most frequent target of these forces—contrary to the justification given by the regional authorities for their existence—were not Liberal guerrillas but rather the unarmed civilian population.

Among the more than thirty-three reports of contrachusma activity and sixty-one reports of Liberal guerrilla violence filed with the governor's office or with his secretary between 1948 and 1953—the vast majority of which were reports of violence in 1952 and 1953—in the Bajo Cauca, Magdalena Medio, and northeastern regions, there is not a single report in which the Conservative civilian police attacked Liberal guerrillas or contrachusma forces and Liberal guerrillas had any kind of intentional armed encounter with each other. Of the sixty-one reports involving Liberal guerrilla attacks or encounters between them and the government's forces, moreover, there was not a single instance in which the police took the offensive and sought out guerrillas in their camps before a guerrilla attack occurred. Encounters between the police and guerrillas typically only took place when the latter assaulted a town in which the police happened to be stationed or when guerrillas led ambushes of policemen to steal their arms, uniforms, and supplies. In the few cases where the police did go after the guerrillas it was only after the guerrillas had already attacked and left behind civilian casualties. Unable to locate their objective, the final police report invariably concluded that the much sought after guerrilla forces had melted into the surrounding hills and been lost from sight.

The police and contrachusma violence that was directed against the civilian population, combined with these forces' evident failure to protect civilians from guerrilla attack, embittered many inhabitants in eastern Antioquia. Among them were moderate Conservatives like Arturo who refused to condone the violent behavior of their partisan brethren and who opposed the use of violence against innocent members of the opposition. They warned the regional government that it was unwise to push local inhabitants too far. The government, they insisted, was in no position to actually restrain violence should local Liberals decide they had endured enough abuse and opt to support or join the incipient, armed Liberal bands that were increasingly active in the region. Juan de Dios Arango, a Conservative engineer in charge of Puerto Berrío's electric plant and a local landowner, for instance, denounced fellow Conservatives for falsely accusing the Liberal opposition of subversive activities solely to legitimize taking jobs away from them. Arango insisted that the local Liberal mayor had never abused Conservatives as some extremists insisted and that his only "crime" was to focus on advancing the development and growth of an area where "progress has been put off for twenty years." The mayor was the first appointee to pay serious attention to finishing much needed sewerage, electricity, and aqueduct projects in the town. *Laureanistas,* bent on punishing moderate Conservatives who refused to collude in the abuse of the opposition were, in Arango's estimation, the real sources of local unrest. In his own case, fellow Conservatives had attempted to force "the undersigned to resign as the head of the electric company" for defending the mayor and for attributing Puerto Berrío's "backwardness" to Conservative-led "intrigues around the distribution of public jobs." Arango, however, had resisted attempts to force him to resign insisting that "under no circumstances can we operate subject to the intrigues of these politicians." He also reminded the governor that while there might be no harm in constantly fiddling with local political appointments to public office in other towns where local needs were less pressing, doing so in a town as strategically important as Puerto Berrío would have disastrous consequences.[52] The local Conservative party committee surprisingly seconded Arango and also pleaded with the governor to restrain local party extremists and to block their attempts to force the removal of the town's Liberal mayor.[53]

Local inhabitants, including many Conservatives, moreover, had been protesting the partisan activities of fellow Conservatives in eastern Antioquia since 1950. The former customs administrator and collection agent of the national finance office in Zaragoza, for instance, complained to the governor that the local mayor had removed him from office and denounced him to the local Conservative committee as "a bad Conservative" for refusing to arbitrarily dismiss Liberal public employees.[54] Two months later in January 1951 Caucasia's municipal registrar narrowly escaped an attempt on his life after he refused to condone the arbitrary treatment of members of the opposition by national policemen and their contrachusma aides.[55] Later that same month, Puerto Berrío's Conservative committee denounced the mayor and national police agents for abusing the town's citizenry when they were drunk (which, the committee assured the governor, was often because both the mayor and police suffered from "alcoholic intemperance"). The mayor and the police had assassinated an unarmed citizen and caused frequent public scandals. This behavior, the committee reminded the governor, "reflects badly on the Conservative government."[56]

The determinants of local violence in eastern Antioquia were hence far more complex than any innate, unavoidable differences between monolithic groups of Liberals and Conservatives—the traditional explanation given for *la Violencia*—might suggest. In many areas there were no innate conflicts, these were created and fed by the state's own agents who capitalized on a few disgruntled, local adherents or otherwise imported them from nearby areas to fan and exploit the flames of partisan difference. It is also apparent from the numerous complaints filed by moderate Conservative public employees and elected officials in peripheral areas that no consensus existed among Antioquia's Conservatives regarding the propriety of using violence for political purposes. In some cases this may have stemmed less from a sense of ideological sympathy with local members of the opposition and more from fears of the economic impact of partisan unrest. But whatever the motivations for the absence of overwhelming local Conservative support for the activities of the regional authorities, what is evident is the need to question a generalized or "inherently" violent concept of partisan affiliation in Colombia as an explanation for *la Violencia*.

For a long time Governor Braulio Henao Mejía was loath to respond to or believe Conservative reports suggesting that the principal catalyst of local violence in eastern Antioquia was the unruly presence and seemingly unlimited arbitrary authority exercised by extremist public officials, contrachusmas, and national police troops. He also ignored suggestions that rivalries between competing Conservative factions played a determinant role in the rise of police and contrachusma influence. But events in western Antioquia, where violence had already grown quite severe and where comparable complaints against extremists had been received by his office, gradually convinced him that there was some truth to both the rumors of police inadequacy and to accusations of arbitrary actions filed against Conservative contrachusmas in areas where violence was present. The governor first voiced his growing doubts about the exact nature and scale of the conflict being played out in Antioquia's peripheral zones in a detailed, confidential letter he sent on March 1, 1951, to his close friend and fellow Antioqueño, Gonzalo Restrepo Jaramillo, the minister of foreign relations in Bogotá.[57] In it the governor confessed that he no longer knew whom to believe nor had he any idea how many men were really up in arms, whether they were "thousands" or simply "whether their extraordinary mobility makes it appear as if there were a great number of them." He also noted that violence only recently attributable to conflicts organized along clear partisan lines no longer seemed so easily classified. "More serious than the initial twisted political inspiration or the gang [*pandilla*] or guerrilla actions directed against the government and the nation's institutions—which is what we had been witnessing until just a couple of months ago," he wrote with evident concern, "is what we are currently witnessing, that is, groups of true vandals who are solely dedicated to pillage as their main motivation and who are now made up of members of both parties." Henao Mejía acknowledged knowing that there were now at least two different kinds of armed groups in Antioquia. Those whose sole purpose was to "steal and, while they are at it, assassinate, burn, and rape" and for whom partisan concerns seemed to play a secondary role, and others who fulfilled a variety of functions ("there are those taking part in several different tasks," that is, both partisan and economic). Liberals and Conservatives were involved in both types of armed bands.

The governor's letter to the minister of foreign relations was mainly motivated by worries regarding the presence of guerrilla groups on the stretch of road from Dabeiba to Turbo in the northwestern region of Urabá. But disappointment in the ability of the police to meet the challenge of Liberal guerrillas and escalating economic banditry elsewhere in Antioquia influenced his change in attitude toward the issue of public order throughout the department. Preoccupied by the ineffectuality of the police, Governor Henao Mejía insisted to the minister of foreign relations that only the complete militarization of regions severely affected by violence (such as eastern Antioquia) could begin to meet the problem of unrest in the department. Only absolute control by the army would do, the governor concluded, because, as he confessed to Restrepo Jaramillo, "our valiant police force—whether because of a lack of manpower or supplies—has been lamentably defeated twice in the last month on occasions in which it could have performed splendidly." The central government, moreover, appeared to have abandoned the region to deal with escalating violence entirely on its own. Although in secret meetings the president had promised the governor needed supplies, arms, radios, and airplanes, Antioquia had still not received any aid. Without the requested materiel, the governor warned, he could hardly be expected to stem "Liberalism's increasingly subversive attitude." As the central government delayed, the conflict in Antioquia intensified. Every day areas of recent colonization and intensive agricultural production were "razed, harvests are stolen or destroyed and workers are assassinated or they flee in the hope of saving their lives." Henao Mejía was convinced that he could win the war against subversion if only the central government would send him adequate support with which to confront it. As such, he concluded his missive on a bellicose note and demanded, "more judges, more arms, more soldiers, but above all much more diligence and cooperation [from the central government]."

Braulio Henao Mejía never received the additional troops and supplies he insisted were necessary to reestablish public order in Antioquia. He was reduced during his entire term in office (August 1950–July 1952) to writing a stream of memorandums to the central government, begging for aid and for additional monies with which to meet the increased expense of public order maintenance in the region. Meanwhile *laureanistas* and other extremist Conservatives publicly upbraided him and portrayed him as an ineffective regional leader who was too timid to impose authoritarian measures to end Liberal subversion. In response to local public order incidents, moreover, Henao Mejía continued to deploy on an ad hoc basis the very policemen whose efficacy he had questioned in his missive to Bogotá. The governor also came to tolerate, whether through inertia or commitment, local Conservative efforts to arm volunteers and to ignore or minimize disturbing complaints from concerned party members regarding the long-term implications of continuing to promote arbitrary and violent policies against the opposition.

The predictions made by moderate Conservatives that the escalation of government repression would invite intense armed Liberal retaliation were ultimately fulfilled when several Liberal armed groups went on an extended rampage against haciendas, mines, and towns that began in February 1952 and lasted through July. By October, guerrilla violence was matched by equivalent levels of contrachusma violence, and rural areas in eastern Antioquia, where public-order matters had not been of pressing concern to the government before 1952, suddenly emerged as some of the departmental sites most severely affected by *la Violencia*.

The Intensification of Guerrilla Conflict

On June 13, 1953, a month before a military coup brought down the government of Conservative president Laureano Gómez, a young woman was captured in Puerto Berrío and brought to Medellín to testify about her life among the Liberal guerrillas who operated in eastern Antioquia.[58] Her name was Angela Rosa and she was twenty-four years old, single, of illegitimate birth, and part of the wave of seasonal laborers who floated from hacienda to hacienda throughout eastern Antioquia looking for work. Angela Rosa had been born in the northeastern mining town of Amalfi, where declining production and the growth of large estates had pushed hundreds of settlers out in search of livelihoods from the late 1920s through the early 1940s. She had been living in another mining town to the south, Maceo, when a local landowner turned her over to the police and accused her of being a spy for the men up in arms against the Conservative government. After her arrest, the chief of the department of criminal investigation in Medellín asked Angela Rosa to recount everything she knew about "where that group of *bandoleros* that operated in your vicinity lived, the number of men up in arms, their names, how they dress, how they obtain food, their leaders, what connections they have with nearby towns and their activities."

The verbatim transcript of her testimony provides a rich account of the ordinary lives and hardships of migrant settlers in the Magdalena Medio region of Antioquia and of the effect of violence on their way of life. The events Angela Rosa recounted in her judicial testimony took place between mid-1952 and May 1953—the year in which Liberal guerrillas were most active in eastern Antioquia and the year in which the greatest number of deaths, expropriations, and general criminal activity were reported for the area.

Angela Rosa began her narrative by disabusing the criminal investigator of his impression that she had "lived" with the guerrillas: "we didn't exactly live with them, but we did live near them and that's how we knew everything they did." Proximity turned to intimacy when sometime in 1952 Angela Rosa and her lover, Alfonso, were informed by the proprietor of the estate where they had been working as tenants that they would have to "get out." Angela Rosa and her companion moved to her stepfather's farm where they stayed for a month. "They were rounding up Liberals in those days supposedly to kill them," and so Alfonso and five other young men "fled to the hills." Angela Rosa and her stepsister Teresa were left behind. After wandering around for six days without sighting the guerrillas, Alfonso returned to the women's side and picked up another friend, Manuel, with whom he planned to renew his search for the "Liberal chusma." Before they set out, however, a contra-chusma group came down from the hills and there was a "shoot-out [*se echaron candela*]." Wounded in the skirmish, Alfonso fled into the hills with Jesús (Teresa's lover) and Pedro to renew his search for the guerrillas while the women sought refuge on another farm (*finca*). Some days later, the men rejoined the women as they were about to move on to a third farm and begged the women to accompany them into the *monte* (hills). Prompted by rumors that the Conservative contrachusmas "were killing women, children, men, and everything in their path," the group traveled and lodged at four different farms in the space of less than a week. The group finally arrived at a farm called "Nuevo Mundo," where Angela Rosa noted that "we had lived before" as sharecroppers or tenants.[59]

A week after the group's arrival at Nuevo Mundo, members of a Liberal band headed by a man nicknamed "Pielroja" (red skin) arrived and insisted the men join their guerrilla group because "they'd be killed there all by themselves."[60] The problem once more became what to do with the women. Alfonso and Jesús insisted that the women go back to their stepfather's farm, but the women refused because "we were scared to go back on our own." They proposed continuing with the men and then stopping at a farm located at a league's distance from Pielroja's camp on the near shore of the Río San Bartolo.[61] Alfonso was still suffering from the wounds from the skirmish with the contrachusma, so Pielroja sent Alfonso back to be nursed by the women on the farm, but agreed to send for Alfonso when "Alfonso was better and they [the guerrillas] had a mission to perform." Pielroja's men kept careful tabs on the recovery of their recruit during the two months of Alfonso's convalescence. When his arm healed, "he joined them on missions and then came back home, and he did that for another month." During the month in which Alfonso accompanied the guerrillas on their "missions," the band attacked one rural neighborhood in the municipality of Yalí and killed five people. They then moved on to Ité where they had an encounter with government forces in which they killed another six men. In July 1952, their month-long spree culminated in an aborted attempt to blow up the railroad bridge at Monos.[62]

Alfonso abandoned the guerrillas after that and sought work on the hacienda where his female companions had found employment. He and the proprietor drew up a six-month contract in which "half the farm was negotiated and [Alfonso] began to sow the fields and fix up the animal pens and beds." At the end of six months, news reached the group that Pielroja's band had recently killed eighteen people in "Las Partidas"—among them a man, his four sons, a son-in-law, and others whom Angela Rosa knew. Around the same time, two other Liberal guerrilla groups arrived at the farm, one led by Capitán Corneta and the other led by a guerrilla leader named Santander. Santander was originally (as his name suggests) based on the other side of the Magdalena River, but he had linked up with the Antioquia-based band led by Captain Corneta and become Corneta's second in command. These two groups, who numbered around 190 men, were about to attack "El Coco," a *corregimiento* near "El Tigre" in the municipality of Amalfi.[63] Once they had successfully burned half the settlement and killed "a lot of people," they moved on to nearby "La Susana" where they burned numerous homes and killed another twenty-five people, among them a woman whom Angela Rosa also knew.[64] After resting three days at Alfonso's farm, Captain Corneta's and Santander's men moved on to join forces with Pielroja's band.

The attack on El Coco and La Susana finally pushed the army into action; they came looking for the guerrillas, surrounded them, and forced them to flee north toward the mining town of Segovia.[65] Government forces killed three guerrillas from a detachment of seven sent to search for salt on one of the farms where Angela Rosa and Alfonso had sought refuge, but four others escaped after killing several miners, among them the father-in-law of the farm's owner. Terrified that the army would kill them, Angela Rosa, her stepsister, the concubine of one of Pielroja's men, and Alfonso fled to a safe house owned by another guerrilla where they stayed for a week while the farm owner built his wife and mother-in-law a hut in the hills where they could hide. Alfonso and Angela Rosa joined the farmer and his family in their hideaway, while Teresa set up house with another of Pielroja's men nicknamed "Relámpago" (Lightning). Three weeks later, Alfonso and Angela Rosa had "a falling out [*un pereque*]" with the farmer and moved onto a farm owned by "Lalo," one of the guerrillas' local suppliers. They had to abandon that farm, too, when Pielroja's men commandeered it a week later.

Resting in a hut hidden in some scrub on the farm "Pescadero," the group heard that forty of Santander's men had arrived at Lalo's farm and were looking for "Amanda, Luis (Amanda's partner), Alfonso, and [Angela Rosa]." They demanded that the men "join up" and that the women become "their [the guerrillas'] women." Hearing this, the women and their companions fled but failed to reach a safe farm before dusk. Ten of Santander's men caught up with them and announced: "OK men, what's the deal here? Either you're Conservatives [*godos*] or maybe we're the Conservatives, but you keep fleeing from us, so we've come for these women, these are our orders. We'll take them with your consent or without it." When the women began to cry, the guerrillas told them they would leave them alone if they stopped crying, but later that night, the guerrillas gang-raped them. "At night they grabbed us and did with us whatever they liked, all of them used us, and since Alfonso and Luis grabbed us back, they got mad because we'd been taken away from them [the guerrillas], and one of them who they call 'Lucero' took his gun from his holster and took aim." Angela Rosa then concluded that "everything calmed down and we went to bed."

Santander's men then left to link up with Pielroja's band, while Alfonso and Luis, apparently after agreeing to rejoin the guerrillas and deliver the women later, set out with Angela Rosa and Amanda in the direction of "El Presidio." There, Luis hoped to sell his only worldly belongings, his shotgun and his poncho (*ruana*), in the hope of cobbling together enough money to enable Amanda to escape to the port town of Puerto Berrío. Instead, the men were accosted by two of Pielroja's band and forced to lead the guerrillas to the women's hiding place. On the road, Alfonso escaped and ran to warn the women to flee. At one of the several farms at which the women stopped to ask for refuge, a servant fed and agreed to lodge them but was discovered by the proprietor and his overseer who turned the women over to the Maceo authorities and accused them of being "spies for the chusma." Angela Rosa and Amanda were eventually sent to Medellín, where the authorities took down their testimony and pressed them for details regarding the whereabouts and strength of the guerrillas.

Six guerrilla bands operated in eastern Antioquia. Pielroja's had seventy men and two women and was based near "La Susana" in Maceo between Puerto Berrío and Yolombó. Santander and Corneta's band had 190 members and had its base in "San Vasconio" near the mining camps of Remedios and Segovia. Vicente Mejía (alias "El Dormido") had eighteen men and three women and was based along the railroad tracks between Maceo and Puerto Berrío. A fourth group, led by "El Chicote," was based in the department of Santander, but Angela Rosa purported not to know of it. Two other bands, led by Rafael Rangel and Trino García, were based on the other side of the Magdalena River near Santander's camp but sometimes crossed the river to operate in Antioquia. Angela Rosa had had no contact with them and could supply no further information (see map 10).

To survive, Pielroja, Corneta, Santander, and Vicente Mejía "went out all the time to rustle cattle."[66] Pielroja's group kept the branded cattle for their own consumption and sold unbranded cattle to an absentee landlord from Maceo who resided in Puerto Berrío. Salt, of crucial significance to the guerrillas' survival and a commodity whose trade was strictly controlled by the authorities, was mainly obtained by stealing what was left out in pastures for cattle. Knowing the dire need for salt by many guerrillas, the authorities frequently poisoned it. To avoid this, guerrillas only stole salt from troughs in pastures where the cattle had just been let out to graze. When I interviewed the former guerrilla leader, Captain Corneta, he said the salt was dyed with methylene blue, but that the guerrillas were so desperate that they washed it off and ate it anyway.[67] The guerrillas obtained other day-to-day necessities such as grains, lard, molasses loaves, and clothes by stealing from nearby farms. Salt, saltpeter, and cigarettes, however, had to be brought in from Puerto Berrío. Several local farm owners and merchants residing in Puerto Berrío colluded to supply these items to the guerrillas. When questioned about the degree

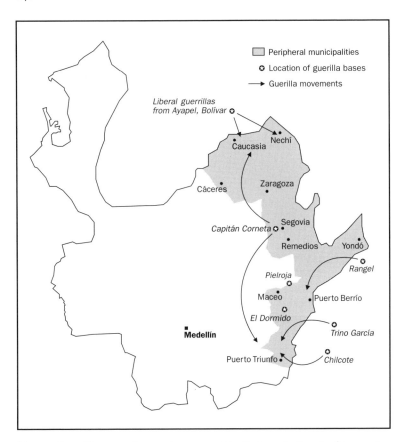

Map 10. Guerrilla operations and movement in Eastern Antioquia. (Source: Instituto Geográfico Augustín Codazzi; Archivo Privado del Señor Gobernador de Antioquia, 1950–1953; Archivo de la Secretaría de Gobierno de Antioquia, 1950–1953)

to which inhabitants other than those in Maceo provided logistical support for Pielroja's men, Angela Rosa responded that "I haven't heard it said that any of the other nearby towns help them out." She was unable (or unwilling) to say whether locals acted as "spies" or informants who relayed information regarding government operations to the guerrillas.

Angela Rosa was able to reel off the aliases of numerous participants in Pielroja's band. But the men under Santander and Corneta, she insisted, were "all strangers to me."[68] Whereas Pielroja's men appear to have been largely local and to have mainly confined their activities to the Maceo/Puerto Berrío area, Corneta and Santander's group was highly mobile and of largely nonlocal origin. Angela Rosa testified that "[Cor-

neta's] band moves around a lot, they say it's been sighted in the department of Bolívar in the Cienagas de Barbacoas as well as Ité, and that lately
they've been seen around Segovia and Remedios in the 'Mata' canyon."
Corneta and Santander's group was also considerably better armed than
Pielroja and his men.[69] Except for a few shotguns and revolvers, the majority of Pielroja's band possessed no guns and was armed only with the
peinillas, or small machetes, commonly carried by agricultural laborers
throughout Colombia. A shortage of weaponry had in fact compelled the
group to scale back their activities to such a degree that "they hardly go
out anymore." In contrast, Corneta and Santander possessed seventeen
rifles — fifteen captured from the police and two marked as army-issue —
several carbines and revolvers, many shotguns, swords (*yataganes*), and
peinillas. Santander and Corneta's men also had stolen police uniforms.[70]
The majority of the bands' participants, however, donned the typical garb
of the *paisano* (khaki pants, shirt, ruana, and straw or felt hat) that enabled them to blend in with local inhabitants and to wander unnoticed
throughout the countryside.

Angela Rosa ended her long account of her experience with the guerrillas with the fate of the group of eight men who had initially set out
in search of the guerrillas less than a year earlier. Alfonso and Luis had
joined Vicente Mejía's band; three other men had met their deaths at the
hands of the government's forces; the whereabouts of two others were
unknown, and Angela Rosa's stepsister's lover had joined Santander.

The Context of Angela Rosa's Narrative

It is a striking feature of Angela Rosa's testimony that *la Violencia* appears
not to have touched her or her neighbors' lives until sometime in mid-
1952. Indeed, her narrative — spanning an approximately eleven-month
period between June 1952 and May 1953 — encompasses almost exactly the
duration of consistent armed conflict in most of eastern Antioquia. Unlike either Urabá or Urrao in western Antioquia, where partisan violence
gave rise to a well-organized, locally-based Liberal guerrilla response by
late 1949 and where a state of nearly continuous armed conflict existed
from then until June 1953, most civilians and hacienda workers in eastern Antioquia largely escaped the effects of intense violence until 1952.
Although there were guerrilla attacks against Antioqueño port settlements and the mining areas around Caucasia since 1948, they had all

been led by guerrilla groups based outside Antioquia proper (from the nearby departments of Bolívar and Santander) and appear to have enjoyed little local Liberal participation or support. Government forces, although quite brutal, had also encountered difficulties in applying a widespread policy of harassment throughout eastern Antioquia. This was due in part to the vastness of the terrain and the lack of infrastructure, particularly around the mining regions of the northeast and Bajo Cauca, but was also due to the relative absence of local Conservative support for such efforts. Despite the use of official violence against organized state workers and miners since 1948, moreover, organized workers had largely succeeded in deflecting or resisting government attempts to eliminate them or usurp their control over local political offices and power.

The turning point in the spread of violence occurred in 1952 when at least one major guerrilla group (under the leadership of the Antioqueño-born Captain Corneta) based in Antioquia proper emerged, and when Governor Braulio Henao Mejía endorsed an incipient expansion of the role and number of paramilitary Conservative forces operating in eastern Antioquia. When Dionisio Arango Ferrer, a longtime supporter of armed Conservative contrachusma groups assumed control of the governor's office in July 1952, moreover, contrachusmas were made primarily responsible for the maintenance of public order in the department. The combination of these two developments shifted the focus of violence away from the harassment and dismissal of workers and political office-holders toward a far bloodier and more generalized violence against rural inhabitants and hacienda personnel.

In a body count of civilian and guerrilla ("*bandolero*") deaths registered by the regional armed forces in 1949, eastern Antioquia reported two civilian deaths (in Amalfi and Cáceres) out of a departmental total of sixteen casualties. In 1950, eastern Antioquia reported twelve dead civilians out of a regional total of forty-nine (concentrated in two towns, Puerto Triunfo/Cocorná and Puerto Perales/San Luis). It was not until 1951 and especially 1952, however, that the number of casualties in the area rose to alarming proportions and constituted a significant percentage of the violent deaths occurring throughout Antioquia. Amalfi, Puerto Berrío, Remedios, and San Luis accounted for 14 percent of the region's total of 468 civilian deaths and 1 percent of the region's total of 502 "*bandolero*" deaths in 1951 (see appendix A.4). But, by 1952 eastern towns accounted for more than half the departmental total of 1,114 civilian deaths and 37 percent of the total number of the region's "*bandolero*" casualties (1,154). This is especially striking as these eastern towns held less than 10 percent of the department's total population. The largest number of deaths in 1951 and 1952, moreover, was registered in Puerto Berrío and its surrounding area, precisely the zone encompassed by Angela Rosa's account (see appendix A.6).

The governor first received reports that a locally-based, armed Liberal group was operating in eastern Antioquia when spies complained that an hacienda owner in Yolombó, who was also a Liberal regional assembly representative, had sent his *mayordomo* to deliver provisions to Liberal guerrillas who were camped out in the hills nearby.[71] Five days later, eight guerrillas appeared on an hacienda in the Alicante region between Puerto Berrío and Yolombó to inquire about the political affiliation of the hacienda's workers. When it turned out that they were all Liberal, the workers' lives were spared, but the hacienda was robbed. By late February the guerrillas were reported to have "taken up positions" around the hacienda "La Gallinera" in the vicinity of Yalí.[72] Meanwhile, in the hamlet of Nechí in Caucasia, guerrillas crossed the border from the department of Bolívar and attacked the Conservative *caserío* "Regencia" (located five leagues from the border with the department of Bolívar), destroyed forty-three houses, left many dead and wounded, and raped most of the settlement's married women. Meeting with no official opposition, the guerrillas escaped via Ayapel, Bolívar, without losing any men.[73] A massive migration of the area's inhabitants ensued, prompting the governor to beg Caucasia's notary "not to formalize during these days of terror, any land deeds, so as to avoid the abuses audacious individuals wish to commit with simple, terrified people."[74] No further guerrilla attacks were reported in eastern Antioquia for about a month.

In April, however, the guerrilla activity flared up once more and lasted until July. Armed Liberals struck in Puerto Nare in early April killing one woman and leaving another eight inhabitants missing.[75] Two weeks later a guerrilla force of between 40 and 150 men marched down from the railroad line near Puerto Berrío and attacked an hacienda in the settlement of Santa Rita in the southeastern municipality of San Luis. The guerrillas left fourteen dead while seventy-five terrified families fled to seek refuge in the hills near the village.[76] The attack on Santa Rita sparked a panic among Conservatives in other parts of San Luis such as Samaná, where rumors of an impending guerrilla incursion forced dispersed rural inhabitants to converge upon the town proper. In their hurry to abandon their properties before the guerrillas arrived, the inhabitants left "troughs filled with corn, hundreds of cattle on different farms, [and] thousands of wandering pigs" while they themselves were "without housing, food, or work."[77] They joined together to send a petition to the governor requesting the establishment of an army post in the settlement to woo back the rural residents who had left "the lands in Samaná uninhabited for fear of the chusma" just at the onset of the planting season. Only a week after Samaná's residents begged the government to send soldiers to protect them, however, an armed Liberal band of forty men, led by the Santander-based guerrilla leader Trino García, crossed the Magdalena River into Puerto Nare and once more spread terror in Antioquia's port towns and the surrounding rural areas.[78]

While Trino and his men attacked the southeast, two other guerrilla leaders, Captain Corneta and Sergeant Santander, were being chased down the mountains by the army in Caucasia. In the absence of any public authorities who could do so, Caucasia's telegraphist took it upon himself to provide the regional government with a public-order report from Tarazá, where he had escaped to after the guerrillas cut the telegraph line in Caucasia proper. He informed the governor that all the stores in the town were closed, that the town's inhabitants had fled, and that the priest and all the nuns from the local girls' school had escaped across the fields to Puerto Antioquia in the company of the town's public officials. Three days later, national police troops fought with the guerrillas when they encountered them attempting to set fire to the government-owned gasoline reserves. The national police assassinated eleven people.[79] Nearby Cáceres, moreover, resembled a ghost town. All of its farms had been abandoned as inhabitants fled in the wake of a guerrilla attack in which fields were razed and houses burned.[80] Corneta and his men eventually escaped via the Cauca River and a month later attacked mining camps in El Bagre, Remedios, and Segovia. Just prior to the attack, local inhabitants warned the governor that there were no policemen, no soldiers, and no arms with which to defend the town.[81] Having robbed the gold mines, Corneta's men proceeded toward Puerto Berrío, where his men and those of Pielroja and Vicente Mejía wreaked havoc on the numerous haciendas concentrated in the area between Maceo, Amalfi, Yolombó, and Puerto Berrío.

On May 18, thirty to forty guerrillas attacked a farm in Virginias. It belonged to a Conservative engineer in charge of Puerto Berrío's electrical plant—the same engineer who had earlier denounced Conservative extremists and warned the governor not to allow the police and contrachusmas to harass local Liberals lest they rise up in arms against the state. Although some of the farm workers managed to escape (many were Liberal), others were captured and killed by the guerrillas.[82] Guerrillas next burned an hacienda in La Susana belonging to a prominent Medellín industrialist family on June 10, then assaulted an hacienda in a place called Alicante in Puerto Berrío and stole all its cattle.[83] Four days later guerrillas attacked again, this time at an hacienda belonging to the same family in Murillo, Puerto Berrío.[84] Within days, other haciendas became the focus of guerrilla attacks in Remedios and all along the railroad line between Cristalina and Puerto Berrío.[85] In a single attack on one farm, twenty-five workers were killed, while in nearby Yalí on June 25, a group of ninety guerrillas assassinated the Liberal hacienda owner, Raul Isaza Sierra, because he employed thirteen Conservative workers and denied it when asked about their political affiliation.[86] Guerrilla attacks on haciendas in Maceo and Puerto Berrío continued through July until finally the flood of guerrilla violence ended with attacks on Shell Oil's Casabe camp and against the Pato Consolidated Mining Company's camp in El Bagre where guerrillas stole gold dust, dynamite, tents, and machines.[87]

The speed and intensity of guerrilla assault on eastern Antioquia shocked the regional government. Although Conservatives residing in the port towns along the Magdalena River in the southeast and in mining hamlets in Caucasia had been the occasional targets of Liberal attack since 1948, such assaults had been sporadic and led by guerrillas based outside Antioquia proper. The typical targets of these early guerrilla attacks, moreover, had not been hacienda workers but rather the offices and agents of the state. In contrast, the majority of guerrilla attacks occurring between February and July of 1952, October through November of the same year, and the first four months of 1953, were led by forces based in Antioquia and conducted as part of a systematic and intensive strategy of human eradication. The principal objects of these later attacks were the mining camps and haciendas that produced the bulk of Antioquia's gold, cattle, and commercial agricultural products. Threats to the region's economy coupled with the fact that attacks were now led by forces based in Antioquia—who were perceived to be likelier to garner the support of local hacienda owners and inhabitants—prompted the regional government to finally treat the issue of public order in the area with the attention it had until then only lavished on questions of public order in western Antioquia. The central problem facing the regional government in early 1952, however, was how to meet public-order challenges emerging simultaneously on several fronts when it lacked sufficient troops and supplies.

On April 29, 1952, Governor Henao Mejía received a telegram from Bogotá's secretary of the ministry of government encouraging the Antioqueño leader to respond to growing guerrilla activity by arming Conservative civilians. To give added force to his message, the secretary forwarded the complaints of numerous Conservatives from towns scattered throughout Antioquia who expressed their discontent with being left at the mercy of armed Liberal bands. He gave Puerto Berrío as a prime example of a town that would benefit from the organization of "personal defense groups."[88] By the time Luis Ignacio Andrade's telegram reached the governor, however, Henao Mejía had already held a meeting with the members of Antioquia's Conservative directorate. Together they agreed to create and arm contrachusmas in towns such as San Luis and Remedios in eastern Antioquia and Caicedo and Titiribí in the southwest. In theory these contrachusma groups were intended to complement, not supplant, official forces when they were too few to defend particular areas against Liberal attack. However, in reality local sponsors seized the opportunity to form paramilitary groups to act independently or in lieu of official troops regardless of whether sufficient official forces existed or not.[89]

The inhabitants of the municipality of San Luis, for instance, bluntly informed the governor that the national police were "cowards" and that "the only solution . . . is to arm all the area's Conservatives so that they can defend themselves, and to give rifles to all the local members of the army reserve who are older than twenty years."[90] Requests for arms soon poured into the governor's office. On each telegram demanding weapons, the governor reassured impatient petitioners: "we have sent arms," and "we have distributed more than one thousand revolvers. We're doing this every day." In a half-hearted attempt to maintain at least the semblance of some kind of control, he also added that he needed "at least the names" of the reserve volunteers before they could be issued uniforms, food, and weapons. He also warned Conservatives in San Luis not to repeat what had happened in the western town of Ituango where Conservatives had also volunteered to form a group of civilian police and then quickly disappeared once arms had been distributed.[91]

This was not the first attempt to organize Conservative civilian police troops in eastern Antioquia. Extremist Conservatives and selected regional authorities had first mobilized them in anticipation of the senate elections of September 1951. Most of these efforts had been concentrated, however, in towns with a modicum of Conservative support and not directly in the mining towns of the northeast or in the Bajo Cauca where Conservative loyalists were few. There was simply not enough local antagonism between members of the two parties in these areas, or the Liberal opposition was too large for Conservatives to seriously contemplate forming paramilitary units to attack Liberal neighbors in these towns. The strength of organized labor in mining towns such as Remedios, Zaragoza, Segovia, and Caucasia, moreover, deterred the emergence of the kind contrachusma-led electoral harassment that had occurred in Liberal towns throughout the southwest between 1946 and 1949. The regional government had also encountered little support from Conservative landowners in eastern Antioquia for their paramilitary project. Local landowners proved uninterested in promoting a partisan agenda for extremist regional authorities if such a strategy meant the possible disruption of tenuous labor markets and valuable production. This left extremist regional Conservatives with only one good option: to import or encourage individuals with no vested economic stake or local bipartisan ties in eastern Antioquia's Liberal-dominated areas to migrate there in order to promote violence in return for material and political rewards.

Thus, it was not until the events of 1952 that the possibility of deploying armed Conservative civilians to usurp power from local Liberal majorities in eastern Antioquia became a reality. The creation or deployment of Conservative civilian forces was ultimately most successful in towns where Liberal railroad and public sector workers had been the victims of official abuse since the death of Gaitán in 1948 and one or two towns where Conservatives were a strong presence. Conservatives in San Roque, for instance, colluded with Conservatives in Maceo and Caracolí who were commissioned by Maceo's parish priest to force Liberals to vote in the 1951 senate elections. Together they obliged Liberals to shout *vivas* to the Conservative party and to parade in the streets on election day "bearing the blue flag [the Conservative party's color] before them to save their skins [*para poder salvar el pellejo*]." Liberals tolerated such humiliation, one man recounted, because they feared the implicit threat of being taken for "a ride" on the train that ran from San Roque to Puerto Berrío, where they would be "decapitated at the Monos railroad station," which was, not surprisingly, one of the targets of guerrilla attack.[92] Other local citizens confirmed that contrachusma reinforcements from Maceo and Caracolí were sent to San Roque to "preach violence and finish off the Liberals."[93]

Contrachusmas recruited and organized in Maceo and Caracolí eventually expanded their activities into towns such as San Carlos, San Luis, and Cocorná in the southeast. In San Carlos a man named Emilio Espinosa, referred to as a "stranger [*forastero*]" by local inhabitants, was said to have arrived mounted on a white steed, waving a blue flag, and leading "a mob of peasants which he'd collected" along the way. With the support of San Carlos's parish priest, Espinosa and his mob recruited unemployed local agricultural workers and "began hacking down Liberal houses and businesses."[94] The possibility of effecting contrachusma violence against local Liberals with no apparent connection to the Liberal guerrillas, however, was contingent on the support of local Conservatives. When the local Conservative mayor of San Carlos interceded to defend a local Liberal town council member and party leader from becoming the contrachusma's victim, the guerrillas "put away their machetes and left."[95] But in places where the contrachusma encountered the support of local officials, they prospered and eventually challenged or usurped the control of less extremist fellow party members. Such forces gradually grew in such a manner as to contemplate penetrating into nearby areas where Conservative support was weaker and where Liberal workers were abundant. Contrachusmas from Yolombó, for instance, spread northward into Yalí and Amalfi, while those from Caracolí mobilized toward Alejandría and Puerto Berrío.[96]

The mobilization of a landless, largely unemployed or underemployed peasant "army" brought to the surface the very real issues of agricultural crisis, land concentration, and declining employment that underlaid many of the tensions between the predominantly agricultural southeast, disappointed colonists in the northeast, and workers in the public and foreign-owned mining sectors. Violence was waged through officially-sanctioned paramilitary units (the contrachusma) that became legitimate channels of expression for long-simmering rivalries and feuds not directly related to partisan differences. The contrachusma were formed and led by ambitious local politicians and priests or by recently appointed public employees such as mayors and police chiefs who were brought into local areas from elsewhere in the department. The use of force against Liberal citizens and uncooperative Conservatives was justified by invoking the defense of religion or preemptive strikes against possible "Communist" subversion. The real purpose, as colluding parish priests and local leaders made abundantly clear when called upon to justify their decision to arm poor civilians before disapproving regional and national critics, was to take away jobs, solve rural unemployment, and restore "order." In other words, the contrachusma became a crucial means of putting right both political and economic wrongs.

Building on these earlier efforts, a consolidated, armed Conservative response to the Liberal guerrilla's presence began to take shape in the port towns on the Antioqueño side of the Magdalena River shortly after the first guerrilla attacks against haciendas in April 1952. The explicit mission of these public order reinforcements was to repel and eradicate Liberal guerrillas and to inhibit the migration of peasants and settlers (*colonos*) crucial to the area's hacienda production.[97] But contrachusma forces were very quickly viewed by significant sectors of the regional population—including many prominent Conservative property holders and a number of Conservative public employees—as a remedy worse than the problem they were meant to alleviate. The contrachusma's violent and arbitrary actions prompted even Conservatives to suggest the adoption of alternative solutions to the problem of public order that did not involve the formation of armed civilian bands. Liberal and Conservative citizens in Cáceres, for instance, jointly signed and mailed the governor a petition in which they openly declared their support for the governor's Pro Paz Initiative, which was announced by both party directorates on the day the governor secretly sent out arms to Conservative civilians, and asked the regional government to promote a colonization project to repopulate the areas devastated by guerrilla violence. They insisted, moreover, that rather than arming more people, the regional state would be better off making its presence felt in the area by appointing legitimate authorities and making a commitment to investing in the area's economic development.[98] This would seem to suggest that locals were fully aware that at least one of the attractions of participating in armed groups was the hunger for jobs and land.

The inhabitants of Cáceres were not the only citizens to suggest a link between the absence of state authority, economic incentives, and the incidence of violence in the Bajo Cauca and the Magdalena Medio. A promi-

nent Conservative family who owned numerous haciendas in the area between Remedios and Puerto Berrío, for instance, joined a Liberal member
of the Sociedad de Agricultores Colombianos and a Liberal member of
Antioquia's legislative assembly, who were also landowners in the Northeast and Magdalena Medio, in a unique private sector offer to Colonel
Luis Abadía, the commander of Antioquia's Fourth Brigade in May 1952.[99]
These landowners offered land to any soldier willing to commit himself
to protect the area's haciendas for five years. The signatories were willing
to alienate a portion of their own lands to the soldiers and to supplement
these with concessions obtained from the reserve of public lands held in
trust by the nation. They also offered to pay for barracks, a landing strip,
and supplies in order to attract a permanent presence of the state's officers
to the area.[100] Both in this letter and in another that these men wrote in
conjunction with others in June, the landowners stressed eastern Antioquia's strategic economic importance. They also implied that the state's
failure to make itself felt and respected in eastern Antioquia had contributed to the region's becoming a major site of violence and an easy target
for attack.

In their June letter, petitioners impressed upon the governor "the extremely serious situation in which the cattle haciendas situated on the
west side of the Magdalena River have been left, especially those located
in the area between Puerto Nare and the shores of the rivers San Bar-
tolomé and Ité, encompassed by the municipal boundaries of Puerto
Berrío and Remedios." Landowners also pointedly reminded the governor of the area's importance as a supplier of agricultural products and
cattle to Medellín and the industrial satellite towns that surrounded it:
"your lordship [Su Señoria] cannot ignore that the haciendas located in
the above-mentioned area hold more than sixty thousand head of cattle,
not to mention the fact that they constitute the pantry of our department.
The farms in that region supply 70 percent of the cattle for Medellín's
cattle fairs. Besides, they also supply a large percentage of the agricultural
products consumed in this city [Medellín], and in many other Antioqueño towns." The petitioners complained that public insecurity in the
area had forced them to limit their purchase of livestock, while the threat
of cattle-rustling had seriously compromised their ability to transport
to markets the cattle ready for slaughter. Landowners were unequivocal
about the effect of a reduction in hacienda productivity. They warned the
governor that prices for meat and agricultural commodities would rise

"exorbitantly" to the detriment of consumers faced with already unstable and escalating price cycles and would "produce serious setbacks in the collective economy." Violence, moreover, was forcing workers to migrate away from haciendas—leading to a scarcity of labor and a concurrent rise in operating costs and demand as former rural producers became urban consumers. Concerned landowners also suggested a number of ways of protecting private property in the region and of avoiding "imminent socioeconomic upheaval resulting from the multitudinous exodus of rural workers." They requested an increased presence of the military and the police, particularly those already familiar with the area (that is, locals); the establishment of a body of armed personnel within certain haciendas to restore the confidence of workers who feared being killed; permanent foot patrols throughout the region; and boats and other means of transportation that might aid in the pursuit and capture of guerrillas.[101]

What is striking about the landowners' appeal for a greater military presence in the area and their offer to "cooperate with the Armed Forces with all the means at our disposal" is that they were members of both parties. The threat posed to private property was attributed by landowners to the presence of "pillage and . . . banditry" which had transformed the region "into the most terrible site of vandalism and ruin," not to violence motivated by partisan differences. Given the highly politicized discourse employed by the regional authorities when referring to the problem of violence, it is notable that the economic motivation behind armed mobilization was made explicit by cattlemen with holdings in the Remedios/Puerto Berrío area, while partisan issues were rarely mentioned. This may have been due, as other evidence would seem to suggest, to the fact that landowners were aware that violence that endangered the region's economic interests was committed by Conservatives as well as Liberals, and they were thus careful not to alienate the regional authorities by directly accusing them of fomenting violence. But it also seems to suggest the persistence of a regional, elite bipartisan attitude that privileged economic development and social calm above distinctly partisan objectives.

The strategies advanced by local hacendados—most of whom were absentee landlords with industrial and commercial interests in Medellín—to end violence suggest that they and the regional government were motivated by quite different concerns in the issue of public disorder. In eastern Antioquia, hacendados affiliated with both parties were equally dependent on a predominantly Liberal workforce and were aware that it was unrealistic and dangerous to attempt to alter its composition by force. Landowners also feared the possible long-term consequences of delegating the maintenance of public order to armed groups of poor individuals in an area characterized since the 1920s by struggles over land and resources, even when such individuals shared the landowner's partisan affiliation. The fate of private property in one particular *corregimiento* during *la Violencia*, "El Tigre" in Amalfi, was well known to all the landowners in eastern Antioquia and vividly illustrates the material basis of landowner fears during this period.

El Tigre

In December 1947 the owners of the Hacienda El Tigre, located on the border between Amalfi and Yolombó in a settlement also known as "El Tigre," complained to Antioquia's *secretario de gobierno* that *colonos* (a term that can mean either "settlers" or "squatters") were invading their lands. To protect their property, they demanded that they be allowed to form private, armed defense groups like those they claimed were organized and paid by the foreign-owned mining companies that operated nearby.[102] Although El Tigre's proprietors did not specifically make reference to it, only six months earlier Governor José María Bernal and his secretary, Eduardo Berrío, had lobbied hard to defeat a measure that would have prohibited the sale of arms and ammunition to civilians. The central government had proposed the measure as part of an effort to limit the escalation of partisan conflict.[103] But the governor and his secretary argued that such a law discriminated against farmers who relied upon shotguns and other firearms to hunt and defend their harvests and animals from thieves. The right to bear arms in self-defense, not surprisingly, quickly became the basis for a government policy of distributing arms to Conservative civilians between 1947 and 1953 and greatly increased the number of hired guns employed by local political bosses and landowners in areas where *colono* disputes were most common.

Two months after El Tigre's proprietors demanded the right to form armed defense groups, Amalfi's town clerk informed the government that the dispute between landowners and settlers over control of the Hacienda El Tigre had been going on for a very long time and that the landowners had already "used violent means to . . . establish gangs of armed men in order to dislodge the settlers." The private land dispute had become a public order matter and the clerk requested the immediate presence of six departmental police agents to keep the peace.[104] The police intervened on behalf of the landowners, but colono attempts to gain recognition of their rights continued. In June 1948 eleven peasants made the trip to the governor's office in Medellín to complain that over the course of several years they had "peacefully" made improvements [*mejoras*] consisting of "houses, gardens, plantings . . . covering a large extension along the mountain 'La Gallinera' " on the contested lands.[105] Yet a man named Luis Restrepo, who claimed he held legal title to the lands they had settled, had expelled, illegally imprisoned, and fined them. Settlers did not dispute the legitimacy of Restrepo's titles (although their validity had yet to be determined), but they insisted on being reimbursed for the improvements they'd made before being forced to move on. When the conflict was still not resolved in August, settlers once more protested that Restrepo was abusing them. He had ordered the police to surround them and had threatened to take away their goods and harvests.[106]

The economic dispute between settlers and landowners in El Tigre eventually intersected with the emergence of partisan violence, and the police and private security forces originally employed to defend the hacienda became the nucleus of a contrachusma.[107] The village in which the hacienda was situated, moreover, became the repeated site of assaults and invasions while squatters and rural peons alike bore the indiscriminate brunt of both contrachusma and Liberal guerrilla violence. Conservative inhabitants reported that the contrachusma attacked farm workers in general, even Conservative ones, "beating [them] up, demanding money, arms, and terrorizing workers as happened to a member of this locality's Conservative committee."[108] Meanwhile, Liberal guerrillas sacked the customs office, stole money and the majority of the liquor stocks, burned down the telegraph office and archives, and destroyed half of the village's houses. The guerrillas then invaded the church and hacked the Virgin of Fátima statue to pieces.[109] The two partisan forces concentrated their fury upon the civilian population but never engaged in combat with each other, even though the goal of eliminating the other was what ostensibly served to justify their mutual existence. By February of 1953, most of the inhabitants of El Tigre had fled, and violence had become so severe that the Caja de Crédito Agrario y Minero (Agrarian and Mining Credit Agency) complained to the governor that even financially desperate "working peoples categorically refuse to go into that region."[110]

El Tigre's situation was widely known to the property holders and working peoples of the northeast, and its history illustrates one facet of the complex situation raised by partisan violence in areas where there were preexisting conflicts over land, labor, or resources. What had begun as a struggle over land between settlers and landowners had opened the way for armed groups (initially sponsored by the landowner to dislodge the discontented settlers who challenged his authority) to gradually assume control of the hacienda and act on their own. "Self-defense" groups certainly dislodged settlers, but they also invited Liberal guerrilla attacks on the area and ultimately created a situation of violence so severe that the original landowners could neither reoccupy their lands nor attract labor to work them. For local landowners the lesson of El Tigre was clear. Empowering armed groups, particularly those who could justify their violent activities by representing themselves as allies of the regional government in an area characterized by struggles over property and labor, was simply too risky a strategy for landowners, even Conservative ones, to adopt.

Logic argued against the creation of informally organized, armed groups regardless of their official objectives. The majority of the area's settlers and workers were Liberals and many were non-Antioqueño migrants. Many of the area's landowners, however, were Conservative absentee landlords whose residence was in distant Medellín. For years before the outbreak of violence, absentee landlords had a system for ensuring a stable labor force and the continued productivity of their lands: they had hired Liberal *mayordomos* (estate managers) and administrators and allowed them to determine the political affiliation of the majority of hacienda workers. Many of the workers were transient or seasonal laborers or tenants with precarious status, who, like Alfonso in Angela Rosa's account, drifted from one limited contract to another to work someone else's land. For the landowners, the advantage of such a system was that it never enabled workers to establish a claim on lands whose status (privately owned or in part usurped from public lands) was often murky. Several prominent industrialists and merchants from Medellín with large properties in the Puerto Berrío/Remedios/Yolombó zone had already had to fight the claims of poor colonos and expelled thousands of them from the land in the 1920s and 1930s.[111]

Paradoxically, the emergence of Liberal guerrillas did not threaten hacienda labor relations or private property in eastern Antioquia as did armed Conservative bands operating in conjunction with the police. This was not because Liberal guerrillas were less violent than the Conservative contrachusma; the list of thefts, assaults, and assassinations perpetrated by Liberal armed groups on the area's haciendas between 1952 and 1953 leaves little doubt as to the guerrillas' brutality. But the guerrillas were primarily interested in supporting themselves economically in order to finance their rebellion against the Conservative government; they were not motivated by land hunger or unemployment. Most of the members of the guerrilla groups operating in the area, moreover, were not native to the department and had not been poor farmers. They were former public workers, miners, and cowboys, not sedentary agriculturalists.[112] What the guerrillas had in common with the majority of workers and mayordomos in eastern Antioquia was a shared political affiliation. Thus, while guerrillas might rob an hacienda or work out a deal with mayordomos to take a cut of the hacienda's production, if the workers were Liberal, the guerrillas tended to leave them and the land alone. Local landowners also appear not to have believed the arguments of the armed forces and regional government that local Liberals were inherently rebellious or indistinguishable from the guerrillas. Indeed, the very small size of most guerrilla bands operating in the area and the overrepresentation of non-Antioqueños in them suggest that while locals may certainly have looked to the guerrillas to defend them from Conservative violence, few flocked to join such bands. For instance, Angela Rosa's companion, Alfonso, and his friends only felt compelled to seek out and join a guerrilla group after Liberal hacienda workers became the target of contrachusma attacks invading from other areas in mid-1952. The threat of unemployment and sudden, forced displacement by a landowner seems to have acted as a stronger catalyst to guerrilla membership than the threat of personal injury inflicted by roving bands of the Conservative opposition or any sentiment of partisan loyalty.

The peculiar structure of the local economy thus intersected with political pressures to create a seasonal labor market in which theft, attacks against the state, and general violence alternated with more traditional employment in mining, clearing pasture land, and agricultural labor. Young men with no other viable means of support and little other means of defense easily shifted in and out of armed bands and from violence to seasonal labor on nearby estates. Guerrilla attacks increased when seasonal work on local estates dried up and declined when the young men whom they recruited found employment clearing forests, sowing fields, breeding cattle, or mining. The structure and operation of the guerrillas therefore adapted to and reproduced the area's seasonal cycles of production and employment without unduly threatening or rearranging these activities.

Collusion between contrachusmas and local authorities, in contrast, transformed indiscriminate robbery into the prelude for more complicated and permanent patterns of extortion and, ultimately, land usurpation. Unlike the Liberal guerrillas, the contrachusmas threatened not only hacienda production, they also affected the stability of the area's labor market since they operated on the assumption that all Liberals (including hacienda workers) were guerrillas or guerrilla sympathizers and that this justified their abuse and elimination. The contrachusma and their police allies also justified a wide range of activities, such as expropriation of cattle and agricultural production and the appropriation of lands, in the name of eradicating subversion and defending the interests of values such as religion, order, and democracy. In doing so, the contrachusma threatened landowners' interests by accusing them, as the Liberal guerrillas could not, of betraying the government by hiring Liberal workers and of being complicit with guerrilla forces.

In January 1953 a Conservative proprietor in San Roque (where contrachusmas were particularly active) complained to the governor's secretary that he had returned to his farm after a two-month absence only to find that it had been overtaken by ten armed men who beat him up and accused him of leading a guerrilla group of forty men against the government.[113] Another Conservative complained that his land had been taken over by a former administrator with the help of the "police quartered in this parish" and that they had barred his own and his workers' entry to his property.[114] Incidents such as these probably influenced the decision of a Conservative owner of several haciendas in Remedios, whose properties had repeatedly been the target of Liberal guerrilla attack, to refuse the local contrachusma leader's offer to set up an armed group within his haciendas' limits. The hacienda owner informed the governor that he rejected the offer of contrachusma protection "spurred by my belief that this [the monopoly of force] is the sole prerogative of the authorities."[115] But he must also have worried that once inside the hacienda there was nothing to keep an incident like El Tigre from happening or nothing to prevent the contrachusmas from eventually usurping control of his properties.

Conservatives who disagreed with the tactics employed by their extremist party members even began to turn the extremists' justification of the need for Conservative militancy on its head. In addition to re-pudiating the use of violence against innocent local Liberals, moderate Conservative citizens in Puerto Triunfo, for instance, accused the contra-chusmas and their civilian supporters of attracting rather than impeding Liberal guerrilla attacks. Conservatives singled out the local police in-spector as the principal instigator of "the assaults which our party mem-bers have been conducting against peaceful settlers of that land." The inspector's actions worried moderate Conservatives because they might goad "the guerrillas that operate in the mountains of Boyacá to organize and attack the port with . . . unfavorable repercussions for the Conser-vative party and the government." The fact that Conservatives were in power and constituted a local majority, moderates insisted, was a poor excuse for provoking the opposition. The Liberal's economic importance weighed heavily with Conservative moderates, many of whom were land-owners. They described local Liberals as "Liberal peoples who . . . are workers who haven't been mixed up in anything" and who had the high-est rate of productivity in the entire Magdalena Medio region. Common sense thus prompted moderate Conservatives to urge the regional gov-ernment not to harass local Liberals in places where "the government lacks adequate police forces to deal with so many disturbances." But their complaints were also motivated by a deeper concern regarding the appro-priate functions of the state. The state should "respect the lives of those citizens in order to maintain the region's tranquility" and not promote and perpetuate violence.[116]

The armed forces and extremist Conservatives, however, rejected the attempt by local moderates to persuade the governor to stop deploying or tolerating official attacks against rural Liberal workers. They suggested that local landowners had enabled their workers and mayordomos to use their privileged position within the haciendas to rob and despoil them at will, and that they were therefore criminal accessories of guerrilla vio-lence. Puerto Berrío's army commander made this point explicitly in re-lation to an hacienda in Murillo just north of the town. The hacienda had been attacked by masked men who bound the watchman and took his shotgun "after all the workers docilely allowed themselves to be tied up." The guerrillas knew exactly where the mayordomo kept a second gun, removed it, and "told the mayordomo to take out his family and all their things because they were going to set fire to the house." The workers were then let go unharmed so that they could "watch their employer's house go up in smoke." Only one person was injured, "an individual affiliated with the Conservative party" whom the attackers had sought "to kill."[117] The owners, the authorities argued, had created the very conditions that now endangered the economic viability of their properties. "The majority of Conservative and Liberal hacendados who do not support the guerrillas, dare not go to their haciendas for fear of being killed. In order to protect their properties from attack they surround themselves with administrators, mayordomos, and workers who are completely disaffected from the government. . . . Liberal hacienda owners are even more prone to do this."[118] Indeed, the army commander asserted, "the bandits are located inside the very haciendas. . . . This makes it extremely difficult to control the situation when there is no sincere desire on the part of the hacienda owners to cooperate with the government in the reestablishment of normalcy." The only possible means of eradicating Liberal banditry, the authorities concluded, was to import "new personnel . . . healthy [*sano*] workers who unlike the rest of this region aren't full of revolutionary ideas." In the military's estimation, this was the only way of "cleansing [*sanear*] the region" and pacifying it.[119] One way of pacifying was to encourage and deploy contrachusmas from the southeast where there was not only a greater Conservative presence but also a large number of landless poor with few if any employment opportunities.

The formation of the contrachusmas or "an army of armed peasants [*campesinos*]," as the parish priest of Yolombó explicitly suggested doing in 1952, had long been advocated by local priests and municipal Conservative committees as an efficient solution.[120] The formation of armed Conservative bands solved the problem of growing enclosure around once public lands in the southeast and accompanying growth in unemployment.[121] The contrachusmas provided jobs for needy Conservatives either by employing them as civilian policemen or by using them to strip Liberals of state patronage jobs and employment on haciendas. The creation of the contrachusma, moreover, was perceived to solve other "problems" as well. Civilian volunteers with a stake in the region were thought to be more committed antagonists of the guerrillas, and they constituted an inexpensive and effective means of supplementing what everyone agreed were insufficient government troops in the area. The contrachusma were also perceived to exert a rehabilitative moral and ethnic presence on the very populations the police in Puerto Berrío suggested were full of "revolutionary" ideas. Contrachusma volunteers were drawn from among "white" migrants from core municipalities who had recently settled in the southeast, and, as such, they became the ethnic shock troops of extremist Conservative interests who attributed local violence to the presence of unruly blacks and non-Antioqueños.[122]

Efforts to persuade the regional government to modify its indiscriminately repressive policies against Liberals in eastern Antioquia were thus drowned out by the arguments of the armed forces and extremist Conservatives who approached the issue of public order as a moral crusade. The repeated defeat of the army and the police at the hands of guerrillas in Urabá, western Antioquia, the Bajo Cauca, and the Magdalena Medio in 1952, moreover, convinced extremists in the regional government of the necessity of adopting more severe — not more lenient — measures to restore public order.

The State's Response to Guerrilla Violence

The role of the military in the containment of civilian conflict was the first aspect of public order policy to undergo a drastic shift in the Magdalena Medio region in mid-1952. By June, the commander of the troops stationed in Puerto Berrío issued a memorandum to hacienda owners and farm administrators in which he announced a series of policies intended to control the hiring and movement of hacienda workers in the region. The armed forces once more accused Conservative landlords of knowingly hiring Liberal mayordomos and having them "hire [*enganchar*]" Liberal workers. The army insisted these were "potential bandits" who robbed and burned haciendas. So, the military announced that, beginning in June, "hacienda proprietors or their administrators will have to put together a registry of hacienda employees" in which the names of all workers, their job descriptions, dates of employment, town of origin, national identity number, and reservist status had to be noted.[123]

When a worker left his job or was fired, whoever was in charge of the hacienda was obliged to "immediately inform the local barracks commander regarding the worker's date of departure and intended destination." The hacienda's registry of workers had to be kept in ink, and owners were obliged to submit it to the local military base for inspection at the beginning of every month. Hacienda employment was also made contingent on the agreement of workers to collaborate with the authorities in the identification and capture of guerrillas. Permits (*salvoconductos*) which enabled individuals to obtain work were to be issued only to those who agreed to help the military and police and only after the "well-known honorability" and "absence of a criminal record" of these individuals had been vouchsafed by employers. Hacendados were forbidden to hire "unfamiliar personnel" or those who couldn't provide the information demanded by the *salvoconducto* process. Anyone found in the region "without his appropriate pass," moreover, was to be "considered a bandit suspect and will be detained by the army and the police," and any worker who lost his pass "will not have a new one issued to him but will be forced to abandon the region."[124]

The effect of these measures on the region's workers was felt only a week after the military issued its memorandum. On July 17, police raided "suspicious" haciendas in the Alicante and La Florida parishes, where they stole cattle and ten *cargas* (125 kilograms) of corn and beans and assassinated thirty workers. On July 22, Puerto Berrío's police arrived in Maceo and its haciendas and killed another forty campesinos they suspected of being guerrillas.[125] Since employment had been made contingent on collaboration with the authorities, moreover, workers increasingly acted as informants in order to remain alive and keep their jobs. Liberals who oversaw Conservative-owned haciendas in Maceo, for instance, reported sighting Pielroja's guerrillas and informed the army that these guerrillas had called in one Liberal worker and charged him with asking the town's Liberal leaders to send supplies. The guerrilla leader had let the workers know that "he thought it very strange that given that Maceo's Liberals knew he and his men were hanging around in those mountains, that no one had offered to help them out with anything."[126] Other Liberals reported that shipments of bullets, shoes, and clothes destined for guerrilla use were being transported between Maceo and an hacienda by the name of "Playa Rica" in Remedios.[127]

The military's aggressive campaign to gain the upper hand over public order matters in eastern Antioquia was somewhat undermined by the reappointment of Dionisio Arango Ferrer as Antioquia's governor in late July 1952. Arango Ferrer had last been named governor the day after Gaitán's assassination when the central government had deemed it necessary to use force to stem outbreaks of Liberal subversion in the department. During his earlier administration, the governor's preference for privately organized, Conservative civilian forces to maintain public order and his violent tactics had elicited an outcry from moderate Antioqueño Conservatives, and he had left office only eight months after his appointment. His reappointment in 1952 reflected the central government's desperation and the extent to which it feared public order had deteriorated in the nation's most important department. Arango Ferrer was no friend of the army.[128] He suspected that sectors of the armed forces were sympathetic to the Liberal opposition or, at the very least, did not endorse the Conservative government's instigation of partisan war, and he feared army hostility might eventually instigate a coup. For this reason, Arango Ferrer was reluctant to increase the power of the military over public order matters. The governor put his trust instead in the police and armed Conservative contrachusma forces, despite overwhelming evidence of their brutality and ineffectiveness. It was these two forces then which he chose to bolster and reinforce in the campaign to restore public order in Antioquia during his tenure from July 31, 1952, until a military coup against Laureano Gómez also toppled him on June 13, 1953.

Shortly after assuming office in August, Arango Ferrer ordered the mayors of Puerto Berrío, Remedios, Maceo, San Luis, Caracolí, and Yalí to contact the presidents of their local Conservative committees. The presidents were asked to send a special delegate to a meeting at the governor's office in Medellín to discuss issues of public order. The delegates were to bring detailed reports of the state of public order in their areas and the names (and national identity card numbers) of potential Conservative volunteers.[129] Arms and supplies were distributed to each of these volunteers. Two weeks later, the armed forces issued a confidential message to all its commanders in Antioquia in which, as a way of regaining the institution's prestige and the public's faith in the army as an effective combatant against guerrilla violence, it announced a policy of no quarter in dealing with Liberal guerrillas. Puerto Berrío, they admitted privately, was one of the places where they deemed their counterinsurgency strategy to have been most deficient and, aside from Urrao and Dabeiba in western Antioquia, the municipio where it was most important to stop violence in the department.[130]

The combination of these two measures — the strengthening of contrachusma forces and the decision to adopt a policy of no quarter against the guerrillas — soon provoked a wave of terror throughout eastern Antioquia. Less than a month after distributing arms and condoning the creation of contrachusmas in Remedios, Maceo, and Yalí, officials and citizens reported widespread assassinations and indiscriminate thefts led by contrachusma forces against the area's citizenry. In late September the mayor of Remedios warned the governor in a coded message that the town's Liberals were fleeing because of a rumor that the Conservative contrachusmas were about to arrive.[131] Meanwhile, the severity of contrachusma violence in Maceo provoked Liberal and Conservative citizens to band together to ambush and assassinate the "contrachusma leader Evelio Carmona" while he was unarmed and his men were confined to their barracks.[132] In Yalí and Vegachí, Yolombó, moreover, the mayor reported accompanying the *visitador administrativo* to investigate reports of contrachusma violence against both Liberals and Conservatives. They found that men under the leadership of Emeterio Castro had assassinated ten peasants, five of whom were Conservatives; looted and robbed Conservatives and Liberals alike; and raped local women belonging to both parties. The *visitador* concluded that the contrachusmas conducted "general extortions" and that they operated "without any control," and he recommended that they "should be totally exterminated" because their behavior only discredited the government. Instead of arming unsupervised and informal paramilitary groups, the *visitador* suggested that the governor would be better off taking up the local hacendados' offer to pay "lodging and . . . the expenses associated with supporting and arming the police" and appointing a police inspector to oversee the region.[133]

Conservative repudiation of partisan violence was even more pronounced in towns where Liberals were an overwhelming majority. A meeting held by moderate Conservatives in Remedios was violently interrupted when the local contrachusma leader burst into the party's headquarters and announced that "he had a list of Liberals to be eliminated approved by [Antioquia's] Conservative directorate." Dismayed, moderate Conservatives immediately telegraphed the governor to ask if this was true. They warned him that if it was true, then the governor was being complicit with "abuses against peaceful citizens whose only crime is to belong to the opposition party." They angrily insisted that "a good 80 percent of all the many tragedies which this town has suffered" were not the product of guerrilla violence but of the contrachusmas who have forced "families of known honorability belonging to both parties" to have to "abandon the city." A month later these same moderate voices reiterated their concerns regarding the activities of the contrachusma and its use against "peaceful Liberal citizens, helpless people who are engaged in working in the countryside." The Conservative mayor complained that abuses were conducted by "a group of Conservatives led by Remedios's treasurer" who had organized "groups that they call contrachusma whose purpose is to go out into the countryside and kill Liberals." The mayor justified his resignation by saying that the contrachusma wanted him "to take part in all kinds of vengeances; things I don't want to accept." It was one thing, the mayor insisted, to go after "those who lend their support to groups up in arms" and "to pursue and punish those whom it can be proven are responsible [for guerrilla violence]," but another thing entirely to assume that simply because they belonged to the opposition that all Liberals were bandits. The local priest and Conservative committee members agreed with the mayor, but the governor did not, and he accepted the mayor's resignation with considerable alacrity.[134]

The police inspector of Puerto Nare similarly denounced the police and their contrachusma aides and accused the governor of violating the public's trust by presupposing that "the mission of lower-ranking employees is to assassinate 'traitors' [manzanillos] in order to pacify the department." If this were the governor's expectation, then Puerto Nare's inspector would resign because "my condition as an honorable man who has a soul entrusted to God will not permit me to stain my name and reputation." The police inspector added that the oft-invoked justification for the state's indiscriminately repressive tactics in the area, the so-called Liberal "chusma," moreover, was "nothing more than people abused by the police who fled to the hills to seek refuge and revenge."[135] The very forces whose reprehensible behavior the police inspector condemned — "people with a bad conscience who call themselves Conservatives, but of the kind that Doctor José María Bernal classifies as rustlers who want to assume ownership of other people's properties," as the inspector's distraught son put it to the departmental secretary eight months later — conspired to remove the police inspector from his post.[136] Colorado's police inspector in the municipality of Caucasia also made it clear that interests that transcended partisan objectives were at the heart of many disputes between the contrachusmas and their opponents. For instance, he attributed accusations leveled against him by local hard-liners — accusations similar to those leveled against Puerto Nare's police inspector — to his refusal to be an "instrument of vengeance" against local Liberals who were "rich and apolitical."[137]

Many Conservative observers residing in the northeast and Magdalena Medio regions were quite simply appalled by police and contrachusma brutality. Their publicly expressed outrage corroborated and ex-

panded upon the critiques offered by the public employees of Puerto
Nare and Puerto Triunfo. The issue at stake was not the legitimate use of
force to defend against Liberal guerrilla assaults. Even local Liberals admitted that the guerrillas were often as bloodthirsty and sadistic as their
Conservative opponents. Rather, what bothered those who denounced
contrachusma and police actions was the indiscriminate use of violence
against civilians simply because they belonged to the opposition. The
state was charged with protecting and not harming citizens, these critics argued, and the official endorsement of paramilitary forces violated
the contract binding citizens and the state. It was one thing, as Arturo in
the Bajo Cauca had argued, when "the bandits commit horrible crimes,
have always committed them, and will continue to commit them," for
they were outlaws ostracized and excluded from civil society. But it was
another thing entirely when "the others, the policemen, are exonerated,
are paid and glorified so that they may pervert their mission of peace for
that of shameless theft and criminality."[138] The same yardstick could not
be used to measure the behavior of those sworn to uphold the law and
those up in arms. Local citizens reminded the regional authorities that a
state that modeled its behavior on the comportment of the very sectors
it was meant to discipline and that justified criminal behavior by arguing
that the means justified the ends risked becoming illegitimate in the eyes
of its citizenry.

The regional government's strategy of promoting contrachusma
forces to combat the guerrillas had three major effects on the situation of
public order in eastern Antioquia. First, it brought to the surface irrec-
oncilable differences within the ranks of the regional Conservative party
regarding questions of public order maintenance and attitudes toward the
opposition. These differences ultimately contributed to catalyzing local
Conservative support behind a military coup in June 1953.[139] Second, the
use of contrachusma forces provoked a violent reaction among the Liberal guerrilla groups operating in the area without significantly lessen-
ing the impunity with which they acted. And, finally, the proliferation of
paramilitary forces condemned the region to becoming the site of persistent conflict long after Liberal guerrillas had given up their arms and
ceased to pose a challenge to the regional authorities or the state.

The months between October 1952 and June 1953, when the deployment of Conservative contrachusma forces in eastern Antioquia escalated, were characterized by brutal acts of vengeance and retaliation be-

tween the Liberal guerrillas, the contrachusma, and the state's official forces (especially the police). The focal point of struggle continued to be the region's haciendas and the civilians who worked on them. First, one group would sweep through the rural areas of towns such as Remedios, Amalfi, and Puerto Berrío raping, killing, stealing, and burning and then the forces of the opposition would follow and eliminate what little was left or would indiscriminantly go after the opposition in nearby communities to exact revenge. El Tigre in Amalfi, Santa Isabel in Remedios, the railroad stations of Virginias, Sabaletas, Cristalina, and San José de Nus in Maceo and Puerto Berrío became sites of repeated martyrdom, assaulted and looted by opposing armed bands until neither people nor goods were left. Those who survived migrated, swelling the number of starving refugees in towns such as Puerto Berrío. By December 1952 the parish priest calculated that Puerto Berrío had at least five hundred unemployed heads of household, an alarming rate of infant deaths due to malnutrition, and an innumerable number of poor, "all the result of banditry."[140]

The distribution of arms by the government, moreover, increased the number of predators in the region, but the carnage and destruction caused by the guerrillas and their ability to elude the authorities did not diminish. Indeed, all that changed was that now instead of one active force that stole, raped, and killed, there were two. These forces rarely if ever faced off against each other in direct combat. Instead, they conducted an intricate dance of evasion, circling and feinting but never crossing, preying mercilessly on the populations unfortunate enough to lie in their path. Civilian casualties in eastern Antioquia amounted to 42 percent of all civilians killed in Antioquia (141 of a department total of 334) as a result of violence between January and May of 1953, but eastern Antioquia accounted for only 20 percent of guerrilla deaths in the department during the same period.[141] The presence of police troops in the area grew, but so did the incidence of violence. There were sixty national policemen stationed in Puerto Berrío and thirty-two in Zaragoza in January 1953 when other violent municipios in Antioquia had fewer than twenty-five agents each.[142] In February there were 97 policemen in Maceo while Urrao in western Antioquia had only 27 agents; and, in March, 138 policemen were stationed in Remedios when the most violent municipios in the southwest (Betulia, Salgar, and Urrao) had 29 agents each.[143] Any justification that the contrachusma were necessary because government forces were absent or insufficient was clearly risible, for more troops were deployed in eastern Antioquia than anywhere else in the region in 1953. In any case, soon even the pretense of combat faded, overshadowed by the lucrative opportunities to usurp and occupy the lands and goods that desperate, frightened people had left behind. By the beginning of 1953 it was clear that the primary sources of instability in the region were the government's own forces.

The "End" of Violence in Eastern Antioquia

Ideologically motivated conflict in eastern Antioquia gave way in 1953 to a war in which the only meaningful objectives of armed conflict were material goods and access to employment. Already by 1952 it was difficult to state with any degree of precision just who made up the various "sides" of the conflict. Generalized competition for goods gave rise to situations like that reported by two hundred colono families from Puerto Triunfo who had fled to La Dorada to save their "seriously threatened lives." They left behind their "homes and plantings, as well as the animals . . . used for agricultural labor." In a petition to the governor begging for protection, they delivered a painful list of those assassinated in their town, all of them poor settlers and hacienda workers. The colonos insisted that the killings and robberies that had forced them to flee "were prepared in Puerto Triunfo by people who were perfectly well known to all" and that this could be corroborated by their "Conservative neighbors . . . who out of good will and Christian spirit had impeded other attacks." The assassins "seek out every possible means to befriend and obtain the passive obedience of the police," but partisan concerns appeared not to be the central motivation for their violent acts. This led the refugees to conclude that the problem was not a partisan one, but rather the result of "social breakdown." "Neither the undersigned, nor the instigators and perpetrators of the depraved acts we have recounted," they insisted, "belong to a single political party."[144]

The refugees suggested that an implicit bargain between themselves and the government had been broken by the events of *la Violencia,* and, in doing so, they expressed a sentiment common among many of eastern Antioquia's inhabitants. The life of the majority of local inhabitants was dominated by the hardship of agricultural labor and by the modest expectation that years of "physical effort to forge wealth and homeland [*patria*] in inhospitable regions" would guarantee them but the barest promise of survival. It seemed relatively little to ask that in return for "years of arduous effort bereft of the smallest comforts . . . and [considering] the payment of our taxes and obligatory contributions" that the government should at the very least "safeguard our lives and tranquility." That the very government entrusted with protecting them promoted violence by empowering individuals such as the police and contrachusmas who "for reasons we cannot fathom obey orders issued by irresponsible persons who are only interested in damaging the government, the region, and private citizens" bewildered the former inhabitants of Puerto Triunfo and deepened the sense of isolation and alienation to which eastern Antioquia's inhabitants had long been condemned.

Indeed, as the number of denunciations of contrachusma violence grew to alarming proportions, and as the number of these filed by Conservatives increased, it became evident that the supporters and detractors of a paramilitary response to the issue of public order were divided by more than partisan differences. What had begun as partisan conflict gradually crystallized along opposing lines of economic interest. Those supporting the formation of contrachusma forces and those who defended them even when their fellow party members denounced them as assassins, tended to be select members of the local clergy accustomed to acting as local political brokers, extremist public officials who gained authority and prestige through their association with armed men over whom they exerted a certain degree of control, and poor Conservative individuals who often migrated from economically depressed areas and volunteered to form contrachusma groups in the hopes of material as well as political rewards. Those who most vocally opposed the contrachusmas, in contrast, were either wealthy property holders, locally-born Conservative public officials linked by interest and friendship with prominent Liberals, or poor Conservatives suspected of disloyalty by their party members because they had long coexisted with and married into the local Liberal majority and refused to collaborate in eliminating their neighbors and kin. Unlike the mixed feelings elicited by the contrachusma, Liberals and Conservatives differed little in their view of the Liberal guerrillas. Landowners affiliated with both parties repudiated the guerrillas' often arbitrary and vindictive acts and attributed many of the area's economic difficulties to their constant cattle-rustling and thefts. Popular Liberal support for the guerrillas was more widespread but seems often to have been largely shaped by circumstance and necessity rather than from any deep sense of ideological communion or identification.

By June 1953 complaints of indiscriminate violence waged against Liberals and Conservatives alike, and shaped largely by economic and not partisan competition, were echoed by inhabitants from all walks of life in eastern Antioquia.[145] The main perpetrators of violence were uniformly described as the very forces charged with controlling public order in the region and protecting its inhabitants' lives. Insult was added to injury, moreover, when the inhabitants were expected to maintain paramilitary groups through forced contributions of 500 pesos or more in towns such as Yalí.[146] The exaction of forced contributions from locals and the direct support provided by the regional authorities enabled well-armed, largely independent bands of roving assassins, legitimized by official authority, to become entrenched in eastern Antioquia. These bands continued to operate long after Liberal guerrilla groups such as those manned by Capi-tán Corneta accepted the military's amnesty in July 1953.[147] By August of 1953, Antioquia's Liberal party directorate warned the military governor that not even the military regime was safe from the contrachusma. The contrachusma were said to be intent on "toppling" the regime with the support of the bishop of Santa Rosa, Miguel Angel Builes, and former governor, Dionisio Arango Ferrer.[148]

Much to the despair of regional moderates, Antioquia emerged as a national leader in the organization and distribution of arms to paramili-tary forces and became a source of reference for other governors and departments wishing to follow its example (see appendix B.2). The gov-ernor of Huila, for instance, enjoined Dionisio Arango Ferrer in April 1953 to share with his regional government "by what means the governor managed the purchase of revolvers and ammunition to arm Conserva-tives in order to counteract bandit actions and maintain public order." The "state-of-the-art" arsenal of recently purchased Winchester repeat-ing rifles and Hornet .22-caliber rifles that was deployed by Antioquia's contrachusma groups had become the source of considerable admiration by Conservative authorities anxious to replicate Antioquia's success in their own regions.[149]

Conclusion

The creation and consolidation of a paramilitary response to problems of public order was perhaps the single most important outcome of the struggle that began as a conflict motivated by partisan differences in east-ern Antioquia. It shaped the emergence of endemic violence around the area's haciendas and mines, and in contrast to what scholars studying the effect of violence on partisan identification in other Colombian regions have suggested, *la Violencia* appears to have undermined, not cemented local loyalty to Colombia's traditional parties.[150] People in towns such as San Roque, San Luis, Maceo, and Cocorná, for instance, turned away from the mainstream of the Conservative and Liberal parties to swell the ranks of dissident political movements that challenged both the traditional two-party system and the legitimacy of the regional government in the decades following *la Violencia*.[151] Incidents such as land invasions and the forcible expropriation of property, moreover, became commonplace in eastern Antioquia wherever Conservative paramilitary forces and government agents had been intensively deployed during *la Violencia*. Towns such as San Roque, Puerto Nare, Nús, Puerto Triunfo, Amalfi, Puerto Perales, Yolombó, Remedios, and Cisneros all reported such incidents in the months following the military coup. Yet the military government had by then already passed a decree to collect the arms that had been distributed to Conservatives under the previous civilian government.[152]

Liberal guerrillas who surrendered and gave up their arms when the military came to power found it impossible to return to civilian life or to their traditional labors as cowboys, public works employees, or miners. The continued presence of the contrachusma ensured that they were mercilessly harassed and forced to migrate. Pushed off lands and barred from working for local mining concerns, several former guerrillas eventually left for the Llanos and joined the incipient leftist guerrilla groups organizing there.[153] Former guerrillas who remained in eastern Antioquia complained that the armed Conservative civilian forces even forbade them from expressing open support for the government of General Rojas Pinilla.[154] The seeds of future armed rebellion that eventually came to characterize the daily lives of eastern Antioquia's inhabitants in the 1960s and 1970s may be traced to the forcible migrations, expropriations, and indiscriminate abuse exercised by the groups to which the state alienated its "monopoly of force" in the 1950s.

Peque, July 2001.
Townspeople carry the
days-old, mutilated
body of a local leader
in the aftermath of
a paramilitary attack.

3. Urabá and Western Antioquia

Urabá and certain areas of northwestern Antioquia had long been viewed as valuable but undomesticated regions. Luxuriant, virgin nature magnified and reinforced perceptions of unlimited economic promise and political danger. Urabá was still largely a jungle in the 1940s, a densely vegetated, insalubrious lowland area wedged between the Pacific lowland department of Chocó to the west and Córdoba (then part of the department of Bolívar) to the east. Cattle ranges and wild pineapple groves dotted the landscape as did forests of valuable hardwoods and coconut trees. On its shark-infested shores were numerous coves where contraband trade flourished. Despite encompassing a significant portion of Antioquia's physical area (13,560 square kilometers), in 1949 Urabá boasted only four municipalities: Turbo, Chigorodó, Murindó, and Pavarandocito. A mere 17,000 individuals, dispersed in widely scattered settlements, constituted Urabá's official population in the census of 1951.[1] Settlements that have since become municipalities such as Mutatá, Apartadó, Necoclí, San Pedro de Urabá, and Arboletes were but small settlements [*caserios*] or *corregimientos* and were subordinated to the jurisdictional authority of either Turbo, Chigorodó, or Pavarandocito (see map 11). Between one oasis of human concentration and another, enormous, often unexplored distances prevailed.

Western Antioquia, in contrast, included fourteen municipalities, covered a physical area half the size of Urabá (6,600 square kilometers) and boasted a population nearly eight times greater (133,000).[2] Most of western Antioquia was broken and steep, crisscrossed by streams and rivers laced with gold, with land too rocky for most kinds of farming. Large sections of it (Frontino, for instance), were still largely covered in unexplored primary forest. With the exception of Cañasgordas where extensive coffee plantations existed, the municipalities of western Antioquia mainly produced cattle, sugar, gold, and commercial agricultural commodities such as cotton (in Dabeiba) or cacao (in Sabanalarga). Much of this production was concentrated in large estates (especially in towns such as Frontino and Ituango) situated at considerable distance

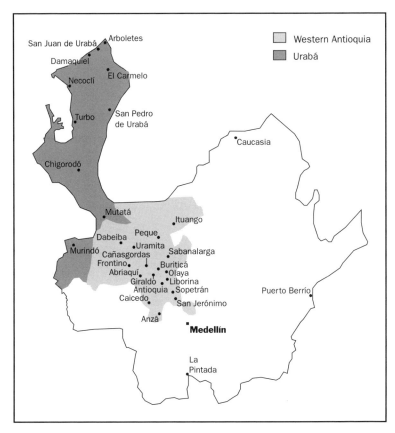

Map 11. Urabá and Western Antioquia. (Source: Instituto Geográfico Augustín Codazzi)

from one another and from each town's urban center, making these areas difficult to patrol or monitor. The absence of paved roads or established mule paths meant that most travel required an expert knowledge of hidden jungle routes or mountain passes or involved navigation. Canoes and dugouts were the principal means of transportation in and out of the labyrinthine channels, rivers, and streams sunk deep in the jungle and known only to experienced guides and longtime local inhabitants.

Antioquia had lobbied hard to gain control of Urabá since the early nineteenth century, but it was not until 1905 after the ignominious loss of Panama to the United States in 1903 that Urabá officially came under the province's jurisdiction.[3] Urabá gave Antioquia access to the Caribbean Sea, a stake in the lucrative trade between Panama, Central America, the

United States, and Colombia and a region rich in forest products, public lands for colonization, and the possibility of extensive agricultural plantations. When Conservative president Pedro Nel Ospina signed a contract in 1926 to begin construction of a road (the Carretera al Mar) linking Medellín to Turbo with a series of interlocking trunk roads, Antioquia's dream of harnessing Urabá's resources finally seemed close to becoming a reality. Communication between the center of Antioquia and Urabá continued to be nearly nonexistent, however, well into the 1950s, despite the initiation of road construction and government-sponsored colonization efforts. Consequently, although Antioquia claimed to control Urabá, on a day-to-day basis most public order matters concerning Urabá were resolved in the departments of Bolívar or Chocó and not Antioquia. In addition, almost all of the region's production was directed north toward Cartagena or Panama, not Antioquia proper. Antioquia could not even be said to have colonized Urabá, for most of the area's settlers were drawn from Chocó, Bolívar, or the Caribbean coast.[4] Matters were somewhat less dramatic for western Antioquia, parts of which (Santa Fé de Antioquia, Buriticá, and San Jerónimo) had been linked to Antioquia since the colonial period because of their importance as mining and commercial centers. Still, the physical location of northwestern municipalities such as Frontino, Dabeiba, Peque, and Ituango (at considerable distance from Medellín and the seat of regional power) and the sparseness of human settlement relative to their vast physical size made these areas isolated and only unevenly integrated into the rest of Antioquia.

Violence altered the administrative arrangements that separated Urabá from western Antioquia, or at least exposed the inconsistencies inherent in this division. For the purposes of this book, I have opted to give priority to the parameters of subregions as they were redefined by violence rather than to the official administrative divisions established by the state (see map 3 on page 6). Indeed, at the time of *la Violencia* the regional government itself ignored its own administrative jurisdictions and, for public order purposes, considered towns such as Ituango to be part of western Antioquia, and Dabeiba to be a continuation of Urabá. There were good reasons for doing so. The guerrilla groups that operated in these areas were often linked to each other. Moreover, the Carretera al Mar emerged as a central locus of violence binding Urabá and western Antioquia into a coherent public order area. And, finally, the movement of goods, people, arms, and official forces during the period of *la Violencia* created a broad circuit of exchange from Urabá through western Antioquia as far as Cañasgordas and back. For instance, cattle-rustling, which constituted a significant aspect of the violence in this region, found one of its central outlets through Ituango and into the department of Bolívar (today the department of Córdoba), thus tying a nominally northern municipality into the western/Urabá complex. For these reasons I will consider the question of violence in western Antioquia and Urabá together.

The Early Years of Violence

The strategic implications of an absence of infrastructure and decades of state indifference in Urabá and western Antioquia became painfully evident in the days following Gaitán's assassination. Buriticá went up in flames while armed *gaitanista* sympathizers who were connected to the mayor by blood and friendship occupied his office and threatened the municipal telegrapher's life when he dared to inform the regional authorities that the entire town was in a state of open rebellion.[5] Indeed, weeks after regional authorities had successfully put down unrest in other parts of Antioquia, Turbo and Peque remained up in arms.[6] Gaitán's death brought to the surface a complex combination of partisan rage and deeply held local resentment against a regional government that for decades had ignored local needs, ruling through imposition without consultation or negotiation. Just four months after the uprisings affecting these towns, the minister of hygiene noted with alarm that these and other towns in western Antioquia and Urabá were among those where sanitary and health services were poorest or nonexistent and where even the obligatory official doctor normally appointed by the state was absent.[7] These towns were also characterized by communication and transportation infrastructure that was so antiquated, modest, or inadequate as to create serious difficulties for both the region's economic development and the state's ability to respond effectively to episodes of disorder. When guerrillas cut the telegraph line that constituted Turbo's only form of communication with Medellín in late 1948, for instance, more than a month passed before the regional authorities were in a position to reestablish radio contact with the area.[8] During that time contraband arms flowed freely from Central America and Panama to supply emergent insurgents along the Carretera al Mar while the area's few regionally appointed representatives were powerless to impede it.[9]

Like most of the rest of the department, however, western Antioquia and Urabá were relatively quiet for almost a year after Gaitán's assassination. But in May 1949 during the heated pre-electoral season latent partisan tensions resurfaced. Liberals and Conservatives accused each other of engaging in acts of intimidation and harassment. Turbo's Conservative minority insisted that the town's Liberal majority had mercilessly attacked the town's Conservative mayor and requested the appointment of a military mayor to provide protection during the upcoming June elections.[10] In contrast, Turbo's Liberal voters and the presidential delegates sent to oversee local elections insisted that military troops were needed to protect not Conservatives but Liberals from intimidation and fraud.[11] As in other Antioqueño areas where Liberals constituted an overwhelming majority, however, Conservative intimidation had little effect on electoral returns in either the west or Urabá. Liberals handily won the June 1949 elections while *gaitanistas* in Turbo, Dabeiba, Peque, and Frontino won majorities in local town council elections.

Had the regional government accepted these Liberal victories and understood that further pressure was unlikely to increase the number of government supporters in Urabá and western Antioquia, it is possible that violence such as that which became prevalent by late 1949 might have been averted. Instead, after a brief respite, the regional government renewed its campaign to intimidate and publicly humiliate members of the opposition in preparation for the November presidential elections. An unrepentant *laureanista* politician of the era confessed that he and other Conservatives corralled local Liberals into the central plaza in towns such as Cañasgordas and stripped them of their *cédulas*. The *laureanistas* then smacked Liberals with the back of a machete to further ensure that local returns for the Conservative candidate could be boosted without impediment.[12] Such tactics often produced the desired outcome of inflating the number of Conservative votes, although they fooled no one as to their fraudulent nature. In Dabeiba, a town where the total number of Conservative votes had never numbered more than 458 before 1951, for instance, 1,974 votes were cast for Laureano Gómez.

The use of public order forces and public employees for partisan purposes during the 1949 elections deepened divisions between local inhabitants in the west and between Liberals in these areas and the regional authorities. Partisan differences overlapped with ethnic antagonisms in a volatile combination that even affected different branches of the government's armed forces sent to maintain order in the region. The intersection of partisan and ethnic divisions among the different branches of the government's armed forces impeded from the very start the possibility of developing a coherent public order policy in Urabá and western Antioquia. Army troops deployed to maintain public order in Urabá in 1948 and 1949 (and later in the 1950s), for instance, were generally drawn from Cartagena's Second Brigade, not the army based in Medellín. The long distances involved in deploying troops to Urabá from Medellín made the use of Antioqueño forces costly and inefficient as they had to be flown in. Soldiers from the department of Bolívar, unlike many of the soldiers recruited in Antioquia, tended to be black and to share the dominant partisan affiliation of the majority of Urabá's inhabitants; that is, they were Liberals. Thus, in contrast to the hostility with which southwestern inhabitants greeted public order forces brought into Antioquia from other Colombian regions, Urabeños embraced soldiers from the department of Bolívar with greater sympathy and support than they gave to regional government forces staffed by Antioqueños. Urabá's Conservative minority, most of whom were migrants and settlers from Antioquia rather than Bolívar or Chocó, in contrast, suspected the troops brought from Cartagena of collusion with the guerrillas and doubted their willingness to defend Conservative lives. These perceptions fed rumors that the army did not support the Conservative government. This was such a commonly held belief in western Antioquia and Urabá by late 1949 that the commander of the Fourth Brigade in Medellín, Colonel Eduardo Villamil, felt compelled to officially warn Governor Eduardo Berrío that a subversive campaign was under way to try to turn the army against the government.[13]

In contrast to the soldiers from the Liberal-dominated, black Caribbean coast sent to patrol Urabá, most national policemen deployed to Urabá and western Antioquia were drawn from traditional, heavily indigenous departments such as Boyacá, Cundinamarca, and Huila where the Conservative party had historically been strong. Conservatives in western Antioquia and Urabá tended to prefer the police to the army because they perceived the former as more sympathetic to their partisan interests, although at times the indigenous identity of many policemen also gave rise to frictions among race-conscious Antioqueño Conservative colonists. The majority Liberal population in the area, in turn, despised the national police for both their ethnic origin and their perceived partisan sympathies. To complicate matters further, Urabá's municipal policemen tended to be overwhelmingly Liberal and locally born and opposed to the national police who were nonlocal and Conservative. Customs officers, who were regionally appointed and among the few government representatives present throughout western Antioquia and Urabá, in turn, were resented by local Liberals both because the customs administration had been conservatized after 1948 and because smuggling constituted a primary and fiercely defended local survival strategy. Long-term cultural, ethnic, and regional differences (whether perceived or real) thus intersected with partisan differences to create the sense of an alignment between specific sectors of the government's forces and the populations over whom they were sent to exercise authority.

The departmental government at first attempted to dismiss as local fantasy the perceptions of partisanship among the armed forces and denied the influence of ethnic and interregional conflicts in the formulation or implementation of public order policies in Antioquia. The regional authorities' own actions, however, belied such denials. When Turbo's citizens led an armed attack against regionally appointed customs agents and injured one of them in November 1949, authorities in Medellín did not send in national policemen, their only available public order troops at the time, because they anticipated the local citizenry would react violently.[14] In early 1950 when Governor Berrío entertained bids from Smith and Wesson for the purchase of two thousand of their .38 "Specials" to improve the region's defenses, moreover, he privileged the distribution of arms to forces whose cultural as well as partisan proclivities were likely to garner local Conservative support. When Conservative committee members in the western municipality of Dabeiba questioned the partisan and ethnic loyalties of soldiers (blacks from Bolívar) and policemen (indigenous recruits from Cundinamarca and Boyacá) sent to maintain public order in the town, the governor liberally distributed arms to locally constituted, volunteer contrachusma groups and culturally acceptable police forces instead. These were groups whose regional and partisan credentials were beyond reproach.[15] Indeed, the governor generally opted to arm Antioqueño-born civilians and police rather than official forces in which non-Antioqueños played an important role, regardless of the tactical needs of these forces.[16] It sent the recently negotiated Smith and Wessons to outfit the reorganized and conservatized customs and border officers (*resguardo de rentas*), trustworthy policemen, and Conservative civilians in select municipalities. None of the new revolvers were distributed to the army.[17]

Once lines were drawn between Liberals and the army on one side and Conservatives, locally formed contrachusmas, and national policemen, on the other (at least in the minds of many of the local inhabitants and the regional authorities), violence escalated dramatically in western Antioquia. In towns such as Caicedo, police agents brazenly destroyed the pictures of Liberal council members and heroes that hung in the town council office and replaced them with posters of Conservative Laureano Gómez. Anyone who attempted to impede the police was arrested and jailed. Policemen then colluded with civilian Conservative forces to paper over the entrance of Liberal stores with the Conservative president's image, warning disgruntled Liberal shopkeepers that they would have to pay a five-peso fine every time the poster was damaged.[18] When asked to investigate and condemn such actions, Jorge Salazar, the police officer in charge of Antioquia's department of criminal investigation, exonerated the national policemen and civilian Conservatives responsible for these violations. The police chief insisted that the army was only issuing permits to bear arms to Liberals in western Antioquia, and that Conservatives therefore had a right to defend themselves from the opposition by any means possible, including arming themselves and employing the police for partisan purposes.[19]

The Organization of Armed Liberal Resistance

Guerrilla groups in Urabá and western Antioquia emerged shortly after the June elections of 1949. Their initial objective was to harass the Conservative government and topple it. They quickly found both considerable local support and a strategically ideal place from which to mount concerted attacks against the state, its representatives (public employees, police, army, customs officers, and so on), and the area's small minority of Conservative citizens. Although many guerrilla bands varying in size from a dozen men to several hundred operated in the area between Turbo in Urabá and Frontino in western Antioquia, several groups stand out both for the range of their activities and their ability to effectively at-

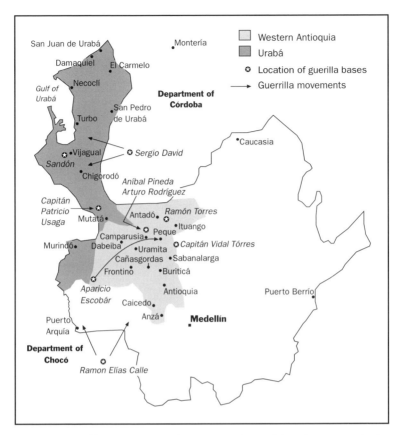

San Juan de Urabá
Montería
Damaquiel   El Carmelo
Necoclí
Gulf of
Urabá
San Pedro
Turbo   de Urabá
Vijagual   ✪ Sergio David
Sandón
Chigorodó
Aníbal Pineda
Arturo Rodríguez
Capitán
Patricio   Antadó.   Ramón Torres
Usaga   Mutatá•   ✪   ✪Ituango
Camparusia   ✪ Peque
Murindó•   Dabeiba   ✪Capitán Vidal Tórres
•Uramita
Cañasgordas   •Sabanalarga
Frontino   •Buriticá
Aparicio   Antioquia   Puerto Berrío
Escobár   Caicedo•
Puerto   Anzá•   **Medellín**
Arquía
Department of
Chocó   ✪
Ramon Elías Calle

•Caucasia

Department of
Córdoba

☐ Western Antioquia
☐ Urabá
✪ Location of guerilla bases
→ Guerrilla movements

Map 12. Guerrilla operations and movement in Urabá and Western Antioquia (Source: Instituto Geográfico Augustín Codazzi; Archivo Privado del Señor Gobernador de Antioquia, 1951, vol. 8, "Asociación, instigación para delinquir." Ministerio de Justicia, Juzgado 82 de Instrucción Criminal, Oficio #0040, 4 Feb. 1951)

tack and elude the authorities (see map 12). One of these groups was led by Sergio David and had its base in the valley between the Sinú, Sucio, and San Jorge rivers in the department of Bolívar (in an area that is now part of the department of Córdoba) immediately north of Antadó and Ituango and east of Urabá.[20] Satellite camps led by members of the David clan along with members of the Arias, Cartagena, Duarte, Velásquez, Higuita, Montoya, Pino, Romero, Serna, Torres, Tuberquia, and Usaga families in turn spread the reach of the guerrillas into Chigorodó, Mutatá, and along much of the Carretera al Mar. An offshoot of the David-led group, under the immediate command of Captain Patricio Usaga, more-

over, established control over the hamlet known as Caucheras near Mutatá where important rubber plantations were located.[21] A second guerrilla group numbering approximately one hundred men operated in El
Carmen, Chocó, across the border from the town of Bolívar, under the
leadership of Ramón Elías Calle, while a third guerrilla base was located
in the municipality of Frontino in a settlement known as "La Blanquita"
within Murrí. In the base in La Blanquita, several dozen guerrillas under
the leadership of Aparicio Escobár manned a cattle-rustling operation
that extended as far as Peque, Juntas de Uramita, Frontino proper, and
Pabón (in Urrao).[22] Other smaller groups or satellites of larger guerrilla
organizations also operated in the area between Sabanalarga and Barbacoas (Captain Vidal Torres), in Cañasgordas (Salomon Marín), Antadó
(made up of former penal colony prisoners), and Vijagual/Apartadó (led
by an individual named Sandón).

The most important of the guerrilla camps operating in western
Antioquia, at least from the perspective of the regional government and
the armed forces, however, was that located in Camparusia (today the
municipality of Armenia) in the town of Dabeiba. The military commander in charge of overseeing the maintenance of public order in Frontino deemed Camparusia the "best organized guerrilla camp in Antioquia and the one with the greatest number of men prepared to enter
into combat with any one of the government's forces."[23] Here, Arturo
Rodríguez Osorio and Aníbal Pineda Torres (the latter a native of the
Urama/Uramita area in Dabeiba) built a nearly impenetrable headquarters where several hundred men and many displaced Liberal families
sought refuge. Although under a separate command, the guerrillas based
in Camparusia were nominally linked to the guerrilla organization led
by Captain Franco in Urrao (in the upper southwest).

Unlike the single men who operated as Liberal guerrillas in eastern
Antioquia and who rarely drew their recruits from among the local population, guerrillas based in the areas of Dabeiba and Chigorodó and along
the Sinú River in Bolívar participated in armed resistance as members of
locally based family clans, although these clans often straddled the border between Antioquia and Bolívar. In a list of men and women sought
by the government as suspected guerrillas, 185 men and women sharing
common surnames or singled out as members of distinct family groups
appear to be the principal source of disorder in the area.[24] The guerrillas
or "*chusma*" (rabble), "*bandoleros*" (bandits), and "*maleantes*" (hooli-

gans) as the government liked to refer to them, initially began their activities as defensive organizations. But their relative isolation, easy access to contraband arms, and the general weakness of the regional government and its forces quickly enabled the guerrillas to take the initiative against the government rather than merely defend local Liberals from it. Within two years of their initial appearance, a number of these armed bands expanded their activities to primarily serve the political and personal interests of powerful individuals in the region. There gradually emerged a flourishing informal market of stolen articles and animals (mules, horses, cattle) of which the guerrillas formed an integral part.

In Dabeiba, for instance, guerrillas took part in what one observer referred to as "all kinds of business deals" and received money and tactical assistance from seven well-known merchants and Liberal political leaders. The interaction and intersection between local civilians and the guerrillas was so great that one of these patrons boasted publicly that "he could stop the bandit rabble from killing any more people" with a single order. Pronouncements such as these led the regional authorities to conclude that civilians and guerrillas were largely indistinguishable and that the civilians were also "the heads of guerrilla bands." [25]

In return for merchandise, food, money, and logistical support, the guerrillas guaranteed their supporters and patrons the ability to travel freely through strategically contested areas. One of the guerrillas' Dabeiba supporters, for instance, had rented fourteen estates for a pittance from Conservative property owners who "were forced to abandon them" precisely because they feared being killed by the guerrillas. The guerrillas accompanied their patron whenever he needed to oversee production "throughout the rural areas and saved him from having to worry about losing his life." For other sponsors the guerrillas acted as enforcers and hit men that eliminated or forced to flee unwanted squatters, workers, or rivals. One landowner contracted the "bandit chief Patricio Usaga so that he would come in the night and kill one of his peons, Justo Giraldo, in his very own home." The guerrillas also acted as private security forces or bodyguards for local landowners. Several landowners "frequently go out to their farms located at some distance from the county seat [and] have been observed now several times in the company of eight or more bandit riflemen [escopeteros]." [26] Even Liberal political leaders in Medellín who were sympathetic to the guerrillas' goal of fighting to restore their party to power, and who occasionally offered the guerrillas advice and instructions, admitted privately that in some cases partisan objectives among the guerrillas in western Antioquia rapidly gave way to more base monetary objectives. Western guerrilla leaders such as Salomon Marín were considered by even supportive Liberal political leaders in Medellín to do "little more than rob people of their money."[27]

The Beginning of Liberal Guerrilla Activity

After months of reported arms smuggling from Panama through Urabá and parts of the Chocó, Liberal guerrillas in western Antioquia led their first major attack against Murrí, in the extreme northwestern corner of the municipality of Frontino in June 1950. They occupied the settlement and stole cattle worth sixty thousand pesos.[28] The regional government had been warned in advance that the attack was imminent — just as the governor was warned some three weeks before a similar attack took place in Caucasia in the Bajo Cauca in August.[29] It made no difference. The regional authorities were simply in no position to respond to unrest on the department's borders. Years of neglect and failure to invest in infrastructure or the well-being of such areas could not be overcome at a moment's notice. The attack on Murrí spread to other areas of western Antioquia, spurring local Conservative officials to report that a guerrilla army of five hundred men was on the verge of taking control of the region.[30] The areas bordering the departments of Chocó to the west and Bolívar to the northwest were places where little other than cattle was produced, but they were crisscrossed by concealed paths and hideaways that made them ideal refuges for men up in arms.

Unable to actually respond to the presence of Liberal guerrillas with permanent forces of its own, the regional government attempted to starve the guerrillas by blocking their supply routes and means of survival. But like so many other policies embraced on different occasions by authorities far removed from the day-to-day realities of the areas they nominally governed, food rationing penalized the local civilian population but did little to deter the guerrillas who operated in their midst. Local landowners sympathetic to the regional government were among the first to insist that food rationing was an ineffectual means of dealing with armed insurrection in the region: "There is a scarcity of chocolate, lard, molasses loaves, and other foodstuffs indispensable to the lives of honest workers in all that area, but to think that the bandits will retreat for lack of food is an error, since there are immense amounts of available corn, . . . cattle, plan-tains, yucas, etc., sufficient for the bandits to live on for many years."[31] Indeed, while the guerrillas supplied themselves through theft and illicit exchanges with smugglers, investors in the Chocó complained that food shortages had raised prices for basic goods in the area to dangerous levels. This created labor problems in the area's mines and in turn had negative repercussions on Chocó's economy and state of public order.[32]

It was clear, moreover, that even in instances where merchants, land-owners, and noncombatants did not necessarily support the idea of taking up arms against the government, there often was little incentive to deny the guerrillas material support, especially if there existed the pos-sibility of considerable profit. The second sergeant inspector stationed in Uramita, who had been accused of collaborating with local Liberals and guerrillas but adamantly denied this to his superiors, gave a persua-sive explanation of why attempts to eliminate the guerrillas with poli-cies such as food rationing were doomed to failure. Uramita's merchants, the inspector insisted, had at first abided by the government's decree forbidding the sale of food or merchandise to those suspected of being guerrillas or guerrilla supporters. But the guerrillas had simply shifted their business to Urama, Juntas de Uramita, and Peque where merchants were perfectly willing to sell them goods instead. As the inspector rightly concluded, "the rabble-rousers [*chusmeros*] can always find provisions in other areas," especially since there were no government forces present to enforce the prohibition against sales to the guerrillas. And the inspector continued, "in this *corregimiento* we could say that all the merchants are purveyors of goods to the bandits since all of them sell their goods with-out asking questions. All they care about is making money."[33] The state's inability to enforce its own policies and laws, in other words, destroyed any incentive for even its most fervent supporters to abide by them. But it also seems true that for many locals partisan differences were simply not compelling enough to stand in the way of doing business with the opposition.

Shortly after the attack on Murrí, three hundred men armed with shotguns, revolvers, and machetes attacked a troop of soldiers in Tucura (today Córdoba) several miles north of Playones in Dabeiba on July 16. The guerrillas wounded four soldiers, committed a series of murders and robberies, and then fled south to attack Playones proper.[34] Attacks occurred simultaneously in Urrao and La Camara in the municipality of Salgar, where guerrillas forced Conservative peasants and workers to leave their haciendas.[35] These events—especially the occupation of valuable estates—obliged the regional government to acknowledge the severity of the threat to state control in western Antioquia and Urabá and prompted it to deploy soldiers and additional policemen to the area. On July 26, Colonel Eduardo Villamil, the commander of the Fourth Brigade in Medellín, ordered the sub-lieutenant and commander of the local barracks in Dabeiba to permanently patrol the road between Mutatá, Dabeiba, and Chigorodó with two cars. He also sent two lower-ranking officers and thirty national policemen from the Antioquia division as reinforcements. Anticipating that the deployment of police would be resisted by both some soldiers and local Liberals, Villamil admonished his subordinates to form mixed police and army patrols and to ensure that the police agents be treated with "respect and kindness by the [army] troops."[36] In the further hope of dispelling rumors that the army was cooperating with the guerrillas, moreover, the colonel insisted that his men penetrate deep into the jungle in pursuit of the bandits and that these bandits be offered no mercy.

A few days later, government officials in Dabeiba were able to report their first minor victory against the Liberal guerrillas when they captured six and detained nine other people suspected of providing supplies from the settlement of "la Montañita," located just outside the town.[37] In other parts of the west, however, in a pattern that would become commonplace, frustrated public officers who were unable to locate the guerrillas wreaked vengeance on the local civilian population instead. In Caicedo, for instance, members of the national police and Conservative volunteers attacked ten inhabitants with machetes and guns in Guasabra, and justified the attack by arguing that this was one of the many *corregimientos* suspected of giving aid to the guerrillas.[38] Excesses such as these prompted bickering and mutual accusations between police and army officials. Only a day after the report by Caicedo's military commander of police abuses against civilians, Colonel Villamil complained to Antioquia's Governor Berrío that Jorge Salazar, the police chief in charge of Antioquia's department of criminal investigation, had overstepped his powers and violated several national decrees. Salazar in turn accused Villamil of being disloyal and a secret Liberal sympathizer.[39] Meanwhile as the police and army exchanged barbs, towns such as Ituango and Caucasia on the border with Bolívar worried aloud about the absence of any government officers to defend them from imminent guerrilla attack.[40]

The expected attack came on August 10 when guerrillas simultaneously struck settlements in Urabá north of Turbo, Dabeiba, Caucasia in the Bajo Cauca, and Urrao. News of the assault first reached the governor's ears not through an official channel, but via the secretary of the regional Conservative party directorate who informed him that numerous Conservatives had been assassinated in Urabá and that Dabeiba's parish priest had been murdered by Liberal guerrillas. Later that same day, the minister of government, Domingo Saresty, forwarded a list to the governor of all those killed in the town. The minister complained that the local mayor and his secretary and the soldiers stationed in the region by the Fourth Brigade had physically impeded national police troops under the command of Major Arturo Velásquez from sending out a group of armed civilian volunteers and policemen to track down the guerrillas, thus "allowing the assassins to go free."[41] These events prompted the minister to rebuke Governor Berrío and to make patent the minister's own lack of faith in the army as a reliable public order force. The minister openly sided with Dabeiba's Conservatives when they declared that "the army Lieutenant Quintero is a social menace as far as we are concerned, for he has become one with the Liberals who are his fellow party members."[42] From this point on, Dabeiba became the site of constant conflict and a major center of contrachusma organization. Dabeiba formed a kind of gateway between Urabá proper and western Antioquia, the last possible geographic staging ground of Conservative paramilitary strength, as it was impossible to rustle up enough Conservatives in Urabá. The town consequently became a major battlefield and suffered Antioquia's greatest number of officially registered deaths as a result of violence between 1949 and 1953. In three and a half years, Dabeiba lost 560 inhabitants or 3 percent of the town's 1951 population of 19,000.[43]

As bad as matters were in Dabeiba, the situation of public order was far worse in El Carmelo and Turbo in Urabá. A week went by before the regional government even acknowledged that the guerrilla invasion had taken place. By August 18, when government forces had still not arrived to take stock of the situation, local observers tentatively reported a death toll of more than fifty Conservatives. When troops finally made it to Turbo on August 21, eleven days after the initial attack, "one thousand" armed men from the department of Bolívar were reported to have attacked El Carmelo once more.[44] The guerrillas looted the "principal stores," assaulted the customs offices, and destroyed the police inspector's office. Two policemen and several customs officers were wounded and one policeman was killed. The number of civilian deaths was difficult to calculate because the bodies of the dead had been thrown into the river where they were torn apart by sharks. The police inspector reporting on the attack pleaded desperately for the governor to send "a strong, permanent contingent of the army" to counter the area's civilian authorities, all of whom "are enemies of the current government" who would take "any opportunity to attack the regional authorities."[45]

The only troops available for deployment to Urabá, however, were members of Cartagena's marine infantry. Turbo's Conservatives thought of *costeños* as lazy and inept and were convinced they "would arrive, get drunk, and do nothing." Whether the infantry did "nothing" is not clear, but it is clear that many of its men disagreed with Antioquia's and the Conservative government's actions against Urabá's Liberal citizenry. This was abundantly corroborated by a letter from one of the infantry's men who was captured several months later by the national police. In it an officer gave testimony of the deep sense of camaraderie that bound the coastal forces to Urabá's population. He expressed a sense of shame because "I and my comrades make up part of the public administration, that is, of this bloodied government, [even though] we did not come to commit assaults against those victims who are only persecuted because they are Liberals. We came to establish safeguards." Posted for duty in the Port of San Juan de Urabá, the officer made evident the weight of racial and ethnic considerations in public order matters: "The port's inhabitants are dark-skinned [*morenos*], but they are noble and respectful of the authorities. We were well received in this settlement, all the settlers loved us because they were able to understand that we were there to guarantee the safety of their property, their lives, [and] their honor and not intent upon assaulting, robbing, or persecuting them, unlike the preceding blue [Conservative] authorities who hid behind their military uniforms to assault their houses, rape their daughters, and murder their fathers. . . ."[46] Sentiments such as these on the part of forces sent from the Caribbean coast prompted Turbo's Conservatives to remind the governor of the area's strategic location between the department of Bolívar and Panama and to request "thousands of soldiers" commanded by high-ranking officers whose political loyalty was beyond question.[47] But it was not until August 29 that Medellín's Fourth Brigade was able to spare additional men to send to Urabá. On that date Colonel Villamil sent six planes full of army personnel for public order maintenance to Turbo.[48]

In the very midst of the repeated guerrilla attacks that took place in numerous peripheral towns along the region's northern borders in August 1950, Antioquia's governor's office changed hands. Eduardo Berrío González, who preferred arming Conservative civilians as volunteer policemen and deploying national policemen to maintain public order and bring recalcitrant Liberal areas to heel—regardless of the effect of such policies on local populations—was replaced by Braulio Henao Mejía. In contrast to Berrío, newly appointed Governor Henao Mejía was a retiring man who maintained cordial relations with the military and was wary of, if not explicitly opposed to, arming Conservative civilians or forming contrachusmas. The new governor was also supportive of the police but was sensitive to deploying them in places where they were hated so much as to catalyze popular rebellion. While former governor Berrío blamed the spread of Liberal violence on the lack of cooperation provided by the commander of the Fourth Brigade whose removal he belligerently reminded the president, "I have been begging the national government to undertake for more than six months," Governor Henao Mejía attributed the ineffectuality of the region's public order strategy to the sheer insufficiency of government troops, not the disorderly or partisan affinities of army officers.[49] A scant two days after taking office on August 22, Governor Henao informed the president that Antioquia simply did not have enough men to suppress the numerous sites of "sedition" in the department. The local army battalion had even been forced to borrow troops from Pereira and Manizales in the department of Caldas to the south.[50] Moreover, far from suspecting the army's loyalty as Berrío or Minister Domingo Saresty had, Governor Henao entrusted the difficult and potentially sensitive task of conducting an in-depth analysis of the reasons for widespread unrest in Urabá to a military officer, Colonel Luis Abadía, who was given broad powers to deal as he saw best with the situation of public order in the northwest.

The State of Public Order in Urabá

If what the regional government hoped for was a glimmer of local identification or sympathy between Urabá's inhabitants and Antioquia's regional government, the colonel's findings were disheartening. Colonel Abadía's report covered five crucial areas in Urabá: San Juan de Urabá, Arboletes and Damaquiel on the Caribbean coast near the border with the department of Bolívar, Necoclí near the Gulf of Urabá, and Turbo, the northernmost point of the Carretera al Mar (the road to the sea, connecting Medellín with Turbo). The army officer first noted to what degree economic interest and class played a role in the perception of guerrilla threat in the region. The region's wealthiest citizens, he noted with ill-disguised irony, were the most likely to complain of the threat of a guerrilla attack. Large property owners "sensed the presence of bandits everywhere." One individual who had "properties and is a rich man" insisted that the *chusma* were stationed near Turbo, while another insisted they "were expected to attack on the same day in San Juan and Arboletes" (an extremely far distance away).[51]

Colonel Abadía was convinced that nervous landowners were mainly moved to request the immediate deployment of military troops by concern for their large capital investments and estates. Local haciendas were so large, the officer noted, that they swallowed up all the land between certain towns or villages. This forced travelers to cross the haciendas in order to move between settlements.[52] Indeed, between 1918 and 1931 twenty-four concessions of public lands were made in Turbo in which the average lot amounted to 1,061 hectares (approximately 2,600 acres), while the average size of forest concessions in Chigorodó between 1900 and 1953 was 15,000 hectares (37,000 acres).[53] The colonel made it clear that fears of economic extortion, rather than partisan-inspired conflict, spurred the numerous rumors of impending disorder in Urabá. Landowners belonging to both parties, for instance, repeatedly alluded to having been "threatened by Hincapie's band," which wandered from hacienda to hacienda soliciting ammunition and supplies or extorting *mayordomos* (estate managers) and workers.

Turning his attention next to the town of Damaquiel, Colonel Abadía noted that one hundred armed civilians had turned up at the port when news of the arrival of government troops spread throughout the town. Thinking that the police had been sent to monitor public order in the area, Damaquiel's citizenry mobilized to forcibly turn away the governor's agents.[54] It was only when they were reassured that the governor had sent the army and not the police that people dispersed and put away their arms. The townspeople's attitude convinced the colonel that many of Urabá's inhabitants felt alienated and suspicious of Antioquia and that it would be foolhardy for the regional government to insist on sending national policemen to patrol the area. The colonel's observations about the inhabitants and conditions present in the settlement of Damaquiel also reveal the degree to which hierarchies of cultural difference imbued and shaped official assessments of local conditions and violence. Damaquiel was described as "painfully abandoned. . . . There is no one who may act as the representative of authority. . . . There is the greatest indolence. . . . The men don't work because of the state of abandonment [and] the hostile and suspicious climate. . . . I found all of them stretched out on their hammocks, the grimace of a defeated race tormented by laziness reflected in their faces." The same was true of San Juan de Urabá, a town in ruins with "multitudes of abandoned houses . . . in the most horrifying state of filth."[55] Moreover, those who had not fled the town after the guerrilla attack in August hid from the authorities.[56]

Finally, the colonel concluded his inquiry by explaining why, purely from the perspective of self-interest, it behooved the regional authorities to take immediate action to remedy Urabá's current state of public disorder: "[Urabá] represents for the national economy one of the most promising sources of future development; and if it attaches itself to Antioquia, the economic features represented by such faraway corners of the department will be of critical and of incalculable value in the future interests of Antioquia."[57] Colonel Abadía's report exposed the colonial fantasies of extraction and wealth that had historically underpinned the regional government's attitude toward Urabá. He suggested that Urabá's integration into Antioquia and the department's control of the peninsula would remain tenuous so long as the area was economically oriented toward the Caribbean rather than Antioquia. The area's rice, lard, corn, and plantains (produced in "large quantities") were shipped to Cartagena and other ports on the Caribbean, while bananas and coconuts had historically been shipped to Panama rather than used to "supply the scarce markets of Antioquia."[58] In other words, as long as few of Urabá's "economic features" were oriented toward Antioquia, the army officer seemed to suggest, Antioquia's dream of political control would remain unfulfilled. There was no official motorboat to patrol the region. Air service was provided haphazardly at the whim of Avianca. Communication from Urabá was accomplished by couriers who traveled by foot or canoe because there were no radio or telegraph lines to link the region to Medellín, and the only government authorities present were customs agents and a sporadic mayor or police inspector.[59] From the colonel's perspective, then, the problem of violence in Urabá was at least as much a result of cultural, political, and economic differences as it was of partisan ones.

The only hope for Urabá's future integration into Antioquia and identification with its values and interests was the completion of the road linking Medellín to Urabá. The colonel was convinced that only the Carretera al Mar could begin to solve Urabá's problems and introduce "progress and economic resurgence." More importantly, the road would also guarantee the assertion of Antioquia's political control and cultural values. The army officer argued insistently for the "need to extend to these areas the moral and civic aspects of the Antioqueño people [*pueblo*], which will ensure the redemption of many men who in these distant regions live a primitive, morally and mentally lax life." However, before any change in Urabá's attitude could be expected to occur, Colonel Abadía warned his regional superiors and the department's civilian authorities that the department would have to prove that "all of Antioquia is truly attentive to them."[60] This was unlikely to occur in the immediate future. Indeed, but a month after the colonel concluded his extended inquiry into the public order situation in Urabá, the region was once more awash in rumors of arms smuggling and imminent guerrilla activity. Guerrillas, moreover, had established a stranglehold over the area stretching from Turbo to Puerto Abaldía in the Gulf of Urabá.[61]

The problem of open insurrection in Urabá ceased to be a strictly regional matter of public order concern by late 1950. By November, incidents of extensive arms smuggling, attacks on private properties, and assassinations had spilled across Antioquia's borders into Chocó and Bolívar and prompted the governors and public order forces of these two departments to express their concern regarding Antioquia's seeming inability to police its own frontiers and internal affairs. The trouble was that Urabá was not and had never been a strictly Antioqueño area; its settlers, trade, investments, police forces, and resources easily bled across multiple administrative and physical borders. It had until very recently been little more than a vast commons of sparsely populated jungle where the state, the law, and its representatives—whether regional or national—were rarely felt. A small army of customs officers, policemen, coast guards, and soldiers with modern forms of communication and transportation would have been needed to submit Urabá's many hidden coves, rivers, and dense forests to the effective surveillance of the regional government. In 1950, however, Antioquia did not even have a motorboat with which to patrol Urabá's coast, much less a central radio station for Turbo, six boat stations, watchposts along the region's roads and rivers, or two planes, items that in December the governor of Cartagena warned Braulio Henao Mejía were absolutely necessary to inhibit the massive contraband of arms through the area and to impede the spread of guerrilla forces.[62]

Indeed, joint efforts by the departmental police forces of Bolívar, Antioquia, and Magdalena to control the trade in illicit arms proved futile. This was not because the smugglers were aided by "Communist ideologies emanating from Russia" as the police liked to insist, but because the government's forces were poorly equipped and lacked almost any logistical support for their endeavor. In contrast, most of the commercial boats owned by merchants based in Cartagena who plied their goods up and down the Arquía River and the banana boats traveling back and forth along the Atrato River were armed with machine guns and rifles and had two-way radios.[63] The government, in contrast, lacked customs officials to stop and search these boats, leaving them free to trade in weapons intended to supply guerrillas employed or hidden along the Carretera al Mar. Reports of just such illicit traffic in Sautatá on the Sucio River—where Abuchar Brothers, a Cartagena-based merchant house, had the region's largest sawmill and logging operation—were frequent.[64] In several cases the regional government received detailed inventories of exactly what and how many arms were passing through Urabá and western Antioquia, the routes through which these were shipped, and who was trading, but did absolutely nothing in response.[65]

The combined effect of the flow of arms to guerrillas and the state's poor performance in western Antioquia and Urabá made December 1950 the most turbulent month in the region since the multiple incidents of guerrilla attack in August. Armed disturbances occurred in Turbo on December 12, while Conservatives in Cañasgordas complained that more than two hundred farms had been invaded by guerrillas and that the two hundred soldiers sent to patrol the area by Medellín's military commander refused to enter the invaded areas to reclaim them.[66] By midmonth the Caja de Crédito Agrario, Industrial y Minero reported that guerrillas were also occupying valuable agricultural areas and leading invasions of public lands reserved by the regional government for rubber development in Villa Arteaga and Pavarandocito.[67] The installations and workers on the experimental rubber plantation in Villa Arteaga — which was jointly operated by a U.S.-Colombian consortium — had been attacked several times in the previous eight months and sustained losses of sixty thousand dollars. Economic loss was accompanied, moreover, by fears of worker starvation and revolt as the regional government's food-rationing policy took its toll on the civilian population.[68] Although they had already sunk $1.2 million into the rubber plantation and were on the verge of producing their first crop, the investors were considering pulling out of the project because government protection was so unreliable and sporadic. Terrified lest such threats become reality, the Caja de Crédito Agrario offered to pay out of its own pocket the expenses of fifty soldiers to be stationed in the area and also offered to fund, in conjunction with the Red Cross, medical and humanitarian aid and services for the area's settlers (*colonos*).[69] By December 27, verbal threats and *boletas* (extortion notes) were circulating along the Carretera al Mar and as far south as Dabeiba. The regional government's own officers admitted that it was impossible to control the "bandits" or to lead a surprise attack against them because everyone in the town — whether from conviction of simply out of fear — informed the guerrillas of government operations before they occurred.[70]

The Militarization of Urabá

The severity of unrest in western Antioquia and Urabá and the repeated defeat and ineffectual performance of official forces prompted regional authorities to once more commission government agents and members of the armed forces to analyze the situation of public order in Urabá. A specially charged visitador (*visitador encargado*) provided the first of these commissioned reports in January 1951. The *visitador* concluded that the towns most affected by violence within the larger western region were Dabeiba, Frontino, Cañasgordas, and Peque, and he attributed the state of constant disorder to the government's inability to impede collusion between the Liberal civilian population in these towns and the men up in arms.[71] A detailed report issued around the same time by a prominent Conservative officer in Caicedo seemed to confirm the *visitador*'s conclusions. But, the Caicedo official added that moderate Conservatives who refused to break off relations with the opposition in areas where their party was weakly represented, the state was largely absent, and the opposition dominated local affairs also posed an obstacle to the establishment of regional Conservative control over the area.[72]

Caicedo had a Liberal majority of 500 voters to 145 Conservative voters, a situation that seriously compromised the influence of the Conservatives on local affairs. In addition, the Conservative mayor contributed to the local Conservatives' continued marginality by being an "enemy of conflict and a friend of the peaceful life." The mayor was on awkward terms with the newly installed and openly reactionary local Conservative committee and the local priest. He was also "economically dependent on Liberals since whenever he buys goods for cash or on credit he does so in the stores and grain dealerships belonging to Liberals, since these are the best. This creates, at the very least, a material obstacle to [conservatizing] administrative affairs."[73] Caicedo's analyst touched on a sensitive but important problem for extremist regional authorities in his report: the regional government enjoyed too little credibility even among its own sympathizers to risk breaking off ties with the opposition or engaging in openly defiant acts that might trigger additional guerrilla attacks. Who would come to their defense were they to do so? Ill-paid, poorly trained, and scarce public order forces, nearly as much at odds with each other as they were with the individuals they were sent to combat? Party officials who rarely ventured beyond the confines of Medellín?

While extremist sectors of the regional government insistently provoked and harassed the opposition in distant areas, they rarely considered the cost of such a policy to local citizens or took into account the government's inability to effectively respond to local Liberal reactions to such harassment. Regional authorities also failed to recognize the degree to which the interests of their party's local membership were intertwined with those of the opposition, whether because of kinship, business, or other long-term associations. For many local inhabitants the demands of extremist sectors within the national or regional Conservative party were unrealistic or simply had little bearing on local affairs. Competing loyalties produced a contradictory response among local Conservatives. Unable to win the support of moderates, local Conservative extremists increasingly preferred paramilitary or unofficial solutions rather than the deployment of either the army or the police to confront guerrilla-led attacks. Moderate Conservatives, meanwhile, distanced themselves from their party and the extremists in it, limiting themselves to unsuccessfully pressing the government to avoid promoting partisan conflict or, in some cases, opting to surreptitiously collude with members of the opposition against regional government officers.

Conflict labeled as strictly partisan simply failed to address the complexities of local strife or the possible existence of long-standing relationships that cut across party lines. Indeed, the bewildered tone in which the governor of Antioquia reported on the composition of the armed bands operating in western Antioquia to the minister of foreign relations in Bogotá made apparent an official tendency to reduce violence to a series of binary oppositions, and this was one of the central obstacles to devising an effective public order policy in western Antioquia. In response to the president's theory that violence in Urabá and western Antioquia was organized and led by members of Medellín's Liberal directorate and that the guerrillas were all former *gaitanistas,* Antioquia's governor was forced to acknowledge that no such clear-cut conclusion could be drawn about the participants in the area's unrest.[74] Instead, the governor ruefully admitted that he had received numerous reports that violence was increasingly motivated by economic rather than purely partisan factors and that among the participants in it were numerous Conservatives— acting in their own armed bands or in groups that included both Liberals and Conservatives.[75]

The difficulty of identifying exactly who was up in arms and why was a point repeatedly alluded to by a number of the analysts charged by the regional government with diagnosing the sources of unrest in the west. Detectives employed by the office of internal security, for instance, insisted that there were no separate guerrilla forces per se, but rather that road workers and guerrillas were one and the same (exactly as military analysts suspected was true of the Bajo Cauca region).[76] Guerrilla activity in the name of a party and union militancy was conflated. This opinion was seconded by a public order report filed by the military in February in which road workers were accused of providing the guerrillas with information, food, and clandestine transportation of arms through Urabá. It proved difficult to separate the interests of organized labor from partisan interests because the Conservative authorities had made it a point to conflate workers, Communists, and Liberals, and because state employees were necessarily the products of a partisan patronage system and therefore tended to belong to whatever party happened to be in power

when they were hired. New road personnel sent to replace those suspected of collaborating with the guerrillas, for instance, were killed by
old road workers (hired during an earlier period of Liberal rule) lest the
former collaborate with or betray their work mates to the army.[77] Road
workers employed on the Carretera al Mar clearly used threats such as
those directed at potential Conservative personnel appointees as a means
of protecting themselves from both dismissal and from partisan discrimination and harassment.

The national forest inspector also suggested that partisan conflict
thinly disguised the struggles between competing economic interests in
the region. The inspector reported that he had gone on a trip to Chigorodó to survey wood concessions leased to several prominent Antioqueño Liberals who owned an important logging and sawmill operation
in the area. In the course of his inquiry he found "that local opinion is
unanimous in asserting that the company has fomented, given aid to, and
sustained the reigning state of insecurity in the area in order to monopolize control of the forest products which abound in the region."[78] Indeed,
the governor had already received earlier reports linking the Surambay
sawmill with the contraband of arms through Urabá.[79] It is difficult to
know, however, whether the inspector's accusations were motivated by
the desire to benefit a group of equally prominent and well-connected
former Conservative officeholders who had also formed a consortium to
exploit a forest concession for wood products in Urabá or by the genu-
ine protests against privatization expressed by locals.[80] The privatization
of extraction from what had long been construed as public lands was
clearly an issue of considerable conflict and concern among local residents and had been for several decades.[81] Either way, more was at stake
in the armed struggles taking place in Urabá than the question of which
party was to control Colombia's fortunes. Reports that linked violence
to the emergence of an important, informal market for the sale of stolen
wood and cattle in which members of both parties were said to take part
further reinforce the impression that in some cases so-called partisan violence masked conflicts more appropriately construed as economic and
personal.[82]

Analysts sent to report on western Antioquia and Urabá all agreed
that the existence of illicit economic networks in which members of both
parties colluded and benefited was dependent upon a continued state
of public disorder. Analysts also believed that local collaboration with

the guerrillas and the reluctance of some Conservatives to participate in the wholesale oppression of the opposition undermined the government's ability to impose order in the area. But the principal determinant of continued unrest in western Antioquia was thought to lie elsewhere. The government's informants concluded that the central impediment to the defeat of armed insurgents was the absence of a collective consensus regarding the legitimacy of using force to impose partisan hegemony. This lack of consensus had created an intractable problem: the persistent refusal of members of the government's party and the armed forces to cooperate with one another or to take part in what was perceived as partisan-motivated violence.

In late January, Turbo's civilian mayor complained that the soldiers stationed to defend the town refused to cooperate with the Conservative civilian authorities or the police to search for and combat the "*bandoleros.*"[83] Two weeks later the governor deployed twenty-nine national policemen to provide backup in Turbo, but Colonel Luis Abadía (the newly appointed commander of Medellín's Fourth Brigade) notified the governor that the police had refused to be put under the command of the army (despite the governor's orders). Indeed, the police had publicly declared they would not cooperate with the army under any circumstances. The regional head of the national police in Antioquia, Major González, was forced to fly out on a military plane to deal with his men.[84] The conflict between soldiers and policemen was temporarily resolved by entrusting them with separate jurisdictions. The police were assigned to defend Turbo and the Vijagual region, while the military was granted jurisdiction over everything else.[85]

Ethnic and partisan tensions between different branches and divisions of the armed forces such as those suggested by Major González contributed to the absence of a united official front against armed insurgence. In January, the major informed the governor of the need to relieve the troops from Cauca and Huila who were stationed in the area because they "adversely affect [the] behavior of Antioquia's troops and are totally undisciplined."[86] The scion of a Conservative Medellín industrialist family who owned a large hacienda in Chigorodó seconded the major's observation. The Conservative hacienda owner warned the governor that so long as responsibility for maintaining public order in Urabá lay in the hands of national policemen who were "*cundiboyacense*" (that is, of indigenous descent) little hope existed of winning local civilian trust or eradicating the guerrillas.[87] In a confidential letter to Laureano Gómez in early 1951, Governor Henao, moreover, attributed the guerrillas' repeated defeat of government forces in western Antioquia to the "lamentable human material of many of the guardians of order" and implied that this was partly a result of their ethnic and regional identity (that is, they were non-Antioqueños and of indigenous descent).[88] Local Conservatives, in contrast, blamed the "Liberal army from the Caribbean coast [*costeños*]" sent to patrol the Carretera al Mar for an increase in guerrilla directed assassinations, robberies, and extortion and accused these of openly supporting the insurgents by selling them saltpeter and arms.[89]

Disputes over the relationship between ethnic identity and the ability to maintain public order were in the majority of cases but an expression of Antioqueño xenophobia and an excuse for what were really conflicts about jurisdiction and prerogative. The regional authorities resented the intrusion of forces appointed from outside Antioquia in the maintenance of public order because they could not so easily subordinate them to a dominant regional ideology or value system. But paradoxically, just as the regional authorities regarded such forces as a threat to their power, localities also resented the intrusion of regionally appointed forces who were perceived to be alien to or not so easily subordinated by local machinations. In late January the Conservative town of Anzá reported that two hundred guerrillas had attacked one of the town's *corregimientos,* which was protected only by six departmental police agents, a single municipal policeman, the police inspector, and three customs officers. The town had been left defenseless because racism had prompted it to refuse to allow the deployment of soldiers from the Caribbean coast in the area.[90] National policemen from Boyacá and Cundinamarca stationed in Dabeiba, moreover, were targeted by guerrillas operating along the Carretera al Mar who knew that black *costeño* soldiers (from Bolívar) stationed in garrisons in Chigorodó and Mutatá would make no effort to aid or rescue the "*cundiboyacense*" policemen.[91]

In the wake of events in early 1951 and after having considered the various reports analyzing the sources of continued and escalating violence in Urabá and western Antioquia, Governor Henao Mejía took a series of steps to assert regional authority over an area he and the central government feared was rapidly escaping the government's grasp.[92] First, the governor set up a meeting between Colonel Abadía of the Fourth Brigade, Major González of the department of security, the chief of the regional office of the national roads department, Antioquia's secretary of public works, and Gregorio Mejía, the Liberal contractor in charge of hiring workers on the Carretera al Mar. These men agreed to station one hundred members of the army corps of engineers on the Carretera al Mar where "bandits . . . harass workers and private citizens, interrupt transportation, rob settlers, and maintain a climate of terror."[93] The regional government also decided to once more rearrange the deployment of troops in the region. Cañasgordas, Peque, Ituango, Dabeiba, and Frontino (western towns) were put under the control of the police while Mutatá, Caucheras, Chigorodó, and Riogrande (towns in Urabá) were assigned to the military.

Regional authorities justified their decision to assign policemen and soldiers to different geographic areas by arguing that the police were posted to areas where there were a greater number of inhabitants and where incidents of violence were more related to "police issues," while the army was sent to patrol areas involving "technical" matters (such as the construction of the road).[94] In reality, however, the reasons for assigning police and army to different public order sites and to which specific areas followed other concerns. Both the central government and Antioquia's regional authorities worried that worker disturbances might imperil the completion of the road. Indeed, in February the governor had confessed that he feared a "massive revolt by workers."[95] It was the fear of alienating the workers (almost all of whom were Liberal) and jeopardizing Antioquia's control and access to important natural resources and trade that ultimately determined the assignment of the army to patrol this zone. In this sense, road workers in Urabá effectively capitalized on their reputation as militants who would stop at nothing to impede dismissal and harassment to force the hand of the regional government much as miners in eastern towns such as Segovia were able to do. In contrast to the considerations shaping the governor's approach to public order matters in worker-dominated areas of eastern Antioquia, however, in western Antioquia the regional authorities were initially more concerned about alienating Conservative supporters who distrusted the army but supported the police. Western Antioqueño towns were also areas where in early 1951 the regional government was convinced that the motivating force of violence was more narrowly partisan, not economically motivated, spurred by cultural differences, or involving organized workers as it appeared to in Urabá.

The regional government's policy changes initially worsened the situation of public order in Urabá. In the first weekend after the placement of army troops along the Carretera al Mar between Mutatá and Dabeiba, a series of guerrilla attacks took place which prompted the governor to report to an alarmed president that "I fear the rebellion is spreading in a dangerous fashion."[96] Indeed, guerrilla activity escalated so dramatically throughout the zone during the last days of February that the *visitador administrativo* in the area recommended bombing Rio Sucio and the guerrilla camps established in Mutatacito and Chadó as the only way of stopping the guerrillas' advance.[97] By March 16, the governor admitted that government forces had been unable to defeat armed men present in Turbo, Riogrande, Micuró, Vijagual, San Juan de Urabá, and Necoclí. He limited himself to ordering scarce army troops to the area to "maintain bases to conduct the necessary sweeps to defend the local citizenry . . . until such time as the governor's office may be in a position to build up its defenses in those areas."[98] But the regional state never managed to increase its ability to protect those areas, and their continued vulnerability simply invited further guerrilla aggression. On March 20, guerrillas took advantage of the fact that army troops deployed in El Carmelo had abandoned the settlement twenty days earlier. The guerrillas attacked the police inspector's office, killed fifty Conservatives, and forced surviving inhabitants to flee in terror.[99] Five days later a group of fifty guerrillas struck again on the outskirts of Turbo. Meanwhile, local Conservatives complained that the soldiers posted to defend the town were drunk and shouted *vivas* to the Liberal party and vulgar insults at the town's mayor and local Conservatives.[100]

By the end of March the government had lost the battle against guerrilla forces in Urabá. The tax collector in Chocó reported that guerrillas controlled Titumate and Tanela and were about to sweep settlements in the Acandí district, an area through which much of the contraband between Antioquia and Panama flowed.[101] Meanwhile, the military officer in charge of overseeing public order in the area between Chigorodó and Cañasgordas reported that despite the presence of military garrisons in Mutatá and Chigorodó and the permanent assignment of soldiers on the rubber plantations in Caucheras, three active guerrilla camps existed between Caucheras and Chigorodó.[102] The army's inability to destroy the camps was partly due, the officer noted, to the inhabitants' general refusal to cooperate with the army and to their political affiliation as Liberals. But he also noted a widespread perception among wealthy hacendados in the area (who did not support the guerrillas) that the army would be unable to defend them if they were to turn in the guerrillas. This, too, contributed to the government's inability to effectively contain unrest. Overwhelmed by the seeming intractability of armed insurrection in Urabá and under considerable pressure from both Liberal and Conservative landowners in the area, Governor Henao Mejía informed his superiors in Bogotá on March 27, 1951, that he had done as much as could reasonably be expected of him and that the only solution to Urabá's violence was to hand over control of the area to the military.[103]

The Locus of Violence Shifts Westward

Once the governor opted to put Urabá completely under military control, the principal theater of armed confrontation shifted away from Urabá toward western Antioquia, particularly to the towns of Peque, Frontino, Cañasgordas, and Dabeiba. Guerrilla attacks in western Antioquia after March 1951, in contrast to those reported for Urabá in 1950 and early 1951, tended to avoid targeting either government offices or public order personnel to concentrate instead on attacking private property and civilians. In an ironic twist — given the governor's supposition that western violence was more partisan than economic — cattle-rustling, extortion of hacienda owners and administrators, forced sales of land, and theft became increasingly common expressions of violence. For instance, in late March four hundred head of cattle and one hundred thirty mules and horses were stolen from Mora Hermanos y Cia.'s hacienda, "Argelia," in Urama and taken to Camparusia, where Liberal guerrilla leader Arturo Rodríguez had his headquarters. The hacienda's administrator was able to identify the thieves by name, and he insisted that they were well known to everyone in the region.[104] A little over a month later, guerrillas led by Aparicio Escobár of Frontino stole another ninety-five head of cattle, and in June another local hacienda and much of its livestock was burned to the ground by ten or so guerrillas. The result was fifty thousand pesos of damage.[105]

Indeed, cattlemen from both parties in Frontino increasingly complained of rustling and of the movement of stolen cattle to Murrí and nearby municipalities.[106] By August it became apparent that established circuits for the distribution and sale of stolen cattle and property exceeded any scale of rustling guerrillas might be engaged in for sheer survival. Mora Hermanos, which had been robbed of several hundred head of cattle and horses in March, once more reported attacks against its properties, this time "Argelia" and "El Palermo."[107] The administrator again knew the thieves and insisted that the identities of those buying the stolen cattle were known as well. The cattle thieves were concentrated in Peque, Juntas de Uramita (Cañasgordas), Antesalas (Ituango), and all along the Sinú River in the department of Bolívar on the border with Ituango, while cattle stolen in the corregimiento of Tabacál in Buriticá were routed through Cañasgordas and Uramita.[108]

In September 1951 the Caja de Crédito Agrario, Industrial y Minero announced that more than seven thousand head of cattle had been stolen in western Antioquia over a period of several months. The institution warned that if the situation continued, within seven or eight months rustling "would absolutely destroy the economy of this important region."[109] To counteract the extensive losses to the Caja's reserves from forfeited loans, the credit agency opted to restrict loans in areas affected by violence, especially those intended to finance the purchase of cattle. The lending organization also requested authorization from its main office in Bogotá to refuse all requests for credit while the situation of public order in the west remained severe. The Caja argued that it was pointless to extend further credit for cattle purchases when the guerrillas had become so bold in the face of the regional government's inability to protect the region as to attack haciendas only six or seven kilometers from the urban core of the area's towns.[110]

The impact of violence on the property and economic interests of western Antioquia's inhabitants, as well as the rising toll of civilian deaths wreaked by guerrilla attacks and the government's inability to effectively impede violence, increasingly prompted some local Conservatives to appeal to the regional government for arms. The mayor and disgruntled Conservatives in Ituango had already offered to organize a group of Conservative contrachusmas to combat the group of six hundred "*bandoleros*" that were stockpiling everything they could steal in the area. The mayor insisted that an armed volunteer force of local citizens was the only effective means of eradicating guerrillas in the area, because the police that had been sent to defend the predominantly Conservative town were "useless."[111] Conservatives in nearby Dabeiba on Ituango's western border had already threatened to create a contrachusma four months earlier in retaliation for the guerrilla attack that had left their parish priest dead. There could be no harm in arming Conservative civilians, Dabeiba's Conservatives insisted, since "no matter how armed we are, . . . we are armed only to defend the public order."[112]

As was true of contrachusma forces that came to operate in other parts of Antioquia such as the Magdalena Medio and Bajo Cauca, those in western Antioquia elicited considerable concern and criticism from members of the government's own party. Some months after Dabeiba's offer to support a local contrachusma, the bishop of Santa Fé de Antioquia, Luis Andrade Valderrama, felt sufficiently alarmed about the course of events in Dabeiba and nearby Cañasgordas to send one of the area's priests for a private audience with the governor in which the former relayed "several very serious observations . . . regarding the situation of public order in that region."[113] The bishop also sent the parish priest of Giraldo to meet with the governor. Giraldo's priest had publicly declared that the only local violence was that created by a perpetually drunken police force. The priest accused the police of being "the sort of evildoers who so deeply dishonor the prestige of the government and who are really only Communists in disguise who are out to undermine the honor of the government."[114] The priest's accusations prompted Bishop Andrade to insist to the governor that those promoting violence should be stopped "regardless of who they may be," a posture which won the bishop accolades from Liberal leader Alberto Jaramillo Sánchez.[115] During a dinner in Medellín at the Nutibara Hotel in July 1951, Jaramillo Sánchez declared that Bishop Andrade was "the only prelate in Colombia who had raised his voice to plead for the restoration of peace and tranquillity" and who had spoken out against the "civil guards" (that is, the contrachusma) created by Dionisio Arango Ferrer in 1948 and the "aplanchadores" sponsored by Eduardo Berrío González soon after.[116] Months earlier, in fact, both Jaramillo Sánchez and Captain Agustín Salcedo, the military attaché of the Fourth Brigade, had sounded the alarm against contrachusma activities in western Antioquia and called for the total disarmament and dissolution of "civic police forces" in the area traversed by the Carretera al Mar. The two men insisted that if soldiers were assigned to control public order in areas affected by violence they would personally guarantee workers' "respect and obedience to the army and the return of workers to their tasks, because they were fully confident that army officers and soldiers would guarantee the security and tranquility of the road workers."[117] To extremist Conservatives such pronouncements served only to confirm long-held suspicions that the army and the Liberal party were working together.

Despite the protests of selected armed forces personnel, the bishop of Santa Fé de Antioquia, numerous parish priests, and Liberal leaders such as Alberto Jaramillo Sánchez, the number of towns opting to create contrachusmas in western Antioquia grew rather than diminished by May 1951. Peque, squeezed between Dabeiba, Cañasgordas, and Ituango, and fearful of an impending attack led by guerrilla leader Aníbal Pineda and three hundred men from the Llano de Urarco, offered to organize volunteers to defend the town in exchange for arms from the regional government. But the few available policemen in the area, Conservative volunteers pointed out, possessed only twenty bullets between them. Faith in the government's forces had reached such a low ebb, moreover, that the parish priest, from the pulpit during Sunday Mass, had exhorted his parishioners to abandon the town, and he fled two days later with several local families.[118] Meanwhile, many Conservative hacienda owners fled south from Pineda's stronghold in the Llanos de Urarco to seek refuge in Anzá, while Peque's Conservatives sought refuge across the Cauca River in the town of Sabanalarga.[119] Partially in response to the wave of refugees seeking asylum and to the presence of guerrillas led by Captain Vidal Torres and Pablo Emilio López who were camped some fourteen kilometers from the *corregimiento* of Barbacoas, Sabanalarga's priest urged the regional government to empower him to arm volunteers and pay them "a daily wage as police auxiliaries" so as to "recuperate lands" and pursue the guerrillas.[120] By June 5, it appears that the governor had heeded the priest's call, for the priest reported that a group of armed civilian police had just succeeded in killing the Liberal guerrilla leader Vidal Torres.[121]

In June the regional government and Medellín's Fourth Brigade reorganized and increased the distribution of soldiers throughout Urabá, along Antioquia's border with Chocó, and in western Antioquia to reflect the intensification of guerrilla and contrachusma activity in the area. The number of soldiers present in the region rose dramatically to three hundred eighty from the mere ninety-two that had previously patrolled the area between Turbo and Frontino.[122] Two weeks later, a message from the armed forces declared Urabá to be the third most violent area in Colombia (following only the Llanos and southern Tolima) and noted that western Antioquia was rapidly becoming as great a matter of public order concern to the central authorities as Urabá.[123]

Several incidents of public unrest fueled the armed forces' increasing preoccupation with western Antioquia. Guerrillas had led an attack against Peque in which they desecrated the local church, hung children alive by meat hooks, and flayed a woman to death. When thirty-five national policemen were sent out to search and capture the guerrillas, however, four ran away and two others were wounded, while the guerrillas lost no men at all.[124] A wiretap conducted by the chief of the security department recorded the reaction of the army officers stationed in nearby Dabeiba whose responsibility it was to provide backup troops for the national policemen under attack in Peque. The transcript of their conversation leaves little doubt that they considered the police one of the central impediments to the effective defense of public order in the region. On hearing that four of the policemen sent to pursue the guerrillas had fled and that the others had stopped their operations simply because some of their number were wounded, Major Peña Sánchez complained to his fellow officer, Major Márquez, that "the police are useless. . . . The moment someone takes a shot at them from the hills, they run." When Major Márquez lamented that he had no other men to send but thirty national policemen as backups, Peña Sánchez grumbled, "man, what a bitch [que vaina carajo]. . . . What I'll do is take fifteen soldiers away from the posts I control and I'll take charge of the matter." To which Márquez slyly suggested, "Better yet, at every post you come to, take the police away from them so they'll [the guerrillas] be screwed, because [police] are what those bastards have been wanting."[125] The thirty policemen, just as Major Márquez predicted they would, attracted another guerrilla attack three days later.[126]

As terrified refugees fled Peque toward Sabanalarga, the priest there once more called upon the regional authorities and local Conservatives to arm and organize contrachusma units to track down the guerrillas and avenge Conservative deaths.[127] But the regional government took other steps in response to the wave of guerrilla activity assaulting Urabá and western Antioquia. In August the government decided to impose a system of salvoconductos, or permits, that limited local mobility within the area covered by the Carretera al Mar. Any person wanting to enter or leave the Carretera al Mar's jurisdiction (that is, between Turbo and Cañasgordas and through Dabeiba and Frontino) could only do so with a government-issued pass. Those found not to have a *salvoconducto* were to be expelled from the area. The new mandate also applied to workers on the rubber plantations in Chigorodó and Caucheras.[128] Just as it would do with hacienda workers in eastern Antioquia in mid-1952, the regional authorities effectively criminalized western Antioquia's workers while making them a captive labor force as well.

The intensification of violence in western Antioquia also prompted the private sector to take steps to mitigate the effects of unrest on local investments. In September, the Federation of Coffee Growers hammered out an agreement with the governor to forestall the possible loss of Antioquia's leading export commodity. Any producer who feared that his crop might be endangered by the threat of violence could immediately request troops from the regional government to collect the harvest.[129] There was good reason to suspect that violent incidents might interrupt the harvest, for senate elections in which Conservatives were the only candidates were to be held at the end of the month. Elections usually meant the widespread distribution of liquor and use of intimidation to force the opposition to vote. Frontino, Buriticá, Dabeiba, and Juntas de Uramita in Cañasgordas all reported electoral disturbances that coincided with the onset of the coffee harvest and all appealed to the government for troops to protect them from attack. In Uramita such threats emanated from the government's own forces as contrachusmas allied with members of the national police "sowed panic" in the rural working population.[130]

Growing fear of the police and their contrachusma aides gripped not only Liberals but also moderate Conservatives who worked with or employed Liberals and who did not support the creation of paramilitary or vigilante groups who might use partisanship to further specific economic interests. The extremes to which such groups could go became apparent when police and civilian Conservatives lined up eleven Liberal peasants employed by the prominent Martínez Villa family in Frontino and shot them dead because they held jobs that might have been filled by Conservative peasants.[131] This incident and another a month later signaled a shift from violence intended to achieve a Conservative monopoly over offices and votes or to limit Liberal guerrilla activities to one in which economic considerations played a determinant role. A group of coffee producers in Cañasgordas informed the governor in November 1951 that eighty "rural police" from Tabacál, Buriticá, were dedicated to "conducting all kinds of abuses such as homicides, major thefts of cattle, hogs, coffee, corn, [and] beans." Things had gotten so bad, the coffee growers complained, that "they had been forced to abandon the region."[132] The growers reported that the rural police had stolen twenty thousand pesos of harvested goods from one store and then burned it down, stolen an additional forty thousand pesos in goods from local farms, and killed many women and children in the *corregimiento* of "El Naranjo." Sixty rogue policemen and their officers, moreover, owned "a store, a cantina, and a butcher shop where they sell the cattle, coffee, [and] corn they've stolen from us" in Tabacál. Seriously alarmed by the possible repercussions of such developments, the regional chapter of FEDECAFE insisted that the regional government conduct a rigorous investigation to ascertain whether or not such accusations had merit. The Federation of Coffee Growers warned that if they did, measures would have to be taken to protect "an economic force of incomparable value to the nation."

In late February 1952, a worried parish priest and members of the municipal conservative committee in Caicedo also reported that the national police stationed in the town and their civilian volunteer aides were not pursuing the guerrillas. Instead, the contrachusma and the police were terrorizing the countryside "abusing women [and] stealing animals and money from innocent peasants."[133] Several western towns nonetheless continued to enthusiastically organize additional Conservative paramilitary units. Caicedo's Conservatives, for instance, were split and, despite earlier complaints of police and contrachusma terror, Caicedo was among those towns reminding Governor Henao Mejía in early April 1952 that he had promised to outfit volunteers with official arms to supplement the insufficient number of available troops to combat the guerrillas.[134] The governor sent nearby Frontino and Cañasgordas more than twenty guns each.[135]

Because they enabled certain local factions to wreak revenge on the opposition with impunity and to use the threat of terror to obtain real material advantages, contrachusma forces were popular despite the evident risks involved in arming untrained local extremists. But locals also preferred unofficial armed groups, because they perceived the government's official forces as inefficient and corrupt, a perception that the government's own policies and attitudes did little to counteract. The parish priest of Ituango, one of the earliest municipalities to call for arming Conservative civilians, for instance, wrote the governor five months after the creation of these to denounce atrocities committed by the national police assigned to defend the town. The policemen, the priest angrily insisted, spent their time "drinking up the government's liquor stocks, killing defenseless and peaceful people, [and] . . . terrorizing the residents who discern in the police an enemy more terrible than the very *bandoleros.*" While Liberal guerrillas took away local people's lands, the police lived off the town's meager public budget and did nothing to stop them. This state of affairs led the priest to muse aloud, "I ask myself if these peasants — who are left unprotected by the government and are subject to extortion by a police force that only obeys depraved instincts — would defend the government should it become necessary."[136]

The police's failure to actively pursue the guerrillas may have been the result of having not been paid, being poorly armed, and knowing that there were no backup forces. But these reasons cannot excuse the repeated reports of police brutality against the civilian population in the areas they were sent to patrol. Complaints of corruption among the government's forces, moreover, were too common to dismiss as exceptional. Uramita reported that national policemen had confiscated seven horses, saddlebags filled with goods, and three *cargas* (loads) of coffee (about 375 kilograms) worth four hundred pesos in early May and colluded with a local civilian who acted as their fence to hide and divide the spoils. The incident came to light when one of the officers sold the items in question but cheated his subordinates out of their share. A vicious, public struggle ensued. Those denouncing the policemen's behavior suggested that incidents such as these were commonplace.[137] The possibilities for profit appear to have been so significant that they attracted the attention and participation of policemen from nearby Frontino. They were said to migrate to Uramita in search of "alternative forms of economic survival" as a way of overcoming the scarcity of food and supplies and lack of pay they suffered in the neighboring municipality to which they'd been assigned.[138]

Collusion between members of the government's official forces and unscrupulous civilians and between civilians and the guerrillas or contra-chusmas reached alarming proportions by June 1952. The military warned the governor of Antioquia that it was imperative to protect rural folk as they transported their goods to market "to free them from the extortion they are subjected to by unscrupulous merchants who capitalize on the region's abnormal state of affairs to advance their own interests."[139] Meanwhile, local merchants spread rumors that guerrilla attacks were about to occur or that the guerrillas were close by in order to terrify farmers into selling their goods for less than their market value and at great profit to themselves.

At first, the illicit activities carried out by the police and local contra-chusma forces were matched by those perpetrated by Liberal guerrillas in the region. Cattle owners detected and reported the development of networks of merchants and even fellow ranchers who dealt in cattle and goods stolen by the guerrillas in early 1951. Evidence of the importance of these newly formed, informal markets and of the indiscriminate theft of goods without regard to partisan affiliation, however, became more frequent in the latter half of 1951. In September, for instance, members of Toledo's Conservative committee complained to the minister of war that a hundred guerrillas armed with shotguns and machetes had recently stolen three hundred head of cattle and thirty beasts of burden from land-owners "without regard to whether the owners are Conservatives or Lib-erals."[140] Both Liberal and Conservative stockmen complained as well that known cattle rustlers haunted the area around Murrí and Rioverde in Frontino.[141]

The possibilities for profit created by a permanent state of dis-order, moreover, affected even the livelihoods of supposedly partisan-motivated guerrilla leaders. In early February 1952, Arturo Rodríguez Osorio, Dabeiba's guerrilla chief, was overheard responding disdainfully to an offer made to him by officers of Medellín's Liberal directorate of one hundred fifty pesos to start a new guerrilla group in the department of Santander. Rodríguez rejected the directorate's offer, boasting that he could easily earn four to five hundred pesos a day leading an indepen-dent, armed band.[142] Indeed, throughout the first half of 1952 reports of guerrilla attacks in which the sole objective appeared to be the theft of cattle and goods abounded. Rapes, torture, and abuse also increas-ingly accompanied these robberies.[143] By March the excesses committed by Liberal guerrilla leader Aníbal Pineda in Dabeiba were so egregious that they prompted disgusted members of his own band to kill him.[144] Three months later, for similar reasons, Patricio Usaga met the same fate at the hands of his followers.[145] In April, the Caja de Crédito Agrario, noted with alarm that guerrilla groups in Urabá had advanced from rob-bery to land occupations (see appendix B.3). Guerrillas took over pri-vately held lands and occupied them against the owners' wishes in Urama (Dabeiba), Urarco (Buriticá), Carepa (Mutatá), Carauta, Murrí, and Platanales (Frontino).[146] Meanwhile, the townspeople of Cañasgordas reported in July that guerrillas based in Camparusia, Dabeiba, had sowed the entire surrounding area with beans and corn and were anticipating a large harvest in August. If no effort were made to put a stop to this, local townspeople warned, the guerrillas would be able to buy arms and food and remain active in the region indefinitely.[147]

In addition to the rise in theft, by mid-1952 the Magdalena region, Urrao, Urabá, and western Antioquia were caught in the grip of an unprecedented wave of homicides. Statistics kept by the armed forces in Antioquia of civilian and guerrilla deaths estimated that 2,225 individuals lost their lives as a result of violence in 1952, more than double the number of casualties reported in 1951 (970) or 1953 (910).[148] Western Antioquia accounted for 34 percent of the officially recorded, violence-related deaths in the department. Indeed, although the number of deaths in western Antioquia was incredibly high what was more horrifying was that the town of Dabeiba accounted for more than 10 percent of Antioquia's officially reported casualties in 1952 (266). This made Dabeiba the second most violent Antioqueño town that year after Puerto Berrío in eastern Antioquia. Other western towns such as Cañasgordas accounted for 6 percent of the departmental total of deaths and Anzá for 4 percent in the same year. One-fifth of Antioquia's *Violencia* casualties in 1952 took place in just three western municipalities (see appendix A.3 and A.6).

The military responded to the rise in violence-related homicides by stepping up its counterinsurgency tactics. But the escalation of military activity, coupled with the proliferation of contrachusma groups, worked to dramatically increase rather than curb violence throughout the region. Events in a single western municipality illustrate this process vividly. Abriaquí had registered no deaths before 1952, but in that year it became the destination point for numerous Conservative refugees from Caicedo and Anzá who were fleeing Liberal guerrilla violence.[149] The refugees began to organize contrachusma forces to combat the guerrillas and to lead forays into the areas where Liberal groups had usurped their properties. Four months after the mass exodus to Abriaquí, the town's mayor reported in distress that "some Conservatives want me to support the killing of peaceful, honest Liberals who have never attempted to rise up against the authorities. They circulate false rumors in which they insist that your lordship [the governor] has ordered the indiscriminate massacre of Liberals and that mayors who don't comply with that order will suffer the same fate."[150] "If it was true" that the governor had ordered the killing of Liberals, the mayor announced, then he would resign. "If mayors cannot offer equal safeguards to all citizens . . . then I beg your lordship to replace me in the post in which I have served loyally during three and a half years without ever violating the rights of others."[151] As it turned out, the newly reappointed governor, Dionisio Arango Ferrer, and his secretary had encouraged mayors throughout the west to organize volunteer Conservative forces and to meet with the regional authorities for the distribution of arms. By the end of 1952, forty-four individuals in Abriaquí had become the victims of violence, twenty-nine of these casualties were supposed *bandoleros* tracked down and killed by newly created paramilitary forces made up of outsider refugees.[152]

Among the many problems incurred by the encouragement of paramilitary forces to fulfill what should have been the sole responsibility of the state and its legally constituted armed forces was the government's failure to supervise. The governor and his secretary, Alfredo Cock, exhorted mayors and Conservative committee members charged with arming civilian volunteers to keep close tabs on the use and location of the arms distributed to contrachusmas.[153] But in most cases, once arms left the governor's office, he ceased to have any real influence over the individuals employing them in the government's name. The majority of arms ended up in the hands of economically and politically influential local *caciques* or public functionaries who failed to report on their status or use.

The lack of control exerted by the regional government over its local followers led to a situation in which all manner of excesses could be justified as the fulfillment of official orders. On October 1, for instance, Conservative volunteers in Toledo and members of the national police stationed in the town joined together to organize a group of fifty-five armed men. They were to link up with Conservative volunteers and policemen in nearby towns ostensibly to pursue guerrillas based in Bocas de Peque and Orobajo in Sabanalarga.[154] Nine days later, however, the local mayor of Toledo reported that instead of pursuing the guerrillas, contrachusma forces and the police had been engaged in cattle-rustling and thefts in both Toledo and Sabanalarga.[155] Conservative farm owners in Uramita, Cañasgordas, meanwhile complained that their cattle had also been stolen by the group.[156] Cañasgordas' mayor—obliged to communicate in code lest local sympathizers of the contrachusma find out and kill him—informed the governor that Conservative contrachusmas were engaging in widespread cattle-rustling, "including from Conservatives," and that he urgently needed ten departmental policemen to keep the contrachusmas in line.[157]

The illicit activities of the contrachusma operating in Dabeiba reached such a high level by December that the town's Conservative mayor recommended they be disbanded immediately. There was an "imperative need to uproot five local Conservatives in order to avoid sending them to jail for a long time," the mayor insisted, for they had been "dedicated to stealing horses and corn, selling them later in the *corregimiento* of Uramita."[158] It must have seemed a painful irony that contrachusma forces were selling goods stolen from their fellow party members to merchants in Uramita who were widely known to be the principal suppliers of the Liberal guerrillas.

Violence, initially waged in defense of particular party interests or to protect the lives of party members against the actions of the opposition, evolved into a free-for-all in western Antioquia. Duty and partisan loyalty gave way to the pursuit of personal accumulation among armed members of both parties and even the government's own forces. Indeed, recruitment into the national police and contrachusma forces became—as it also did in eastern Antioquia—a way for the government to channel in nonthreatening ways poor rural men's resentment in areas where lands were concentrated in the hands of a few, and the only available employment was as poorly paid peons on local haciendas. By directing violence against members of the opposition of similar social status, local authorities deflected aggression away from the stark economic and social inequalities typical of an economy that revolved around cattle ranching and large sugar estates dominated by hacienda owners who doubled as political bosses. Partisan competition and repressive state policies produced a Hobbesian world in western Antioquia in which the opportunity for profit (sometimes but not always mediated by desire for revenge or partisan hegemony) gradually emerged as the only viable objective of violence by late 1952.

The Regional Government Responds to the Breakdown of "Order"

In January 1953, national policemen stationed in Frontino set out on a mission to capture guerrillas and the stolen cattle they had hidden on the outskirts of the town. Several days later the police returned with two

hundred eighty animals they had confiscated from outlying farms without regard to the owners' affiliation or their possible relationship to the
guerrillas. Forty head of cattle were entrusted to the mayor to hold while
their "rightful" owners were supposedly located and contacted, while
the remaining two hundred forty head of cattle were taken by the police
to an hacienda in Musinga, Frontino. A prominent member of the local
Conservative committee owned the hacienda and he was the individual
with whom "the deal was to be clinched." The hacendado then resold
the stolen cattle captured by the police to other Conservative hacendados in the area. When the mayor protested, the local committee members
intervened to have him removed.[159]

Simultaneously, the Caja de Crédito Agrario, Minero y Industrial complained that the state of disorder in nearby Frontino (caused, it implied,
by the increasingly violent activities of the contrachusma) had made "it
almost impossible to obtain labor" in the area.[160] Alarmed by reports
that local Conservatives were at each others' throats over whether or not
to support armed Conservative volunteers and that some Conservatives
were colluding with Liberals in open defiance of their party's interests,
Dionisio Arango Ferrer asked Antioquia's Conservative directorate to
send a *visitador especial* to Dabeiba, Cañasgordas, and Frontino to report
on the state of the party in the region and the role of armed Conservative
forces in the promotion of local violence.

The *visitador*'s report on Cañasgordas revealed (unintentionally perhaps) a sordid, corrupt, divided, and violent society riven by faction-
alism, family feuds, local animosities, personal jealousies, vindictive-
ness, greed, conflicts between haves and have-nots, and struggles over
power.[161] The report excused homicides and brutality as "youthful excesses" and dismissed opponents of partisan extremism such as the priest
or mayor or an elderly patrician political leader as corrupt, sexually licentious, or senile. Nepotism and collusion ran rife and were treated as unremarkable aspects of a local political culture in which both the regional
and central government were powerless to confront the complex machinations of cliquish, family-defined *roscas* (patronage networks). Locals
routinely defied the governor or any government official that attempted
to restrain or condemn their actions. A Conservative who dared to suggest that Liberals were not safe was met with the steely reply that "the Liberals could hardly meet with better treatment than we have given them,
[I cannot understand] why some people should go around saying that

it's impossible to live in Cañasgordas, that the persecution here is horrible." As proof of their kindness toward the opposition, local Conservatives noted that "the bust of [General] Santander is intact even after the Liberals have persecuted us so many times." Meanwhile the mutilated bodies of those opposing the contrachusma rotted amid clouds of flies on outlying farms.

Egregious acts of violence by Conservatives were blamed on an implausible "Liberal conspiracy." Liberals had supposedly agreed to "pass themselves off as Conservatives in order to commit crimes in the name of the Conservative party." When it proved impossible to get around the fact that a well-known Conservative had engaged in violence, the *visitador* found an explanation for that, too. "Emilio Cifuentes (Milo), is a Conservative from head to toe and has a reputation for being a terrible bandit," the *visitador* acknowledged, but "What has he done? He always goes on missions accompanied by the police and other civilian Conservatives. He has attacked areas where a bandit has surely been." Indeed, when performed by the Conservative contrachusma, violence was excused as the unfortunate product of economic necessity rather than personal ambition. The *visitador* insisted that "it cannot be argued that he [Cifuentes] only robs defenseless people for his own personal enrichment. He is married, has three kids, and is very poor." Another Conservative assassin, Samuel Ruiz, was lauded for being "principled and well mannered" even though he had robbed the Liberal coffee hacienda of which he was the administrator. Finally, "Rapidol," another contrachusma leader, was described as a paragon of virtue who "prohibits his followers from committing theft, the rape of women, etc." Unfortunately this appears to have been Rapidol's death sentence, for disgruntled members of his own band murdered him.

The *visitador* found that none of the men participating in Dabeiba's or Cañasgordas's contrachusma was an army reservist even though the regional government had specified that only reservists could be issued arms. Indeed, in some cases, members of the contrachusma did not even possess a national identity card and therefore could not be tracked down legally for any crime they might commit while supposedly acting in the government's name. Contrachusma recruits were uniformly described as poor, young, married, with many children, and employed as day laborers, several of them on haciendas owned by local Liberals. Wealthy hacendados and *tienda* (store) owners who dominated the local economy and political decision-making in the town stood in counterpoint to the perpetually underemployed reserve army of rural laborers. The *visitador* reported that some landowners and merchants supported the contrachusmas, seeing in them a vehicle for the expansion of their own influence and the opportunity for considerable profit. Others vehemently opposed the contrachusma, terrified lest a ragtag band of underemployed, resentful, armed poor men eventually challenge their property rights and their right to determine the fortunes of the party within the municipality. Indeed, the portrait that emerged from the *visitador*'s observation of western Antioquia's local Conservative party committees and the qualities of those serving on them is pathetic and devastating.

In Dabeiba, the local pharmacist was the president of the municipal Conservative committee, but he was opposed by an hacendado originally from the southwestern town of Fredonia. The hacendado harbored ambitions to "be Dabeiba's political boss [*gamonal*] since, according to his own words, he's got money and he's white." The hacendado from Fredonia's opposition to the committee's president was supported by the committee's former secretary, who was the administrator of various local haciendas belonging "exclusively to Liberals." The former party secretary was accused of buying and selling goods and cattle with Liberals, even suspected "bandits." These two opposed the creation of the contrachusma and refused to make a "voluntary" contribution to the local party committee to underwrite the contrachusma's activities. This led the *visitador* to conclude that the contrachusma's detractors were nothing more than "three or four rich guys who aren't even from Dabeiba, and there's no telling which of them is a worse Conservative." The quotas, which these men refused to pay, were exacted from both public employees and local party members to support party activities. The wealthy received letters requesting a contribution of five hundred pesos with an accompanying note from the party president "energetically warning members that [the committee] was demanding the quota because of the apathy which they have always shown when it was time to serve the party in this municipality." Wealthy members who refused to contribute were threatened with death, while public employees who did not pay a percentage from their salaries were fired and replaced with those who would.

Those contributing to the party coffers could demand certificates stating that they and their dependents, workers, or friends were "Conservatives in Good Standing," a document which was a prerequisite for obtaining employment on local haciendas and for avoiding assassination by the local contrachusma. When an hacendado refused to pay his assigned quota, for instance, the committee informed him "not to ask the committee for recommendations or any favors since if he [the member] wouldn't serve the party then the party wasn't obliged to do anything for him." Nepotism, moreover, was well inscribed in this system of doing politics. Favorites and relatives of those in good standing were routinely paid to act as intermediaries and messengers between the local committee and the regional government.

In the course of describing the way politics worked in Dabeiba, the *visitador* also provided a brief synopsis of its operation in the nearby western municipality of Sabanalarga. Like public employees in Dabeiba, those hired in Sabanalarga also had to pay a forced contribution to the local party committee; this resulted in the creation of a system of bosses who distributed patronage and subverted any possible neutrality among those they helped hire. When candidates needed to be fired or replaced, they were simply accused of "being turncoats [*manzanillos*]," "keeping concubines," or "drunkenness." In Sabanalarga a pair of "uneducated" brothers filled the offices of mayor and judge. The tax collector was the brother of the president of the local Conservative committee. The committee president was a cousin of the mayor and the judge. The local *inspector de corregimiento* was an uncle of both the tax collector and the committee president; the town clerk was related by marriage to the inspector, and the customs agent was a first cousin of the town clerk. The Conservative president's two daughters were public school teachers who had gained their appointments by falsely accusing the two teachers before them of being party traitors.

If the local party committees in Dabeiba, Cañasgordas, and Sabanalarga were dens of competing private interests and petty rivalries, the state of the Conservative party in Frontino, perhaps the most important and largest western municipality, the governor's special envoy reported, was even worse. To begin with, the seventy-year-old medical doctor who had historically been the president of the local Conservative committee refused to collaborate with the newly appointed president or any of the newly elected members. He informed the *visitador* that he considered "some of them little better than bandits and the rest idiots." The doctor was a "respected" man but opposed by a faction of the town's Conservatives because he continually berated them and publicly declared that he would like to "see them all in jail, doing worse sentences than those merited by the acknowledged bandits [that is, the Liberal guerrillas]." The *visitador* concluded that such a violent assessment of his party members' behavior was due to the doctor's "nervous state that impedes him from seeing political reality with seriousness and good judgment." Those accused of being brutal assassins by the former president were, in the *visitador*'s estimation, nothing more than "boys, enthusiastic about politics, but clean and honest when it comes to respecting other people's property and human life." But despite this vindication of local Conservative comportment, even the *visitador* concluded that the majority of those currently serving on the local party committee were "incapable of working in politics" and that the only useful member was a local mechanic although even he "doesn't exactly possess excellent abilities."

The Conservative party's problem in Frontino boiled down to a simple one: the likeliest and most desirable candidates for committee membership were primarily landowners and merchants suspected of colluding, doing business with, and hiring Liberals. The unreliability of such wealthy Conservatives had created the opportunity for individuals whom the *visitador* essentially characterized as part of a lumpen class—poor, unemployed or underemployed, and "resentful"—to finally enter politics. These were the shock troops of right-wing ideological movements everywhere. The lumpen allied with *arrivistes*—individuals with a modicum of wealth or status who hoped to dislodge those who had historically ruled local fortunes through a strategy of terror and intimidation. The *visitador* envisioned the contrachusma not as appointees to the committee, but as its enforcers. They would constitute the popular support necessary to give the current committee the strength to withstand opposition from Conservatives such as the former committee president. Depending exclusively upon armed goons clearly posed problems for a local party committee, but these seemed less serious obstacles than those posed by the neutrality or bipartisanship of the wealthy. As an example, the *visitador* mentioned the names of three brothers who owned several haciendas in Santafé de Antioquia, Cañasgordas, Frontino, and Dabeiba, and whose cousins owned Antioquia's Conservative daily *El Colombiano*. Using their influence on Frontino's Conservative committee, all three had repeatedly requested and obtained certificates attesting to the Conservative affiliation of the workers on their haciendas even though most of these were actually Liberal. Workers such as these typically carried two forms of identification—a Conservative certificate and a Liberal party identity card—that they showed selectively, depending upon who was asking.

The composition of Frontino's reconstituted Conservative committee included a fair share of landowners, but unlike the hacendados deemed unworthy by the *visitador,* the landowners supported the formation of the contrachusma. This may have been due in part because, aside from "defending" the party's interests, the contrachusma also served the land-owners' illicit economic ambitions. Three of the hacendados named to the committee were in the process of being investigated for purchasing stolen cattle from policemen and their Conservative civilian aides during supposed raids to free the region of Liberal guerrillas. The hacenda-dos in question had joined forces with the policemen and contrachusma to recuperate cattle and goods they had earlier lost to the Liberal guer-rillas. This they appear to have done with great success as less than two years after their initial losses all of them owned new estates nearer to the urban core and had bought cafés and stores in town. It was commonly known in Frontino, the *visitador* acknowledged, that the new committee members had become wealthy dealing in cattle and goods "brought from places affected and unaffected by violence . . . and even from farms be-longing to Conservatives, and that they kept the proceeds from the sales to themselves . . . without being authorized by anyone."

The *visitador* acknowledged that local party members were hope-lessly divided and that those who most adamantly defended the organiza-tion of armed civilian Conservative groups were also those most deeply involved in benefiting economically from *la Violencia.* They purchased stolen cattle and goods, resold them, and used the contrachusma as their own private army to terrorize and eliminate those who disagreed with them or posed a challenge or obstacle to their economic ambitions. The *visitador* made no effort to hide his findings, he freely admitted that those supplying the Liberal guerrillas were "weak but entrepreneurial Con-servatives from Dabeiba, Uramita, and Nutibara" and that prominent committee members were engaged in robberies against their own party members. Even the police were assessed disdainfully as "Boyacenses" (in-digenous people from the department of Boyacá) who robbed and ex-torted for "personal gain" and who "frequently engaged in annoying snubs and humiliations directed at Antioqueño members of the police and the general citizenry, provoking highly inconvenient arguments." Ultimately, however, the *visitador* was willing to overlook the misbehavior of Conservatives such as the "ardent boys" who, with dubiously acquired wealth, made up the contrachusma, the police, and the hacendados, because "at least we can be sure of their political affiliation."

All that mattered, the *visitador* suggested in his report to the governor, was an unquestioning loyalty to the party regardless of the moral or ethical nature or real motivations of those acting in its name. The unruly behavior of the contrachusma, for example, was not only exonerated by the *visitador,* he even recommended that party fervor expressed as violence could be put to good use by the regional authorities in other areas. He thus concluded his report by recommending that contrachusma members accused of murder and robbery be recruited as policemen and sent to other Liberal-dominated towns such as Puerto Berrío "so that they can have a change of pace. This way they could be removed from Cañasgordas where they've become a nuisance, and their valor could be put to use under the discipline of the police in specific needy areas." It is unsurprising that the police enjoyed so little esteem from the civilian population when the government and its representatives envisioned the institution as a channel through which lower-class aggression could be safely and legitimately played out against the populations of marginal areas who, from the government's perspective, were colonized by undesirables.

The Denouement of Western Violence: 1953 and Beyond

Two months before General Rojas Pinilla toppled the Conservative government of Laureano Gómez in June 1953, the situation of public order in Urabá and western Antioquia remained as severe as it had been in 1950. Cattle-rustling had become a permanent feature of the area's economy despite repeated decrees intended to strangle the export of livestock from the region and repeated forays conducted by the police and army to dislodge the guerrilla camps that they argued were the conduits for stolen animals in the region.[162] Guerrillas, moreover, continued to successfully lead attacks against civilians, rural workers, and the state's officers despite the increased number of troops stationed in the area.[163] The only tangible change in the area's public order situation was the increasingly entrenched character of the contrachusma. Municipal authorities who came to regret arming civilians would remember the first months of 1953 as the point at which the armed men they organized to defend against Liberal guerrilla forces took on a life of their own.

In a long, coded message that Caicedo's mayor sent the governor in April, the mayor lamented that when he had attempted to expel the local contrachusma by arranging a distant mission, the members of the group had threatened to return and "form a new guerrilla group with the Montoyas."[164] Also, local leaders in one town increasingly deployed the contrachusma to extend their control over individuals in another. Those organized by the mayor of Dabeiba, for instance, were sent to operate in Chigorodó where they assassinated three adults and six children in April and then with impunity returned through the hills to their home base.[165]

The government and its forces, meanwhile, were still a largely ineffective and absent presence in the region. Workers and mule drivers in Uramita, Cañasgordas, suffered assaults along the main road through the town because of the absence of military posts in San José, San Benito, and Aguadas, while moonshine flourished in Chigorodó because all of the customs officers had been forced out of the zone.[166] Disorder that initially appeared to be a horrifying but temporary product of partisan conflict in late 1949 had thus become endemic and difficult to categorize by 1953. Conservatives who had initially supported any government effort intended to stem the tide of Liberal guerrilla thefts and assassinations gradually came to lose faith in the ability of the regional authorities or the armed forces to defeat the guerrillas or maintain public order. In many instances, the police whom local extremists had insisted were the only force whose partisan identity made them trustworthy, proved as disorderly and rapacious as the armed opposition. Some Conservative landowners even went so far as to urge the regional authorities not to appoint national policemen to oversee local public order matters, because the police force "sweeps away any human element in its path."[167] Private citizens ultimately offered to underwrite the cost of public defense—as landowners in eastern Antioquia had also done—in order to ensure the minimal protection of their lives and economic interests.[168] Other Conservatives opted to arm bands of Conservative civilians to fulfill the government's responsibility to protect private property and lives, while others withdrew their support from the government and their party and colluded with members of the opposition in order to defend their personal interests.

But disillusion also set in among those initially supporting the creation of contrachusma groups as these increasingly proved to have agendas that transcended a subordinated role as strict defenders of partisan interests. By 1953 local attitudes toward the contrachusma and Liberal guerrillas mirrored to some degree those present in eastern Antioquia. Moderate Conservatives and established local landowners or businessmen with no stake in deploying armed members of their party to attack Liberal workers or the properties of the opposition with whom they had shared business interests, opposed the contrachusma, often at considerable risk to their own lives. *Arrivistes* and locals resentful of collaboration between an old guard and the opposition, or resentful of the opposition's control of local affairs, seized upon the contrachusma as a medium for simultaneously advancing their personal fortunes and settling old scores.

Poor Conservative farmers, settlers, and day laborers, who bore the brunt of guerrilla attacks, supported or participated in the contrachusma out of self-interest or in self-defense as it became apparent that the government's forces could provide little protection. Some eventually came to regret their participation as the indiscriminately vindictive nature of these forces became increasingly evident. A similar phenomenon occurred among poor Liberals who initially supported the guerrillas but eventually could see little difference between one criminal organization and another, both of whom taxed, assaulted, and stole from them indiscriminately. Disorder, in other words, created both unparalleled opportunities for some and tragedy for others. Lands and properties were cleared of unwanted and troublesome squatters and tenants.[169] Some local merchants packed up and left, others capitalized on the emergence of new informal markets of stolen goods. The marginally employed or poor found an alternative source of economic survival as members of private armies and political offices and party committees were rearranged to reflect newly acquired fortunes and recently achieved status.

Of course, all of this occurred at considerable cost. Western Antioquia alone accounted for 40 percent of all the officially registered deaths caused by violence in the department between 1949 and May of 1953 and for 41 percent of all the deaths registered in the six worst months of *la Violencia* between August 1952 and January 1953. In real terms, these percentages represented a total of 1,700 deaths in western Antioquia, nearly two-thirds of which occurred in just three towns: Dabeiba (561), Cañas-gordas (368), and Frontino (170).[170]

The trajectory of violence did vary, however, between Urabá and western Antioquia, as did its long-term impact to some degree. Urabá, considered by the armed forces as Colombia's third most violent area in 1951, actually registered relatively few deaths between 1949 and 1953. Two percent (seventy-seven) of the department's total casualties occurred in Urabá, while only four deaths were registered in 1952, the year in which the rest of the department recorded the most deaths from violence.[171] It is significant that the bulk of officially registered deaths in Urabá occurred during 1951 (sixty-three) in the months before the regional government relinquished control of the area to the military and pulled out the national police. For while Urabá accounted for a very low percentage of the region's total *Violencia* deaths, it accounted for a considerable percentage of the political prisoners (that is, captured guerrillas) interned in Medellín's "La Ladera" prison (32 percent) (150) (see appendix A.6). In contrast, civilian and guerrilla casualties in western Antioquia were high while the number of guerrillas captured and imprisoned amounted to only 10 percent (fifty) of those jailed.[172]

The explanation for this discrepancy may lie in the entrenched presence of the contrachusma in western Antioquia and its relative absence in Urabá. The majority of those held in "La Ladera" from Urabá were captured after the military took control of Urabá. With the exception of the portion of the road in Dabeiba controlled by the military (which accounted for the majority of the prisoners from western Antioquia [thirty-three of fifty]), in contrast, almost no prisoners were taken in western Antioquia after 1952 when the contrachusma became particularly active in the area. These facts lead to several conclusions. Contrachusma groups began to operate extensively in western Antioquia in late 1951 and early 1952. They received an added impetus and additional arms from the regional government after July 1952. The greatest number of deaths in the area were registered between August 1952 and January 1953 when these groups were most active. Urabá, on the other hand, experienced very little contrachusma activity (except for sporadic attacks led by contrachusma groups organized in Dabeiba against the section of the Carretera al Mar that linked Dabeiba to Mutatá) and registered very few deaths after 1951. This would seem to suggest that violence was directly proportional to the presence of irregular forces, especially the contrachusma. When the government relinquished control of Urabá to the military (most of whom were from the department of Bolívar) in March 1951, for instance, violence in Urabá declined substantially.

In other words, the unprecedented rise in civilian casualties seems directly related to the presence of paramilitary forces in western Antioquia rather than to conflict between the armed forces and guerrillas or guerrilla-led activities. Indeed, a summary of the town of Peque's ills, provided by the parish priest in the immediate aftermath of the military coup, gives a sense of the intransigent and significant impact of paramilitary violence on the region even after the military government had come to power. Father Blandón Berrío informed Píoquinto Rengifo, Antioquia's new military governor, on June 27 that approximately eleven thousand inhabitants had lived in Uramita (Cañasgordas) and Peque prior to *la Violencia*. By mid-1953, however, only three thousand exiles inhabited the town of Peque proper, while several hundred former residents were dead and another seven thousand inhabitants were holed up "in the hills, surrounded by misery, lack of clothing, hunger, and sickness." They were too terrified to come back to the town for fear of losing their lives, not to the Liberal guerrillas, but to contrachusma groups still active in the surrounding area (see appendix B.4).[173]

It is little wonder that the priest of Liborina seized the pulpit to denounce the contrachusma and to declare during a Mass in late May 1953 that "the government led by Braulio Henao Mejía had been a disaster, but that under Dionisio Arango Ferrer it was worse."[174] In a long missive addressed to Governor Dionisio Arango Ferrer in June, former governor Fernando Gómez Martinez in fact argued that the main instigators of violence in western Antioquia were the contrachusma groups endorsed and armed by the regional government. Gómez Martinez also accused Arango Ferrer's administration of reassigning public employees indicted for criminal behavior instead of firing and jailing them; of illegally detaining suspects and arbitrarily executing them with the aid of the national police; and of using torture to obtain confessions even when evidence obtained in such a manner had been declared illegal and inadmissible by Colombia's highest court.

The former Antioqueño governor used the excesses of the paramilitary forces endorsed by the state in Cañasgordas to illustrate his accusations. After a unit shot at each other in a public dispute over goods they had recently stolen from innocent local inhabitants, they forced "the inhabitants, especially Liberal women, to don mourning clothes while the republic's armed forces acted as the honor guard to the funeral procession as it wound its way to the cemetery."[175] Shortly after this incident, the town's contrachusma erected a bust in Arango Ferrer's honor that confirmed the degree to which their existence had been the product of the governor's support.

The contrachusma were, in fact, the big winners in western Antioquia. They continued to operate long after August 1953 when the government officially demanded the return of arms distributed by the former regional government and after local Liberal guerrilla groups had been captured or voluntarily taken advantage of the military government's amnesty policy.[176] Their continued presence made it impossible to heal the wounds of inhabitants exhausted by a conflict many of them had neither condoned nor understood. Caicedo's priest, who prefaced his criticism of the contrachusma by identifying himself as a lifelong Conservative loyalist, emphatically denounced the persistent effect that armed civilian Conservative groups had on local life. In July, shortly after the military took power, he held a reconciliation Mass on the feast of the Virgin of Mount Carmel to reincorporate Liberals who had stayed away from the church during the previous four years. His good intentions were ruined, however, when "three guys of the very lowest Conservative scum in this town, . . . three men who were probably once *recalzados* [Liberal converts to Conservatism] and implicated in the great robberies conducted by the famous Montoya Giraldos who led the contrachusma," erupted in the churchyard and dragged away several "peaceful" Liberal congregants and imprisoned them.[177] Elsewhere policemen and contrachusmas continued to work for private interest groups and individuals to intimidate workers and deny them their legal rights.[178] By August, reports were circulating in Juntas de Uramita and Cestillal, Cañasgordas, that one hundred contrachusma were in the hills between these two villages and were organizing "throughout western Antioquia" "to topple the government."[179]

Although all of the Liberal guerrillas once active in western Antioquia and Urabá surrendered or had been eliminated by October 1953, homicides, cattle-rustling, and forced displacement of workers, squatters, and rural property owners grew rather than diminished.[180] In western towns such as Sabanalarga, Cañasgordas, Dabeiba, Caicedo, Uramita, and Frontino, citizens of both parties complained to the military governor that "four or five layabouts have been dedicated to sowing terror," forcing people to flee and then seizing their lands.[181] The perpetrators of disorder organized publicly and were well known to all. Lists of those forming the contrachusma as well as their sponsors in towns such as Cañasgordas, Uramita, Buriticá, and Frontino were repeatedly sent to the governor and to various private sector entities such as the Caja de Crédito Agrario, the regional Federation of Coffee Growers, and the Conservative and Liberal regional party directorates during the several months following the military coup.[182] But the very sectors of society that might have been counted on to put a stop to privately motivated disorder—the local clergy, political leaders, prominent businessmen and landowners, police, and public employees—were precisely those most enmeshed in the perpetuation of paramilitary violence in the region. The list of future victims in Buriticá, for instance, was routinely submitted in advance to the parish priest for approval.[183]

The incidence of forced land abandonment as a result of contrachusma terror became so severe in western Antioquia that the Caja de Crédito Agrario warned the governor that it would have to deny any credit to these regions until the destabilizing contrachusmas were eradicated.[184] Antioquia's Auditoria General del Departamento (regional comptroller's office), moreover, officially declared that the bulk of the cattle stolen in Uramita, Frontino, and Chigorodó had been taken with the collusion and participation of the authorities and the government's forces.[185] Indeed, the local Conservative party members whom the Conservative directorate's *visitador especial* had found guilty in Frontino a year earlier of colluding with the authorities to resell stolen cattle and force out tenants and farmers, were once more accused in November 1953 of leading "gangs of assassins and thieves" to terrorize the inhabitants of Cañasgordas, Dabeiba, Frontino, and Buriticá.[186]

It is impossible to draw an absolute correlation between paramilitary violence, land concentration, the growth in property values, and the expansion of large-scale commercial production of sugar and cattle in western Antioquia as a result of *la Violencia*. Some data does suggest, however, that violence supported by powerful economic agents in selected western municipalities and parts of Urabá affected by contrachusma violence had long-term repercussions on local land markets and forms of production. Regional *catastro,* or property tax assessment records, contain the number of properties assessed in a given year and their total value in each municipality from 1941 through 1961.[187] Dividing total municipal land values by the number of municipal properties and the resulting value by the number of inhabitants recorded by the respective population census, enables us to form a general picture of land trends in the immediate aftermath of *la Violencia* (see appendix A.7 and A.8).

While the departmental average for the number of properties per capita in Antioquia between 1941 and 1958 was .13, towns in western Antioquia and Urabá figured among the fifteen Antioqueño municipalities with the least number of properties per capita. The average number of properties per capita in Turbo, Sabanalarga, Santa Fé de Antioquia, and Dabeiba was half or less than half the departmental average. The towns experiencing the greatest increase in the value of properties per capita in Antioquia between 1941 and 1958, moreover, were those dedicated to the production of cattle, commercial agriculture (such as sugar processing, cacao, rice, rubber, and coconuts) and wood extraction. These included Chigorodó and Turbo in Urabá, and Buriticá, Anzá, and Ituango in western Antioquia. Land values in these areas outstripped even the value of land in industrial towns, the traditional leaders in land values in Antioquia through 1941. For the period encompassed by the land tax survey of 1958 and 1961, moreover, the town with the greatest increase in the average value of property was Frontino. This was the very municipality where the contrachusma was most actively mobilized by up-and-coming businessmen and landowners to promote their economic interests and where the strongest evidence for the collusion of these forces in land usurpations and cattle-rustling was collected by the regional authorities.

Indeed, both the absolute and relative growth of property values in western and Urabá towns was phenomenal between 1941 and 1958 and again between 1958 and 1961. Chigorodó went from an average value per property of 419 pesos in 1941 to 5,900 pesos in 1958 and 20,975 in 1961. Dabeiba experienced a similar rise in property values during the same period, climbing from 876 pesos in 1941 to 5,064 in 1958 and 21,661 in 1961. Frontino whose average property value amounted to 842 pesos in 1941 and 1,687 pesos in 1958, posted the fourth-highest average property value in all of Antioquia by 1961 (25,063 pesos). Sabanalarga, a major center of contrachusma organization, registered the department's third-highest average property value in 1961. It had risen from an average of 865 pesos in 1941 to 3,568 in 1958 to 28,781 in 1961.

While the completion of the Carretera al Mar may partially account for the rise in property values in towns such as Turbo, Chigorodó, and Dabeiba, it cannot account alone for either the concentration of land ownership or increase in land values in the area: The road did not run through either Sabanalarga or Frontino, the western municipalities with the highest growth in average property values. What all the towns experiencing the most dramatic increases in average local property values had in common was the presence or operation of well-organized paramilitary forces supported by and deployed in cattle-rustling, theft, worker elimination, and land usurpation by sectors of the economically powerful.

Conclusion

The military coup that brought an end to Conservative rule failed to bring peace to western Antioquia. This was at least in part a result of the fact that beyond the partisan antagonism that had fueled initial unrest in Antioquia, *la Violencia* had laid bare the weakness of the state's authority and invalidated any claim to a monopoly of force in Colombia. It was true that the guerrillas in western Antioquia had access to arms, logistical information, and supplies that exceeded on occasion those available to the government's own forces, but the cause of continuing violence in the region was not primarily instigated by the Liberal guerrillas. It was the lack of consensus within the regional and central government and within the regional Conservative party, coupled with an absence of trust between the government and its own armed forces, that first doomed the state's efforts to contain unrest in the region. Moreover, when the state handed over responsibility for the maintenance of public order to armed, informally constituted groups of partisans, it lost legitimacy and credibility not only among the alienated opposition but also among many of its own supporters.

   Whatever the nature of the disputes initially catalyzing unrest in western Antioquia and Urabá—and in most cases these disputes were partisan, although inextricably linked to economic and cultural issues as well—by the official conclusion of *la Violencia,* Liberal guerrilla containment and the imposition of partisan hegemony were not the overriding objectives of public order forces. Indeed, it is hard to escape the impression that for distinct local sectors what began as partisan violence eventually evolved into unprecedented opportunities for personal profit that, contrary to the stated objectives of groups such as the contrachusma, required the persistence and not the conclusion of violence to thrive. In effect, the state and local forces not only promoted violence, they maintained it long after the justification of unrest—the existence of organized armed insurrection led by members of the opposition—had ceased.

Betulia, March 2000. People
are displaced in the aftermath
of repeated battles between
paramilitaries Autodefensas
Unidas de Colombia (AUC)
and members of the Fuerzas
Armadas Revolucionarias de
Colombia (FARC) guerrillas
on the border between Urrao
and Betulia.

4. Urrao and the Southwest

AUTHOR: Why weren't you killed?

GRACIELA URREGO, GUERRILLA COMPANION: Because God was on our side and the devil was on theirs.

Seeing as how the inhabitants of La Mina and La Guamala have given great support to bandits [*bandoleros*] since the War of the Thousand Days, [I], the undersigned, without consulting with my superiors, but with the best intentions, ordered the complete disoccupation of these hamlets. . . . There is no reason to offer safeguards to the enemy in places where the families of honorable Conservatives cannot live. — Major Arturo Velásquez Acosta

The area most associated with *la Violencia* in Antioquia is the southwest, specifically Urrao. Its experience has been the benchmark by which regional violence between 1946 and 1953 has historically been measured. Yet, in many ways the trajectory and character of violence in the southwest followed a quite different path from what was typical of violence in eastern Antioquia, the west, and Urabá, the other areas of Antioquia where violence was severe. Part of the reason why *la Violencia* and the southwest have become synonymous may have to do with the fact that in certain ways southwestern violence appears to conform most exactly to what became, in hindsight, the idealized version of *la Violencia*. Conservatives opposed Liberals, Liberals took up arms to defend their party, and when the military toppled the Conservative government of Laureano Gómez, Liberal guerrillas put down their arms, accepted amnesty, and *la Violencia* came to an end. It is a tale of loss and tragedy, but it is also heroic and familiar: a tale in which the two sides and their objectives were clearly drawn in a pattern reminiscent of the nineteenth century's civil wars. Or, as the wife of Urrao's former guerrilla leader succinctly put it, "We knew what we were fighting about then, but what are they fighting about now?"[1]

In the southwest, there were no outside migrants, militant unionized workers, ethnic hatreds or overt rivalries over resources and land to muddy the development of *la Violencia* or to suggest that its ultimate purpose had been more complex than a straightforward partisan dispute. A recognizable language existed—the language of traditional partisan politics—to constitute a familiar frame of reference among Antioqueños and other Colombians for thinking about violence, regardless of how extreme, as the product of age-old hatreds. When what was fought over were principles and loyalties intelligible to all, the conflict between people who had only shortly before been neighbors, friends, business associates, and kin could be infused with a kind of nobility (and inevitability). This was particularly the case when the objectives of struggle in the southwest seemed not to call into question the distribution of power in Colombian society or its basic economic and social arrangements as it did in eastern Antioquia, the west, and Urabá.

Violence in the southwest is worthy of study precisely because its trajectory seems to have differed so markedly from the way violence evolved elsewhere in Antioquia during the same period. The most commonly accepted version of *la Violencia,* in other words, was the regional exception, not the rule. Yet, even in the southwest where violence appears to have reproduced an uncomplicated version of *la Violencia*—a conflict waged exclusively around partisan issues—ambiguity as to the exact objectives of violence also surfaced by 1952, particularly in relation to the distribution of land and jobs. The presence of a struggle over land in certain southwestern towns, especially those characterized by large estates, suggests that *la Violencia,* at least in Antioquia, was a dress rehearsal for the explicitly Marxist-inspired land struggles that emerged in the 1960s and that are still a critical determinant of Colombian violence today. If this was so even in an area of supposedly traditional settlement, what inhibited violence in the southwest from becoming the vicious internecine struggle over material resources and rights that it ultimately became in eastern and western Antioquia?

Why did violence manage to remain relatively contained in the southwest? Why was the state able to eventually defeat the guerrillas without recourse to the paramilitary organizations to which it alienated its authority over public order in other parts of Antioquia? And, finally, why was Urrao, the southwestern epicenter of *la Violencia,* able, as other regions affected by violence were not, to heal the vestiges of fratricidal conflict and reknit the bonds of collective identity in the aftermath of *la Violencia*?

Redefining the Geographic Parameters of Southwestern Violence

The term "southwestern violence" is a bit of a misnomer. As a map of the towns affected by violence in the southwest makes clear, violence was not a generalized phenomenon throughout the southwest (see map 13). While nearly all the towns of the coffee-producing southwest experienced some electoral conflict between 1946 and 1949 and/or suffered from violence spearheaded by regional Conservative appointees, only Urrao, Betulia, Salgar, and, to a lesser degree Concordia and Bolívar experienced violence generated by conflicts between armed Liberal guerrillas and government forces from 1950 to 1953.[2] Of these five towns, four were important coffee producers, although in Urrao, where the guerrillas were concentrated, coffee played but a minor role in the local economy. What linked these five towns into a coherent area of violence was the emergence of armed Liberal resistance in Urrao. Violence radiated out from Urrao to affect surrounding municipalities. For these reasons, in the analysis which follows, the bulk of the narrative will focus on Urrao and only secondarily on the four southwestern and two western municipalities that fell within the radius of Urrao's influence.

While technically Urrao is considered part of the administrative subunit known as *suroeste* (southwest), it resembles and is linked by interest and location more appropriately with the administrative area known as *occidente* (the west). The municipality is situated in a broad valley crisscrossed by clear streams and the Penderisco River. To the west, dense jungle forms a natural boundary between Urrao and the Pacific lowland department of Chocó, while to the northwest Urrao abuts the sparsely settled municipality of Murindó in Urabá. Tropical highlands (the Paramo de Frontino) separate Urrao from Frontino and the Urabá peninsula to the northeast. The southwestern coffee belt ends at Urrao's southern border. Situated between wilderness and "civilization," Urrao formed an intermediate space or gateway between the frontier of traditional Antioqueño settlement and the less explored territories of Chocó and Urabá.

With the exception of several hamlets along Urrao's southern border where smallholder coffee farms flourished, the town's economy revolved around ranching, the cultivation of sugarcane, the manufacture and sale of moonshine, contraband, *guaqueria* (the unearthing and sale of items from Indian burial grounds), and subsistence farming. The more acces-

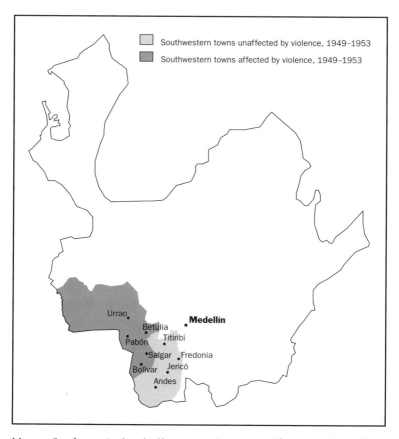

Map 13. Southwest Antioquia (Source: Instituto Geográfico Augustín Codazzi; Archivo Privado del Señor Gobernador de Antioquia, 1949–1953; Archivo de la Secretaría de Gobierno de Antioquia, 1949–1953)

sible land was concentrated in large estates, some of whose twentieth-century titleholders were descended from colonial owners. A considerable amount of land, however, remained as *tierras baldías,* or public lands, covered in dense forest and jungle. Nearly four thousand square kilometers of total land made Urrao Antioquia's second largest municipality by area (after Turbo in Urabá) with a population of approximately twenty thousand at the onset of *la Violencia.* However, this population was concentrated, and the vast majority of the municipality's territory was uninhabited.

Urraeños perceived themselves and were perceived by other Antioqueños as independent, rebellious, fierce individuals with a reputation for licentious behavior and an iconoclastic attitude toward life. Like frontier towns elsewhere in Latin America, economic survival and social comportment in Urrao often revolved around activities at the margin of licit society.[3] The fortunes of many otherwise "respectable" inhabitants were the product of the opportunities for illicit gain offered by Urrao's unique topography and location. Contraband had flowed freely since colonial times from the Gulf of Darien through the Atrato River in Chocó and from there into Urrao's countless hidden paths and streams. Locals had developed ingenious systems for smuggling goods and arms in and out of the region, and these systems stood them in good stead during *la Violencia.*

Smugglers capitalized on local beliefs in witchcraft and animism by camouflaging contraband in coffins that were paraded through the jungle borders of the municipality by men dressed in sheets and accompanied by flickering torches in the dead of night. The fear of encountering angry spirits effectively deterred both regional customs officials and local policemen from pursuing such incidents too closely, and this was a boon to armed insurgents who knew the terrain and the power of local superstition only too well. The tenacity of local resistance was expressed as well in a long tradition of moonshine distilleries which no amount of aggressive customs revenue pursuit had ever managed to dislodge. Regional customs agents still ruefully complained in the 1950s that Urrao's illegally produced local cane liquor (*tapetusa*) was so popular that it consistently forced the regional liquor monopoly to reduce its prices just to compete.

Nonconformity took social as well as economic forms in Urrao. Middle-class norms of piety and respectability that formed the basis of the regional ideal of Antioqueño comportment rarely operated in a consistent fashion there. Many of the town's residents typically lived in free union rather than in legally sanctioned marriages, and the rate of illegitimate births was considerably higher than the regional norm.[4] The town abounded in taverns and brothels. These facets contributed to Urrao's regional stereotype as a place of loose morals and radical political tendencies. Coffee farmers from nearby towns whose behavior was closely scrutinized by parish priests and the Legion of Mary perpetuated Urrao's fame as a moral-free zone by fleeing to it during holidays to find release in prostitutes and drink.

In addition to its reputation as a place of "misrule" where the restrictions of conservative, smallholder, ultra-Catholic society could be temporarily shed, Urrao was famous for the independent spirit of its local inhabitants and their defense of local autonomy.[5] The town's reputation dated back to the colonial period when Urrao became a place of refuge for free people of color, runaway slaves, and others fleeing the restrictions of Santa Fé de Antioquia's mining and ranching economy to the northwest. The area's natural attractions—its lush vegetation, gentle hills, and sparsely inhabited valleys of well-irrigated land and abundant woods—offered a respite from colonial scrutiny and demands. Antioquia's archives are filled with lengthy petitions and drawn-out lawsuits initiated by Urrao's lowborn, free people of color against abuses exercised by powerful landlords and colonial bureaucrats. Although few such petitions were successful, a precedent of local resistance and an unwillingness to subordinate local needs to established rules of hierarchy and power continued to form an important aspect of local lore and self-representation in Urrao throughout the period of *la Violencia*.

Urrao was also famous as a center of Liberal fervor in a historically Conservative department. Liberals had always controlled the majority of the town's public offices and wealth. This did not change when the Conservative party came to power in 1946, but, like other Liberal towns in the 1940s, local Liberals were divided. The bulk of the town's Liberals voted for the official party candidate, Gabriel Turbay, in the 1946 presidential election, but *gaitanistas* were in control of the local town council in 1947.[6] Urrao's Conservatives, who constituted perhaps 20 percent of the town's eligible electorate, primarily identified with the moderate politics of Mariano Ospina Pérez, although some support for Laureano Gómez existed as well. It was not until the assassination of Jorge Eliécer Gaitán in April 1948, however, that local Liberals had any sense that their monopoly over local authority might be endangered by the rise to power at the regional and national levels of the Conservative party.

As news of the assassination spread, Liberals in towns to the south of Urrao, such as Andes and Venecia, especially those characterized by a concentration of men employed by the railroad and in public road construction, organized demonstrations to protest the Liberal leader's death with the support of Liberal municipal policemen and local public employees. Governor Dionisio Arango Ferrer responded to these protests by promoting the formation of Conservative volunteer forces. These were concentrated in the southwestern municipality of Andes and in Bolívar.

Arango Ferrer also deployed army troops to guard against possible insurrection in Fredonia, Jardín, Andes, Betania, Tarso, Pueblorrico, Salgar, Bolívar, Betulia, and Urrao, but fears of imminent rebellion proved unwarranted.[7] No incidents of unrest or partisan skirmishes were reported either in Urrao or in other southwestern municipalities during the year following Gaitán's demise.

In February 1949, however, Urrao's mayor and the Liberal town council president wrote Antioquia's governor (by then moderate Fernando Gómez Martinez) to request an immediate audience. A variety of administrative issues were beginning to create tensions among the local citizenry.[8] The parish priest, an ardent *laureanista* named Manuel Zapata, was accused of conspiring to establish a meat monopoly and of increasingly intruding on the secular prerogatives of the municipal authorities in an attempt to consolidate his position as a local power broker.[9] A marginalized Conservative schoolteacher was making threatening noises about the local Liberal monopoly of offices and was clamoring to be appointed as town clerk. Embroiled in a bitter battle with a divided municipal council in Medellín and threatened with the city's bankruptcy, Governor Gómez Martinez paid scant attention to Urrao's complaints. The governor then unpleasantly surprised the town by appointing a Conservative mayor without consulting local officials. The newly appointed mayor snubbed Urrao's Liberal officeholders and refused to collaborate with the local municipal council. It seemed increasingly evident that the regional government was intent on eclipsing the authority of Urrao's Liberal majority and its elected representatives.

Administrative tensions involving predominantly Liberal municipal councils and Conservative appointees to municipal public office emerged in other southwestern towns around the same time in early 1949. A month after the events in Urrao, the recently appointed Conservative mayor of Valparaiso informed the governor's office that he had uncovered a dynamite-making operation, ammunition, and arms in a local Liberal politician's house, and accused the politician of preparing a local revolt against the Conservative authorities.[10] Two weeks later the mayor and police chief of Jericó assaulted two Liberal *visitadores fiscales* (regionally appointed legal aides) who had been sent to review irregularities in the municipal account books. Moreover, in Bolívar, where the memory of Gaitán's assassination and the Conservative repression in its aftermath was still fresh, disturbances on the April anniversary of the fallen leader's death prompted the governor to deploy ten policemen to preempt the spread of unrest to nearby municipalities.[11]

Neither escalating tensions between members of the Liberal and Conservative parties nor the usurpation of local authority by Conservative appointees, however, impeded predominantly Liberal southwestern towns such as Urrao from returning a resounding victory for Liberal candidates in the municipal council elections of June 1949. Seven Liberals—four of them self-described *gaitanistas*—and two moderate Conservatives won seats on Urrao's town council. Temporarily emboldened by their ability to resist Conservative pressure without resort to violence, Urrao's political leaders continued to express their grievances with the regional government through petitions, letter-writing campaigns, and bipartisan meetings of local party representatives.

By September 1949, however, peaceful attempts to oppose the regional government's conservatization campaign had come to naught. The mayor who had been named by the governor preferred to coordinate his activities with Father Zapata rather than cooperate with Urrao's popularly elected officials. Real municipal power began to rest increasingly in the reactionary priest's hands. He hand-picked victims for public humiliation and beatings and directed the local police to carry them out. On September 30, 1949, Liberals and moderate Conservatives from the town council called an emergency meeting to discuss the deterioration of relations between the parties and the priest's excesses. But the mayor, whom the council had especially invited, failed to attend.[12] Two weeks later, a procession led by Conservatives from nearby towns and Urrao's few *laureanista* supporters took over the town square. Bearing aloft the statue of the Virgin of Fatima, a small group of drunken, armed men shot up the bust of Liberal hero Rafael Uribe Uribe in Urrao's central plaza.[13]

Fights escalated in the aftermath of the Virgin's appearance. Brawls broke out in local taverns and served as dress rehearsals for the organization of Liberal armed resistance. Chócolo, who became a prominent member of Urrao's Liberal guerrillas, heckled and insulted departmental police agents and local Conservatives from the safety of the cantina Cantaclaro in December 1949. "Go ahead and abuse us you son of bitch Conservatives [*godos*], our day is coming soon!" the town heard him shout defiantly, as unsympathetic *laureanistas* stared. Conservative complaints in the town judicial records dismissed Chócolo as an "antisocial" who "provokes peaceful citizens . . . inciting them to fight" and a "rabble-rouser" who flaunted his relationship with a prominent Liberal lawyer and politician as proof of his impunity and power.[14] But Chócolo's outburst served as a warning about the growing unease of the town's Liberal majority whose only outlet was through raucous insults issued under the protective guise of inebriation.[15]

The presidents of the local Liberal and Conservative parties, in contrast, were careful to eschew any incendiary action. They preferred to respond to violence by sending the governor reports in which they accused the mayor and the police of encouraging citizens to loot stores and attack the town's inhabitants. They sent copies of their complaints to regional and central authorities, Medellín's private producer associations (FENALCO, FEDECAFE, and ANDI), and the city's principal industrial boards (Coltejer, Fabricato, Litografía de Bédout, and Cervunion).[16] Urrao's party leaders seem to have still been laboring under the impression that a threat to the local economy would mobilize the region's elite against the local spread of violence. But the region's elite was enmeshed in its own ineffectual attempt to restrain the regional government from engaging in partisan activities and proved deaf or too impotent to address Urrao's petition. Instead, those daring to make public the misuse of authority by Conservative public appointees were met with swift reprisals by local extremists. One individual's office and its contents were set afire, another's gas station was threatened with arson, a moderate priest was beaten up, and a prominent moderate Conservative committee member was forced to leave town or be killed.[17] In the days that followed these events, local *laureanistas* destroyed or invalidated local Liberals' national identity cards, while Father Zapata directed the police to conduct lynchings and *aplanchamientos*.[18]

When the central government declared a state of siege in November, the president of Urrao's town council, who was a Liberal, and his close friend and fellow council member, a moderate Conservative, decided to act independently of their respective party directorates and take the matter of public order into their own hands. The two men were concerned that violence waged by the regional authorities and Conservative outsiders would irreparably alter what had been competitive but not openly violent relations between local members of the two parties. They also feared that their own ability to influence events in the town was rapidly ebbing away as regional appointees and previously marginal elements within the town insinuated themselves into positions of power. These men resolved to consult the two institutions they continued to believe could still influence government policies and the town's fate: the church and the military.[19] Separately and secretly, so as not to arouse the suspicions of the regionally appointed local authorities, each traveled to meet the bishop of Santa Fé de Antioquia, the ecclesiastical head of Urrao's parish, and the commander of Antioquia's army base in Medellín. They begged Bishop Luis Andrade Valderrama to remove Father Zapata and begged Colonel Eduardo Villamil to send soldiers to regulate the behavior of the police.

The religious and military leaders to whom these councilmen appealed were not chosen haphazardly. Each had forged a reputation of tolerance and rectitude and had publicly expressed disapproval of partisan violence. For several years prior to *la Violencia,* Bishop Andrade Valderrama had issued letters warning parish priests under his authority to abstain from using partisan rhetoric or the pulpit to influence politics.[20] In retaliation, extremist Conservatives spread rumors that the bishop was conspiring in a possible "general uprising led by Liberals."[21] Colonel Villamil was similarly distrusted by sectors of the Conservative regional bureaucracy as his attitude of neutrality was misinterpreted as advocacy of Liberal interests.[22] Both Andrade Valderrama and Villamil agreed to help Urrao's elected representatives. The offending priest was eventually posted elsewhere, and in the interim a less partisan prelate was appointed to mitigate Father Zapata's influence in Urrao. The deployment of soldiers was equally remembered by locals as a significant deterrent to police abuses. Urraeños insisted that until 1951 when Colonel Villamil was removed from his post in Medellín, and aerial strafing against local guerrillas began, the army occupied a neutral, even sympathetic presence within the town.[23] But despite the attempt undertaken by Urrao's Liberal and Conservative representatives to mediate incipient partisan conflict in nonviolent ways, they proved unable to prevent the emergence of Urrao as a prime site of armed Liberal and Conservative struggle between 1950 and 1953.

The Organization of Urrao's Liberal Guerrillas

Local lore states that a man named Juan de Jesus Franco arrived in Pabón, a southern hamlet in Urrao near the border with Betulia and Salgar, with nothing more than the clothes on his back, a letter of introduction from national Liberal party leader, Carlos Lleras Restrepo, tucked in his shoe, and the change from the bus fare given to him by Liberal party head-quarters in Medellín.[24] In June 1953 after the Conservative party had been toppled from power, in a letter to Antioquia's military governor, Pío-quinto Rengifo, Franco gave his reasons for taking up arms and his choice of Urrao as the site for an armed insurrection. A lifelong Liberal who had taken little overt part in party affairs before *la Violencia,* Franco claimed that his political education began when he attended a meeting held at Medellín's Liberal party headquarters shortly after Gaitán's assassination. During the session, armed Conservatives attacked the Liberal offices, de-stroyed party propaganda, and vandalized the premises. After the melee, several Liberals were hauled off to prison. Franco was among them.

This event convinced Urrao's future guerrilla leader that only arms could defend his party and restore it to power. He approached the Lib-eral directorate and asked the members to cover his travel expenses to Urrao. Dubious, but figuring there was little to lose, the directorate sup-posedly agreed.[25] Franco's choice of Urrao was shaped by a prior stint in the army and police; he had once been stationed in the western town and found its difficult, broken terrain, proximity to the jungles of Chocó, and staunchly Liberal population advantageous for mounting an insur-rectionary group. The story may be more apocryphal than true; despite Franco's signature at the end of his public apologia for taking up arms, it was a member of Medellín's Liberal directorate, not the guerrilla leader himself who penned the missive to Antioquia's military governor. Con-cerned lest Franco "go down as a mere bandit," the Liberal party officer had felt compelled to justify the emergence of armed popular rebellion and to reassure the regional authorities that such groups had been politi-cally motivated, not merely criminal, and that their ideology had been Liberal not Communist.[26]

When Franco arrived in Urrao he found the vestiges of an earlier armed group organized by a man named Arturo Rodríguez. Rodríguez, whom Liberal leaders in Medellín later referred to as a glorified bandit (*bandolero*), had left about a dozen men with a few shotguns wander-ing about the hills outside town when he abandoned Urrao and moved to Dabeiba. Rodríguez ultimately established one of Antioquia's most powerful guerrilla camps (Camparusia) in Dabeiba.[27] Shortly afterward, Franco was joined by a strapping, blue-eyed, blond recruit, known affec-tionately as "*El Mister,*" who came from the department of Valle and contributed his Liberal fervor and machine gun to the local effort to form a guerrilla band. As news of Franco's arrival spread throughout the region, young Liberals who were persecuted in their towns of origin flocked to Pabón, the village where the guerrillas established their main headquarters. In addition to men from Urrao, others came from Salgar, Caicedo, and parts of Betulia. The majority of guerrilla recruits, however, were local men and boys from Urrao. No men, the guerrillas later fiercely insisted, had joined from Altamira, the Betulia parish dominated by the reactionary priest, Manuel Vargas, who personally recruited and armed Conservative civilian volunteers to counter Urrao's guerrillas.

Franco's men eventually ranged across most of the western region of Antioquia (see map 14). Pabón's forces were linked to guerrilla bases in Camparusia and worked the areas along the Carretera al Mar connecting Antioquia to Urabá, west along the border with the Chocó (with Ramón Elías Calle's men in El Carmen, Chocó), and south and southeast through Salgar, Bolívar, and Caicedo. There were infrequent reports of guerrillas sighted as far south as Jardín in the heart of the southwestern coffee zone, and as far north as Mutatá in Urabá, but the core of Franco's group was concentrated in the hills and jungle between the Chocó, Urrao, and Dabeiba. Their range of operation included Urrao, Caicedo, Betulia, Salgar, Bolívar, Anzá, Santa Fé de Antioquia, Peque, Frontino, Dabeiba, and various towns in the Chocó such as El Carmen. To great advantage, the guerrillas established their bases in what government agents later ruefully concluded was "a relatively inaccessible region."[28]

Official estimates of the size of the guerrilla group varied between eight hundred and several thousand.[29] However, former guerrillas calculated that a core group of one hundred fifty permanent men, which could swell to three hundred or more in times of combat, was a more realistic assessment of the number of men up in arms in Pabón.[30] The marked difference between these estimates of the group's size reflects the government's initial failure to defeat the guerrillas. In order to excuse the ineptitude of government forces, particularly the police, it became necessary to wildly exaggerate the enemy's number, arms, and range. The guerrillas also contributed to misperceptions about their number. To improve their negotiating position with the central state, they claimed to have incorporated many more recruits than the actual number of men who reported to the Fourth Brigade seeking official amnesty after the military came to power in June 1953.

Map 14. Guerrilla operations and movement from Urrao (Source: Instituto Geográfico Augustín Codazzi; Archivo Privado del Señor Gobernador de Antioquia, 1949–1953; Archivo de la Secretaría de Gobierno de Antioquia, 1949–1953)

Initially, all those who wanted to join the guerrillas were accepted. Recruitment became more selective in late 1950 and early 1951 as the members of Franco's band became wary of possible spies and were unwilling to integrate those prompted to join the guerrillas by a romantic notion of the outlaw life or who were motivated solely by revenge. Only those who could produce a letter of introduction from their respective Liberal party committee — and, some said, who knew the secret handshake — could hope to be admitted.[31] The guerrillas were organized in a series of camps, each of which was under the leadership of a single man, typically a member of the guerrilla's *plana mayor*, or junta. Each camp had between twenty and forty recruits who operated over a specific territory. Military

hierarchy defined the guerrilla group's internal structure of command: at
the top a supreme commander (Captain Franco), next a group of about
twenty lieutenants and sergeants, and, at the bottom, the rank and file.[32]
Assignments were made on a daily or weekly basis and posted on a camp
blackboard. Officers were armed with rifles or automatic pistols; rank and
file soldiers used shotguns or machetes. Only officers had "official" caps
(*kepis*) and sported police or army fatigues, the other men were dressed
as *paisanos,* that is, in common rural civilian dress: ruana, khaki pants,
white shirt, and felt or straw hat.[33]

Franco's men built a foundry to repair and manufacture arms, appointed a number of male cooks who never engaged in combat, and employed male nurses. Medicine and food were prepared and stored in the
guerrilla camps but were rationed out to individual guerrillas so that they
could take them home to share with their wives and children. The guerrillas set up mobile *rancherías* (groups of huts) a short distance from
headquarters so that women remained in constant contact with their hus-
bands, lovers, and kin up in arms. Supplies, clothes, ammunition, and
smuggled goods were kept in the rancherías, as well as sewing machines
for the manufacture of uniforms. A distinctive feature of Urrao's guerrillas — one not found in any of the other guerrilla forces operating in either
Antioquia or the rest of Colombia — was the incorporation of Catholic
ritual into daily guerrilla life. Guerrilla encampments boasted a portable
altar and shrine for the three figures of guerrilla devotion: the Virgin of
Mount Carmel, the miraculous Child of Buga, and the Holy Trinity.[34] Before each battle the guerrillas would gather around the makeshift altar
and say the rosary or recite the *trisagio.*[35] One member of the guerrillas
was always on duty to ensure that the altar was carried away to safety
should government forces ever attack the camp. Many years later members of the group insisted that they had lost so few men despite the heavy
militarization of the region because "God was on our side and the devil
was on theirs."[36] Father Ramirez, who eventually replaced Father Zapata,
visited the camps to say Mass, conduct baptisms and marriages, and con-
sole the guerrillas. (Disapproving Conservatives said the priest drank and
danced with the guerrillas, too.) With the exception of the male nurses
and cooks — employed rather than women to "avoid possible jealousies"
among the men — the guerrillas reproduced the coordinates of rural domestic life within the camps.[37]

The core of the armed organization was made up of clansmen. Seven

Urrego brothers from Caicedo, who had moved to Urrao with their sisters (one of whom, Graciela, became Franco's common-law wife) were joined by families such as the Cañolas and Cartagenas. The list of guerrillas incarcerated after *la Violencia* in "La Ladera" prison in Medellín or listed in Urrao's parish registry of the deceased is rife with networks of uncles and nephews, sons and fathers, brothers and cousins. They joined up all together or individually as they rotated between guerrilla activity and scratching out a living as farmers and day laborers (*jornaleros*). Recruitment and conflict frequently grew out of long-standing family feuds. Liberal Urregos, for instance, joined Franco, while their longtime enemies, the Cossios and Montoya Montoyas from Caicedo, made up the ranks of the police and Conservative contrachusma in nearby towns.[38] The intricacies of kin-based loyalty—in which many families included members affiliated with both parties, especially through marriage—and dispute meant that Conservatives sometimes joined the guerrillas as well. The men who formed part of Urrao's guerrillas were well and widely known to the local population. A large number of the town's families had at least one near or distant relative involved in guerrilla activities. When testimony was taken from civilians who had had contact with Franco's band, they frequently referred to the guerrillas by name, situating them within established local family networks and neighborhoods. One Urrao farmer noted, for instance, that when he was stopped by guerrillas who patrolled the rural areas and who exacted a kind of tax on goods transported to and from peasant fields, he "was perfectly familiar with" three of the five men who accosted him.[39]

Urrao's womenfolk played a pivotal role in maintaining the link between civilian and armed resistance in ways that seem not to have been reproduced to such a degree in any of the other guerrilla occupied areas within Antioquia. Women served as spies, messengers, providers of food and clothing, carriers of arms, and informal sentries.[40] They penetrated the police lines when the town was occupied, shifting critical information across a broad network of rumor and gossip that wrapped the town in a close-knit relationship of conspiracy and complicity. Like the *soldaderas* (camp followers) of the Mexican Revolution, Urrao's women followed the guerrilla camps from place to place ensuring that life was organized like a household, where religious devotion, regular conjugal relations, and ritualized festivities reproduced local customs and formed an integral part of war.[41] In the lulls between armed encounters, women and men held the threat of death at bay with boisterous drinking and dancing enlivened by impromptu music strummed on rough-hewn instruments. Women were so intimately a part of guerrilla organization that government spies sent to observe the composition of the guerrilla camps around Urrao reported with astonishment the presence of "at least fifteen women."[42]

The omnipresence of women among Urrao's guerrilla forces appears to have ensured the maintenance of social and sexual norms of conduct dictated by local custom.[43] Unlike other areas of Antioquia, for instance, guerrilla warfare in Urrao appears not to have involved the systematic use of rape or sexual mutilation. In areas where guerrillas were made up largely of nonlocals or *forasteros* and where the battlefront and home-fronts were divorced from each other, in contrast, rape, sexual abduction, and mutilation appear to have been common.[44] Much of the guerrillas' popular support was contingent upon avoiding rape or torture in their treatment of civilian enemies and the local population. Indeed, Urrao's guerrillas became known for sparing women and children in villages or settlements they attacked—often warning them in advance of an attack—and concentrating their violent activities against male heads of household and the police.

Women within Urrao who had no direct contact with the guerrillas and who felt ambivalent about the use of popularly led violence against a legally elected (if disliked) government, agreed that the guerrillas had distinguished themselves from many of the government's troops precisely because they did not widely engage in rape. The daughter of the local Liberal Party chief, who noted with distaste that the guerrilla leader Franco was a swarthy, impulsive, hard-drinking man, nonetheless pointed out that he was able to maintain discipline over his followers. In fact, Franco imposed the death penalty upon members of his band who took part in the two acts which he considered violated the norms of legitimate warfare: rape and torture.[45] Although this draconian measure met with resistance within the guerrilla group and was not consistently obeyed, it constituted an important way in which the guerrillas could differentiate themselves from the authorities.[46] This is not to say that rape did not occur, but rather that a widespread perception existed—corroborated by testimony and judicial records—that it was a tactic more frequently employed by the authorities than the guerrillas. At the very least, rape was punished harshly by the guerrillas.

Cross-class cooperation and support for the guerrillas in the interests of local and partisan defense was another critical component of Urrao's experience during *la Violencia*. That is, while cross-class alliances and collusion certainly characterized relations between members of the Liberal guerrillas in eastern Antioquia, Urabá, and western Antioquia, in Urrao the end result of this was not the advancement of the interests of specific landlords or merchants but the defense of the town and the Liberal party. A woman of elevated social class within Urrao remembered waiting every night until her husband fell asleep and then crawling across the floor of their bedroom to the balcony that faced the town's main street. Outside, police sentries posted at the doors of prominent Liberal homes would chat with each other and let slip strategically important information about troop deployments, arms, and reinforcements. The woman would eavesdrop, memorize the information, and pass it on to her sister who in turn passed it on to members of the guerrilla group. Another sister, known as a local Mata Hari, made it her duty to flirt with local policemen in the hopes of extracting valuable information.[47]

In this manner, the web of complicity was drawn to incorporate nearly everyone in the town. The Sisters of the Poor, who ran the local hospital and dispensed medicine, sent the guerrillas penicillin and other drugs on the sly. Local merchants—before the town was so heavily policed that it became impossible to smuggle out food or merchandise—sold the guerrillas matches, candles, lard, cigarettes, and cloth, while local farmers, including several Conservatives, sent the guerrillas food and molasses loaves. Even children had a role to play as they used their routine ubiquity to drift between the police station, the army headquarters, the school, the streets, and home, picking up information, observing details, acting as the town's "ears."[48] So pronounced was the degree of everyday conspiratorial participation in Urrao that the regional authorities came to regard the townspeople in their entirety as enemies. Nowhere else in Antioquia did *visitadores* or army officials who were sent to analyze the situation of violence report as they did for Urrao that "the majority of the local people are untrustworthy since they are all partisans of the *bandoleros* who inhabit the hills surrounding the municipality and who they absolutely adore."[49]

Even if it were not true that everyone in the town "adored" the guerrillas, the very fact that the authorities thought so and assumed that the town as a whole could not be trusted, encouraged and reinforced a sense of local identity and collective purpose. This sense of collective involvement enabled local inhabitants to justify having taken up arms against the government. This local sense that they were invested in a just cause and that it had been the government that had left them no option but to take up arms extended beyond Liberal party lines to incorporate Conservatives who refused to actively endorse the use of violence for partisan purposes against their neighbors. The Conservative in charge of the local airport—a critical point of contact and access between Medellín, the cattle-rich towns around Urrao, and strategically placed Urabá—was removed in 1951 because his lifelong friendship with several prominent local Liberals made him suspect of complicity with them.[50] Conservative telegraphers who were thought to sympathize with local Liberals suffered the same fate. For the first two years of armed struggle (1950–1952), the tight interaction between guerrillas and the civilian population made it nearly impossible for the regional administration and its troops to locate, penetrate, or attack the guerrilla groups. Even when the regional authorities succeeded in choking off outside support to the guerrillas and reduced them to intermittent defensive attacks by 1953, the struggle between guerrillas and authorities never advanced beyond one of attrition and stalemate; neither side could win an outright victory.

The Initiation of Guerrilla Conflict

The first incidents of organized guerrilla violence in the southwest took place not long after the November 1949 presidential election and Chócolo's drunken outburst in the Cantaclaro bar. On December 1, several dead and wounded Conservative peasants were found on outlying farms that had been burned to the ground in the vicinity of Concordia and Betulia.[51] The event set off a battle between the soldiers and the national police troops who were sent to investigate the crime and pursue the guerrillas.[52] This blatant show of internal dissension within the government's forces encouraged the guerrillas to think that undermining the Conservative government would prove a relatively simple affair. Soon after this incident, rumors similar to those which had become common in western Antioquia and Urabá flourished. In towns such as Salgar and Betulia, rumors alleged that the army was sympathetic to the Liberal rebels and that the police were the minions of the Conservative government.[53]

The national police's extensive use of intimidation and physical violence (beatings, armed assaults, and arson) during the November presidential elections was the immediate catalyst for the armed retaliatory Liberal attacks which began against Conservatives in December 1949. The behavior of the police and their Conservative civilian aides even prompted the commander of Medellín's Fourth Brigade, Colonel Eduardo Villamil, to advise the minister of government in Bogotá — because his requests to Governor Eduardo Berrío had been ignored — of the need to remove the departmental police agents stationed in Betulia and Venecia. These policemen were led by Captain Arturo Velásquez, an officer who made no bones about his Conservative sympathies and who the military commander noted "had been [in the area] too long, making it impossible to pacify the town without replacing the agents responsible for leading local abuses." With the support of Conservative civilians, drunken national police agents had on several occasions fired their guns at the unarmed Liberal citizenry several times until, finally, the army interceded to disarm them.[54]

During the first half of 1950, violence around Urrao was limited to periodic assaults on coffee and cattle haciendas in Urrao proper and the *corregimiento* of La Camara in Salgar and did not involve warfare between armed groups of Liberal and Conservative antagonists or the guerrillas and the armed forces. The guerrillas forcibly dislodged Conservative peasants from areas such as La Camara and took over their properties. Franco's men also secured control of Puerto Arquía on the Chocó border and killed the Antioqueño authorities stationed to monitor the entry of contraband through the port.[55] These initial acts of violence met with no organized government response because the number of police and army troops stationed in Urrao was insufficient to allow for deployments into the countryside. Instead, the mayors of Betulia, Salgar, and Concordia gathered together national policemen, one hundred Conservative civilian volunteers, customs agents from Betulia, and policemen and Conservative civilians from Urrao and stationed them along the Betulia and Urrao border.[56] These forces were used to keep at bay guerrillas in Pabón after rumors began to circulate in late June 1950 that they were planning a major attack.[57]

By July, however, the expected guerrilla attack had failed to materialize. Instead, Pabón's guerrillas focused on rustling cattle from Conservative haciendas such as that owned by Francisco Ospina Pérez, the Colombian president's brother, in Concordia.[58] In the meantime, the mayor of Betulia (where no guerrilla actions had yet occurred) took it upon himself

to appoint and arm additional "civic" policemen, that is contrachusmas.
Colonel Villamil made it clear to Governor Berrío that the mobilization of contrachusmas in Betulia constituted an unnecessary provocation
since in his opinion there were more than enough national policemen
and soldiers assigned to the area to oversee public order matters.[59] The
guerrillas, in any case, had not yet engaged in any major confrontation,
thus avoiding actions that might force them into a showdown with the
government's forces. Instead, they continued to force Conservative peasants off lands that were located in areas of difficult access, selectively ambushed the police and stole their arms, and penetrated and took control
of important coffee plantations in the settlements of El Planchón, La Margarita, and La Camara in Salgar.[60] The guerrillas were biding their time,
building up their store of arms, gaining control of territory, and eliminating local Conservative men who might be recruited by the contrachusma.
Unlike the sporadic guerrilla attacks that took place during this period
in eastern and western Antioquia, Urrao's guerrillas targeted members
of the opposition and estates, not government offices or officers for attack. By late July, the local Conservative committee reported that Liberal
guerrillas operating in La Camara numbered two hundred and that they
were well armed as they had attacked "defenseless" Conservatives and
their single police escort with a machine gun.[61]

By August 1, Conservatives in Urrao and Salgar were in a panic. They
demanded that the government immediately deploy one hundred fifty
men to defend the area and its economy from guerrilla assassinations of
Conservatives, the usurpation of coffee estates, and cattle-rustling.[62] But
despite his earlier assurances of sufficient personnel to oversee the region,
the commander of the Fourth Brigade was unable to provide more than
fifty national policemen to the town because of all his other troops were
already deployed elsewhere in anticipation of violent protests against
Laureano Gómez's inauguration as president. The guerrillas had astutely
waited until just before the inauguration to strike, knowing that Liberal
protests were likely to explode in numerous places and that the government's forces would be reduced and dispersed. The military commander
was forced to concentrate his few men within the urban perimeter of the
towns likeliest to erupt in violence, leaving the guerrillas free to act unimpeded in the countryside. The commander could do little otherwise, for
as he pragmatically noted, "with the existent personnel at my disposal we
can only attend to the public defense needs of the urban center and under

no circumstances the hamlets or villages where the *bandoleros* are actually located."⁶³ Meanwhile, fear of property attacks similar to those occurring daily in Salgar and Urrao convinced other southwestern towns that it was pointless to rely on the regional or central government to supply troops. They requested and bought arms from the regional government to arm contrachusmas instead.⁶⁴

Numerous assassinations of Conservatives occurred in and around Urrao in early August 1950 at exactly the same moment in which Liberal guerrilla forces in the Bajo Cauca, Urabá, and western Antioquia went on a similar spree of killing and house burning. Indeed, from this moment on, every major guerrilla attack that took place in Urrao or its immediate environs was echoed in similar guerrilla attacks throughout Antioquia.⁶⁵ The national police and their contrachusma aides retaliated against the wave of assassinations by killing ten Liberal peasants in the hamlet of Guasabra in the western municipality of Santa Fé de Antioquia, but they did not attempt to penetrate guerrilla-dominated territory in Urrao itself.⁶⁶ Two weeks into August, another fifteen Conservatives were assassinated in rural Urrao, while more Conservatives were forced to give up their farms and goods to the guerrillas.⁶⁷ When the number of Conservative refugees seeking asylum within Urrao's town limits swelled to more than a hundred, local Conservatives impatient with the government's failure to attend to their pleas for help threatened to "mobilize two thousand men in the southwest to avenge the blood of our fellow party members."⁶⁸ Then, as suddenly as guerrilla attacks had begun, they stopped. No further violent incidents were reported during the next three months, which was the period of the main coffee harvest season.

The guerrilla's activities during the early days of August set the temporal pattern and general character of future violence in the southwest. Attacks occurred most frequently in July and August before the onset of the main coffee harvest—a period in which large numbers of men were without jobs or partially unemployed and beginning to be desperate for food and money. Guerrilla activity was next most intense in February, March, and April, just before and at the onset of the *travesia,* during the coffee crop's second flush. The second harvest typically employed less than half the labor force of the main harvest. Guerrilla activities were preceded by the *boleteo* (written messages sent to threaten potential victims and exact a forced contribution); the penetration of isolated or unpatrolled villages and settlements; the confiscation of land, arms, and food; widespread cattle-rustling; and selective assassination and arson. If the victims of guerrilla aggression were police agents, they were typically shown no mercy. Before entering an area and burning it down, guerrillas sometimes advised Conservatives to leave if they were not "*sapos*" ("toads" or informants) for the regional government or contrachusma sympathizers. Peasants too poor or unable to travel to Medellín to seek refuge were forced to seek asylum within the nearest town.[69]

Guerrillas were slower to consolidate their presence and activities in Urrao than were guerrilla groups elsewhere in Antioquia, but once they did, violence quickly escalated and spread. In December 1950 guerrillas resumed their assassinations of Conservative peasants in Urrao and nearby Betulia and then attacked Urrao's army barracks and the town itself in the early hours of the morning of December 14.[70] Nearly two weeks passed before the government was able to lead a retaliatory attack, but on December 27 the military strafed and mortared the area of Guasabra in Betulia where guerrilla forces had pushed out Conservative peasants and established a base of operations. Unfortunately, as the military itself admitted some time later, the deployment of heavy armament against the guerrillas proved largely ineffective. The logistical implications of transporting men and arms to guerrilla-occupied areas made the government's approach known to everyone in the area long before the actual initiation of military activity. By the time troops arrived in Betulia, the guerrillas had melted into the surrounding hills and taken their stolen livestock with them.

Capitalizing on the weakness of the government's forces and their inability to penetrate into isolated regions of guerrilla support, Franco's men aggressively spread and consolidated their presence and control over a broad territory. The guerrillas occupied the settlements of Orobugo, Santa Isabel, Pabón, and San José in Urrao and took control of northwestern Betulia during the first half of 1951. By May of that year the guerrillas had bases in the neighboring department of Chocó, up through the region of Urabá, and in the southwest. Reports of killing, arson, and theft increased accordingly, although the intensity of these varied from area to area. Betulia complained that the guerrillas recruited young peasant men, engaged in widespread cattle theft, extorted and intimidated wealthy townspeople, and went on rampages burning the homes of Conservative peasants and resettling Liberal peasants or their own guerrilla recruits in such areas.[71] But in Salgar and Concordia, complaints regarding the presence of the guerrillas focused primarily on their extensive cattle-rustling and coffee theft rather than on the assassination or displacement of peasants.

The elimination of members of the opposition from particular hamlets appears to have obeyed the logic of personal feuds, partisan differences, and intermunicipal rivalries, and it was in the context of forcibly displacing individuals from such contested areas that the greatest incidence of brutality was reported. On two separate occasions in 1950, Antioquia's Conservative party representatives prefaced their pleas for government action, additional judges, and public order personnel with descriptions of guerrilla barbarity directed against their party members. Summing up the events of the year, they reported that by late December twenty Conservatives had been assassinated in Urrao during the preceding months and that the preferred guerrilla tactic was to invade regions and kill "everyone," women and children as well as adult men. Guerrillas were accused of raping and sexually mutilating women in the presence of their families. The killings were done "with a truly horrifying degree of cruelty and butchery."[72]

Without denying the veracity of these reports, I found that explicit references to sexual violence and mutilation were rare in official reports, judicial testimony, or the complaints regarding violence perpetrated by Urrao's guerrilla forces that were forwarded to the governor's office in Antioquia.[73] In contrast, complaints of extortion, cattle-rustling, and the forced displacement of people from settlements that were about to be burned to the ground were the most commonly reported incidents of violence. Indeed, when more sensationalist accounts were invoked in reports of public disorder, they tended to constitute a rhetorical strategy, a prelude to far more detailed and lengthy complaints of economic violence.[74] The report of twenty dead Conservatives in Urrao, for instance, dedicated less than a paragraph to mourning the victims of violence or describing what had happened to them but spent more than two pages detailing the economic and social effects of tolerating such violence. The guerrilla actions "seriously injured the local economy because of the abandonment of rural areas [and] harvests" while "the considerable number of people left without employment [who] suffer the rigors of hunger and misery" constituted "a real social problem." "Banditry," moreover, had begun to spill over into adjacent municipalities. The complaint's principal concern was once more the economic effect of violence: "several incidents of coffee looting had already occurred, as had orders to hand over significant sums of money."[75] Affluent hacienda owners from Urrao, for instance, had begun to relocate to Betulia to seek protection in what had emerged as a contrachusma stronghold. The *corregimiento* of Buchadó, on the Chocó side of the border with Antioquia, Salgar, and Concordia, and the hamlets along the Carretera al Mar also reported similar incidents of economically motivated out-migration.[76]

The few local accounts (typically written by Conservatives) alleging acts of barbarity or torture that were sent to the regional government tended to be viewed with some skepticism, perhaps because conflicting versions so frequently surrounded a single event. Regional authorities also appear to have suspected that exaggeration and sensationalism were strategies used by local Conservatives to justify demands for arms and the right to organize paramilitary organizations that might well exceed or escape the control of either the party or the regional government.[77] Betulia's request for one hundred fifty reinforcements and the appointment of a "trustworthy" army officer—a ploy characteristically used to replace appointed officers who would not conform to local civilian demands—after a guerrilla attack spilled over into the municipality, for instance, elicited a restrained response from the commander of the Fourth Brigade. He advised his second in command in the area to "safeguard your independence, don't allow yourself to be counseled by civilians who, in order to be believed by you, should present evidence and not mere rumors."[78]

In his instructions to his subordinate, the army commander touched upon a sensitive issue at the heart of public order matters and violence in Antioquia. The interests of those affected and taking part in *la Violencia* were many and complex, and gossip and rumor created an atmosphere of confusion and distrust. Death might be swift, but reliable firsthand reports describing the conditions in which it occurred were few. Days or even weeks might elapse before the regional or central governments received news of local affairs, and a similar amount of time might pass before government agents or troops were deployed to the scene of violence. Delays and conflicting reports made the identification of the perpetrators of violence nearly impossible. Confusion led the governor of Antioquia to complain in private to his friend the minister of foreign affairs in March 1951 that he no longer knew what violence was about. Liberals and Conservatives attacked their own party members as well as the opposition, reports of the size and reach of guerrillas were unreliable and constantly shifting, and internal divisions within the party made consensus about public policy impossible.[79] Three months later when Urrao's Conservative committee president berated the governor for "doing nothing to stem the tide of violence" affecting the southwest, Governor Henao responded in frustration that it was difficult to know exactly what to do "since our fellow party members in areas affected by violence suggest different strategies not only regarding the deployment of the armed forces but also with regard to the tactics these should adopt."[80]

In a rough draft of a letter to President Laureano Gómez in the same year, the governor was forced to acknowledge, moreover, that his repeated orders that public officials be impartial and respect the opposition's civil rights were routinely subverted or ignored.[81] For example, in April 1951 the governor had ordered the engineer in charge of overseeing public road construction between Urrao, Betulia, Concordia, and Bolombolo to speed up work on the section between Concordia and Bolombolo as a way of facilitating troop deployments to the southwest. Betulia's mayor and police chief, however, arrested the workers and threatened to kill them because they were "Urraeños-Paboneños" (i.e., suspected Liberals and guerrilla sympathizers). When the engineer confronted Betulia's authorities about disobeying the governor's orders, the mayor belligerently responded, "that I should come and complain in person and then I'd see that the same thing would happen to me." The mayor then sneeringly instructed the engineer to tell the governor that "if the government is interested in finishing the section of road between Bolombolo and Concordia, they should request personnel from the mayor and he'd have these ready in half an hour, but that he wasn't about to accept *forasteros* around there."[82]

A city-bred professional had run up against the ugly underbelly of power at the municipal level. There, petty tyrants like the "group of police agents [*polizontes*] who radiate aggression everywhere" ruled with impunity and could submit regional appointees like the engineer to the humiliation of having his belongings ransacked "by a bunch of illiterates." As the engineer (who was a Conservative) sadly concluded, "you'd have to have experienced the pain to understand what it felt like."[83] Little wonder then that governors like Braulio Henao did not know whom to believe and how many men to deploy in defense of public order. Towns in the same region could report that the guerrillas "are not very numerous" and six months later that they numbered a thousand.[84] Indeed, military strategists eventually came to suspect that such conflicting rumors were either a guerrilla strategy to distract and disperse the government's limited forces in order to facilitate guerrilla attacks on unpatrolled areas or they were the ploy of local authorities to further their own private vendettas and interests.

Growing Fears of the Economic Effect of Violence

In August 1951, largely in response to events in Urrao, Governor Braulio Henao Mejía sent an urgent request for arms to the minister of government in Bogotá. Less than two-thirds of the department's national police force was armed (750 out of 1,150), and many of its weapons were outdated or unserviceable.[85] Four months earlier, the governor had notified the president that the soldiers stationed in Urrao needed six new automatic rifles to meet the quality and number of guerrilla arms.[86] An inventory of arms provided by an ex-guerrilla and cross-referenced with the list of arms submitted by the guerrillas when they sought amnesty in 1953 confirms that Franco's men were well provisioned. They possessed machetes, peinillas, 200 *escuadras* (automatic pistols), 95 revolvers, 150 shotguns, 400 rifles, 3 machine guns, and 23 boxes of ammunition.[87] It was also rumored that Liberals obtained contraband arms from the Caribbean through Urabá and that the department of Valle had sent Urrao's Liberals a machine gun to aid in the area's defense.

By 1951, the fears of economic decline in the heart of the department's coffee region and the anxiety that the guerrillas were better armed than the armed forces—and also were rapidly gaining ground in the southwest where the regional government had historically regarded itself as exerting effective control—spurred the regional government to take the threat of armed insurrection in the area very seriously. While the number of people killed was not spectacular, the loss of cattle was. Guerrillas reported with some glee that they had survived for an entire year on the cattle confiscated from the haciendas of their former enemy, Father Zapata, and former president Mariano Ospina Pérez (whose family owned land in Urrao).[88] In the same month Urrao's Conservative committee (which had been keeping careful records and periodically updating them for the regional authorities) insisted that 3,000 head of cattle had been stolen in Urrao alone, 300 houses had been burned and, 59 Conservatives had been murdered since late 1949.[89] Similar calculations prompted the Caja de

Credito Agrario, Minero y Industrial to insist that the only way to restore order in the area would be to deploy one thousand men to patrol the area in and around Urrao. Had such a measure been implemented, it would have tied up almost all of Antioquia's available troops.[90] Instead, the regional government settled on a two-pronged course of action. Cannon and machine-gun fire had proved ineffective in stopping the guerrillas, and the government's forces had been unable to penetrate the enemy's networks of local support.[91] The governor decided that the army should shift tactics and use military planes to bomb guerrilla camps while imposing severe restrictions on the sale of all goods and the movement of cattle in the region.

On September 30, the army bombed Bocas de Peque to stop a guerrilla retreat from the area.[92] Two weeks later, a joint operation by the air force, army, and national police used planes to bomb and strafe a guerrilla-held area near "La Despensa." Stolen cattle were recovered, but the government's forces found only women and children in the area and no guerrillas.[93] On November 15, aerial strafing was directed against the guerrillas' main camp in Caríazul on the Cerro de Pabón.[94] This time, the guerrillas knew in advance about the government plan to bomb them, and they reacted accordingly. Franco spread his people throughout the targeted area and used cattle as decoys. The bombs killed eighty head of cattle, but only three humans. The army claimed a victory even though no guerrillas were captured, while the guerrillas congratulated themselves on foiling the government's attempt to destroy them and their followers.[95]

The initiation of bombing in 1951 marked a shift in the struggle between the guerrillas and the government. Any real or purported secret agreement to avoid confrontation between the guerrillas and army leaders stationed in Urrao came to an end. Franco was said to have declared that from now on "they [the guerrillas] were to shoot at any helmet [*cachucha*]," and the army expanded its definition of bandits to include anyone who might be perceived to aid the guerrillas or disagree with the Conservative government.[96] Increasingly, moreover, a division of labor and tactics began to characterize official responses to guerrilla violence. The military concentrated its efforts upon eradicating guerrilla camps and supply lines, bombing them or conducting pincer movements involving the coordination of troops in several municipalities, but avoided one-on-one retaliatory sweeps in the towns affected by guerrilla action.[97] The police and civilian Conservative forces, on the other hand, tended to respond to guerrilla attacks by selectively targeting Liberal-dominated hamlets and settlements regardless of whether or not these were areas where guerrillas were present or had recently struck. After a series of guerrilla assaults on hamlets in Urrao in August 1951, for instance, police and contrachusmas attacked supposed subversives and Liberal civilians in towns such as Salgar and Betulia where no guerrilla actions had taken place.[98]

During the main coffee harvest of 1951, guerrilla and government military activity ceased as it had the year before, but on January 23, 1952, a troop of "six hundred guerrillas" resumed their activities by attacking El Yerbal in Betulia. Two weeks later, twenty-five guerrillas attacked a Conservative hacienda in Urrao, destroying the house and killing the Conservative mayordomo. Next, on February 18, the guerrillas killed seven soldiers in Pabón, burned down eight houses near the town of Betulia, and torched six more houses and assassinated two conservatives near Morelia in Concordia. The guerrillas culminated their spree in early March by leading an ambush on the government's forces in Urrao, killing three soldiers, three policemen, and wounding five others.[99] No government action against the guerrillas took place until mid-March, nearly a month after the guerrillas first initiated their attacks. The government's failure to respond to guerrilla assaults on the region prompted Urrao's Conservative party committee to complain that the death toll of Conservatives killed by the guerrillas in Urrao had risen to seventy-six and to denounce Governor Braulio Henao Mejía's administration for being incapable of defeating the guerrillas.[100]

As was true of Conservatives in western Antioquia, southwestern Conservatives had been pressing since the time of Gaitán's assassination for the right to organize their own armed groups as a way of responding more rapidly to guerrilla attacks. These groups were already active by 1950 in towns such as Betulia, but despite frequent threats to "take matters into their own hands," few permanent contrachusma groups had actually emerged in the southwest between 1950 and 1952. Municipal requests for arms or for additional logistical support to expand already established contrachusma forces were given added impetus in 1952, however, when local Conservatives—like their counterparts in eastern and western Antioquia—began to lose faith in the state's ability to defend them or their properties. Conservative patience with the regional governmental response to guerrilla attacks wore out around the time that Governor

Braulio Henao Mejía also began to despair of ever possessing sufficient troops to adequately patrol the region.

Conservatives in the southwest were also increasingly likely to view the national police with whom they shared a common political affiliation as cowardly, poorly armed, and too intent on lining their own pockets to be reliable allies in the struggle against Liberal guerrillas. Conservative charges that the police were ineffectual and corrupt were confirmed just a short time after the guerrilla attacks of early 1952. The townspeople of Salgar accused the police of ignoring the guerrillas but assassinating the mayor and engaging in extensive robberies against haciendas in both Salgar and Bolívar. Locals then interpreted the inadequacy of state forces through the lens of regional and ethnic xenophobia. The problem, local officials insisted, was that the police were not Antioqueños: "When the police were made up of men from Antioquia who were drawn from the same areas in which they were posted to serve, these sorts of assassinations and robberies never occurred nor was anyone's life ever vulnerable as it is today when one sees every policeman as a potential murderer or thief. This state of affairs can only be explained by the fact that the police are not from Antioquia and are brought from other parts of the country where the life of the citizenry has no value."[101] A month later, when twenty soldiers were found dead in Concordia, local Conservatives insisted that they not be sent any more "outsider" policemen but rather be given twenty rifles with which to arm themselves.[102]

Betulia's Conservative citizens, moreover, devised what they considered to be a perfect plan to defeat the guerrillas that avoided dealing with the police or the military, which they did not trust. They proposed giving "honorable people" a shotgun so that they might defend themselves, and they pushed for passage of a law that would exempt self-defense killings from being tried as homicides. They also demanded that rural Liberals be denied any commodities not produced on the land itself (such as salt, clothing, and cigarettes). This would make them suffer just as Conservatives displaced from their homes did. They insisted as well that any Liberals found to act as spies for the guerrillas be treated as criminals just as the guerrillas were.[103]

The growing desire for revenge made the struggle between government forces and the guerrillas more brutal. In an encounter between policemen and guerrillas in the *corregimiento* of El Yerbal in Betulia in March 1952, men led by Franco's right-hand man, the guerrilla leader

"El Mister," shot three police and tore out the eyes and tongue of one of them.[104] Such acts made it politically more difficult for Governor Henao Mejía to resist local demands that he distribute arms "so that locals might form *chusmas* and gangs [*pandillas*] that would perpetrate the same actions as the Liberals do and, in this way, apply the law of an "eye for an eye" [*la ley del talión*]," as one disapproving Conservative public employee in Titiribí put it.[105] Whether he was aware of the danger of endorsing what amounted to an official license to mete out justice or not, the governor eventually capitulated to local demands for arms. Both Concordia and Betulia were among those receiving government-issued guns later that month.[106]

The strengthening of paramilitary responses to guerrilla attacks initially had the same effect in the area surrounding Urrao as it did in other parts of Antioquia: it increased rather than lessened the intensity of local conflict. With only a brief respite in July, Urrao's Liberal forces led assaults against La Camara in Salgar, several different hamlets in Betulia and Urrao, Morelia in Concordia, and the area of Anocozca between Urrao, Abriaquí, and Caicedo. They cleared these areas of Conservative settlers between June and August, right before the beginning of the main coffee harvest, in a deliberate effort to create a broad swath of exclusive Liberal-controlled territory that emergent contrachusma forces would find impossible to penetrate. The government, as usual, did not immediately respond to these attacks. Instead, when the guerrillas returned once more to their bases to concentrate on the coffee harvest in October, the military organized a pincer movement to block the guerrillas' escape route from Guasabra in Caicedo to La Encarnación in Urrao. This netted the government 247 head of stolen cattle, enabled them to destroy all the guerrilla camps and safe houses along the way, and to kill forty-five men up in arms.[107]

At this point, the struggle in Urrao developed in directions that profoundly affected the outcome and long-term consequences of violence in the region. The elimination of Conservative men who might have swelled the forces of contrachusma groups based in Betulia, Caicedo, and Concordia ensured that Conservative paramilitary organizations were never able to achieve the influence, size, or impact that such forces grew to have in western or eastern Antioquia. By killing men, the guerrillas capitalized on the weaknesses of the patriarchal family-farm model that dominated in the southwest. A highly individualistic, extensive nuclear family made up of a husband, wife, and many children was the dominant form of household organization in the areas of traditional settlement within Antioquia. Once the patriarch of such a family and his eldest sons were killed, no one remained to exact revenge but a widow who was encumbered (in most cases) by several dependent minors. Unable to work or defend the land, women and their children typically abandoned it and migrated. This strategy of clearing potential sites of opposition proved so successful that eventually policemen under the direction of officers such as Arturo Velásquez adopted it as well. Conservatives in Altamira in 1953 complained that 270 widows and their dependent children had been forced into exile in the *corregimiento* after the police killed all the Liberal men in nearby San Mateo.[108]

The guerrilla policy of killing and displacing Conservative families and forcing survivors to migrate and abandon their lands might have been expected to create or renew an upswell of local support for official attempts to combat the guerrillas. But excesses committed by national police troops deployed in Betulia, Salgar, and Caicedo, and the police's tendency to respond vindictively rather than strategically to guerrilla assaults, introduced an element of uncertainty and random terror that ultimately undermined local support for the government even among Conservative property holders. The police cast their retaliatory net so broadly that they indiscriminately attacked Liberals and Conservatives alike; merely inhabiting an area in which the guerrillas operated was enough to be deemed an accomplice of them. The indiscriminate attacks led by the government's police forces ultimately prompted private producer associations and members of the regional economic elite with extensive properties in the southwest to pressure the regional government to avoid using the police to supervise or protect the local coffee harvest. It was only in the southwest where powerful institutions such as FEDECAFE held sway that sufficient political muscle could be exercised to limit the police presence which had come to be acknowledged throughout Antioquia as one of the primary instigators of unrest. This probably saved more civilian lives than any other single action undertaken during the period of *la Violencia*. In contrast, the military's sporadic but intense campaigns to eradicate guerrilla headquarters, escape routes, and supply lines—a policy that had called down upon the governor's head the vociferous derision of extremist Conservatives—finally began to have some success in the war against armed insurrection.

The implications of these combined elements in the struggle between government forces and local insurgents were far-reaching. First, the conflict in and around Urrao never evolved into an escalation of paramilitary forces and crude, indiscriminate killing as it did in western and parts of eastern Antioquia. The ability to avoid such an outcome was aided by the relatively tight control wielded by the military over the police troops assigned to support its tactical maneuvers in the region and by the military's general reluctance to endorse or conduct joint operations with local contrachusma forces. The influence of powerful landowners in control of the production of Colombia's main export commodity was also crucial in this regard. Second, the struggle between insurgents and the army assumed the characteristics of a war waged between armed equals that, aside from the conscious elimination of Conservative men by guerrillas in selected hamlets, tended not to be indiscriminately directed at broad sections of the civilian population.

Casualty statistics tend to support the conclusion that "regular," as opposed to "irregular," warfare spared civilian lives and made a reconciliation between opposing armed factions possible in the aftermath of *la Violencia*. Reconciliation was difficult to achieve in areas where partisan conflict evolved in complex directions that included struggles over cultural, racial, and ethnic identity and where the responsibility for combating guerrillas and maintaining public order was primarily entrusted to paramilitary forces. Army and church records from 1949 to 1953 indicate a rise in the number of civilian deaths beginning in 1951 that reflects a general intensification of violence in and around Urrao.[109] The army recorded only one violent civilian death in 1950, but the number of recorded violent deaths rose to 49 in 1951 and 67 in 1952. Clashes between guerrillas and the government also appear to have increased in 1951. While the army recorded no guerrillas among the dead in either 1949 or 1950, for instance, 102 and 84 guerrillas were listed as casualties in Urrao in 1951 and 1952, respectively. More than half of the total civilian casualties recorded by the armed forces over a three-year period occurred in 1952. Of these, fifty occurred before August when contrachusma forces briefly expanded and accompanied the police on missions to wreak revenge on hamlets where no guerrillas were based (see appendix A.5).[110]

While it is certainly possible that the military consciously underestimated the number of civilian deaths and inflated the number of guerrillas killed to give its struggle greater legitimacy, local church records echo the details of official deaths registered by the army. Urrao's parish priest noted that 39 of the 452 deaths recorded in the parish registry of 1950 were the result of violence.[111] By 1951, the number had grown to 60, while in 1952—the year in which the greatest number of violent deaths were officially recorded in Antioquia—twice that many people (123) were registered as having died by violent means. Many of the dead were Liberal guerrillas. In 1953, in contrast, when most violent activity in the area was reduced to one-on-one combat between the armed forces and the guerrillas and direct attacks of guerrilla encampments, official civilian casualties declined to five.

The latter half of 1952 proved seminal for other reasons as well. In the year and half before the army initiated aerial strafing, Urrao's guerrillas had been able to capitalize upon divisions within the forces sent to control public order in the region. However, after mid-1952, greater consensus and coordination among the government's forces limited the guerrillas' ability to move easily within the region. Guerrilla access to support and supplies became increasingly difficult. Cattle-rustling continued unabated, but the government's successful attempt to limit the trade in other basic necessities such as cigarettes, matches, fuel, and salt forced the guerrillas to overextend themselves. They were obliged to seek out towns further afield where government checkpoints were less common or less effective. The search for salt was perhaps the most fraught with danger and the most urgent. Guerrillas desperately raided salt bins left out in pastures for cattle only to find that they had been poisoned by government agents hoping to force the guerrillas to surrender.[112] An important surreptitious exchange between guerrillas and merchants from towns such as Salgar, Bolívar, Ituango, and Puerto Arquía in the Chocó had to be negotiated to replace the loss of supplies from within Urrao itself.

The civilian population was also affected by government control of basic commodities and restrictions on the transportation and sale of cattle and agricultural goods that were imposed with growing intensity between March and October of 1952. The management of day-to-day survival for Urrao's civilian inhabitants became increasingly arduous. A strict system of police roadblocks emerged to limit the mobility of peasants from the surrounding countryside who traveled into Urrao on market day to buy and sell their produce, baptize their children, use the coffee credit agency, and catch up on local news. Those entering and exiting the town were individually searched to ensure that they did not carry goods that might be used to supply the guerrillas. Since the government suspected that "all of the local merchant community sends the guerrillas presents and sells them cloth and food," it implemented a system of rationing in which families were allowed to purchase and carry only the basic items needed to survive over a period of a few days.[113] Urraeños got around this by selling to third parties, smuggling out items at night, or transporting goods along the mule paths, contraband routes, and streams that crisscrossed the town and only locals knew about. But, by the end of 1952, general hardship and hunger wore down guerrilla and civilian resistance in Urrao.

The military's destruction of guerrilla bases in Caríazul on the Cerro de Pabón and government-imposed rationing gradually forced the guerrillas to scale back their activities. They either retreated into the Chocó or blended back into the agricultural working population in areas such as La Camara in Salgar. The guerrillas withdrew from open conflict in the middle of August 1952 and maintained a low profile through January of the following year. The guerrillas' decline in activity, however, was countered by a concurrent intensification of police and contrachusma activity in the area. The rise of paramilitary forces temporarily shifted the focus of violence onto the unarmed civilian population. Refugees from Urrao's countryside flooded the town, while food restrictions, constant surveillance, and the gradual intrusion of violence within the town limits made life increasingly unbearable. Individuals who had been children in Urrao during *la Violencia* remembered that mutilated bodies and fetid corpses became a familiar presence in the early morning along Urrao's main street. Children stumbled over dead bodies on the way to school or witnessed public works trucks as they dumped their macabre load before their terrified eyes.[114]

In January 1953, the attacks that had become characteristic of the seasonal cycle of violence in the southwest were resumed, but the guerrillas were noticeably weakened. They limited their activities to quick cattle theft and petty robbery of basic staples from haciendas in Caicedo, Urrao, and Salgar.[115] They resumed assassinations of Conservatives and government officers in March but conducted them in an almost haphazard fashion. Most casualties occurred when guerrillas, in the course of stealing cattle or moving their camps inadvertently stumbled upon or were surprised by government troops rather than from a conscious effort to eliminate members of the opposition.[116] In June, there were local reports that Urrao's guerrillas were active in the southwest and still engaged in robbing, arson, and assassination, but no official reports of guerrilla violence were filed with the governor's office. Guerrilla strength had essentially dissolved by late 1952. The concerted efforts of the regional government to block supplies and the movement of cattle — the sale of which was absolutely forbidden between the municipalities affected by violence around Urrao, much to the despair of local ranchers — ultimately eroded the economic basis of survival for armed Liberal revolt.

The end of *la Violencia* in Urrao was almost anticlimactic. Two months after the military led a coup against Laureano Gómez's government in June 1953, Captain Franco and several guerrilla officers were ambushed and captured in a local cantina. The guerrilla leader and trusted members of the *plana mayor* had, with considerable trepidation, agreed to meet a delegation of government representatives to discuss the conditions for a peaceful surrender. Suspecting a possible trap, several guerrillas had hung back and stationed themselves at various points in the town, but armed government agents surprised them and took Franco prisoner on August 26, 1953.[117] Franco and his surviving officers were sent to "La Ladera" prison in Medellín and, not long after, his followers surrendered their arms and accepted the political amnesty offered by General Rojas Pinilla's government. Most of Urrao's former guerrillas served sentences of several months, while Franco — the most sought-after guerrilla leader in Antioquia — was imprisoned for nearly three years. Upon his release, his unabated popularity prompted him to launch a career as a Liberal politician, but the fear that he would usurp and upstage them moved local Liberal leaders in Urrao to pressure the regional party to channel Franco's ambitions elsewhere. For a few months before his death in a mysterious drowning accident in the San Jorge River in the Chocó, Juan de Jesus Franco traveled up and down the Colombian Caribbean as an official spokesman (and hero) for the Liberal party.

Inspired by their parish priest, the citizens of Urrao marked the conclusion of armed conflict in the zone in a unique fashion. For several years, Father Ramirez had carefully kept track of the place and cause of death of his parishioners even when he had not buried them. Those who died as a result of violence had been denied Catholic burial since 1948, because they were presumed to have violated divine law in rising up against a legitimately elected government. The local priest had disagreed with this policy, but was too prudent and too closely observed by extremist Conservatives to violate it during *la Violencia*. Instead, he enlisted the relatives of the dead to provide information regarding the circumstances of death and the probable location of the bodies. After the military coup, the priest drew his parishioners together and instructed them to dig up the remains of all those who had died without the benefit of Catholic ritual. The priest and Urrao's citizens (of both parties) organized a procession and conducted a collective burial to mark the end of *la Violencia*.

Two secular rituals were also used to mark the end of *la Violencia* in Urrao. First, local Liberals raised money to hire the sculptor who had originally made the bust of Rafael Uribe Uribe that had graced the town's central square before the violent intrusion of the Virgin of Fatima in October 1949. They commissioned him to make a statue that was identical to the first. When it was ready, the municipal authorities and party leaders installed it in the central plaza amid considerable pomp. Second, the town purchased a bronze plaque and dedicated the main road leading into Urrao to Captain Juan de Jesus Franco. The entry to Urrao is still known as the "Avenida Capitán Franco," a tribute to a rebel leader without precedent in any other part of Antioquia.

No contrachusma groups survived in Urrao, although remnants briefly continued to disturb the countryside around Salgar, Bolívar, and Betulia for several months after the military came to power.[118] Still, they were too weak to constitute the threat to property and power typical of paramilitary forces active in western and parts of eastern Antioquia after June 1953. Former guerrillas who remained in the area, in contrast, enjoyed such widespread respect and legitimacy that several of them later went on to become town councilmen and officeholders in Betulia, the center of local Conservative opposition during *la Violencia*. And, in what can only be understood as a peculiar twist of history, when violence once more emerged in Urrao in the late 1950s it was led not by vindictive Conservatives seeking revenge against their Liberal adversaries, but by members of Alfonso López Michelson's Movimiento Revolucionario Liberal (MRL) who opposed the agreement to return to civilian government known as the National Front.[119] Having experienced the hardships of an outlaw life—"*la mala vida*," as the guerrillas called it—Franco's ex-combatants were unwilling to take up arms again, and their refusal made them the target of their fellow party members. Ironically, Liberal violence achieved what local Conservatives during *la Violencia* had not: former guerrillas were forced by the followers of the MRL to abandon their lands and move elsewhere, many of them joining the growing waves of rural migrants leaving for towns such as Itaguí, Envigado, and Medellín.

The Defeat of the Guerrillas

What motivated the regional government to intensify its efforts against Urrao's Liberal guerrillas so dramatically in late 1952? And what motivated them to charge the army, not paramilitary groups or the police, with the primary responsibility for combating the guerrillas? Several possible explanations exist, the most significant of which may be the ignominious assassination of ninety-six soldiers in the Llanos in July 1952. This event prompted the military to rethink its counterinsurgency strategy in Colombia and the central government to take more seriously regional complaints that "our resources of arms and men continue to be notoriously insufficient."[120] In the specific case of Urrao, moreover, the escalation in government attacks against guerrilla forces was also surely influenced by two other issues: a growing perception among regional authorities that the guerrillas posed a threat to property arrangements and production in what was considered the very heartland of Antioquia's economy and, also, the guerrillas' enduring popularity among the local population.

In June 1952, Governor Henao Mejía informed the minister of government in a coded message that there had been "a rebirth of political violence during the previous two weeks" in which Urrao's guerrillas had killed first eighteen and then another thirty male peasants.[121] The victims, the governor insisted, were consciously, not randomly chosen. Aside from the "war of nerves" that these assassinations had produced in the area, other events and information regarding the guerrillas' activities in the region combined to worry the governor that something more sinister than exclusively partisan violence was afoot. Urrao's Conservative committee had warned the governor a year earlier that the guerrilla leader, Captain Franco, was "beginning to redistribute lands in the extensive area between Pabón and its immediate vicinity."[122] The committee accused one guerrilla of being a professional real estate agent who was buying up and speculating in devalued lands owned by Conservatives who were forced to abandon the area. At the time, the governor had paid little attention to these reports.[123] In August, however, Urrao's

Conservative committee members again insisted that men, not women and children, were the primary targets of guerrilla violence and, further, that the men were killed only when they ignored the warnings to leave that were given before hamlets were attacked.[124] A month later, all of the Conservative-owned haciendas in Pabón had been abandoned and taken over by guerrilla forces. The Caja de Credito Agrario calculated that to recapture the occupied haciendas and "pacify" the area would require stationing five hundred soldiers in Pabón.[125]

Complaints of land usurpation also began to emerge from towns such as Salgar, where most land was held in large estates. The owner of a large coffee estate in La Camara complained that guerrillas had taken over private properties in the hamlet and appropriated parts of the coffee harvest since 1950 and that they were planning to do the same in 1953. In contrast to what was happening in Urrao, the estates in La Camara were not being destroyed or taken over directly by the guerrillas. The majority of La Camara's inhabitants were Liberal, as were the majority of *mayordomos,* but the estate owners were sometimes Conservative. To impede outright land confiscation, *mayordomos* and guerrillas from Urrao had worked out a deal: in return for not destroying haciendas, *mayordomos* received half the coffee production while the owner's share was given to the guerrillas.[126] Witnesses also began to report that guerrillas were paid a wage and that they alternated between making war and sowing fields on empty public lands and usurped properties.[127] Alarm began to spread among Antioquia's authorities that partisan violence masked more profoundly unsettling and radical objectives. The language employed by the guerrillas in official communiqués in 1952 contributed to this impression. In response to a peace initiative mediated by Urrao's Father Ramirez in March 1952, Captain Franco signed his decision to decline taking part in the initiative by referring to himself as the representative of "guerrillas and workers."[128]

By early 1952, the occupation of lands by guerrillas and the selective eradication of Conservative inhabitants prompted calls by government supporters for a razed-earth policy.[129] The replacement of Governor Braulio Henao Mejía in July 1952 by hard-liner Dionisio Arango Ferrer, moreover, removed any remaining obstacles to such a plan. Policemen and contrachusmas led the vanguard in areas perceived to be guerrilla-"infested." They targeted any area perceived to be under the influence of a guerrilla band—regardless of the political affiliation of the area's inhabitants — since anyone who succeeded in continuing to farm, or who could still travel between fields and home was automatically assumed to be a guerrilla sympathizer.[130] The extremes to which this policy could be taken became evident in early 1953. Conservatives who opposed the razed-earth policy in Betulia complained that contrachusma groups based in Altamira, Betulia and, El Socorro, Concordia, "do not operate where there are guerrilla bases, but in peaceful areas where everyone is dedicated to working their agricultural properties. [This] has discredited the government because it is the local authorities in such areas who support those abominable crimes."[131]

The struggle between partisan forces had become a struggle over who should have the right to inhabit, control, or farm particular areas, and the determination of that right was increasingly shaped by historical perceptions of conformity and rebellion. Or, as the infamous police chief of Betulia, Major Arturo Velásquez, succinctly put it when justifying his decision to raze two settlements and kill everyone in them: "Seeing as how the inhabitants of la Mina y la Guamala have provided great support for bandits since the War of the Thousand Days [1899–1902], the undersigned [Arturo Velásquez Acosta, Jefe Fracción], without consulting my superiors but acting with the best of intentions, ordered the disoccupation of those hamlets. . . . I felt quite sorry to do so, but I believe that where the families of honorable Conservatives can't live, there is also no reason to protect the enemy."[132] It is not my intention to underestimate the significance or depth of partisan feeling that influenced the vindictive desire to sweep clean areas of inhabitants belonging to the opposition during *la Violencia*. But several factors make it implausible to argue that politics alone shaped the emergent conflict over land even in the supposedly "nonradical" violence of the southwest. First, much of the property around which struggles occurred was concentrated in large estates. Second, the coffee frontier had effectively closed several decades earlier and with it the opportunity to own land had become more remote. Third, struggles over access to agricultural employment were intense, which suggests that jobs were increasingly insufficient and hard to come by in the region. As a whole, the department of Antioquia's census of employment by sector recorded a decline of more than two hundred thousand agricultural jobs between 1938 and 1951.[133] While census figures may reflect errors in calculation, even before *la Violencia* the number of worried editorials in Medellín's newspapers regarding high unemployment figures, scarce food, and the need to implement price controls on basic commodities would seem to support the idea that agricultural areas were experiencing a crisis. Most agricultural employment had historically been concentrated in the coffee-producing southwest and the eastern municipalities nearest Medellín. The presence of adverse economic and social conditions must necessarily be taken into account in any consideration of the ultimate impact of violence on the region. Additional data, moreover, reinforce the impression that economic considerations — however subconscious or ideologically undeveloped they may have been among the guerrillas — were intimately interwoven into the partisan concerns that underwrote armed conflict in the region.

After a military coup toppled the Conservative government in June 1953, Urrao's guerrillas would surrender only after a number of conditions were met. Among them were several that exclusively addressed the issue of credits, government aid to promote colonization, tools, seeds, and the distribution of lands to amnestied guerrillas and to "poor peasants and their families."[134] If no social agenda underpinned armed insurrection, why would demands of this nature have occupied such a significant portion of the terms of political surrender? Guerrillas also demanded that no individuals who might have exercised authority in the locality as national policemen, contrachusmas, or extremist public employees be allowed to resume positions of power in the area or be entitled to reside there. In addition to the intense animosity that would likely have characterized relations between these forces and the guerrillas, competition over scarce resources and an attempt to undo the speculative gains which some of the government-sponsored groups had achieved during *la Violencia* clearly preoccupied the guerrillas.

The guerrillas, moreover, did not voluntarily give up their arms as lore would have it. Indeed, in July of 1953 Captain Franco issued a preemptory "decree" from the mountain strongholds of western Antioquia informing Colombia's new military government of his terms for the negotiation of peace and belligerently signed it, "Mayor Franco, Commander, The Revolutionary Forces of the West and Southwest, General Guerrilla Headquarters." The tone of "Decree no. 53" is that of one military commander to another, not a subordinate to his superior as the subheading of the document attests: "Document by which certain dispositions regarding public order in the southwest, west, and north of Antioquia are decreed. These shall also apply to the department of El Chocó. The Guerrilla

Command exercising the rights conferred upon it by the High Command of the Main Revolutionaries."[135] Was this bluster? Or had Urrao's guerrilla forces moved in the direction of the Communist-led, Llanos forces whom they openly admired?[136]

But perhaps the most startling piece of evidence pointing to the importance of struggles over land in the evolution of southwestern violence was the solution for bringing *la Violencia* to an end that was suggested by ecclesiastic officials and moderate Conservatives in 1952. In March, the Conservative daily *El Colombiano* explicitly stated that violence was the result of an absence of "social justice."[137] Certain sectors of Antioquia's elite seemed to recognize publicly that mixed in with partisan hatred was an inchoate but real anger born of economic despair and the declining possibilities of ownership, opportunity, and mobility in rural Antioquia. The auxiliary bishop of Medellín, Buenaventura Jaureguí, declared publicly in April that a policy of "parceling out lands" would ensure "the salvation of the rural folk [*campesino*]."[138] This pronouncement was followed in May by an article in *El Colombiano* urging a four-point program for ending violence in the countryside. The newspaper suggested that the government "should begin to parcel out large estates [and] popular and agricultural credits should be increased" to build roads and homes with the aid of loans provided by the Instituto de Credito Territorial (Land Credit Institute). *El Colombiano* also suggested that small industries should be encouraged and subsidized with government assistance in municipalities suffering from the effects of violence.[139]

To my knowledge, no other Colombian region raised the issue of land redistribution as a central determinant of any peace negotiation to end *la Violencia* and certainly not at such an early date. Nor is there evidence in studies of other areas affected by violence of official sources that publicly attributed *la Violencia* to social and economic inequity, rather than partisan differences. Yet in Antioquia a sector of the regional elite hailed the implementation of a land redistribution program as "a mission of Christian charity [to guarantee the] patriotic defense of Colombian society and the preservation of true peace."[140] The newspaper followed up these suggestions with an editorial recommending that "wherever a situation of disorder exists and it is possible to parcel out haciendas, this should be done because nothing makes a man more orderly and responsible than attachment to the land and knowing himself to be a property owner."[141]

This was the regional political ideology of *convivialismo* writ large.

The pragmatism characteristic of Antioqueño bipartisan politics before the advent of single-party rule in 1930 once more reasserted itself
in *El Colombiano*'s analysis of the causes of violence and its needed
solutions. Antioquia's elite had always perceived a close correlation between citizenship and property ownership and were convinced from the
days of Acción Católica and the encyclicals of Pope Leo XIII that material well-being was crucial to the maintenance of social harmony and
political order. At the time of *la Violencia,* a core of regional political
leaders understood the need to rethink property and economic arrangements and the degree to which so-called partisan conflicts were linked to
broader structural conflicts in Colombian society. In hindsight it seems
nothing short of tragic that they were ignored. How much later blood-
shed might have been averted if a timely reform program had been implemented like that suggested by *El Colombiano*'s owners in 1952?

When Governor Braulio Henao Mejía was forced to resign in July because he had been unable to put an end to violence, *El Colombiano* reiterated its belief that the catalysts of violence had been neither moral nor
partisan. They insisted on attributing widespread regional unrest instead
to "the lack of food, housing, [and] education" and considered these as
"the true obstacles to achieving peace."[142] Interestingly, *El Colombiano*
specifically noted that the policy of distributing land to assuage violence
should not be limited only to Urrao. This would seem to suggest that
Urrao had emerged as the prototype for official land distribution schemes
as a solution to violence. Some Conservative extremists suggested that
no amount of land redistribution could alter the fundamentally rebellious nature of the town's inhabitants and that the only solution to the
area's problems would be to "recolonize Pabón with Conservatives from
Marinilla" and other eastern Antioqueño towns.[143] But the regional government ignored such suggestions and, when in the early 1960s the
National Land Redistribution Institute (INCORA) was founded as part of
an agrarian reform program, Urrao was among the first municipalities in
Antioquia to break up and redistribute haciendas.

Sometime in late 1952 or early 1953, moreover, the regional government commissioned a secret report regarding the nature of unrest in
Urrao and western Antioquia from what appears to have been a United
States government agent.[144] After providing an overview of the effect of
la Violencia on Urrao and the surrounding rural hamlets, the agent concluded:

Undoubtedly in the beginning [of guerrilla activity] there was a touch of politics in the acts of the bandits, they proclaimed themselves Liberal patriots, and it is almost certain that at that time they were aided by some Liberals, politics being what they are in Colombia. . . . Later, once they understood the true nature of the Liberal bandits, the majority denied them any further support and then they were treated the same way the Conservatives were. . . . It is very doubtful that there is an upstanding Liberal [*de bien*] who is now supporting the bandits.[145]

The agent went on to describe a ruined local economy in which estate owners could no longer visit their properties for fear of being killed, the wealthy had purchased plane tickets and fled, the cost of living had skyrocketed, and the only remaining inhabitants were those too poor to leave town.[146] All of this led the author of the report on Urrao to conclude that "the poor are on the verge of dying of hunger. For them it is no longer a matter of politics but a question of sheer individual survival."[147] But, even worse, the agent insisted that the public was convinced that the Colombian government had no interest in ending the conflict in Urrao: "Those who were once strong Conservatives have changed their minds. They haven't exactly become Liberals but there is no doubt that many believe that Urrao has been made a pawn in a political chess game in which the town has no bet. In other words, that the government isn't really interested in eliminating the bandits because as long as these remain active, the government will have an excuse to maintain the State of Siege."[148]

And the agent added, "Men who have empty stomachs and who see their relatives dying of hunger are desperate men. . . . Urrao is rapidly getting to the point of being fertile ground to receive Communism; not because people like it or because they understand what Communism means but simply because the Communists offer them an exit from their present difficulties. A similar situation exists in many parts of the world today."[149] Like the moderate Conservatives of *El Colombiano,* moreover, the author of this report also believed that addressing people's material needs had to be the first step in bringing violence to an end (and inhibiting the spread of Communism). "The only solution" to the region's problems, the agent argued, "is to obtain work for all those who are unemployed. . . . It is of the utmost importance to improve the morale of the people. Otherwise, anything could happen, none of it good."[150] The solution lay in expanding public works construction and military fortifications in the region so as to hire as many people as possible. The military fortifications were to be supervised and led by "the Army Engineering Corps with infantrymen of Indian descent (Quichua [*sic*]) from Nariño . . . because (a) they are accustomed to high altitudes and cold weather; (b) they are good people in the jungle; (c) by nature are inclined to be strictly disciplined so long as they have good officers; and (d) they'd probably like the work."[151] While these fortifications were under construction, all of the peasants in the area were to be removed. After "the cleansing [*limpieza*], these peasants [*campesinos*] may return to their lots and keep working without fear."[152]

Beyond extensive logistical recommendations intended to guide the development of a counterinsurgency strategy in the region, the report concluded its recommendations with a disquisition on the nature of local guerrilla strength, its connections to Communism, and the dangers that Communism posed to Colombia and Urrao. Interestingly, the agent believed that the local guerrillas had never numbered more than "two hundred altogether and no more than fifty men in any single band," figures that, while not too distant from the estimate Franco's own lieutenants gave of their group, were far below those bandied about by the government or even later researchers.[153] The agent also noted—as had former guerrillas and local Conservatives—that it was persistently "rumored that the active bandits receive a monthly salary of 120 pesos. If there is any truth to this [rumor], it is surely not Colombians who are supplying the money, but they may nonetheless be acting as the agents of outsiders [*forasteros*]."[154]

The report identified the centers of Communist infiltration in Colombia as the eastern Llanos and Western Antioquia (from Urabá to Urrao). But, "in terms of continental strategy, the Llanos in and of themselves cannot be considered important, although they may be used to constantly threaten Bogotá and so divert the attention of the government away from the area where the Communists are actually planning to do considerable damage."[155] The topography of the Atrato River Valley, the agent speculated, made it ideal for "supplying submarines," and "planes could also easily be hidden in that area [the valley below the Atrato River]. Based in the Atrato, submarines could harass traffic traveling along the Panama Canal and, using guided missiles, could damage the Gatún locks. Amphibian planes pose the same danger."[156] Urrao's guerrillas would be the smokescreen behind which Communist agents could hide, but because of the enormous sums of money involved in mounting such a project, a mechanism other than legitimate bank transfers would have to be found to launder sufficient cash to underwrite the Communist take-over of Colombia. The agent rightly noted that smuggling would prove to be the government's Achilles' heel, for the absolute lack of customs agents or other government officials deployed around Urabá's numerous points of entry or ports made it unlikely that Communists would get caught. The locals, for instance, would have little incentive to report the presence of Communist smugglers: "they won't inform for two reasons, first, for fear that the Communists will take revenge and, second, because they won't want to forfeit what will seem to them like very good wages."[157] The leaders of this smuggling plot to introduce Communism, the author of the report insisted, "come from Guatemala, since it is that country where the Communists' general headquarters for Latin America is located."[158] This was of course the moment at which U.S. propaganda and military efforts were under way to topple President Arbenz in Guatemala by accusing him of being a Communist.

The informant ended his report on the Communist danger lurking in Urrao with a dire warning to the Colombian government:

It is clear that if the state of misery continues in Urrao and other municipalities west of the Cauca River, the Communists will have a huge reserve of people from which they will be able to recruit whatever number they need when the time comes to assume control. Once the war begins, the Communists can deliver arms and officers to train natives. These will be used only in the jungle to defend submarine bases, . . . precisely the same model used by Communists in Malaysia, Indo-China, and Burma, and that they are using in Brazil and Bolivia, to say nothing of Colombia.[159]

One can dismiss conclusions such as those included in the agent's synopsis of the state of public order in Urrao and western Antioquia as little more than extreme propagandistic reactions in an emergent Cold War era of which Colombia was not immune. Colombia's Communist party was tiny, its followers were mainly concentrated among skilled artisans (typesetters, shoemakers, tailors) in cities, enclave workers along the Magdalena River, and certain urban intellectuals. There is no evidence that there were any Communist sympathizers in Urrao or its surrounding areas. But however risible predictions of a Communist takeover may have been, they nonetheless point to real anxieties about the presence of economic and social conditions perceived to be conducive to revolutionary activity in particular areas of Colombia.

Indeed, economic subsidies, technical assistance, the distribution of public lands, cheap credit, and the creation of additional public works jobs did in fact come to be adopted by Antioquia's authorities as part of a plan developed in 1953 to restore public order and rehabilitate areas affected by violence. Former guerrillas indicated that the extension of cheap credits, cattle stock through the Fondo Ganadero (Cattle Fund), and the distribution of public lands in and around Urrao had made it possible for them to eventually reinsert themselves into civilian society and survive economically after *la Violencia.*

Yet, to those intimately involved with Pabón's guerrilla forces, the notion expressed by the government agent that guerrilla objectives had deviated from the limited agenda endorsed by the official Liberal directorate and evolved into the precursor for Communist takeover in Colombia would have been deeply shocking. The testimony of Graciela Urrego, Captain Franco's widowed common-law wife, vividly underscores just what made the experience of *la Violencia* in Urrao so different from the experience of violence in other parts of Antioquia and so difficult to encompass in loaded, catchall phrases such as "radical" or "traditional."

In the mid-1980s, Graciela Urrego lived with an unmarried sister in a modest house located on the main road leading into Urrao, the same road named after her famous guerrilla husband, Captain Juan de Jesus Franco.[160] The municipal authorities had given her the house as a token of gratitude after Franco's death. But for the house and a precarious income secured by the sale of homemade sausages (*chorizos*) and popsicles (*paletas*), Graciela Urrego would have been penniless. The house stood not far from the gas station where all the trucks and buses traveling the intermunicipal roads were serviced, a place where Medellín's Liberal directorate and the local guerrillas had exchanged reports and messages via sympathetic drivers and attendants during *la Violencia.*

The world described by Graciela Urrego was divided into "good" and "bad" rather than Liberal and Conservative. She noted how there had been "good" Conservatives, for instance, who helped the guerrillas by selling needed supplies or providing crucial information and protection against despised, imported police troops and unscrupulous *arrivistes* who exploited the opportunity for personal gain and offered themselves as informants. "Bad" Conservatives included government troops who harassed and raped the women who traveled back and forth between the town and their rural residences. But there were "good" Conservatives among the government ranks, too. Guerrilla sympathizers who were among the lower ranks of the government troops sent to patrol the region warned the guerrillas and townspeople in advance about which officers to avoid or when sweeps were to be conducted against them. Indeed, Graciela was convinced that well before Franco's arrival in Urrao, a pact had been made between Eduardo Villamil, the army commander of Medellín's Fourth Brigade and the national Liberal leadership. The army commander and the Liberal leadership, she was convinced, had agreed to foment the creation of Liberal guerrilla forces throughout Antioquia and to ensure that the army would not oppose or engage in combat with them.

Graciela Urrego held as an incontrovertible truth that Liberal leader Carlos Lleras Restrepo had sanctioned the guerrillas' existence; his motto "*Fé y Dignidad*" (Faith and Dignity) was their rallying cry. As "supreme commander," Lleras supposedly sent instructions by secret code to members of Medellín's Liberal party directorate who in turn relayed these to the guerrilla leadership in Urrao. Whether or not this was true is less important than the fact that such a belief enabled Urrao's guerrillas to view themselves as individuals engaged in the legitimate defense of their party's interests rather than as mere outlaws or, more dangerously, as radicals intent upon restructuring the local terms of property tenure and labor.

Graciela Urrego remembered the period of armed resistance as both a terrible and wonderful experience. She retained—as did many other Urraeños—a sense of satisfaction or pride tinged with a sense of profound sacrifice; the taking up of arms was seen as an unfortunate but ultimately noble enterprise. And, the men and women who took part in defending their lives and the Liberal party were loyal citizens forced by circumstances beyond their control to engage in a deeply sacred struggle.

In interviews, former guerrillas and their companions repeatedly contrasted the ideals that motivated their armed struggle with contemporary guerrilla struggles in Colombia. Only those who had never had a choice but to retreat into the hills, they insisted, would willingly choose such a life—hence the reason for Urrego's and other former guerrillas' deep disapproval and contempt for contemporary Marxist-based guerrilla organizations. And, had she been aware of the "American" informant's report that posited Urrao as the next springboard of world Communism, Graciela Urrego would have been apoplectic.

Graciela Urrego's faith in her party was unshaken even when a high-ranking regional Liberal political leader came to see her in 1958 and demanded that she hand over any documents that might have been left by Franco or his command from the "old days" of *la Violencia*. The Liberal leader—originally from Peque—insisted to Urrego the need to destroy any "compromising" materials. She remained loyal even as young Liberal politicians who had been too young to take up arms or had fled to the safety of Medellín during *la Violencia* invoked her husband's name and lied about their participation in Urrao's guerrillas to enhance their chances of being elected. She remained unwavering in her loyalty when Liberals who opposed the National Front agreement turned upon the old Liberal guerrillas of *la Violencia* and forced them to migrate away from Urrao.

She remained silent and loyal throughout, buoyed by the memory of collective hardship and loss, of friendships that for a brief period had erased the barriers of class in Urrao and bound people together in a single endeavor. She was oblivious to the seminal role drawn for Urrao in the struggle for world domination. Nor did it occur to her that the guerrillas' mild redistribution efforts might have alarmed the government of the time, just as the takeovers of property led by the Marxist guerrillas she disapproved of continued to worry the same Colombian state in the 1990s. To Urrego, *la Violencia* had only been about the fight to guarantee the Liberal party's right to take part in shaping the course of Colombian history, not about the advancement of self-interest or the first stage in the creation of a new national order.

Who was right regarding the ultimate objectives and organization of Urrao's guerrilla forces or about the meaning of motivations underlying violence in the town? Graciela Urrego or the U.S. adviser to the Colombian government? If one accepts the inherent duality of historical process, no contradiction need lie at the heart of the apparent differences in interpretation between Urrego's account and that of the American agent. The point of *la Violencia,* even in supposed areas of "traditional settlement" where partisan objectives were the guiding force behind armed insurrection, is that it was multifaceted and ambiguous, that politics and economic considerations can never be considered as discrete forces, that class struggle could be waged within the confines of Conservative and Liberal ideologies without the participants in these conflicts seeing any contradiction in the demands for land and the restoration of their party to power.

Conclusions

Urrao's experience during *la Violencia* was paradoxically Antioquia's most unusual. The town took up arms against the Conservative government reluctantly and as a last resort when all possible democratic means of protest were exhausted or cut short by the state itself. There was no major support for Laureano Gómez locally, nor were the town's Liberals and Conservatives involved in violent contestation with each other between 1946 and 1949. No rebellion took place in the town after the assassination of Jorge Eliécer Gaitán in April 1948. Instead, violence emerged in response to the concerted attempts of the regional government to undermine the authority and legitimacy of the town's own democratically-elected representatives. These attempts were perceived locally as a transgression of unspoken but powerful expectations governing the relationship and negotiation of power between municipal authorities, the regional government, and the central state.

Although conflict in Urrao emerged along partisan lines, it was also more complex than this. Neither the Liberal nor the Conservative parties were monolithic. The behavior of two of Urrao's town councilmen and many of their local cronies are a telling example of the internal divisions within the parties. Memories of an older, regional tradition of bipartisan compromise and pragmatism, moreover, shaped local expectations that partisan differences could be resolved via negotiation rather than arms. This bipartisan "memory" or tradition, however, came into conflict with the new politics of extremism and partisan hegemony. Urraeños took up arms only after a long period of official harassment foreclosed the democratic possibilities of negotiating an end to conflict. In this, Urrao's experience differed from what occurred in the eastern part of Colombia where, aside from the mining towns of the northeast where unionized miners appealed to their rights as citizens to contest state harassment, no municipal tradition of political negotiation between towns and the regional state seemed to operate and where violence was introduced from outside the department rather than from within.

Although Urrao's Liberal guerrillas might not seem to have differed much from the multiple armed groups that sprang up all over Antioquia during *la Violencia,* at a deeper level, they were different. Their success was predicated in part on their ability to intersect with and build upon a preexisting history of local identity and resistance. Unlike guerrillas in other parts of Antioquia (except parts of Urabá and western Antioquia in which local clans also played a strong role), moreover, Urrao's guerrillas grew out of and were intimately linked to Urrao's civilian population rather than arbitrarily or artificially imposed from outside. This characteristic not only endowed the guerrillas with enormous popular legitimacy and support, it ensured that in the aftermath of violence Urrao's townspeople were able to feel justified and proud of their activities during *la Violencia.* This in turn enabled Urrao to enter into a process of reconciliation, to grieve collectively as no other Antioqueño town did, and, in the course of this, to transcend the horrors of war and mutual brutality.

The regional and central government's attitude toward violence in the southwest also influenced the outcome of partisan conflict in Urrao and contrasts strongly with the way the regional authorities approached the issue of partisan unrest elsewhere. First, although various towns within Urrao's range demanded and received arms to form contrachusma forces with which to combat the guerrillas as western and eastern Conservatives also did, the regional government never delegated public order responsibilities in Urrao to the contrachusma and the police as they did in other parts of Antioquia. Very early on, and despite the scarcity of trained personnel, Antioquia's regional government opted to rely on the army in their struggle to stem guerrilla activity. The regularization of conflict and the avoidance of random, vindictive strikes against Liberals in retaliation for guerrilla attacks became a seminal feature of public order strategy in Urrao. This distinguished Urrao's experience from the proliferation of paramilitary forces which became common in other Antioqueño areas severely affected by violence and saved the town from the persistent vendettas that became a permanent feature of other formerly violent areas after 1953.

Violence in Urrao also never gave way to the sorts of landlord-led paramilitary forces bent on eliminating squatters and consolidating control over land and resources common to western Antioquia. Nor did largely autonomous armies of Conservative peasants intent on stripping jobs and lands away from nonextremists in the east emerge in Urrao. Yet, *la Violencia* in Urrao did grow to involve conflicts that transcended purely "partisan" objectives. Indeed, although on the surface violence in Urrao seemed to conform to the paradigm of "safe" partisan conflict, in reality regional authorities recognized the development of armed conflict in the southwest as at least partially the result of emerging structural inequalities in Antioquia's social and economic organization and production.

Urabá. Rural folk
flee guerrilla attacks
in the Chocó and are
marshalled by the
Colombian army into
a displaced persons'
camp in Antioquia.

Epilogue

When I've been digging and I'm tired and don't want to do any more, I think how it could be me in the grave I'm working on. I wouldn't want someone to stop digging for me. . . . —Manuel, member of a forensic team in Guatemala in Michael Ondaatje's *Anil's Ghost*

When Violence Ceases to Be Academic

I finished the research for the project that eventually evolved into this book between 1989 and 1992. During two long stretches I lived in my parents' apartment in downtown Medellín, just two blocks from the Parque de Bolívar and the Metropolitan Cathedral in the heart of Medellín's commercial and financial district. From my window I heard the daily bustle of street vendors hawking *aquacates* and miracle liver-spot creams such as *concha nacar* and the constant backfire of noisy buses on the Bello circuit. The past and present seemed intimately intertwined as peddlers— the heirs to a regional tradition of snake-oil salesmen—vied comfortably with late-model automobiles and computer-controlled commercial operations. At the glass-enclosed paean to architectural modernism— the Edificio Argos—on the corner of Bolivia and the Avenida Oriental, working people waited patiently to board buses back to distant suburbs. At night I watched from my balcony as the crowds gathered at the steps of the cathedral to witness and applaud the boisterous show put on by local transvestites. On the surface there seemed nothing to suggest that fifteen minutes away young men in the city's poorer neighborhoods were being gunned down on street corners, that prostitutes, the homeless, and street children were nightly victims of "social cleansing," or that less than a few miles outside the city's limits rural folk were caught in the crossfire of guerrillas, right-wing death squads, and the armed forces. Businesses bustled, the streets were clean, the phones worked, glaring examples of misery were absent. I was struck by the possibility of multiple, dissonant, lived realities and often thought that a similar bifurcation must have characterized the average Antioqueño's experience during *la Violencia*. I began to understand how the memories and trauma of *la Violencia* were mediated by such subjective factors as social, physical, and cultural place. On the eve of the military coup in 1953, violence was one thing to the urban dweller who was constantly reminded by entrepreneurs and the authorities of the region's unstoppable prosperity and of the harmony that reigned within Medellín's factories. It was quite another to the rural folk in peripheral towns where the stench of burned bodies permeated hamlets and miserable women and children fled a razed-earth policy perpetuated by paramilitary groups with the support of government agents. It is this contingent, divergent, and unstable aspect of violence that I have tried to analyze in this book.

As I concluded my research, narcotics traffickers known as the *"Extraditables"* (led by the now-defunct Medellín drug lord, Pablo Escobar) stepped up their campaign of assassination targeting policemen and public figures to protest the threat of extradition to the United States. The governor of Antioquia, the regional head of the national police, the Liberal presidential candidate, Luis Carlos Galán, numerous local judges, and several university professors were brutally killed in the space of a few months. Every weekend, moreover, the corpses of thirty to forty young men — inhabitants of the lower-class neighborhoods that ring Medellín and are popularly known as the *comunas* — swelled the death count in addition to the politicians and public employees that constituted the alarming balance sheet of local terror. The line separating the focus of my research and daily lived existence increasingly blurred. In the mornings I worked on analyzing the data I had extracted from various local and regional archives and tried to make sense of the violence of the 1940s and 1950s. In the afternoons I took a cab to the Universidad de Antioquia and conducted closed workshops with researchers examining the emergence of death squads and youth assassin gangs in Medellín and peripheral areas such as Urabá, the Magdalena Medio, and the Bajo Cauca. I tried to see how or if the violence I studied and contemporary violence fit together. With the help of researchers from the Instituto de Estudios Regionales, we drew up maps that linked the young men from the city's most violent neighborhoods with emergent paramilitary violence in peripheral towns. At night I returned home to join in the collective evening experience of the broadcast news, to gaze numbly at bloody images of lifeless bodies, and to anesthetize the pain with the inanity of the evening soaps. I would finally fall asleep late in the evening only to leap up in terror hours later at the sound of a bomb that seemed to explode only a block or two away.

Once a week several professors from the departments of economics, psychology, history, political science, sociology, and education came together in a remote seminar room at the Universidad de Antioquia to try and make sense of the chaos that seemed to engulf us. We wrote position papers and acted as informal consultants to the mayor on the subject of violence in Medellín, the city with the dubious distinction of being the international "cocaine capital" and having the world's highest homicide rate. Several colleagues were in the midst of concluding an oral history project with inhabitants of the region then most heavily affected by the narcotics trade and armed violence (the Magdalena Medio). As I read the transcripts of these interviews I was repeatedly struck at how despite being asked about violence in the 1980s, those interviewed came back again and again to their memories of *la Violencia*. Reports in the daily papers and the reaction of Antioquia's political leaders and economic elite to the contemporary escalation of violence in the region, moreover, served to reinforce my sense of déjà vu.

During *la Violencia* and now today, complex, overlapping-yet-distinct phenomena are indiscriminately attributed to a single catalyst. In the 1950s, members of the Conservative government dismissed *la Violencia* as a partisan-based problem that could be solved through the deployment of greater force, ignoring the danger posed by locally sponsored armed groups that arose to fulfill the function of public authority abandoned by the state. In the last decade of the twentieth century, various Colombian administrations dismissed the problem of contemporary violence as one that was essentially reducible to a single issue (the emergence of the narcotics trade or leftist insurgency) and concluded as their predecessors did that selectively directed repression could bring about peace. Like their predecessors, recent administrations have ignored the danger posed by the proliferation of publicly endorsed but privately armed groups entrusted with the duty of maintaining public order. If during *la Violencia* the central culprits of violence were seen by officials as small bands of Liberal/Communist guerrillas and criminal delinquents, they were often grouped together under the generic rubric of "bandits" or "revolutionaries." Moreover, in the contemporary period, naming has been similarly imprecise. Narcotics trafficking, political dissidence, leftist insurgency, criminality, and civil disobedience are indiscriminately lumped together under the convenient denomination of first the unruly, urban slum dweller (the *sicario*) and, more recently, the "narco-guerrilla." In both instances civilians are likeliest to bear the brunt of stepped-up campaigns of violence (exercised by the state or its "enemies") rather than the armed groups supposedly responsible for promoting violence in the first place.

A comparison of past and present violence—an exercise suggested by the very people most affected by violence and whose lives have been fundamentally altered by the experience of violence in the last fifty years—highlights the significance of the Antioqueño experience during *la Violencia* and the continuities and ruptures between what might on the surface appear to be an unchanging and endemic situation of constant strife. For instance, what would it mean if violence tended to recur in the same places over time? And, if violence today still tends to be largely concentrated in the areas that were most violent at mid-century—when in principle the underlying causes of violence were quite different from what they are now—then what relationship might there be between mid-century violence and contemporary violence? Is it possible that to understand Colombian violence—not just *la Violencia*—we must ask different questions and draw different connections than the ones that have historically oriented studies of violence?

A great deal of emphasis, for instance, has been placed on the importance of partisan labels in the formation of Colombian identity and the incidence of Colombian violence. Indeed, most analysts of the violence have tended to focus almost exclusively on the nation's political history, analyzed from a top-down perspective, and traced through the history of the Liberal and Conservative parties. This book confirms that the parties were undeniably important. Partisan conflicts and differences were significant in shaping people's beliefs and comportment in Colombia as well as in producing the environment in which *la Violencia* developed. However, the Antioqueño case also makes evident that partisan identity and individual notions of citizenship and identification with the state varied quite considerably within Colombia. Ultimately, the notion of monolithic Colombian parties does not explain how people understood their participation in the parties, how politics functioned at the local and regional level or why strong identification with a particular party should have inevitably led to violence.

The variety of experiences characterizing *la Violencia* in Antioquia instead suggests the importance of considering how class, ethnicity, kinship relations, local power distribution, geography, and concepts of citizenship intersect to shape people's sense of identity and their willingness or refusal to accept violence as a legitimate political tool. In Urrao, for instance, a long history of cooperative relations between a minority of moderate Conservatives and a majority of moderate Liberals combined to ensure that local politicians exhausted nonviolent, democratic avenues of protest against the intrusion of extremist regional appointees intent on marginalizing the town's historically recognized leaders. The refusal of some regional authorities to respect the mandate of locally elected officials or to negotiate with them to resolve partisan differences eventually prompted the emergence of armed opposition groups who challenged the state, but violence was not the town's first or preferred approach. In parts of Urabá, in contrast, where no prior history of cooperation with the regional government existed and where few democratic mechanisms for the exercise of political opposition functioned, violence often appeared as the only viable response available to local inhabitants against regional authorities and policies perceived to be repressive and exclusionary.

Despite my suggestion that the history of a particular population or area's relationship with the regional or central state was a determinant factor in the way *la Violencia* evolved in Antioquia, the issues at stake during the conflict bear a greater relationship to contemporary Colombian violence than they do to the partisan-based civil wars of the nineteenth century. The "empleo-mania" (patronage-based hiring frenzy) that historian Charles Bergquist found partially fed the partisan disputes that resulted in Colombia's greatest nineteenth-century civil war, the War of the Thousand Days, for instance, appears to have been far less pronounced in Antioquia than elsewhere in Colombia. Competition for the government sinecures and access to patronage positions and influence that were controlled by the central state through partisan monopoly simply do not appear to have motivated widespread support for the War of the Thousand Days in Antioquia. But perhaps the main reason why *la Violencia* does not appear to have been a direct legacy of nineteenth-century civil conflict, however, is that it was fueled by a peculiar confluence of factors that emerged in the twentieth, not the nineteenth, century. Among these factors was the growing centralization of power in Bogotá (at the expense of local and regional power); the closing of the coffee frontier and its promise of social and economic mobility to the poor through land ownership; the expansion of industrialization without a commensurate increase in employment by mid-century; and the growing privatization of land and resources on the periphery (the traditional outlet for disappointed settlers and workers).

The closure or restriction of traditional avenues of mobility, moreover, coincided with the rise of a distinctive middle sector in both parties that was anxious to construct an electoral machine explicitly based on lower-class support. Therefore, "sectarian populism"—an important component, although not necessarily that which led to the greatest intensity of violence in Antioquia—was a phenomenon relatively new to regional, mid-twentieth-century politics. In other words, though purported ideological differences between the parties existed in both the nineteenth and twentieth centuries, the issues that fed off such partisan differences and enabled *la Violencia* to develop into intense and even endemic strife were recent in Antioquia and geographically circumscribed. It is not coincidental that the areas most severely affected during *la Violencia* were also those experiencing the greatest economic and social dislocation and transformation during the decades immediately preceding the violence, or that electoral conflict did not necessarily lead to widespread violence in core areas within Antioquia. Severe violence in twentieth-century Antioquia was the result of an intersection between geography and social unrest rooted in structural inequalities in which partisanship played a role, but not necessarily a determinant one. In contrast to the nineteenth century, moreover, the leaders of armed movements during *la Violencia* were local individuals of middle- and lower-class origin, not members of the elite (as had generally been true of nineteenth-century civil wars).

In many instances, mid-twentieth-century violence was not the spontaneous result of inherent local partisan conflict but was rather consciously spearheaded by selective sectors of the regional state or tacitly encouraged by local bosses to advance interests that had little or nothing to do with ideological differences. Armed groups were privately financed but operated in the name of the state. These findings are not unique to Antioquia's experience of *la Violencia*. Gonzalo Sánchez's work on Tolima, Keith Christie's work on Caldas, and other regional studies have suggested the existence of state-directed violence and the connection between paramilitary organizations (referred to as "pajaros" or "contrachusmas") and certain governors, regional bureaucrats, and officers of local and regional Conservative party directorates. But, while regional studies have suggested the existence of state terror as a generalized policy and assumed that such a policy was mandated from Bogotá (that is, the central state) where it enjoyed the unequivocal support of a monolithic Conservative government, the evidence from Antioquia suggests a far more complex picture of the evolution of state-sponsored violence. Regional and local authorities rather than a central state played determinant roles in promoting private terror in Antioquia and shaped the attitude of both inhabitants and party officials toward the use of violence as a political tool.

There was no consensus in Antioquia regarding the use of either official violence or the tacit endorsement or toleration of privately sponsored violence for partisan ends, however. Numerous towns and even members of the ruling Conservative party rejected the use of both official violence and private forms of terror as legitimate mechanisms for resolving civil conflict. Violence—terror, repression, homicide, forcible displacement, and rape—moreover, was selective, and the determination of its use by official forces was largely shaped by the nature of the relationship between the regional authorities or state and local populations. This relationship, moreover, was in turn shaped by ethnic, cultural, and socioeconomic factors, rather than partisan considerations alone. It was far easier, for instance, to justify and impose a regime of terror against individuals or areas perceived to deviate from a sociocultural norm of Antioqueñidad than it was to do so in centrally situated towns perceived to embody idealized regional values and practices. Thus, the direction, form, incidence, and intensity of violence was determined not only by the majority political affiliation of a particular population, but by a combination of factors that included the nature of the local economy, the distribution and use of land, the racial and ethnic identity of the inhabitants, the degree of conformity to a regional ideal of political and social organization, and the relative strength of either local forms of collective organization or the state's own ability to assert it's authority. For example, miners in Segovia were able to successfully impede the conservatization of their municipality and the violent imposition of regional appointees through active resistance and reliance on a history of radical collective association. The regional authorities' prior experience with Segovia's mining community deterred even adamant Conservative extremists from deploying paramilitary forces to repress local Liberals despite the local inhabitants' political dissidence, militant union activity, and evident failure to conform to the values of Antioqueñidad. A history of collective association and dissident political mobilization was cemented by shared cultural and ethnic practices in Segovia, while a history of alienation from the regional authorities reinforced a powerful sense of local identity and a tradition of resistance. Faced with concerted opposition in an area of strategic resources and production, the regional authorities backed down in their confrontations with the inhabitants of Segovia.

If other than strictly partisan factors shaped the regional state's decision to engage in repression rather than negotiation with local populations during *la Violencia* and if these factors shaped local perceptions of the legitimacy of the state and the legitimacy of using violence to resist the intrusion of state-sponsored violence, then we must rethink our understanding of the causes of violence and of why violence was concentrated in some areas while other areas with a similar political outlook went relatively untouched. Rethinking the causes of violence and why it took particular forms in particular areas, moreover, also requires a rethinking of the seemingly generic and generalized character that has been historically attributed to *la Violencia*.

It is difficult to know how representative the pattern of violence experienced in Antioquia may have been of violence in other parts of Colombia at mid-century. In part this is true because no other study of *la Violencia* has focused on the significance of factors other than partisanship and class as explanations of violence. The conflation of geography, strategic resources, an absent state, contrasting cultural and ethnic identities, and political dissidence in the Antioqueño areas where violence proved most severe, would nonetheless seem to suggest parallels or comparisons to other episodes of selectively intense violence in twentieth-century Latin America. For instance, in its recent inquiry into the thirty-six-year-old Guatemalan civil war in which some two hundred thousand Guatemalans were disappeared or killed, the Guatemalan Truth Commission acknowledged the role that a complicated history of racism, political intolerance, selective indigenous support for leftist insurgency, and the protection of specific economic interests played in making some groups and areas of Guatemala more likely to bear the brunt of counterinsurgency terror than others.[1] Similarly, the Peruvian state also identified specific regional populations as hotbeds of radical support for the Maoist insurgents in its recent struggle against Sendero Luminoso, tailoring its actions in such areas both in relation to the ethnic and cultural identity of the local population and the level of perceived local support for the state.[2] In both the Guatemalan and Peruvian cases, an a priori identification of particular groups as culturally distinct, coupled with a history of hostility between state and citizen, contributed to both the intensity of seemingly generalized violence and the approach applied by the state to stamp out local insurgent support. The point of the comparison to the Antioqueño case is not to suggest a simple causal relationship between racism and violence, but rather to suggest how histories of perceived difference can fundamentally shape the relationship between the state and specific groups and increase the potential for conflicts to be resolved through repression rather than negotiation. The current conflict in Chiapas, Mexico, also illustrates the intersection of ethnicity, geography, and violence. There, an area historically rich in resources, in which ownership of the land is largely concentrated in a few hands, houses a population at the margins of economic survival that is also perceived as ethnically and culturally distinct from the inhabitants of central Mexico. Much as was true in Colombia during *la Violencia,* in contemporary Chiapas, regional authorities direct, or tacitly endorse, privately sponsored armed groups to defend capitalist production and a traditional party system against indigenous insurgents and the threat of Communism.[3]

In Colombia, moreover, the coincidence of ethnicity and culture, geography, and class has persisted beyond the period of *la Violencia* to define the parameters of contemporary violence and its primary victims. The Solidarity Network, a Colombian government agency that deals with the problem of internal displacement, estimates that fighting between paramilitary groups, guerrillas, and the army has forced 1.5 million of Colombia's 40 million people to relocate since 1985. Half of these displacements have taken place between 1996 and 1999.[4] Human rights analysts estimate that the number of displaced people in Colombia is the greatest in the Western Hemisphere, but in contrast to the internal refugees in similarly war-torn societies such as Chechnya or Kosovo, Colombian refugees "are not readily distinguishable by their ethnicity, language, or religion." Paul Oquist estimated in his 1980 study of *la Violencia* in Colombia that some two million people were displaced by violence between 1948 and 1966, a time span and number of refugees comparable to that characterizing contemporary Colombian violence. The individuals forced to relocate during *la Violencia,* like contemporary refugees, were also not considered to have been distinguishable by "their ethnicity, language, or religion," although the *Violencia* refugees were in their majority distinguished by their partisan identity. In reality, however, the notion that refugees both during *la Violencia* and in contemporary Colombia are indistinguishable from the nondisplaced population is only partially true. Several organizations that track contemporary human displacement have noted the disproportionate presence of individuals of Afro-Caribbean and indigenous descent (from the Chocó, Magdalena River Valley, and Urabá, for instance) — many of whom are women and children — among the refugees of violence in Antioquia and Colombia as a whole.[5] Increasingly, moreover, those forced to relocate to cities such as Medellín eschew internment in refugee camps or the official label of "displaced person" for fear of the term's negative associations. Current refugees from peripheral areas fear that their towns of origin are assumed by urban inhabitants to be "nests" of leftist sympathizers and that their presence in particular neighborhoods will provoke retaliation by right-wing paramilitary groups.[6]

During *la Violencia* competition for scarce employment and resources in cities such as Medellín influenced tensions between established inhabitants and newly arrived rural migrants fleeing violence. But urban tensions were also shaped by perceived cultural differences between an established population drawn primarily from nearby, centrally situated municipalities and refugees from peripheral towns in western, northern, northeastern, and far eastern towns (Ituango, Frontino, Dabeiba, Caicedo, Urrao, Remedios, Caucasia, Puerto Berrío, and the port towns along the Magdalena River). These towns were thought to be "unruly" and "different" even before the advent of violence. In Alonso Salazar's interview-based account of the emergent youth assassin groups in Medellín, his respondents repeatedly allude to both a history of physical displacement from peripheral towns in the aftermath of *la Violencia* and the reproduction of violence within their families as factors that influenced their decision to become hired guns for the narcotics trade.[7] What is significant is not whether a direct correlation in fact existed, but that the perception of a relationship between geographic origin, cultural identity, and violence should have persisted and been reproduced among the very people likeliest to take part in and be affected by violence. For Salazar, the coincidence of these factors confirms the existence of a "culture of violence" in Antioquia. But I would suggest something different.

I see a continuation of the perception of dissidence and resistance attributed by the regional authorities to inhabitants from the periphery during *la Violencia* that was used to justify repression against them. Rather than a "culture" of violence, Antioqueño violence must be read against the backdrop of a history of internal colonialism and exclusion in which multiple points of difference between regional authorities and local inhabitants existed over such issues as land and resources, access to political power, and the right to self-determination. These differences have been conveniently reduced to a question of inherent rebelliousness perceived by regional authorities to threaten some idealized Antioqueño stability, regardless of the time period in question.

In current analyses of the problem of violence and internal displacement in Colombia, the victims of violence are also often characterized as "ordinary civilians" who find themselves caught in the crossfire of what are considered by international observers to be "armed groups that have been warring with increasing ferocity since the 1960's."[8] But this perception—that the problem of civilian displacement in which "ordinary" people are forced to relocate dates mainly from the emergence of leftist insurgency—is largely erroneous. *La Violencia,* not the 1960s, is the point of departure for understanding current violence. Indeed, another similarity between the contemporary period and *la Violencia* is that then, as now, the majority of those displaced are less "victims caught in the crossfire" between armed groups, than the primary targets of those armed groups.[9] In other words, only very recently in Colombia have the paramilitary groups, guerrillas, and the Colombian armed forces begun to consciously combat each other, rather than directing their actions, as has historically been the case, against an unarmed civilian population suspected of aiding or tolerating the presence of the "enemy."

As was also true during *la Violencia* (at least in Antioquia), violence in contemporary Colombia is the responsibility of both the left and the right, but the majority of those currently displaced have been forced to move by the presence of right-wing paramilitary groups, while leftist groups (the equivalent of *la Violencia*'s guerrilla groups) are responsible for approximately a third of all displacements, and the Colombian Army for less than 5 percent.[10] In both periods, moreover, paramilitary groups have grown up with the tacit support of selected members of the regional government and even the armed forces.[11] Indeed, the precedent for the current right-wing paramilitary phenomenon in Antioquia—which has now spread to other parts of Colombia, but which was first explicitly endorsed and supported by an Antioqueño governor and other regional officials and members of the departmental bourgeoisie as a quasi-official policy—may be traced back to the endorsement of the contrachusma and the legal arguments made by Antioqueño governors to justify the arming of independently organized civilian groups during *la Violencia*. The catalysts for the emergence of privately organized terror groups both during *la Violencia* and now, moreover, are nearly identical: the defense of strategically located valuable resources in areas where the state exerts little authority and does not command the loyalty or identification of the majority of the local population.

While the growth of paramilitary organizations is hardly unique to Antioquia, there are aspects of regional political practice and self-perception that have contributed to the enthusiasm with which privately organized forms of public order maintenance have been embraced in the department from the period of *la Violencia* to the present. Long before the advent of partisan strife in the 1950s, Antioquia's affluence, demographic and physical size, strategic resources, and pronounced sense of regional identity enabled it to act with considerable autonomy vis-à-vis the central state and even the national directorates of the two main parties. Regional autonomy coupled with a deeply ingrained sense of local pride persuaded Antioqueños and their leaders that they were better able to rule their department's fortunes and determine its policies than authorities based in Bogotá. A refusal to follow Bogotá's lead may paradoxically have enabled much of Antioquia to elude the partisan conflict that engulfed and paralyzed other Colombian regions between 1946 and 1949. But regional defiance of central government dictates and disagreements within the leadership of the Conservative party eventually meant that when violence did become severe in the department, governors such as Braulio Henao Mejía found themselves isolated and unable to obtain needed arms and support from the central government with which to squash armed guerrilla groups operating in peripheral areas. Faced with an absolute incapacity to maintain public order in far-flung areas where violence threatened regional control and resources strategic to Antioquia's economy, regional officers—some reluctantly, others enthusiastically—endorsed the creation of local paramilitary forces to combat guerrilla insurgency. Even after it became apparent that such groups preferred to attack civilians rather than pursue guerrillas and that they were no less prone to collusion and theft than their supposed enemies, Antioquia's authorities continued to justify the brutal actions of such groups by appealing to notions of regional identity and the defense of regional interests. The contrachusma, it was alleged, were Antioqueños through and through — unlike the national police or members of the armed forces whose "alien" customs and origins (that is from the Afro-Caribbean coast or the indigenous areas of Boyacá) endangered the very stability of Antioquia's cultural identity. Racism, regional isolationism, and desperation combined to justify terror in the name of defending departmental sovereignty and honor during *la Violencia.* This set a dangerous precedent whose reverberations may still be felt in the regional endorsement of rural and urban *autodefensas* and *convivirs,* the privately financed and publicly endorsed security or self-defense organizations that have sprung up throughout Antioquia in the wake of the armed forces' perceived inability to protect the lives and interests of rural and urban capitalists.

In the 1980s and 1990s, Antioquia once more felt abandoned by the central government and was forced to face alone an escalation of violence due to narcotics trafficking. As it became apparent to regional officials that the army and police — poorly trained and paid and too scattered to seriously engage in combat with leftist guerrillas or insufficiently motivated to go after popular narcotics dealers — would not be able to defend against a rising tide of kidnappings, homicides, and theft, Antioquia's authorities and selected members of the regional bourgeoisie once more decided that only regionally paid and organized forces made up of "dyed-in-the-wool" Antioqueños could hope to control violence. Monthly contributions elicited from harried cattle ranchers in guerrilla-controlled territories have gradually given rise to paramilitary forces whose brutal efficiency far surpasses that of the Colombian army or police. Like their predecessor organization — the contrachusma — paramilitary forces in contemporary Antioquia and Colombia have gone far beyond the initially limited mandate of self-defense to "cleanse" entire populations perceived for a variety of reasons to "deviate" from the accepted norms of political belief, economic organization, or personal association.[12]

The coincidence between the areas most affected by violence in the 1950s and the areas currently most affected by violence in Antioquia today, and the state's endorsement of a paramilitary solution to violence in those areas both then and now, is striking.[13] Although the issues that have spurred conflict in those zones have shifted over time, many of the elements that currently contribute to making some areas more violent than others—and the state's role in promoting that violence—are decades old. Then as now, violent areas constitute important vectors of contact and exchange with both the outside world and other Colombian departments and are poorly policed and regulated. Mutual mistrust and a history of indifference or incapacity to make the rule of law felt in such areas condemn relations between the state and local inhabitants to failure. These features ensure that the inhabitants and resources located in these areas continue to be the foci of brutal competition for control between the state and illicit forces—whether made up of political insurgents, paramilitary forces, or narcotics and contraband traffickers—just as they were during *la Violencia*. The main avenues of access for illicit arms, goods, and narcotics, for instance, continue to be centered in northwestern Colombia in the regions of Urabá and parts of the Chocó. In these areas, forces on either side of the ideological divide confront each other to dominate power in specific territories, often at the expense, but also with the tacit support of the state and its official bureaucracy. In fact, just as was true during *la Violencia,* it is sometimes difficult to discern exactly who is collaborating with whom and for what purpose in these contemporary episodes of violence in peripheral areas.

The situation of the Magdalena Medio area of Antioquia underscores both the continuities in violence over time and the complexity of the issues contributing to the endemic character of violence in peripheral zones. When narcotics traffickers emerged as a powerful force in Colombian society in the 1970s and increasingly laundered their illicit profits through the purchase of land in departments like Antioquia, they sought out areas such as the Magdalena Medio. Here, the Pablo Escobars and the Rodriquez Gachas of the underworld came into conflict with leftist guerrillas embroiled in a much older battle with large property owners of estates and extractive industries like mining. As newly enriched, large landowners with unparalleled access to state-of-the-art arms and abundant personnel, narcotics traffickers were able to ally with local landowners (and members of a beleaguered military) to form ruthlessly effective and extensive paramilitary forces with which to eradicate potential peasant protest and combat leftist insurgents. The result has been extraordinarily bloody. But even in its modern manifestations, contemporary violence in the area, which may seem far removed from *la Violencia,* continues to bear vestiges of that earlier conflict. The local inhabitants in mining and ranching communities such as Segovia, Remedios, and Puerto Berrío still identify with dissident political parties and militant labor unions just as they did at mid-century.[14] They still consider themselves to possess a cultural identity different from that of Antioqueño officials based in Medellín, and they still appear to those officials as defiant, godless, and rebellious peoples who invite the massacres and repeated political assassinations that have been their recurrent fate.

The case of la Violencia in Antioquia thus further suggests the need to rethink the definition and use of certain analytical categories such as "region," "state," and "citizen" in studies of violence. To begin, at least two Antioquias existed. One—an idealized Antioquia—was a place where people had a modicum of access to social and economic mobility; land ownership was a real possibility; communities were linked by strong common beliefs, Catholicism, and specific social practices and values; and people preferred to do business rather than take up arms. The idealized Antioquia seemed an unlikely candidate for an outbreak of widespread conflict at mid-century and, in fact, never experienced significant levels of violence. The "other" Antioquia—where land was concentrated in a few hands, where agribusiness estates and cattle ranches dominated production, where landless migrants and seasonal workers defined the labor market, and where extractive industries not subsistence farming was the norm—is an Antioquia whose existence is barely acknowledged. The residents of this other Antioquia have historically been viewed with distrust and have been excluded from real participation in regional power. For these Antioqueños, both la Violencia and contemporary violence represent but a more extreme manifestation of the hostility and alienation that has historically characterized their relationship to the regional state.

As a category of analysis, "region" is usually defined in relation to seemingly unproblematic administrative and physical boundaries without regard for the complicated cultural, economic, ethnic, and social implications that may shape perceptions of regional identity and define exclusion or inclusion in regional and central structures of power.[15] Yet regions and departments are not homogeneous and neither are the relations and structures of authority that operate in them. The Antioqueño case points to the need to restructure the typologies and analytical categories by which the study of violence has traditionally been approached. This would call for a remapping of violence in Colombia that would likely reveal nodes of conflict with shared characteristics and commonalities that transcend "departmental" boundaries in the official definition of the term. If the criteria by which violence in regions were redefined, it would be possible to discern continuities over time even when some of the factors contributing to the emergence of violence shift or expand. Surely such knowledge would give us a much better basis from which to address the issues that contribute to producing recurrent episodes of violence in particular areas and give greater promise of arriving at nonviolent solutions in the future.

In this study I have suggested that not everyone included within the physical parameters of the state of Antioquia necessarily or automatically could lay claim to Antioqueño identity. I have also suggested that the construction of regional identity—and hence the right to claim citizenship and take part in decision-making or make demands of the state—was predicated on a constantly negotiated, unstable, and highly exclusionary notion of sociocultural propriety. The import of this redefinition of the concept of region and citizenship is multiple. Many analyses of *la Violencia* (and certainly two of the most influential ones—Daniel Pécaut's and Paul Oquist's) have drawn attention to the importance of the power (or absence) of the state in Colombian society and in the definition of Colombian identity. Leaving aside for the moment the question of whether a central state existed at all in Colombia or whether it collapsed in the face of violence, what if no consensus existed among Colombians as to what constituted the state or what their relationship to it might be? What if more than one notion of the state existed and this were heavily influenced by local and regional experiences? This study of Antioquia is not the first to suggest that the concept of the central state in the context of the Colombian *Violencia* is a potentially problematic or even irrelevant category of analysis for understanding individual perceptions of authority or power on the ground. For most Colombians the central state was an abstract concept and power was largely exercised and determined locally or regionally, not in Bogotá. In the Antioqueño case, moreover, it is evident that the central state possessed very few means of making its authority felt at the regional or municipal level, and that it relied in large measure on the complicity or cooperation of local and regional authorities for even its tenuous presence on a day-to-day basis.

But the Antioqueño case also suggests that local inhabitants developed and deployed notions of the central state that were inextricably shaped by their understandings of the workings of power in their localities and within the regional state. These understandings in turn influenced their ability to claim citizenship and access power structures. Perhaps one of the most remarkable aspects of studying the course of *la Violencia* in Antioquia is the discovery of the degree to which people—ordinary people who sometimes couldn't write their names and had never been to Medellín or had much contact with government—believed in the political system and made use of it. Regional inhabitants insisted on writing petitions, vocalizing their dissatisfactions, and articulating their notions of the proper function of the state and its obligation to its citizens even when the individuals who held regional positions of power belonged to the opposition. These same people—and they were surprisingly numerous—regardless of their party affiliation, often and fearlessly made clear to local and regional officers their disagreement with the use of violence as a political tool. They often went so far as to include their national identity numbers after their names on countless letters and petitions so that they could be easily identified and located. They engaged in acts of civil disobedience by refusing to pay the policemen who were imposed by the regional government and were empowered to divest locally elected leaders from their rightful municipal offices. Ordinary people also risked their lives to save the lives of neighbors and family members targeted by violence, just as many Colombian journalists, judges, academics, and ordinary folk do today. And they saw through the claims of political legitimacy made by armed groups on both sides of the ideological fence as motivated by little more than ill-disguised ambition rather than honor.

The experience of Antioquia during *la Violencia* suggests that Colombians were much more sophisticated about politics and their expectations of the state than they are usually given credit for. It is significant—and I have felt compelled to highlight the phenomenon in this study—how many people resisted partisan violence and refused to take part in paramilitary violence (including landowners who might have been expected to benefit from it). They did so even when the state offered them the possibility of doing so with impunity. It is equally significant that many Antioqueños attempted to use the law and nonviolent mechanisms—such as voting, petitions, editorials, civil disobedience—to influence the state and its policies, and it is important to acknowledge that mechanisms did exist to mediate negotiated solutions to conflict. But it is equally important to note that such mechanisms of nonviolent resolution to conflict were not present or accessible everywhere and that a direct correlation appears to exist between the possibility of a negotiated solution to violence (or even its preclusion) and the impossibility of any response but repression on the part of the state or armed resistance on the part of a local population.

It is tempting to yearn for a period in Colombian history when the differences that generated violence seemed black and white — easy to understand and pinpoint. It is equally tempting to want to draw a clear distinction between the origins and purpose of violence in the 1950s and that which affects Colombia today, to want to view the two as separate and distinct and violence as a whole as isolated, chaotic, and extraordinary. Finally, it is tempting to believe the powerful and by now largely internalized idea that there is something unique or peculiar to the Colombian case, some intractable cultural propensity that makes violence there inevitable and endemic. But there is no such animal. If one listens carefully, if one ignores the cacophonous dissonance of simplistic assessments, echoes of the stories of violence recounted here can be heard amid the survivors of the conflicts in Rwanda, Northern Ireland, Bosnia, Chechnya, Guatemala, or Sri Lanka. I have tried to hear the stories behind the stories, to piece together fragments of lost stories and stories too horrifying to want to remember or retell. At times I have wanted to shut out those stories, to cover my ears, to run away from violence, including the potential for it that lies unrecognized in all of us. But the dead surrounded and tugged at me, while the living would not let me rest, reminding me that even when I no longer wanted to that I must tell their stories. Finally, I hope that I have betrayed neither those who died nor those who survived and entrusted their tales to me over these many years.

Appendix A: Tables

Table A.1. Deaths due to violence in 25 most violent municipalities, 1949–1953

Municipality	Deaths	Percentage of total deaths	Cumulative percentage	Population, 1951	Deaths per 1000 of 1951 population
Dabeiba	561	13.31	13.31	18,972	29.57
Puerto Berrío	546	12.96	26.27	16,099	33.92
Urrao	428	10.16	36.43	20,624	20.75
Cañasgordas	368	8.73	45.16	17,975	20.47
Remedios	191	4.53	49.69	11,867	16.10
Frontino	170	4.03	53.73	10,557	16.10
Yolombó	156	3.70	57.43	26,465	5.89
Betulia	135	3.20	60.63	9,528	14.17
Antioquia	129	3.06	63.69	12,185	10.59
Caucasia	129	3.06	66.75	3,479	37.08
Peque	129	3.06	69.81	5,884	21.92
Anzá	125	2.97	72.78	5,920	21.11
Cisneros	97	2.30	75.08	7,876	12.32
Salgar	95	2.25	77.34	18,715	5.08
Sabanalarga	88	2.09	79.43	4,954	17.76
Buriticá	74	1.76	81.18	6,655	11.12
Ituango	71	1.68	82.87	19,179	3.70
Cáceres	62	1.47	84.34	6,292	9.85
Maceo	62	1.47	85.81	8,978	6.91
Turbo	58	1.38	87.19	14,434	4.02
San Luis	56	1.33	88.51	6,702	8.36
Caicedo	52	1.23	89.75	5,473	9.50
Cocorná	48	1.14	90.89	19,026	2.52
Bolívar	47	1.12	92.00	18,677	2.52
Abriaquí	44	1.04	93.05	3,131	14.05
All others	293	6.95	100.00	1,268,993	0.23
Department total	4,214	100.00		1,568,640	2.69

(Source: AGA, 1953, vol. 9, "Informe sobre la acción del bandolerismo, 1949–1953," Medellín, 11 May 1953; DANE, Panorama Estadístico de Antioquia, siglos xix y xx, table 2.1.6.1, pp. 78–81)

Table A.2. Deaths due to violence, 1949–1953, by subregion

Region	Deaths	Percentage of total deaths	Cumula- tive per- centage	Popula- tion, 1951	Deaths per 1000 of 1951 population
Magdalena	608	14.43	14.43	25,077	24.25
Occidente	1,706	40.48	54.91	124,314	13.72
Bajo Cauca	232	5.51	60.42	19,530	11.88
Urabá	77	1.83	62.24	17,309	4.45
Nordeste	519	12.32	74.56	123,746	4.19
Suroeste	835	19.81	94.38	249,150	3.35
Norte	80	1.90	96.27	127,937	0.63
Oriente	141	3.35	99.62	269,126	0.52
Sur	3	0.07	99.69	77,562	0.04
Central	13	0.31	100.00	534,889	0.02
Department total	4,214	100.00		1,568,640	2.69

(Source: AGA, 1953, vol. 9, "Informe sobre la acción del bandolerismo, 1949–1953," Medellín, 11 May 1953; DANE, Panorama Estadístico de Antioquia, siglos xix y xx, table 2.1.6.1, pp. 78–81)

Table A.3. Percentage population change by subregion, 1918–1964

Region	1918–1928	1928–1938	1938–1951	1951–1964
Urabá	14.00	12.70	46.70	339.80
Norte	10.00	16.00	7.30	22.40
Bajo Cauca	16.90	52.70	50.10	175.20
Nordeste	18.50	19.40	12.40	16.20
Magdalena	81.60	49.20	38.90	74.90
Occidente	19.80	21.50	5.60	26.50
Suroeste	20.60	10.70	7.80	14.40
Sur	28.70	2.90	10.80	15.30
Oriente	20.30	14.50	21.90	25.30
Central	36.10	26.70	95.20	111.40
Departmental	22.80	17.50	32.10	57.70

(Source: DANE, Panorama Estadístico de Antioquia, siglos xix y xx, table 2.1.6.1, pp. 78–81)

Table A.4. Civilian and "bandit" deaths, 1949–1953, by subregion

Region	Civilians	"Bandits"	Totals
Urabá	73	4	77
Norte	54	26	80
Bajo Cauca	155	77	232
Nordeste	228	291	519
Magdalena	353	255	608
Occidente	648	1,058	1,706
Suroeste	346	489	835
Sur	3	0	3
Oriente	113	28	141
Central	8	5	13
Totals	1,981	2,233	4,214

(Source: AGA, 1953, vol. 9, "Informe sobre la acción del bandolerismo, 1949–1953," Medellín, 11 May 1953)

Table A.5. Deaths by year and subregion, 1949–1953

Region	Number of deaths						Percentage of total					
	1949	1950	1951	1952	1953	Total	1949	1950	1951	1952	1953	1949–53
Bajo Cauca	1	0	0	159	72	232	6	0	0	7	8	6
Central	4	1	2	4	2	13	25	2	0	0	0	0
Magdalena	0	0	60	473	75	608	0	0	6	21	8	14
Nordeste	2	0	10	395	112	519	13	0	1	17	12	12
Norte	1	0	62	17	0	80	6	0	6	1	0	2
Occidente	0	30	545	706	425	1,706	0	60	56	31	47	40
Oriente	0	12	1	120	8	141	0	24	0	5	1	3
Sur	1	1	1	0	0	3	6	2	0	0	0	0
Suroeste	6	6	226	390	207	835	38	12	23	17	23	20
Urabá	1	0	63	4	9	77	6	0	6	0	1	2
Department	16	50	970	2,268	910	4,214	100	100	100	100	100	100

(Source: AGA, 1953, vol. 9, "Informe sobre la acción del bandolerismo, 1949–1953," Medellín, 11 May 1953)

Table A.6. Political prisoners, La Ladera Prison, Medellín, 1950–1953

Town of origin	Number of prisoners during year					Percentage of total prisoners from place of origin by year				
	1950	1951	1952	1953	1950–1953	1950	1951	1952	1953	1950–1953
Amalfí	0	0	1	0	1	0.00	0.00	0.60	0.00	0.20
Antioquia Vieja	0	0	1	6	7	0.00	0.00	0.60	4.70	1.40
El Bagre	0	0	0	1	1	0.00	0.00	0.00	0.80	0.20
Betania	0	0	1	0	1	0.00	0.00	0.60	0.00	0.20
Betulia	1	0	0	0	1	1.50	0.00	0.00	0.00	0.20
Buriticá	0	0	0	1	1	0.00	0.00	0.00	0.80	0.20
Cañasgordas	0	2	0	1	3	0.00	1.80	0.00	0.80	0.60
Caucasia	7	5	5	1	18	10.30	4.40	2.80	0.80	3.70
Chigorodó	0	3	0	0	3	0.00	2.60	0.00	0.00	0.60
Chocó	0	1	0	4	5	0.00	0.90	0.00	3.10	1.00
Dabeiba	6	1	15	11	33	8.80	0.90	8.30	8.70	6.70
Frontino	0	3	2	0	5	0.00	2.60	1.10	0.00	1.00
Ituango	7	2	7	0	16	10.30	1.80	3.90	0.00	3.30
Liborina	0	0	0	3	3	0.00	0.00	0.00	2.40	0.60
Medellín	0	0	1	1	2	0.00	0.00	0.60	0.80	0.40
Mutatá	1	6	2	1	10	1.50	5.30	1.10	0.80	2.00
Necoclí	1	0	1	0	2	1.50	0.00	0.60	0.00	0.40
Neguá (Chocó)	0	0	3	0	3	0.00	0.00	1.70	0.00	0.60
Peque	0	3	0	0	3	0.00	2.60	0.00	0.00	0.60
Puerto Berrío	10	15	74	31	130	14.70	13.20	41.10	24.40	26.60
Puerto Perales	9	0	3	2	14	13.20	0.00	1.70	1.60	2.90
Quibdó	0	9	19	9	37	0.00	7.90	10.60	7.10	7.60
Quinchía (Caldas)	0	0	0	10	10	0.00	0.00	0.00	7.90	2.00
Remedios	0	0	1	0	1	0.00	0.00	0.60	0.00	0.20
Riosucio (Chocó)	0	0	0	18	18	0.00	0.00	0.00	14.20	3.70
San Luis	0	0	0	1	1	0.00	0.00	0.00	0.80	0.20
Segovia	0	0	3	0	3	0.00	0.00	1.70	0.00	0.60
San Juan de Urabá	5	8	3	1	17	7.40	7.00	1.70	0.80	3.50
Tagachí (Chocó)	0	0	0	1	1	0.00	0.00	0.00	0.80	0.20

Table A.6. Continued

Town of origin	Number of prisoners during year					Percentage of total prisoners from place of origin by year				
	1950	1951	1952	1953	1950–1953	1950	1951	1952	1953	1950–1953
Titiribí	0	0	1	0	1	0.00	0.00	0.60	0.00	0.20
Turbo	20	54	8	22	104	29.40	47.40	4.40	17.30	21.30
Uramita	0	1	1	0	2	0.00	0.90	0.60	0.00	0.40
Urrao	1	1	27	2	31	1.50	0.90	15.00	1.60	6.30
Yalí	0	0	1	0	1	0.00	0.00	0.60	0.00	0.20
Total	68	114	180	127	489	100	100	100	100	100

(Source: SGA, 1953, vol. 7, "Presos políticos liberales en la cárcel 'La Ladera' por orden de la Cuarta Brigada," 8 May 1953)

Table A.7. Number of property holdings by municipality, 1941, 1958, 1961

Municipios	1941	1958	1961
Abejorral	5,213	4,895	6,317
Abriaquí	354	635	542
Alejandría	606	978	919
Amagá	3,035	3,508	3,478
Amalfí	1,928	3,542	2,873
Andes	4,192	6,969	6,223
Angelópolis	819	1,235	1,087
Angostura	1,604	2,707	2,072
Anorí	771	1,923	1,752
Antioquia	850	4,652	4,177
Anzá	915	1,329	1,183
Arboletes		1,260	3,281
Armenia		1,260	
Barbosa	1,743	3,630	3,185
Bello	2,752	12,631	13,619
Belmira	896	1,002	1,304
Betania	1,009	2,133	954
Betulia	1,277	1,956	1,906
Bolívar	2,382	3,238	1,638
Buriticá	498	1,158	3,270
Cáceres	375	1,820	1,098
Caicedo	832	1,253	2,330
Caldas	1,739	3,011	3,815
Campamento	520	1,708	1,262
Cañasgordas	1,829	4,178	1,737
Caramanta	835	2,640	4,058
Carmen de Viboral	4,388	4,481	2,304
Carolina	1,630	1,624	4,699
Caucasia		2,556	1,561
Chigorodó	289	799	2,655

Table A.7. Continued

Municipios	1941	1958	1961
Cisneros	1,922	2,154	781
Cocorná	3,403	4,271	1,502
Concepción	859	1,547	4,744
Concordia	1,763	2,259	1,303
Copacabana	2,158	3,211	3,643
Dabeiba	1,536	2,781	1,929
Don Matías	1,431	1,387	2,431
Ebéjico	2,392	4,406	1,432
Entrerríos	911	1,096	3,110
Envigado	2,957	7,804	8,169
Fredonia	4,031	5,005	955
Frontino	1,884	1,969	3,722
Giraldo	364	1,072	1,884
Girardota	1,499	2,846	2,483
Gómez Plata	1,323	2,124	830
Granada	2,073	5,563	1,580
Guarne	2,318	3,134	4,402
Guatapé	779	1,270	3,017
Heliconia	1,502	1,589	1,356
Itagui	1,371	7,233	8,787
Ituango	3,327	2,968	1,475
Jardín	1,981	2,354	3,352
Jericó	2,123	3,126	2,154
La Ceja	2,682	4,002	2,453
La Estrella	1,148	1,806	1,953
La Unión	977	2,318	3,047
Liborina	1,445	3,097	2,001
Margento		1,526	2,502
Marinilla	3,144	4,225	1,157
Medellín	29,883	114,006	87,617
Montebello	1,722	2,714	3,921

Table A.7. Continued

Municipios	1941	1958	1961
Murindó		266	3,724
Mutatá		650	51
Nariño	1,481	3,414	573
Nechí	970		2,836
Olaya	650	848	720
Pavarandocito	79		4,536
Peñol	2,843	4,683	798
Peque	756	849	1,913
Pueblorrico	1,980	2,262	3,392
Puerto Berrío	2,128	3,908	1,543
Remedios	815	1,950	1,657
Retiro	1,067	1,880	5,917
Rionegro	4,356	7,459	1,655
Sabanalarga	329	1,632	2,145
Salgar	939	2,344	1,988
San Andrés	987	2,095	2,996
San Carlos	1,020	3,184	1,906
San Jerónimo	1,377	2,050	2,365
San Luis	2,727	1,999	1,759
San Pedro	1,703	1,910	2,150
San Rafael	1,452	2,313	3,196
San Roque	3,154	4,133	4,065
San Vicente	2,416	4,831	5,032
Santa Bárbara	2,300	5,749	3,850
Santa Rosa de Osos	2,052	4,252	2,510
Santo Domingo	2,763	3,314	3,390
Santuario	2,673	4,482	2,066
Segovia	2,033	1,684	8,062
Sonsón	6,554	15,060	3,243
Sopetrán	2,362	4,324	3,704
Támesis	3,870	4,817	697

Table A.7. Continued

Municipios	1941	1958	1961
Tarso	844	765	2,059
Titiribí	2,514	2,596	1,009
Toledo	386	1,297	2,626
Turbo	907	2,595	4,098
Urrao	4,414	4,708	1,239
Valdivia	693	1,497	1,251
Valparaiso	905	1,519	1,420
Venecia	1,189	1,795	1,100
Yarumal	4,573	6,869	5,474
Yolombó	3,591	4,411	2,827
Zaragoza	812	1,778	1,110
Department	206,853	417,746	363,643

(Source: DANE, Panorama Estadístico de Antioquia, siglos xix y xx, table 17.1.3.5, pp. 638–41)

Table A.8. Change in average property values in 25 most violent municipalities, 1941–1961

Municipality	Deaths 1949–1953	Average property value 1941	1958	1961	Percentage change in average value 1941–1958	1958–1961	Average annual percentage change in value 1941–1958	1958–1961
Frontino	170	842	1,687	25,063	100	1,385	6	462
Caicedo	52	360	2,493	30,797	592	1,135	35	378
Sabanalarga	88	865	3,568	28,781	312	707	18	236
Cocorná	48	1,814	2,099	8,985	16	328	1	109
Dabeiba	561	876	5,064	21,661	478	328	28	109
Cisneros	97	431	4,147	15,038	863	263	51	88
Antioquia	129	1,054	3,498	6,383	232	82	14	27
Caucasia	129	n.d.	7,498	9,085	n.d.	21	n.d.	7
Buriticá	74	222	4,815	23,299	2,064	384	121	128
Urrao	428	653	5,337	12,902	718	142	42	47
Peque	129	461	4,884	13,275	959	172	56	57
Cañasgordas	368	1,065	4,539	6,721	326	48	19	16
Betulia	135	1,418	13,443	30,454	848	127	50	42
Abriaquí	44	1,588	7,194	9,548	353	33	21	11
San Luis	56	462	4,507	8,721	876	93	52	31
Yolombó	156	1,273	8,893	11,135	598	25	35	8
Salgar	95	3,571	21,598	12,321	505	(43)	30	(14)
Puerto Berrío	546	2,529	20,427	17,549	708	(14)	42	(5)
Bolívar	47	1,821	20,655	20,726	1,034	0	61	0
Cáceres	62	1,540	14,567	5,950	846	(59)	50	(20)
Ituango	71	625	10,051	13,976	1,509	39	89	13
Remedios	191	602	10,268	12,608	1,606	23	94	8
Anzá	125	456	9,035	13,591	1,882	50	111	17
Turbo	58	577	14,017	9,378	2,329	(33)	137	(11)
Maceo	62	n.d.	n.d.	n.d.	n.d.	n.d.	n.d.	n.d.
Department	4,214	1,539	10,183	17,632	562	73	33	24

(Source: DANE, Panorama Estadístico de Antioquia, siglos xix y xx, table 17.1.3.5, pp. 638–41)

Appendix B: Maps

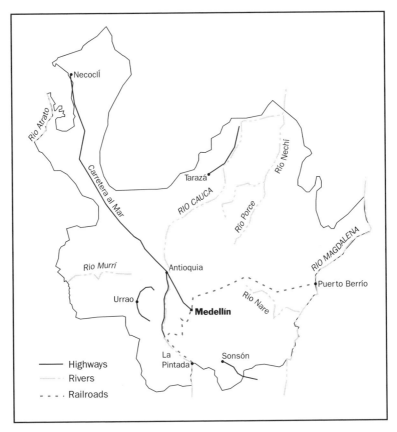

Map B.1. Antioquia: Rivers and highways
(Source: Instituto Geográfico Augustín Codazzi)

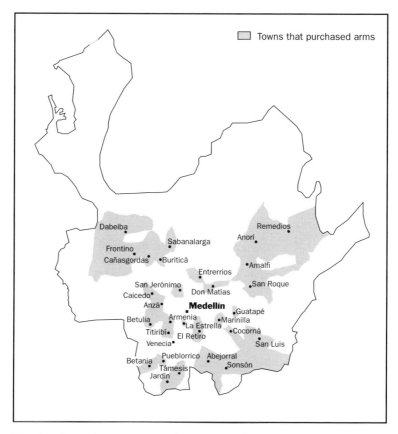

Map B.2. Contrachusma arms purchases, 1950 and 1953
(Source: Archivo de la Secretaría de Gobierno de Antioquia, 1950 and 1953)

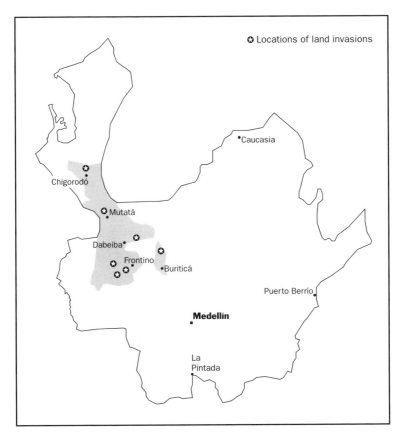

Map B.3. Land invasions by guerrillas in Western Antioquia
(Source: Instituto Geográfico Augustín Codazzi; Archivo de la Secretaría de Gobierno de Antioquia, 1952, vol. 6, Caja de Crédito Agrario, April 28, 1952)

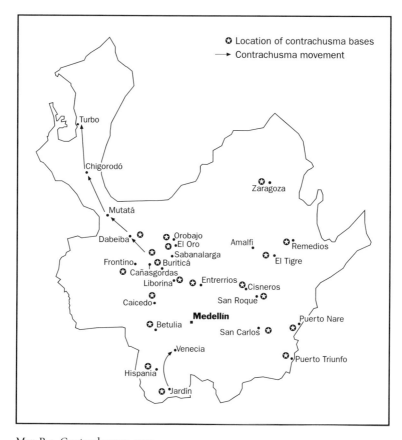

Map B.4. Contrachusma, 1953
(Source: Archivo de la Secretaría de Gobierno de Antioquia, 1953)

Notes

Introduction

1 Colombia is divided into administrative units known as "departments" that are equivalent to "states." In this book I will use the terms "province," "department" and "region" interchangeably to refer to Antioquia and other Colombian states.

2 *La Violencia* refers to the episodic phenomenon of Colombian civil unrest that occurred between 1946 and 1966. No exact consensus exists regarding the beginning or endpoint of the Violence. Some scholars argue that violence began as early as the 1930s, others date its inception to the election of Conservative Mariano Ospina Pérez as president in 1946, and many mark the assassination of Liberal leader Jorge Eliécer Gaitán as the "real" beginning of *la Violencia*. Regardless of the exact date, most scholars agree that the "classic" period of violence — waged between Conservatives and Liberals primarily in defense of traditional nineteenth-century partisan banners — ended with the military coup of General Rojas Pinilla on June 13, 1953. Subsequent years of violence are generally divided into stages characterized by military government (1953–1957), the substitution of partisan concerns with social banditry (the mid-1950s through the early 1960s), and, ultimately, the emergence of contemporary armed leftist guerrilla movements (after 1965). A fuller elaboration of the complexity of *la Violencia* is provided below and in note 57 below.

3 Scholars dedicated to the study of violence in Colombia are informally known as "violentologists."

4 Departamento Administrativo Nacional de Estadística (DANE), *Colombia estadística* (Bogotá, 1987), table 1, 1951; DANE, *Panorama estadístico de Antioquia* (hereafter, PEA) (Bogotá, 1981), table 2.1.6.1, "Población por sexo, según municipios: censos de 1938–1951," pp. 78–79.

5 Scholars debate the total number of deaths caused by *la Violencia*. The lowest estimate of deaths is 200,000 while other estimates are as high as 400,000. I have relied on the statistics calculated by Paul Oquist in *Violence, Conflict, and Politics in Colombia* (New York: Academic Press, 1980), table 1.1, "Distribution of Violencia Fatalities for the Ten Most Affected Departments, 1946–1957," p. 6. Nationally, the provinces of Viejo Caldas (listed by Oquist as "Caldas Antiguo" and currently divided into the provinces of Caldas, Quindío, and Risaralda), Tolima, Norte de Santander, and Santander were ranked respectively as first, second, fourth, and fifth in terms of total casualties.

6 Oquist, *Violence, Conflict, and Politics*, table 6.2, "Migrations, Fatalities, and Land Parcels Lost due to La Violencia," p. 227.

7   Charles Bergquist is perhaps the scholar who most forcefully suggested the existence of a link between coffee and violence. See Bergquist, *Labor in Latin America: Comparative Essays on Chile, Argentina, Venezuela, and Colombia* (Stanford: Stanford University Press, 1986), p. 361. Bergquist's assumption was not unreasonable; several of the regions suffering the greatest number of casualties during *la Violencia* (Tolima, Viejo Caldas, and Antioquia), for instance, were also important centers of coffee production. Coffee production, however, may have been a less important variable in determining the intensity of violence in particular localities than other factors such as geographic location, the nature of the relationship between localities and the regional and central states, and the local structure of land tenure and relations of production. I discuss the intersection of production, geography, and violence later in this chapter.

8   PEA, table 2.2.7, "Defunciones, según causas 1943–1945," p. 91; table 2.2.8, "Defunciones, según causas 1946–1952," p. 92; and table 2.2.9, "Defunciones, según causas 1953–1959," pp. 93–95.

9   National census records for the years between 1943 and 1953 are inconsistent and, when compared to statistics kept during the same period by the governor's office and the armed forces, appear to be seriously flawed. The censuses of 1943 and 1945, for instance, do not include the category "homicide," although the latter is included in census statistics of deaths after 1946. There is, moreover, a big jump (more than 2,000) in the number of deaths ruled "*mal definidas*" (ill-defined) by the census between the years 1944 and 1945. See PEA, table 2.2.7, "Difunciones, según causas 1943–1945," p. 91. This category continued to be included in the census after 1946, but the statistical jump recorded between 1944 and 1945 declined by the same amount (2,000) between 1945 and 1946. Between 1946 and 1953 the number of deaths deemed "ill-defined" grew by 1,000 or more per year and reached a peak of 9,151 in 1951 (or two and a half times the number registered in 1946). In the meantime, the category "homicide" registered an increase from 120 in 1946 to 397 in 1951. The peak of registered homicides (705) occurred in 1952, the year in which violence-related statistics kept by the governor's office also peaked. An additional category of deaths called "Otras muertes violentas o accidentales" remained relatively constant between 1943 and 1945, declined between 1946 and 1949 (except in 1947), and then rose back to 1943 levels (approximately 600 or so per year) after 1950. See PEA, table 2.2.8, "Difunciones, según causas 1946–1952," p. 92. Selected parish death registry records, such as that of the municipality of Urrao (one of the five towns in which the number of officially registered deaths due to violence was highest) confirm the impression that violence-related deaths began to occur during the last months of 1949. This parish's records are particularly useful because the priest noted whether a death was the result of violence and where and how it had taken place. See Archivo Parroquia, Registro de funciones, "Partidas de funciones," 1948–1954, vol. 12, Urrao, Antioquia.

10   Archivo Privado del Señor Gobernador de Antioquia (hereafter, AGA), 1953, vol. 9, "Informe sobre la acción del bandolerismo," 1949–1953, Medellín, 11 May 1953. The report divided the dead into "*civiles*" (civilians) and "*bandoleros*" (bandits).

11   I am not suggesting that towns where no casualties occurred did not experience partisan tensions; however, these tensions generally did not result in a significant number of casualties.

12   As scholars have argued, this might seem to suggest that the violence in the southwest was some of the worst in Antioquia. But Urrao, as I explain below, was in many ways atypical for the southwest: it produced little coffee and was connected more directly to the Chocó and western Antioquia than to the coffee zone to the south. Urrao, moreover, was but one town in the southwest; the majority of other southwestern towns were not severely affected by the violence between 1949 and 1953.

13   The government usually referred to Liberals who took up arms as *bandoleros* (bandits) or *chusma* (rabble), not guerrillas. Achieving state legal recognition that these armed citizens were politically motivated individuals rather than criminals became a serious point of dispute between Liberal and Conservative officers and the Colombian state. In this text I refer to armed guerrilla groups with an explicit political objective as "guerrillas."

14   The term "*paisa*," a variation on "*paisano*," or fellow countryman, is colloquially used to refer to the inhabitants of Antioquia.

15   David Bushnell, *The Making of Modern Colombia: A Nation in Spite of Itself* (Berkeley: University of California Press, 1993), p. vii.

16   The relationship between rural violence, identity, modernization, and the construction of the nation-state in the late nineteenth and early twentieth centuries is explored in a number of works, among them: Ana Maria Alonso, *Thread of Blood: Colonialism, Revolution, and Gender on Mexico's Northern Frontier* (Tucson: University of Arizona Press, 1995); Euclides da Cunha, *Rebellion in the Backlands,* trans. Samuel Putnam (Chicago: University of Chicago Press, 1967); John Lynch, *Argentine Dictator: Juan Manuel Rosas, 1829–1852* (New York: Oxford University Press, 1981); Florencia E. Mallon, *Peasant and Nation: The Making of Postcolonial Mexico and Peru* (Berkeley: University of California Press, 1995); Domingo Sarmiento, *Facundo, or, Civilization and Barbarism* (New York: Penguin, 1998); Richard W. Slatta, *Gauchos and the Vanishing Frontier* (Lincoln: University of Nebraska Press, 1983); Paul J. Vanderwood, *Disorder and Progress: Bandits, Police, and Mexican Development* (Wilmington, Del.: SR Books, 1992).

17   Among the many works examining the effects of anti-Communist "dirty wars" and counterinsurgency in Latin America, see Kees Koonings and Dirk Kruijt, eds., *Societies of Fear: The Legacy of Civil War, Violence, and Terror in Latin America* (New York: St. Martin's Press, 1999); Jennifer Schirmer, *The Guate-*

malan Military Project: A Violence Called Democracy (Philadelphia: University of Pennsylvania Press, 1998); Robert M. Carmack, ed., *Harvest of Violence: The Maya Indian and the Guatemalan Crisis* (Norman: University of Oklahoma Press, 1988); Brian Loveman and Thomas M. Davies Jr., ed., *The Politics of AntiPolitics: The Military in Latin America,* rev. ed. (Wilmington, Del.: SR Books, 1997); Timothy P. Wickham-Crowley, *Guerrillas and Revolution in Latin America: A Comparative Study of Insurgents and Regimes since 1956* (Princeton: Princeton University Press, 1992).

18   Examples of Latin American conflict in which race, ethnicity, geography, and politics intersected to produce violence of genocidal proportions before the second half of the twentieth century may be found in Robin L. H. Derby and Richard Turits, "Histories of Terror and the Terrors of History: The 1937 Haitian Massacre in the Dominican Republic" (paper presented to the Committee on Latin American History at the annual meeting of the American Historical Association, New York, 29 December 1990); and Nelson Reed, *The Caste War of the Yucatan* (Stanford: Stanford University Press, 1964).

19   The most striking parallel of a coterminous and comparably drawn-out internecine struggle to the Colombian case is the war between Catholics and Protestants in Northern Ireland. See Allen Feldman, *Formations of Violence: The Narrative of the Body and Political Terror in Northern Ireland* (Chicago: University of Chicago Press, 1991), and "Violence and Vision: The Prosthetics and Aesthetics of Terror," *Public Culture* 10, no. 1 (1997): 24–60. In terms of participants, magnitude, geographical scope, and complexity, other recent examples of brutal internal conflict such as that between Hutu and Tutsi or Serb and Croat might also be compared to the Colombian case. See Liisa Malkki, *Purity and Exile: Violence, Memory, and National Cosmology among Hutu Refugees in Tanzania* (Chicago: University of Chicago Press, 1995); and Rob Nixon, "Of Balkans and Bantustans: 'Ethnic Cleansing' and the Crisis in National Legitimation," *Transition* 60 (1993): 4–26. The latter piece reproduces a photograph of a Muslim soldier holding the severed head of a Serb—a pose identical to that captured many times during *la Violencia.* See also Arjun Appadurai, "Dead Certainty: Ethnic Violence in the Era of Globalization," *Public Culture* 10, no. 2 (1998): 225–47. Appadurai reminds us of the need to include an approach to ethnic violence that relies on ideas about the stranger—a figure that is repeatedly alluded to in tales of *la Violencia*—not just the notion of collective violence that is "a product of propaganda, rumor, prejudice, and memory."

20   Bushnell, *The Making of Modern Colombia,* p. 117.

21   Helen Delpar, *Red against Blue: The Liberal Party in Colombian Politics, 1863–1899* (Tuscaloosa: University of Alabama Press, 1981); Charles W. Bergquist, *Coffee and Conflict in Colombia, 1886–1910* (Durham, N.C.: Duke University Press, 1978); and Daniel Pécaut, *Orden y violencia: Colombia, 1930–1954,* 2 vols. (Bogotá: Siglo Veintiuno Editores, 1987).

22   Bushnell, *The Making of Modern Colombia*, p. 74; and David Bushnell and Neill Macauley, *The Emergence of Latin America in the Nineteenth Century* (New York: Oxford University Press, 1988).

23   Bushnell, *The Making of Modern Colombia*, pp. 144–45.

24   For a lucid discussion of Colombia's two-party system and the civil wars of the nineteenth century, see Bergquist, *Labor in Latin America*, pp. 290–94.

25   Bushnell has pointed out that no one knows exactly how a death count of 100,000 was originally arrived at and suggests that it may well be "too high," see *The Making of Modern Colombia*, p. 151.

26   The following account of the Reyes's administration relies heavily on chapter 10 of Bergquist's seminal study, *Coffee and Conflict in Colombia*. For a comprehensive overview of the development of the Colombian economy, particularly the evolution of the export economy, see José Antonio Ocampo, *Colombia y la economía mundial, 1830–1910* (Mexico, D.F.: Siglo Veintiuno Editores, 1984), and "Los orígenes de la industria cafetera, 1830–1929," in *Nueva historia de Colombia*, ed. Jaime Jaramillo Uribe, vol. 5 (Bogotá: Planeta, 1989), pp. 213–32.

27   Bergquist, *Coffee and Conflict*, pp. 227, 254.

28   Bergquist, *Coffee and Conflict*, p. 261. For a different perspective on the political and social impact of coffee production on the consciousness and political mobilization of coffee workers employed by large estates, see Michael Jiménez, "The Limits of Export Capitalism: Economic Structure, Class, and Politics in a Colombian Coffee Municipality, 1900–1930" (Ph.D. diss., Harvard University, 1986).

29   Luis Ospina Vásquez, *Industria y protección en Colombia, 1810–1930*, 3d ed. (Medellín: FAES, Editorial Lealon, 1979), pp. 396–97. Ospina notes that between 1910 and 1930 "the situation was such that any political party would have had to think twice before declaring opposition to this era of 'progress.'" And, he adds, "the most influential men within Liberalism, some of whom did so from their positions as directors which they had accepted when the practice of mixed [bipartisan] ministries were in effect, supported protectionism." On the effects of bipartisan policy-making in Antioquia, see my own "Genesis and Evolution of La Violencia in Antioquia, Colombia, 1900–1953" (Ph.D. diss., Harvard University, 1992), chapters 3 and 4.

30   See Bergquist, *Labor in Latin America*, pp. 345–46, and Miguel Urrutia, *The Development of the Colombian Labor Movement* (New Haven: Yale University Press, 1969), p. 99, for discussions of how the Banana Strike of 1928 discredited the Conservative government; and Gonzalo Restrepo Jaramillo, *El pensamiento conservador* (Medellín: Tipografía Bedout, 1936), pp. 46–59, on the reaction of some Antioqueño Conservatives to the issue of the clergy's "intrusion" in the election of 1929.

31   Mariano Arango, *El café en Colombia, 1930–1958: Producción, circulación y política* (Bogotá: Carlos Valencia Editores, 1982), p. 60, and *Café e industria, 1850–*

1930, 2d ed. (Bogotá: Carlos Valencia Editores, 1981); Jesús Antonio Bejarano, *Ensayos de historia agraria colombiana* (Bogotá: Fondo Editorial CEREC, 1987); and José Antonio Ocampo and Santiago Montenegro, ed., *Crisis mundial, protección e industrialización* (Bogotá: Fondo Editorial CEREC, 1984).

32   Richard E. Sharpless, *Gaitán of Colombia: A Political Biography* (Pittsburgh: Pittsburgh University Press, 1978), pp. 15–17.

33   Pécaut, *Orden y violencia,* 1:171. For an in-depth analysis of Alfonso López Pumarejo's first administration, see Alvaro Tirado Mejía, *Aspectos políticos del primer gobierno de Alfonso López Pumarejo, 1934–1938,* Instituto Colombiano de la Cultura (Bogotá: Grafica Cabrera e Hijos, 1981).

34   Pécaut, *Orden y violencia,* 1:274.

35   Gonzalo Sánchez, *Las ligas campesinas en Colombia* (Bogotá: Editorial Tiempo Presente, 1977), p. 36, and Hermés Tovar Pinzón, *El movimiento campesino en Colombia durante los siglos xix y xx* (Bogotá, 1975), pp. 62–65.

36   The most thorough examination of the evolution of Colombian land laws, development of the frontier, and emergence of conflict over public lands may be found in Catherine LeGrand, *Frontier Expansion and Peasant Protest in Colombia, 1850–1936* (Albuquerque: University of New Mexico Press, 1986), p. 108. For an examination of labor unrest on large coffee estates in Tolima and Cundinamarca, see Bergquist, *Labor in Latin America,* pp. 314–16.

37   A thoughtful treatment of the López administration may be found in Richard Stoller, "Alfonso López Pumarejo and Liberal Radicalism in 1930s Colombia," *Journal of Latin American Studies* 27, no. 2 (1995): 367–97.

38   Bushnell, *The Making of Modern Colombia,* p. 188; LeGrand, *Frontier Expansion,* p. 150; Sánchez, *Las ligas,* p. 125.

39   Daniel Pécaut, *Política y sindicalismo en Colombia,* 2d ed. (Bogotá: Ediciones Culturales, 1982), p. 224. Ann Farnsworth-Alvear explores the growth of textile production during these years in Medellín and the response of workers and factory owners to the emergence of Communist labor mobilization in *Dulcinea in the Factory: Myths, Morals, Men, and Women in Colombia's Industrial Experiment, 1905–1960* (Durham, N.C.: Duke University Press, 2000), especially chapter 5.

40   Bergquist, *Labor in Latin America,* p. 343.

41   Arango, *El café en Colombia,* p. 60; *El Colombiano,* 14 Feb. 1953, 19 Feb. 1953, 20 Feb. 1953, and 27 Feb. 1953. Coltejer's profits increased by a factor of twenty between 1940 and 1949 from 830,000 pesos to 16,520,000. See "Coltejer Profits Reports," in *Vidas y empresas de Antioquia: Diccionario biográfico, bibliográfico y económico* (hereafter, VEA), ed. Alfonso Mejía Robledo (Medellín: Imprenta Departamental de Antioquia, 1951), p. 220.

42   Miguel Urrutia, *Historia del sindicalismo en Colombia,* 3d ed. (Medellín: Editorial Lealon, 1978), p. 192–93.

43   John Martz, *Colombia: A Contemporary Political Survey* (Chapel Hill: University of North Carolina Press, 1962), p. 40.

44   Vernon Lee Fluharty, *Dance of the Millions: Military Rule and the Social Revolution in Colombia, 1930–1956* (Pittsburgh: University of Pittsburgh Press, 1957), p. 81.

45   Pécaut, *Política y sindicalismo*, p. 197, and Urrutia, *Development of the Colombian Labor Movement*, p. 155.

46   Pécaut, *Política y sindicalismo*, p. 197.

47   Herbert Braun has provided the most persuasive and thorough exploration of the rise of emergent, non-elite politicians in the period preceding *la Violencia*, and especially the impact of Jorge Eliécer Gaitán on Colombia's elite-dominated political arena in *The Assassination of Gaitán: Public Life and Urban Violence in Colombia* (Madison: University of Wisconsin Press, 1985). See also Carlos Miguel Ortíz Sarmiento, *Estado y subversión en Colombia: La Violencia en el Quindió, años 50* (Bogotá: Fondo Editorial CEREC, 1985), pp. 175–79, for details of the rise of local political hopefuls around the figure of Conservative Gilberto Alzate Avendaño. In Antioquia, a number of these non-elite political figures emerged: Eduardo Berrío González, governor from 1949 to 1950, who began his own dissident movement to champion municipal interests in Oriente (the east); and Aníbal Vallejo Arbeláez, who was raised a Liberal but switched over to Laureano Gómez's faction of the Conservative party. See Christopher Abel, *Política, iglesia y partidos en Colombia* (Bogotá: FAES–Universidad Nacional de Colombia, 1987), p. 119.

48   Martz, *Colombia*, p. 52.

49   Braun, *Assassination of Gaitán*, pp. 164–72, estimates the material cost of damage in 1948 to be nearly 5 million pesos, while estimates of the dead range between 549 and 2,585. For a visual catalogue of the impact of the Bogotazo, see Carlos Delgado, ed., *El 9 de abril en fotos* (Bogotá: El Ancora Editores, 1986).

50   Arturo Alape, *El Bogotazo: Memorias del olvido* (Bogotá: Editorial Pluma, 1983), pp. 272–82 and pp. 364–93.

51   VEA, "Instituto Colombiano de Seguros," p. 302; Abel, *Política*, p. 277; Martz, *Colombia*, p. 112.

52   Colombia, *Decreto del Estado de Sitio*, Nov. 1949.

53   Laureano Gómez was an extremely controversial figure in Colombian politics. He has been depicted as both a brilliant defender of Conservative values and the intellectual author of violence against the Liberal opposition during *la Violencia*. The earliest attempt to understand Gómez took a psychoanalytic turn, see José Francisco Socarras, *Laureano Gómez: Psicoanalisis de un resentido* (Bogotá: Ediciones Librería Siglo XX, 1942). No thorough analysis of Gómez's presidency exists, but James Henderson's *Las ideas de Laureano Gómez* (Bogotá: Tercer Mundo, 1985) provides a good intellectual biography of Gómez. For a more recent treatment of Gómez as a historical figure, see Arturo Abella Rodriguéz, *Laureano Gómez* (Bogotá: Espara, 2000).

54   José Gutiérrez Gómez, president of ANDI, cited in *El Colombiano*, Medellín, 1950; cited again in *El Colombiano*, Medellín, 11 April 1953.

55   General Gustavo Rojas Pinilla's regime has prompted surprisingly few scholarly analyses, but see Fluherty, *Dance of the Millions,* and Silvia Galvis and Alberto Donadío, *El Jefe Supremo: Rojas Pinilla en la violencia y en el poder* (Bogotá: Planeta, 1988).

56   Richard Weinert, "Violence in Pre-Modern Societies: Rural Colombia," *American Political Science Review* 60 (June 1966): 340–47; Fluharty, *Dance of the Millions;* Robert Williamson, "Toward a Theory of Political Violence: The Case of Rural Colombia," *Western Political Quarterly* (March 1965); and James L. Payne, *Patterns of Conflict in Colombia* (New Haven: Yale University Press, 1968). The persistence of banditry and feuds in Latin American countries such as Brazil and Mexico at the end of the nineteenth and in the early twentieth centuries was often cited, for instance, to illustrate the struggle between a more traditional social, political, and economic order to one guided by secular values and identified with modernization; see da Cunha, *Rebellion in the Backlands;* Todd A. Diacon, *Millenarian Vision, Capitalist Reality: Brazil's Contestado Rebellion* (Durham, N.C.: Duke University Press, 1991); Eric Hobsbawm, *Primitive Rebels: Studies in Archaic Forms of Social Movement in the Nineteenth and Twentieth Centuries* (New York: W. W. Norton, 1965); Gilbert M. Joseph, "On the Trail of Latin American Bandits: A Reexamination of Peasant Resistance," *Latin American Research Review* 25, no. 2 (1990): 7–53; Linda Lewin, "The Oligarchical Limitations of Social Banditry in Brazil: The Case of the 'Good' Thief Antonio Silvino," *Past and Present* 82: 116–46; Richard W. Slatta, *Bandidos: The Varieties of Latin American Banditry* (New York: Greenwood, 1987); and Vanderwood, *Disorder and Progress.* On aggression fueled by status deprivation, see Williamson, "Toward a Theory of Political Violence," p. 35. Florencia Mallon suggests that perhaps the strong relationship forged between peasants and specific parties during the nineteenth century was equally present in the Mexico and Peru, see *Peasant and Nation.*

57   The literature on *la Violencia* is too vast to mention in its entirety here, but the most significant studies written since the 1970s include: Charles Bergquist, Ricardo Peñaranda, and Gonzalo Sánchez, eds., *Violence in Colombia: The Contemporary Crisis in Historical Perspective* (Wilmington, Del.: Scholarly Resources, 1992); Braun, *The Assassination of Gaitán;* Comisión de estudios sobre la violencia, *Colombia: Violencia y democracia, Informe presentado al Ministro de Gobierno* (Bogotá: Universidad Nacional, 1987); Medófilo Medina, *La protesta urbana en Colombia en el siglo veinte* (Bogotá: Ediciones Aurora, 1984); *Once ensayos sobre La Violencia* (Bogotá: Fondo Editorial CEREC y Centro Gaitán, 1985); Oquist, *Violence, Conflict, and Politics in Colombia;* Pécaut, *Orden y Violencia en Colombia;* Gonzalo Sánchez and Donny Meertens, *Bandoleros, gamonales y campesinos: El caso de la Violencia en Colombia* (Bogotá: El Ancora, 1983); Gonzalo Sánchez, *Los días de la revolución: Gaitanismo y 9 de abril en provincia* (Bogotá: Centro Gaitán, 1983); Gonzalo Sánchez and Ricardo Peñaranda,

ed., *Pasado y presente de la Violencia en Colombia* (Bogotá: Fondo Editorial CEREC, 1986).

Studies of *la Violencia* in specific regional or municipal contexts include: Jaime Arocha, *La Violencia en el Quindío: Determinantes ecológicos y económicos del homicidio en un municipio caficultor* (Bogotá: 1979); Darío Betancourt and Martha L. García, *Matones y cuadrilleros: Origen y evolución de la Violencia en el occidente colombiano, 1946–1965* (Bogotá: Tercer Mundo Editores, 1990); Julio Casas Aguilar, *La Violencia en los Llanos Orientales* (Bogotá: ECOE Ediciones, 1986); Ulises Casas, *De la guerrilla liberal a la guerrilla comunista* (Bogotá, 1987); Apolinar Díaz Callejas, *El 9 de abril 1948 en Barrancabermeja: Diez días de poder popular* (Bogotá: El Labrador, 1988); Darío Fajardo, *Violencia y desarrollo: Transformaciones sociales en tres regiones cafetaleras del Tolima, 1936–1970* (Bogotá: Fondo Editorial Suramérica, 1978); James D. Henderson, *When Colombia Bled: A History of the "Violencia" in Tolima* (Tuscaloosa: University of Alabama Press, 1985); Carlos Miguel Ortíz Sarmiento, *Estado y Subversion en Colombia;* and Maria Victoria Uribe, *Matar, rematar y contramatar: Las masacres de la Violencia en el Tolima, 1948–1964* (Bogotá: CINEP, 1990).

For overviews of the literature on *la Violencia* see Catherine LeGrand, "La política y la *Violencia* en Colombia, 1946–1965: Interpretaciones en la década de los ochenta," *Memoria y Sociedad* 2, no. 4 (1997): 79–109; Carlos Miguel Ortíz Sarmiento, "Violencia política de los ochenta: Elementos para una reflexión historica," *Anuario Colombiano de Historia Social y de la Cultura* 18–19 (1990–1991): 245–80; and Gonzalo Sánchez, "La Violencia in Colombia: New Research, New Questions," *Hispanic American Historical Review* 65, no. 4 (1985): 789–807.

58   The historiography of the Mexican Revolution is extraordinarily rich and too complex to summarize here. Among the more significant attempts to interpret the causes and significance of the revolution, see Alan Knight, "The Mexican Revolution: Bourgeois? Nationalist? or Just a 'Great Rebellion'?" *Bulletin of Latin American Research* 4, no. 2 (1985): 1–37; Jaime O. Rodríguez, ed., *The Revolutionary Process in Mexico: Essays on Political and Social Change, 1880–1940* (Los Angeles: Latin American Center, UCLA, 1990); and Gilbert M. Joseph and Daniel Nugent, eds., *Everyday Forms of State Formation: Revolution and the Negotiation of Rule in Modern Mexico* (Durham, N.C.: Duke University Press, 1994).

59   Martz, *Colombia;* Robert H. Dix, *Colombia: The Political Dimensions of Change* (New Haven: Yale University Press, 1967) and Alvaro Echeverri Uruburu, *Elites y proceso político en Colombia, 1950–1978* (Bogotá: FUAC, 1987).

60   Ortíz, *Estado y Subversión,* pp. 28–29, suggests the importance of regional residence and class in the formation of partisan identity in the Quindío, but no study of *la Violencia* has pursued the issue of the relationship between ethnic and racial origin and politics.

61   This was the central premise of scholars such as Weinert and Williamson, and

also Steffen W. Schmidt in "La Violencia Revisited: The Clientelist Bases of Political Violence in Colombia," *Journal of Latin American Studies* 6-7 (May 1974-1975): 97-111, and "The Transformation of Clientelism in Rural Colombia," in *Friends, Followers, and Factions,* ed. Steffen W. Schmidt et al. (Berkeley: University of California Press, 1977); and Pécaut, *Orden y violencia.*

62   The main proponent of this thesis was Paul Oquist, but Richard Maullin in *Soldiers, Guerrillas, and Politics in Colombia* (Lexington, Mass.: D. C. Heath, 1973) also insisted that the central government exercised very little power at the local level and over extensive parts of Colombia.

63   Pécaut ascribed to this theory as did Ortíz Sarmiento.

64   Braun, *The Assassination of Gaitán;* Ortíz Sarmiento, *Estado y subversión.*

65   Both Sánchez and Schmidt argued that Gaitán had introduced the question of class into politics.

66   Sánchez, *Los días de la revolución;* Díaz Callejas, *El 9 de abril 1948 en Barrancabermeja.*

67   Arocha, *La Violencia en el Quindío,* and Tovar Pinzón, *El movimiento campesino en Colombia* argued that struggles over land were important features of *la Violencia* in both coffee-producing and frontier cattle areas. Gonzalo Sánchez, "La Violencia y sus efectos en el sistema político colombiano," *Cuadernos Colombianos* 9 (January–April 1976): 1-44, argued that organized labor was crushed as a result of violence after 1949, and Pécaut, *Política y sindicalismo,* agreed.

68   Oquist and other analysts of Colombian politics use the term "hegemony" to describe the monopolistic control of the central state by a single political party. Such a strategy precludes the possibility of collaboration by the political opposition and, in fact, entails their exclusion from all government and public, patronage-determined offices or jobs.

Some Colombian scholars have suggested that too little is known about the degree of integration between local, regional, and national spheres of power in Colombia to support Oquist's notion of the significance of "breakdown" of the national state on the emergence of violence. See Jesús Antonio Bejarano and Marco Palacios in *Once ensayos sobre la violencia,* pp. 304-5.

69   Pécaut, "Acerca de la Violencia de los años cincuenta," p. 43.

70   Braun, *The Assassination of Gaitán,* pp. 20-28.

71   Ibid., p. 7.

72   Ibid., pp. 82-86. Braun notes, "Everything that was physical about Gaitán became deeply symbolic. . . . While the political leaders were repelled by Gaitán's behavior, his followers rejoiced at the earthy exploits that made him look like one of them," p. 82.

73   Ibid., p. 53.

74   Ibid., p. 35.

75   Arocha, *La Violencia en el Quindío;* Betancourt and García, *Matones y cuadrilleros;* Fajardo, *Violencia y desarrollo;* and Henderson, *Cuando Colombia se desangró.*

76 Sánchez, "La Violencia y sus efectos," p. 19.

77 Ibid., p. 15.

78 Ibid., p. 24–26.

79 Ibid., p. 34; Fajardo, *Violencia y desarrollo,* p. 100.

80 Ortíz Sarmiento, *Estado y subversión en Colombia.*

81 Ibid., pp. 38 and 42.

82 Ibid., pp. 46 and 49.

83 A *vereda* is the equivalent of a village. A *municipio* (municipality) is a rural county governed by a mayor and municipal council.

84 Ortíz Sarmiento, *Estado y subversión en Colombia,* pp. 122 and 129.

85 Ibid., p. 69.

86 Ibid., pp. 322–24.

87 Philip Corrigan, "State Formation," in Joseph and Nugent, eds., *Everyday Forms of State Formation,* p. xvii, emphasis in the original; Derek Sayer, "Everyday Forms of State Formation: Some Dissident Remarks on 'Hegemony,' " in *Everyday Forms of State Formation,* p. 371, emphasis in the original; Philip Abrams, "Notes on the Difficulty of Studying the State," *Journal of Historical Sociology* 1, no. 1 (1988): 58–89.

88 Ibid., p. 375.

89 Ibid., p. 376, 377.

90 Many authors have noticed differences between the behavior of Liberals and Conservatives in Antioquia and those in other parts of Colombia and attributed these differences in large measure to the region's economy, the role of the Church, the region's mountainous location, and the cohesive nature of a primarily merchant elite. See, for instance, Bergquist, *Coffee and Conflict in Colombia;* Delpar, *Red against Blue;* Luis H. Fajardo, *The Protestant Ethic of the Antioqueños?: Social Structure and Personality* (Cali: Ediciones Departamento de Sociología, Universidad del Valle, n.d.); and Jorge Orlando Melo, "La política de 1904 a 1946," in *Historia de Antioquia,* ed. Jorge Orlando Melo (Medellín: Editorial Presencia and Suramericana de Seguros), pp. 143–59.

91 For the importance of these "consociational" forms of elite organization and their influence on state policy, see Jonathan Hartlyn, "Consociational Politics in Colombia: Confrontation and Accommodation in Comparative Perspective" (Ph.D. diss., Yale University, 1981); Hartlyn, "Producer Associations, the Political Regime, and Policy Processes in Contemporary Colombia," *Latin American Research Review* 20, no. 3 (1985): 111–38; Echeverri Uruburu, *Elites y proceso político en Colombia;* and Eduardo Sáenz Rovner, *La ofensiva empresarial: Industriales, políticos y violencia en los años 40 en Colombia* (Bogotá: Tercer Mundo, 1992).

92 Roldán, "Genesis and Evolution of La Violencia," chapter 3, pp. 127–83, and chapter 4, pp. 188–238.

93 SGA 1953, vol. 8, letter from Horacio Correa M. to Governor Dionisio Arango Ferrer (hereafter, DAF), Medellín, 28 May 1953.

94   Ibid.

95   This is evident in hacienda and mining hiring patterns in Antioquia where workers belonged to whatever party happened to predominate in the geographic area regardless of the partisan affiliation of the owners.

96   *La Defensa,* 23 Feb. 1949.

97   This phenomenon was not limited to Antioquia. Betancourt and García, *Matones y Cuadrilleros,* p. 57, describe a similar situation in their study of Valle, although their emphasis and conclusions differ from mine.

98   LeGrand, *Frontier Expansion and Peasant Protest in Colombia,* p. 163 and appendix D: "Public Land Grants and Conflicts by Municipality, 1827–1931," pp. 185–204; and Fajardo, *Violencia y desarrollo.* In a twist on this theme, Betancourt and García argue that the municipios in northern Valle where agrarian conflicts emerged in the 1950s were those where there had been Liberal-directed violence in the 1930s. See Betancourt and García, *Matones y Cuadrilleros,* p. 150.

99   See LeGrand, *Frontier Expansion,* appendix D for a detailed list of Antioqueño municipios reporting public land conflicts in the first three decades of the twentieth century.

100   Betancourt and García, *Matones y Cuadrilleros,* p. 43, for instance, note that violence in Valle was most intense along the coffee-producing mountain zones colonized by Antioqueños. They suggest that this violence had more of the character of "partisan confrontation" and seemed to be organized along patron-client networks that observed kinship and cultural ties between dependents and coffee estate owners where both sectors belonged to the same party. Although the authors do not make this argument, the problem of violence may be both partisan and cultural, that is, waged by Antioqueños belonging to different classes but sharing similar values and beliefs and a similar embeddedness in proprietary relations against those who were non-Antioqueño in origin.

101   Manuel Uribe Angel, *Geografía general del estado de Antioquia* (Paris, 1886).

102   *Progreso,* 4 Dec. 1927, 326. The magazine *Progreso* was the organ of Medellín's Sociedad de Mejoras Públicas (Society of Public Improvements). Its editorial board and contributors included Antioquia's most prominent statesmen, merchants, and policy makers. In its pages, capitalism, urbanization, rural society, moral values, class conflicts, and concepts of regional identity, autonomy, and power were explicitly and vocally debated. As such it provides an unparalleled window into the thought and discourse of Antioquia's bourgeois leadership, who shaped both public policy and social mores in the region.

103   Hermés Tovar was the first to note the impact of the 1929 coffee crisis on migration and ensuing land struggles in new frontier areas as a result of these newly displaced colonists; see Tovar, *El movimiento campesino,* p. 61. Interviews conducted by researchers in 1988 with individuals who were first-generation residents in eastern peripheral towns such as Cocorná, Yolombó, and San Roque confirm this phenomenon. Transcripts and cassette recordings of these inter-

views may be accessed at the Instituto de Estudios Regionales (INER), Universidad de Antioquia, Medellín.

104   *Tierras baldías* or *terrenos baldíos* are "public domain land, the ownership of which is vested in the nation." This is Catherine LeGrand's definition in *Frontier Expansion*, p. 265. See also ibid., appendix D.

105   The literature on colonialism is too great to summarize here. Among the works that have directly influenced my understanding of the phenomenon are: Homi K. Bhabha, "The Other Question: Difference, Discrimination, and the Discourse of Colonialism," in *Out There: Marginalization and Contemporary Cultures,* ed. Russell Ferguson et al. (Cambridge: MIT Press, 1990); Jean Comaroff and John Comaroff, *Ethnography and the Historical Imagination* (Boulder: Westview Press, 1992), pp. 155–78 and pp. 235–62; Frederick Cooper and Ann Laura Stoler, Introduction to *American Ethnologist* 16 (1989), special issue "Tensions of Empire: Colonial Control and Visions of Rule"; Ann Laura Stoler, "Making Empire Respectable: The Politics of Race and Sexual Morality in Twentieth-Century Colonial Cultures," *American Ethnologist* 16 (1989): 634–60, and "Sexual Affronts and Racial Frontiers: European Identities and the Cultural Politics of Exclusion in Colonial Southeast Asia," *Comparative Studies in Society and History* 34, no. 3 (1992): 514–51; and Nicholas Thomas, *Colonialism's Culture, Anthropology, Travel, and Government* (Princeton: Princeton University Press, 1994).

106   For a discussion of the construction of preconceived "signs" or "historically determined sets of root-metaphors," see Sander L. Gilman, *Difference and Pathology: Stereotypes of Sexuality, Race, and Madness* (Ithaca: Cornell University Press, 1985), p. 22. Gilman posits that three basic categories of difference "reflect our preoccupation with the self and the control that the self must have over the world": sexuality, illness, and race. Traits specifically associated with sexuality (concubinage, promiscuity, prostitution, free union, and so on), race (fetishism, superstition, sloth, maliciousness, darkness, filth) and illness (insalubrious climate, fevers, malaria, "weakness") are all present in the Antioqueño construction of frontier difference. For an example of the ways in which such categories are applied and implicated in situations of violence, see Malkki, *Purity and Exile.*

107   For an analysis of the issue of race in shaping regional identity and cross-departmental relations in Colombia, particularly between the Chocó and Antioquia, see Peter Wade, "Race and Class: The Case of South American Blacks," *Ethnic and Racial Studies* 8, no. 2 (April 1985): 233–49, and *Blackness and Race Mixture: The Dynamics of Racial Identity in Colombia* (Baltimore: Johns Hopkins University Press, 1993). More recently Nancy Appelbaum has explored the coincidence of racial imaginings and geography in the construction of identity for the department of Caldas. See "Remembering Riosucio: Region, Ethnicity, and Community in Western Antioquia, 1850–1920" (Ph.D. diss., University of Wisconsin, Madison, 1997).

108   For the relationship between middle-class values and citizenship in Europe, see George Mosse, *Nationalism and Sexuality: Middle-Class Morality and Sexual Norms in Modern Europe* (Madison: University of Wisconsin Press, 1985). Sander Gilman has shown how stereotypes of difference (the creation of a category of the "other") are intimately linked to the question of control: "No matter how this sense of control is articulated, whether as political power, social status, religious mission, or geographic or economic domination, it provides an appropriate vocabulary for the sense of difference." See Gilman, *Difference and Pathology,* pp. 20–21. The relationship between specific traits and places or groups of individuals associated with a specific geographic or cultural space and its impact in shaping notions of identity and policy are explored as well by Andrew Parker et al. in *Nationalisms and Sexualities* (London: Routledge, 1992), and in Doris Sommer, *Foundational Fictions: The National Romances of Latin America* (Berkeley: University of California Press, 1991). Perhaps the classic Latin American text to make explicit both the nature of a bourgeois code of values and the relationship between race, culture, and place is Domingo F. Sarmiento, *Facundo, or, Civilization and Barbarism* (New York: Penguin, 1998). The last quote in this sentence is from Stoler, "Sexual Affronts and Racial Frontiers," p. 536.

109   *Progreso,* 11 Oct. 1927, 294. The term "sana" is used here to denote both physical and moral health. For more information regarding the composition and activities of Antioquia's bourgeoisie and the overlapping of public and private power in the province, see Roldán, "Genesis and Evolution of La Violencia," especially chapters 3 and 4.

110   Uribe Angel, *Geografía de Antioquia,* pp. 255 and 296. See also Uribe Angel's description of Remedios, p. 177, Zaragoza, p. 187, Frontino, p. 257, and Cocorná, p. 282. Uribe Angel wrote before the region of Urabá came under Antioquia's jurisdictional control, but, for the purposes of his analysis, he defines the region of Frontino as incorporating Urabá. Uribe Angel's formulations were reproduced and widely disseminated through such classic regional tracts as *Monografías de Antioquia* (Medellín, 1941) and in foreign descriptions and analyses of Antioquia such as P. L. Bell, *Colombia: A Commercial and Industrial Handbook,* U.S. Department of Commerce, Bureau of Foreign and Domestic Commerce, Special Agents Series no. 206 (Washington, D.C.: Government Printing Office, 1921). In her study of family and culture in Colombia, Virginia Gutiérrez de Pineda assesses and deconstructs the relationship between ethnicity, cultural differences, and geography embedded in regional identity and mentality. See Virginia Gutiérrez de Pineda, *Familia y Cultura en Colombia* (Bogotá: Instituto Colombiano de Cultura, DANE, 1975), pp. 373–74, 411–13. See also her tables and charts relating illegitimacy, free union, and Catholic marriage by ethnicity and geographic location. Last quote in the sentence by Restrepo Jaramillo, *El pensamiento conservador,* pp. 263–64.

111   I understand hegemony in a Gramscian sense as "[depending] for its hold not only on its expression of the interests of a ruling class but also on its accep-

tance as 'normal reality' or 'commonsense' by those in practice subordinated to it," Raymond Williams, *Keywords: A Vocabulary of Culture and Society* (Oxford: Oxford University Press, 1976), p. 145. Gramsci argues that for hegemony to work "the leading group should make sacrifices of an economic-corporate kind. But there is also no doubt that such sacrifices and such a compromise cannot touch the essential; for though hegemony is ethical-political, it must also be economic, must necessarily be based on the decisive function exercised by the leading group in the decisive nucleus of economic activity," Antonio Gramsci, *Selections from the Prison Notebooks of Antonio Gramsci,* ed. Quintin Hoare and Geoffrey Nowell Smith (New York: International Publishers, 1971), p. 161.

112 James Parsons, *La colonización antioqueña en el occidente de Colombia,* 3d ed. (Bogotá: Carlos Valencia Editores, 1979), p. 19.

113 Ibid., and see table 1, "Composición Racial en Antioquia," p. 20.

114 Anderson, *Imagined Communities,* p. 7. Anderson adds that "regardless of actual inequality and exploitation that may prevail . . . the nation is always conceived as a deep, horizontal comradeship."

115 Stoler and Jean and John Comaroff have shown in their work on Indonesia and South Africa, respectively, that the process of colonial identity formation is a two-way street: colonizers construct the other (the colonized) in relation to their desired sense of self, but the latter is also transformed and shaped by the colonial experience.

116 Peter Sahlins has noted the important role which the intermediate area between France and Spain known as Cerdanza played in the gradual emergence and consolidation of national identity on either side of and within this contested site. See Peter Sahlins, *Boundaries: The Making of France and Spain in the Pyrenees* (Berkeley: University of California Press, 1989), pp. 8–9.

117 I sometimes use the term "middle sector" to describe the status and rank of emergent professional politicians in mid-century Antioquia. Some, but not all, of these men belonged to the middle class. More than a class designation, "middle sector" indicates the middle rank these rising politicians occupied in the party hierarchy.

1. Medellín and Core Municipalities

1 For a representative look at how Antioquia's elite and statesmen liked to represent themselves and be represented, see Mejía Robledo, VEA; Academia Antioqueña de Historia, *Un Siglo de Gobierno en Antioquia, 1886–1986* (Medellín, 1986); Tulio Ospina, *Protocolo Hispanoamericano de la urbanidad y el buen tono,* 3d ed. (Medellín: Felix de Bedout e Hijos, 1930), especially chapter 1, "El Civismo"; and the magazine *Progreso,* 1912–1939, various issues.

2 The following analysis of the political, social, economic, and ideological differences that divided emergent professional politicians from the elite in Antioquia relies extensively on my "Genesis and Evolution of *La Violencia,*" chapter 5.

3 See Gómez's scathing indictment of Antioqueño congressmen in his parliamen-

tary address of 1940, "Ser Congresista Liberal y Serlo Conservador," pp. 575–78 and "El peor enemigo: El moderado," p. 826 in Colombia, Camara de Representantes, *Laureano Gómez: Obras Selectas,* part 1, vol. 15 (Medellín: Editorial Bedout, 1981).

4   Farnsworth-Alvear analyzes the anti-Communist fears of the Liberal press and regional politicians during López's first administration in Antioquia in *Dulcinea in the Factory,* pp. 133–41.

5   Bergquist, *Coffee and Conflict in Colombia,* p. 4; and Melo, "La política de 1904–1946," p. 145.

6   Liberal Jesús Echeverri Duque, for instance, was reluctant to countenance worker militancy and was almost lynched by the unemployed in Medellín during his term as governor. He was eulogized in the terms often used to refer to Conservative politicians affiliated with or influenced by the Jesuits. See *Un siglo de gobierno,* p. 155–56. Even public works were infused with religious meaning in the political discourse used by the pre-1910 generation of leaders such as Liberal governor Camilo C. Restrepo. Celebrating the construction of the Carretera al Mar; Restrepo declared to the regional *Asamblea* in 1930, "With Gonzalo Mejía [a Liberal] and Tobón Quintero, Father Arteaga and Father Máximo, [who have been] apostles of this work, we shout 'to the sea, to the sea,' without pause, with faith in our destiny, and to the sea shall we go, 'viva God!' we shall go," quoted in *Un siglo de gobierno,* p. 119.

7   PEA, table 2.1.6.1, "Censos de 1905–1912," pp. 75–76; "Censos de 1918–1928," pp. 77–78; "Censos de 1938–1951," pp. 78–79.

8   PEA, table 2.1.7, "Población por zonas, según municipios, censos 1938–1973," pp. 82–83.

9   Alexander Payne, "Crecimiento y cambio social en Medellín, 1900–1930," *Estudios Sociales* 1 (September 1986): 165. Payne notes that a significant number of those migrating to Medellín were university students, some from regions other than Antioquia as well.

10 Helg, *La educación en Colombia,* pp. 162–63.

11 Many elite Liberals felt the same way. Elite members of his own party joined moderate Conservatives to organize protests against López's education project and to protect the elite monopoly over education. Tomás Rueda Vargas and Agustín Nieto (elite Liberals) both opposed López's official education plan of 1935. See Helg, *La educación en Colombia,* pp. 162–63 and p. 173.

12 Helg, *La educación en Colombia;* and Miguel Angel Builes, *Cartas Pastorales del Excelentisimo Señor Miguel Angel Builes Obispo de Santa Rosa de Osos,* 2 vols. (Bogotá: Empresa Nacional de Publicaciones, 1957).

13 Helg, *La educación en Colombia,* p. 209. Such an interpretation jibes with Aline Helg's own conclusions about the destruction of Catholic schools and institutions during the riots after Gaitán's assassination in Bogotá. She argues that such violence was intended to express a popular repudiation of the elitist values

of such institutions whose continued domination of education was predicated upon and ensured the exclusion of non-elites from power. Helg's argument is particularly persuasive since she demonstrates how elite Liberals had been among the most adamant opponents of López's educational reforms precisely because they perceived these as an attack against elite power.

14   Various interviews conducted by the author with Emma Londoño de Mejía, the widow of José Mejía y Mejía, Froilan Montoya Mazo, Aníbal Vallejo Alvarez, and Manuel Mejía Vallejo, Medellín, 1985–1987. See also Roldán, "La política en Antioquia, 1946–1958," in *Historia de Antioquia,* ed. Jorge Orlando Melo (Bogotá: Editorial Presencia, 1988).

15   This is an impression drawn from numerous interviews with individuals active in politics during this period such as Aníbal Vallejo Alvarez, Froilan Montoya Mazo, and Bernardo Ospina Román, and by the perusal of the personal correspondence of these and other individuals such as José Mejía y Mejía, his widow, Emma Londoño de Mejía, Fernando Gómez Martínez, and Belisario Betancur.

16   Ibid.

17   Pécaut, *Orden y violencia,* vol. 1, p. 192; and Mauricio Archila, "Paternalism and Social Relations in the Early Stages of Colombian Industrialization," paper presented at the Latin American Labor History Conference, Yale University, 21 April 1990, p. 18.

18   Ibid., p. 19. See also statistics on food prices in Medellín, 1949–1953, compiled from reports on the "Movimiento de la Feria de Ganados Verificada el día 8 de octubre 1952," put together by the Secretaría de Agricultura y Fomento de Antioquia, Sección de Estadística y Publicaciones in AGA, 1952, vol. 4; and *El Colombiano,* 21 Oct. 1949; 16 Sept. 1950; 14 Oct. 1951; and 18 Nov. 1953. For reports of government-instituted food price controls, see *El Colombiano,* 7 July 1950.

19   Archila, "Paternalism and Social Relations," p. 19.

20   Colombia, Departamento de Antioquia, *Anuario estadístico, años 1944, 1945, 1946,* appendix 2/4, "Estadística electoral."

21   PEA, table 20.1.1.3, "Población ocupada, por ramas de actividad económica, Censos 1938–1973," p. 751.

22   *La Defensa* is a Catholic newspaper founded in Medellín in 1919 whose contributors identified themselves first as Catholics and second as Conservatives. In the 1930s *La Defensa* often acted as the official mouthpiece of Acción Católica. It was an outspoken critic of bipartisan elite cooperation and Liberal control of public sector jobs and patronage.

23   Governors were appointed by the president and mayors were appointed by governors. Municipal councils were popularly elected, and they in turn appointed and paid the municipal police, town clerk (*personero*) and other municipal offices such as town scribe (*escríbano*). Police inspectors and work inspectors were appointed by the governor.

24   On the coffee zone, see AGA, 1947, "Telegramas," no. 1513, 1 Oct. 1947, reporting

irregularities in an all-Conservative hamlet in Andes; AGA, 1947, "Telegramas," no. 1148, 3 July 1947 regarding violence during the coffee harvest in Jerico; AGA, 1947, "Telegramas," no. 1431, 1 Sept. 1947, reporting violence waged by a drunken, Conservative mayor against Liberal citizens while the police stood by in Betulia; and AGA, 1947 "Telegramas," no. 1252, regarding violence in Bolívar, 25 July 1947. On the industrial belt, see AGA, 1947, "Telegramas," no. 1477, 23 Sept. 1947, naming military mayors to towns such as Envigado and Bello which reported electoral disturbances. The northern towns included Valdivia, Ituango, Sopetran, and Ebejico. Aníbal Vallejo Alvarez, interview with the author, and AGA, 1947, "Telegramas," no. 1513, San Jeronimo, 4 Oct. 1947.

25   Colombia, *Memoria de hacienda, Francisco de Paula Pérez, 1929, 1931, 1946* (Bogotá: Banco de la República, 1990), "Auxilios," 1945, pp. 53–66.

26   Colombia, DANE, *Estadística Electoral,* 16 March 1947 and 5 Oct. 1947, pp. 308–15; 5 June 1947, pp. 274–80; and 27 Nov. 1949, pp. 280–81.

27   AGA, 1947, "Telegramas," no. 1452, from a member of the Jurado Electoral (electoral jury) appointed to oversee voter registration, Caramanta, 19 Sept. 1947; AGA, 1947, "Telegramas," no. 1513, from the mayor of Andes who complained that the Jurado suspended the registration of Conservative voters in the *corregimiento* of San José de Buenos Aires, Andes, 1 Oct. 1947; AGA, 1947, "Telegramas," number illegible, Yolombó, 2 Oct. 1947; and AGA, 1947, "Telegramas," no. 1556, Itagüí, 5 Oct. 1947.

28   Centro Cultural Jorge Eliécer Gaitán, Bogotá, Correspondencia de Jorge Eliécer Gaitán, letter from Aureliano Guerra, Daniel Guerra, and Francisco Espinosa, Antioquia, 22 Jan. 1947. Gaitán won a seat on the regional *asamblea,* as did five other men (Conrado Sosa, Jesús García, Luis Atehortúa, Amador de J. Guerra, and Luis Octavio Velásquez) and their *suplentes* (replacements or stand-ins). Colombia, Departamento de Antioquia, *Anales de la Asamblea de Antioquia,* Medellín, 22 April 1947, Año 32:1.

   In the *asamblea,* senate and representative races of March 1947, 72 percent of the Liberal voters in Andes voted for Gaitán; this dropped to 33 percent by the *concejo* (municipal council) elections in October 1947. In March, 69 percent of Bolívar's Liberal voters voted for Gaitán, but none voted for *gaitanista* candidates in October. In Ituango in March 74 percent of the Liberal vote went to Gaitán, but no votes were cast for *gaitanistas* in local *concejo* elections in October. The same pattern occurred in Olaya and Caramanta where the March election garnered, respectively, 81 percent and 96 percent of the Liberal vote for Gaitán and then none in October's contest. Ebéjico had a more consistent loyalty to *gaitanistas,* voting for this movement's candidates in local, regional, and national elections from 1947 through 1949 (80 percent of the Liberal vote in March 1947, 43 percent in October 1947, and 33 percent of the Liberal vote in March 1949). DANE, *Estadística Electoral,* 16 March 1947, 5 Oct. 1947, and 5 June 1949.

   Segovia did not vote for Gaitán in the March 1947 elections but delivered

75 percent of its Liberal votes to *gaitanistas* in local elections in October 1947. Remedios, like Segovia, did not vote for Gaitán in March 1947, but gave local *gaitanista* candidates 39 percent of the Liberal vote in the *concejo* election of October.

29   DANE, *Estadística Electoral,* 16 March 1947, 5 Oct. 1947, and 5 June 1949. See also this volume appendix C for statistics on dissident voting in Antioquia in the 1947 election for *asamblea, concejo,* congress, and the senate.

30   These towns had the misfortune to be located near Conservative redoubts. Olaya and Pueblorrico were the two most severely affected by the conservatization process. Olaya went from having an electorate that was 80 percent Liberal in 1945 to one that was only 26 percent Liberal in 1949. Pueblorrico dropped from a Liberal total of 71 percent in 1945 to 16 percent in 1949.

31   AGA, 1947, "Telegramas," no. 1045, from José María Bernal (hereafter JMB) to Carlos Echeverri, Jesús Saldarriaga et al., Caramanta, 4 June 1947.

32   PEA, p. 306. The coffee farms of Titiribí, in fact, were the most concentrated in Antioquia, averaging 66,000 coffee trees per farm. In contrast, the average coffee plantation in Fredonia, the region's largest volume producer of the bean, had 8,250 trees. See PEA, table 7.1.2.2.5, "Número de plantaciones, cafetos y maquinaria según municipios," p. 306.

33   AGA, 1947, "Telegramas," no. 1106, from Rafael Azula Barrera, Secretario General de la Presidencia to JMB, 21 June 1947.

34   Cáceres had existed since colonial times when it attracted settlers searching for gold mines, but it experienced only sluggish growth until the early to mid-twentieth century when the expansion of important cattle haciendas owned by members of Medellín's industrial bourgeoisie and members of the Ospina family awakened an interest in the town, *Monografías de Antioquia,* p. 94. The town had one of the region's lowest turnouts by eligible voters, see Colombia, Departamento de Antioquia, *Anuario estadístico, años 1944, 1945, 1946,* appendix 2, 4, "Estadística electoral: Resultado de las elecciones para Presidente de la República en el Departmento de Antioquia, el día 5 de Mayo de 1946."

35   AGA, 1947, "Telegramas," no. 1367, from Eduardo Berrío González (hereafter EBG) to Rafael Azula Barrera, 28 Aug. 1947.

36   Colombia, Departmento de Antioquia, *Anuario estadístico, años 1950–1952,* (d) Café—volumen aproximado de la producción cafetera en Antioquia—1952 (sacos de pergamino de 62 1/2 kilos), p. 9.

37   Melo, "La Política en Antioquia," p. 152.

38   AGA, 1947, "Telegramas," no. 1259, from JMB to the mayor of Fredonia, 27 July 1947; AGA 1947, "Telegramas," no. 1260, from JMB to Mariano Ospina Pérez (hereafter, MOP), 28 July 1947.

39   AGA, 1948, "Orden Público," (hereafter, O.P.), telegram to the Governor, 9 June 1948.

40   AGA, 1948, "O.P.," telegram to the Governor, 16 June 1948.

41   *El Colombiano,* 17 July 1950; the Junta de Rentas oversaw the operation and col-

lection of perhaps the single greatest source of regional revenue — the tax on the state liquor and tobacco monopoly — and as such wielded considerable clout in the region's administrative affairs. About 40 percent of Antioquia's revenues were generated by the liquor and tobacco tax.

42   AGA, 1948, "O.P.," Governor to the Ministro de Gobierno (hereafter, MinGob), 9 Sept. 1948.

43   Urrutia, *Development of the Colombian Labor Movement*, p. 85 and pp. 93–107; and Pécaut, *Orden y violencia*, pp. 194–95, pp. 205–7; p. 238, n. 67, and p. 241, n. 83.

44   Ivan Darío Osorio, *Historia del sindicalismo antioqueño, 1900–1986* (Medellín: Tipografía y Litografía Sigifredo, n.d.), p. 71.

45   Letter from Froilan Montoya Mazo in Medellín to Jorge Eliécer Gaitán, Centro Cultural, Jorge Eliécer Gaitán, *Correspondencia de Jorge Eliécer Gaitán,* Centro Gaitán, Bogotá, 17 Sept. 1946.

46   All but two of these towns — Betulia and Ebéjico — were located on the periphery.

47   Pécaut, *Política y sindicalismo,* p. 215.

48   Ibid., p. 240, n. 81.

49   AGA, 1947, "Telegramas," no. 1044, June 1947. While the government's response to the workers' demands was clearly motivated by the desire to simultaneously weaken the union and replace Liberal workers with Conservatives, it bears remembering that a precedent for such actions was established during the 1934 railroad strike in Antioquia, when a Liberal governor, Captain Julián Uribe Gaviria, declared that strike illegal, dismissed workers by accusing them of being Communist sympathizers, and then replaced them with hand-picked Liberal workers loyal to the mainstream and elite-led wing of the party.

50   AGA, 1947, "Telegramas," no. 1285, Governor to Shell Oil Company, Casabe, 1 Aug. 1947.

51   Like many other contemporaneous Latin American authoritarian governments — Perón and Vargas in Argentina and Brazil spring to mind — the *laureanistas* used a nationalist rhetoric and nationalist principles to justify both the suppression of "internationalist" groups such as the Communist Party and the promotion of native industrialist and economic interests against international competition.

52   PEA, p. 406. AGA, 1953, vol. 7, "Memorándum" describing the sources of revenue to pay for regional public works projects, n.d. 1948.

53   AGA, 1953, vol. 15, n.d. 1946 and 1947.

54   Quoted in Osorio, *Historia del sindicalismo antioqueño,* p. 73.

55   Ibid.

56   Other towns where Gaitán's assassination sparked unrest were Rionegro, Remedios, Turbo, Segovia, Zaragoza, San Jerónimo, Caucasia, Amagá, Angelopolis, and Cañasgordas.

57   *Varones Ilustres,* p. 196; "Mensaje del Gobernador," in Francisco Duque Betan-

cur, *Historia del Departamento de Antioquia,* 2d ed. (Medellín: Editorial Albon-Interprint S.A., 1968), p. 990; and Sánchez, *Los días de la revolución,* pp. 48–49.

58 AGA, 1948, "O.P.," Bolívar, telegram to the Governor, 10 April 1948.

59 Ibid.

60 AGA, 1948, "O.P.," El Carmen del Atrato, telegram to the Governor, 11 April 1948.

61 AGA, 1948, "O.P.," Andes, telegram to the Governor, 12 April 1948.

62 AGA, 1948, "O.P.," Dionisio Arango Ferrer to Darío Echandía, Bogotá, regarding the Shell Oil camp in Casabe, 23 April 1948.

63 AGA, 1948, "O.P.," President, Bogotá, telegram to the Governor, 1 June 1948.

64 Ibid., 9 June 1948.

65 *El Colombiano,* 29 July 1950.

66 Interview with Carlos Uribe Echeverri, quoted in VEA, pp. 513–14.

67 VEA, p. 352; and Academia Antioqueña de Historia, *Un siglo de gobierno,* pp. 199–200.

68 Academia Antioqueña de Historia, *Un siglo de gobierno,* pp. 199–200.

69 It is best not to take accusations of "Communism" or the constant use of the term "Communist" too seriously, particularly in the Antioqueño context where the party was small. Liberals were persistently conflated with Communists in Conservative discourse during this period as were any groups making popular demands or critical of Conservative rule. Regardless of the actual ideological orientation, accusations of being a Communist were bandied about freely whenever the status quo appeared threatened or popular sectors rebelled. Academia Antioqueña de Historia, *Un siglo de gobierno,* p. 200.

70 Ibid.

71 AGA, 1951, vol. 2, telegram from Braulio Henao Mejía (hereafter, BHM) to the Ministro de Gobierno, Bogotá, 1 Aug. 1951.

72 SGA, 1948, vol. 2, communication from Dionisio Arango Ferrer (hereafter, DAF) to Visitadores Administrativos, 13 July 1948.

73 These are too numerous to list here, but representative complaints may be found in SGA, 1949, vol. 2, telegram from Bello, 7 Aug. 1949; SGA, 1949, vol. 2, telegram from Betulia, 23 Dec. 1949; SGA, 1949, vol. 2, telegram from Yolombó, 4 Dec. 1949; AGA, 1949, "Papeles del Señor Gobernador (1949–1950)," telegram from Betulia, 4 Jan. 1950; AGA, 1950, vol. 8, telegram from Medellín, 30 May 1950; AGA, 1950, vol. 8, telegram from Caicedo, 24 April 1950; AGA, 1951, vol. 2, telegram from Giraldo, 16 July 1951; AGA, 1951, vol. 5, *El Colombiano* complains of police brutality, Medellín, (no specific date) 1951; AGA, 1952, vol. 3, telegram from Puerto Berrío, 25 Oct. 1952; AGA, 1952, vol. 4, telegram from the local inspector, Puerto Nare, calling customs officers "a public menace, a corps of assassins," 8 Oct. 1952.

74 The *visitador administrativo* is a holdover from the Spanish colonial period when agents of the Spanish king were appointed to conduct a *visita,* or assessment, after a viceroy or governor had finished his term in office. Colombian visitadores

acted as government agents sent to collect information and submit reports on topics as varied as public order, malfeasance, or party discipline.

75   SGA, 1949, vol. 4, communiqué from the departmental detectives to Jorge Salazar, Jefe del Detectivismo, regarding Jardín, 20 April 1949.

76   Ibid.

77   *El Colombiano*, 16 Jan. 1949; *El Colombiano*, 8 Feb. 1949; and *El Colombiano*, 5 Feb. 1949.

78   *La Defensa*, 23 Feb. 1949. *"Nueve abrileños"* was the colloquial term by which right-wing Conservatives referred to Gaitán's followers.

79   Ibid.

80   SGA, 1949, vol. 4, Federación Nacional de Comerciantes to the Governor, 5 Feb. 1949.

81   Ibid.

82   *La Defensa*, 8 March 1949, 11 March 1949, and 12 March 1949.

83   Marceliano Vélez, quoted in *Varones Ilustres de Antioquia: Biografías de los académicos de números fallecidos* (Medellín: Editorial Universo, 1978), p. 20, and Clodomiro Ramírez quoted in *Varones Ilustres de Antioquia*, p. 68.

84   Alejandro López quoted in Alberto Mayor Mora, *Etica, trabajo y productividad*, 2d ed. (Medellín: Ediciones Tercer Mundo, 1985), p. 219; and see Tulio Ospina, *Protocolo Hispanoamericano de la urbinidad y el buen tono*, 3d ed. (Medellín: Felix de Bedout e Hijos).

85   Mayor Mora, *Etica, trabajo y productividad*, p. 219.

86   *El Colombiano*, 25 Feb. 1949.

87   *El Colombiano*, 8 March 1949.

88   *El Colombiano*, 12 March 1949 and 24 March 1949.

89   *El Colombiano*, 6 March 1949.

90   *El Colombiano*, 24 March 1949.

91   *El Colombiano*, 2 April 1949.

92   Alfonso López Pumarejo's son had been involved in a scandal concerning a boxer named Mamatoco a few years before this remark, and I am assuming that referring to the governor by this name in this context was intended to suggest that he kowtowed to the Liberals. AGA, 1949, "Archivo Privado del Señor Gobernador de Antioquia" (hereafter, APSG), letter from a visitador administrativo to Fernando Gómez Martínez (hereafter, FGM), Medellín, 30 March 1949.

93   SGA, 1949, vol. 2, telegram from EBG to FGM regarding Salgar's mayor, 11 Feb. 1949.

94   AGA, 1949, "APSG," telegram from Puerto Berrío, 25 May 1949; telegram from Remedios, 25 May 1949; AGA, 1949, "MinGob," telegram regarding Sopetran, 30 May 1949.

95   AGA, 1949, "APSG," telegram, regarding Cisneros, 8 April 1949, and AGA, 1949, "MinGob," telegram regarding Itagüí, 18 April 1949.

96   AGA, 1949, "MinGob," telegrams regarding Itagüí, 19 April 1949 and 1 May 1949.

97   AGA, 1949, "MinGob," telegram from Bogotá, 6 May 1949.

98   SGA, 1949, vol. 5, Sindicato Ferrovario de Antioquia to the Governor, 10 Jan. 1949.

99   SGA, 1949, vol. 5, Sindicato de Trabajadores Frontino Gold Mines, Segovia to the Governor, 23 March 1949, emphasis in the original.

100 AGA, 1950, vol. 6, Public road workers in Yolombó to the Governor, 23 April 1949, and AGA, 1950, vol. 6, Public road workers in Yolombó and Segovia to the Governor, 27 April 1949.

101 AGA, 1950, vol. 6, Bogotá, Ministro Gobierno to the Governor regarding public road workers in Yolombó and Segovia, 30 April 1949.

102 AGA, 1949, "MinGob," Bogotá to Medellín, 11 May 1949.

103 SGA, 1949, vol. 4, FEDETA to the Governor, 7 May 1949.

104 SGA, 1949, vol. 2, Conservative Committee, Yarumal to the Secretaría de Gobierno, Antioquia, 28 May 1949.

105 AGA, 1949, "MinGob," telegram from Bogotá, 30 April 1949.

106 AGA, 1949, "MinGob," telegram from Andes, 18 May 1949.

107 AGA, 1950, vol. 6, telegram from Bolívar, 18 May 1949.

108 AGA, 1949, telegram from Yarumal to FGM, 18 May 1949.

109 AGA, 1949, telegram from San Roque, 8 May 1949; AGA, 1949, "MinGob," telegram from Caracolí, 9 May 1949; AGA, 1949, telegram from San Roque, 11 May 1949.

110 SGA, 1949, no volume number or date, Jairo de Bedout to the Secretario de Gobierno de Antioquia (hereafter, SecGobAnt) regarding Olaya, 25 March 1949.

111 SGA, 1949, vol. 4, Detectives to Jorge Salazar Restrepo, Jefe Departamento de Investigación Criminal, regarding Jardín, 20 April 1949.

112 *El Colombiano,* 23 May 1949.

113 AGA, 1949, "APSG," telegram from Ricardo Moreno to FGM regarding Remedios, 25 May 1949.

114 *El Colombiano,* 24 May 1949.

115 AGA, 1949, "APSG," telegram from Puerto Berrío, 3 May 1949.

116 AGA, 1949, telegram from Caracolí, 6 June 1949; AGA, 1949, telegram from San Rafael, June 1949.

117 AGA, 1949, telegram from Titiribí, 9 June 1949.

118 *El Colombiano,* 12 June 1949.

119 *El Colombiano,* 5 April 1949, 12 May 1949, and 17 May 1949.

120 *El Colombiano,* 10 Aug. 1949.

121 Liberal majorities in some towns also swelled in response to Liberals fleeing from nearby areas where they did not constitute a majority or where Conservative intimidation was more severe or effective. Such "target towns," places where the increase in the number of Liberal voters was disproportionate to the natural increase of the local population between 1945 and 1949, reflected the possibility that there was an influx of voters from elsewhere or fraud. The increased pres-

ence of Liberal voters in certain towns was also a result of cross-departmental migration, particularly in Puerto Berrío where ports such as Puerto Nare were attracting fleeing Liberals from Santander and Boyacá.

122   Aníbal Vallejo Alvarez (a regional *laureanista* leader), interview with the author, Medellín, 1987.

123   For instance, Bolívar and Betulia exported violence to Bolombolo, Venecia; Santa Barbara exported violence to Valparaiso; Yolombó exported violence to Amalfi; Bello exported violence to Rionegro; and so on.

124   These towns were: Abriaquí, Alejandría, Angostura, Belmira, El Carmen del Viboral, Entrerríos, Granada, Ituango, Jardín, Jericó, Liborina, Nariño, San Andrés, San Luis, San Pedro, Santa Rosa, San Vicente, and Yarumal.

125   Consequently, the majority of conservatized towns were located in the southern and southwestern coffee-producing areas (Andes, Armenia, Bolívar, Caramanta, Fredonia, Montebello, Tarso, Valparaiso) while the rest were scattered in the northeast (Anorí, San Roque, and Yolombó), west (Olaya, Sabanalarga, and Sopetrán), and center (Barbosa and Bello).

126   *El Colombiano,* 10 Aug. 1949.

127   AGA, 1949, "MinGob," Directorio Liberal to Colonel Régulo Gaitán, 22 June 1949.

128   AGA, 1950, vol. 6, mayor of Bolívar to FGM, 5 July 1949.

129   AGA, 1949, "MinGob," Directorio Liberal to Colonel Régulo Gaitán, 26 June 1949.

130   AGA, 1949, "MinGob," MinGob Bogotá to EBG regarding Bolívar, 6 Aug. 1949.

131   AGA, 1949, "Telegramas," Santuario's mayor to FGM, 6 July 1949.

132   *El Colombiano,* 22 Aug. 1949 and 23 Aug. 1949. Jorge Aristizábal, John Gómez, Darío Ramírez Gaviria, Jaime Posada Angel, and Gilberto Zapata Lotero represented the Liberals, while Manuel Yepes, Darío Londoño Villa, Francisco Ospina Pérez, Jorge Escobar, Mario Saldarriaga, and Eduardo Isaza Martínez represented the Conservatives.

133   AGA, 1949, "APSG," Juez Tercero, Medellín to EBG, 6 Sept. 1949.

134   AGA, 1949, "MinGob," telegram from Puerto Berrío to MinGob, Col. Régulo Gaitán, Sept. 1949.

135   SGA, 1949, vol. 5, Sindicato Ferroviario de Antioquia to the Governor, 11 Oct. 1949.

136   Ibid.

137   SGA, 1949, vol. 2, Venecia, Fuerzas Armadas to Comandante, 4th Brigade, Medellín, 27 Dec. 1949.

138   AGA, 1950, vol. 7, telegram, 17 Oct. 1949, and *El Colombiano,* 3 Oct. 1949.

139   AGA, 1950, vol. 6, telegram from the president of the Federation of Coffee Growers to EBG, 31 Oct. 1949.

140   Sergeant Bedoya would later be sent to the Magdalena Medio region to organize contrachusma forces on the haciendas there.

141   AGA, 1949, "APSG," telegram from MinGob Andrade to EBG, Nov. 1949.

142 AGA, 1949, "APSG," telegram from MinGob Andrade to EBG, 9 Nov. 1949.

143 AGA, 1949, "APSG," telegram from MinGob Andrade to EBG, 7 Nov. 1949.

144 AGA, 1949, "Telegramas," Conservative mayor to EBG, 21 Nov. 1949; AGA, 1950, vol. 9, Departamento de Seguridad to EBG, 21 Nov. 1949.

145 *El Colombiano,* 21 Nov. 1949 and 22 Nov. 1949.

146 *El Colombiano,* 23 Oct. 1949.

147 *El Colombiano,* 29 Oct. 1949.

148 *El Colombiano,* 9 Nov. 1949.

149 *El Colombiano,* 11 Nov. 1949, 21 Nov. 1949, and 24 Nov. 1949.

150 Decree no. 2136, 18 July 1949.

151 AGA, 1950, vol. 9, telegram, 26 Nov. 1949 and 29 Nov. 1949; AGA, 1949, "Telegramas," telegram, 30 Nov. 1949; AGA, 1949, "APSG," Rentas to EBG, 5 Dec. 1949; and AGA, 1950, vol. 9, telegram regarding troops for Medellín, 3 Dec. 1949.

152 AGA, 1950, vol. 7, telegram, 27 Nov. 1949 and AGA, 1949, "MinGob," telegram from MinGob to EBG, 1 Dec. 1949.

153 AGA, 1949, "Telegramas," telegram, 11 Dec. 1949.

154 AGA, 1949, "APSG," telegram reporting on events in Concordia and Betulia, 1 Dec. 1949.

155 AGA, 1949, "Telegramas," the priest of San Juan de Urabá to EBG, 14 Dec. 1949.

156 SGA, 1950, vol. 2, Directorio Conservador de Antioquia (hereafter, DiConsAnt) to the SecGobAnt, 5 Dec. 1950.

157 AGA, 1949, "APSG," Sindicato del Ferropacifico to the Governor, 19 Nov. 1949.

158 SGA, 1950, vol. 1, circular no. 065/A, Colonel Carlos Bejarano, Director General de la Policia Nacional, Bogotá, to the Governor, 21 Jan. 1950.

159 AGA, 1950, vol. 9, MinGob to the Governor regarding Venecia, 27 June 1950.

160 AGA, 1950, vol. 9, Colonel Villamil to the Governor regarding Betulia, 10 July 1950.

161 AGA, 1949, "APSG," Governor Valencia, Chocó to Eduardo Berrío, 10 Nov. 1949.

162 AGA, 1949, "APSG," Colonel Villamil to MinGob, 4 Jan. 1950.

163 AGA, 1950, vol. 9, Medellín, Ricardo Posada to Maríano Ospina Pérez, 30 May 1950.

164 Ibid.

165 *El Colombiano,* 7 Feb. 1950.

166 Aníbal Vallejo Alvarez, interview with the author, Medellín, 1987.

167 Oquist, *Violence, Conflict, and Politics,* p. 177.

168 *Rosca* means "inner circle" or "clique," with the added sense of dirty politics or favoritism behind it.

2. Bajo Cauca, Magdalena Medio, and the Northeast

1 Ernesto Guhl, *Colombia: Bosquejo de su geografía tropical,* vol. 1 (Bogotá: Biblioteca Básica Colombiana, 1975); James Parsons, *Antioqueño Colonization in Western Colombia,* 2d ed. (Berkeley: University of California Press, 1968).

2 Gloria Isabel Ocampo, "Hacienda, parentesco y mentalidad: La colonización

antioqueña en el Sinu," *Revista Colombiana de Antropología,* 26 (1986–1988): 23–
32. Ocampo raises questions similar to my own regarding the usefulness of observing official administrative distinctions when analyzing the organization of
production, labor, and political comportment in regions such as the Bajo Cauca.

3   SGA, 1948, vol. 3, DiConsAnt to Secretario de Gobierno de Antioquia (hereafter,
"SecGob"), Aníbal Vallejo A., 19 Nov. 1947.

4   SGA, 1948, vol. 1, Visitador Administrativo to Governor, 13 July 1948.

5   Ibid. and *Monografías de Antioquia* (Medellín; n.p., 1941), p. 386.

6   *La Defensa,* 5 Feb. 1949.

7   *La Defensa,* 16 Feb. 1949.

8   SGA, 1949, vol. 3, Visitador Administrativo to Governor, 31 March 1949.

9   SGA, 1949, vol. 3, Visitador Administrativo, Caucasia to Governor, 31 March
1949.

10 Ibid.

11 SGA, 1949, vol. 2, Conservatives, Zaragoza to Governor, 9 April 1949; SGA 1949,
vol. 2, "O.P.," Colonel Eduardo Villamil to Governor regarding Puerto Berrío,
11 April 1949; SGA 1949, vol. 3, Jairo de Bedout regarding Remedios to Governor,
12 April 1949.

12 SGA, 1949, vol. 2, DiConsAnt to Governor, 12 May 1949.

13 AGA, 1949, "Telegramas," Presidente de la República to Governor, 12 May 1949.

14 SGA, 1949, vol. 2, Directorio Conservador, Caucasia to Governor, 12 April 1949.

15 SGA, 1949, vol. 3, Rafael O'Brien Cadavid to comandante de la Polinal, 16 Aug.
1949.

16 SGA, 1952, vol. 12, Antioquia, Secretaría de Obras Publicas, "Informe para el Sr.
Gobernador de Antioquia," Medellín, 10 Nov. 1952. The composition of workers
in the gold mines and Shell Oil's Casabe camp was described as "98 percent
costeños and santandereanos." AGA, 1952, vol. 12, Shell Oil Camp, Yondó,
Remedios, 10 Nov. 1952.

17 SGA, 1948, vol. 1, Asamblea General Del Sindicato de Trabajadores de Pato Consolidated Gold Dredging Ltd., "Proposicion #1," January 1948.

18 Ibid.

19 Similar claims around citizenship were made by Mexican workers in the Parral
district in the early twentieth century. See William E. French, "Progreso For-
zado: Workers and the Inculcation of the Capitalist Work Ethic in the Parral
Mining District," in *Rituals of Rule, Rituals of Resistance: Public Celebrations and
Popular Culture in Mexico,* ed. William Beezeley, Cheryl English Martin, and
William E. French (Wilmington, Del.: Scholarly Resources, 1994), p. 202.

20 AGA, 1948, "O.P.," telegram to Governor, 14 Sept. 1948.

21 AGA, 1948, "O.P.," telegram, 8 Nov. 1948.

22 AGA, 1949, "APSG," Comité Conservador to Governor, 9 June 1949.

23 AGA, 1949, "APSG," telegram to Governor, 23 July 1949.

24 AGA, 1949, "APSG," Manuel Marín to Governor, 8 Sept. 1949.

25   AGA, 1953, vol. 9, "Informe sobre la acción del bandolerismo," Medellín, 11 May 1953.

26   AGA, 1949, "MinGob," MinGob to Governor and to SecGob, Sept. 1949.

27   SGA, 1949, vol. 3, Polinal to Governor, 16 Sept. 1949.

28   SGA, 1949, vol. 4, Sindicato Ferrovario to Governor, 11 Oct. 1949.

29   AGA, 1949, "Telegramas," Presidencia de la República, 7 Nov. 1949.

30   SGA, 1949, vol. 2, "O.P.," 1 Nov. 1949.

31   AGA, 1949, "Teleg-Presidencia de la República," part of a report dated 29 Nov. 1949, but filed by the Governor on 20 Dec. 1949.

32   SGA, 1949, vol. 2, Fuerzas Armadas de Colombia to Governor, 20 Dec. 1949.

33   SGA, 1949, vol. 2, "O.P.," 24 Dec. 1949.

34   AGA, 1950, vol. 4, Sindicato de Trabajadores de la Shell to Governor, 10 Jan. 1950.

35   AGA, 1950, vol. 3, Shell Oil legal representative, Remedios to Governor, 3 June 1950.

36   AGA, 1950, "APSG," DiConsAnt to Governor, 15 June 1950.

37   AGA, 1950, "Telegramas," Colonel Eduardo Villamil to Governor, 4 Aug. 1950.

38   AGA, 1950, "Telegramas," telegrapher to Governor, 9 Aug. 1950.

39   AGA, 1950, "Telegramas," Colonel Villamil to Ministro de Guerra (hereafter, MinGuerra), 12 Aug. 1950.

40   AGA, 1950, "Telegramas," Colonel Villamil to Governor, 10 Aug. 1950.

41   AGA, 1950, "APSG," Inspector de Policía, Montelibano to Governor, 10 July 1950.

42   AGA, 1949, "APSG," Bolívar to Antioquia, 12 July 1950.

43   SGA, 1951, vol. 1, Governor to Polinal, Bogotá, 13 July 1950.

44   AGA, 1950, vol. 2, DiConsAnt to Governor, 11 Sept. 1950.

45   AGA, 1949, "APSG," 3 Nov. 1950.

46   AGA, 1950, vol. 5, Turbo, 12 Dec. 1950; SGA, 1951, vol. 1, Urrao, 14 Dec. 1950; AGA, 1950, vol. 5, Puerto Perales, 12 Dec. 1950.

47   AGA, 1950, vol. 6, 19 Feb. 1951.

48   *Aplanchar* is the verb used to describe beating someone with the flat part of a machete; *aplanchamiento* is the noun describing the action itself.

49   AGA, 1950, vol. 4, registrador municipal to the Governor, Jan. 1951.

50   AGA, 1951, vol. 7, Departamento de Seguridad to the Governor, 10 Jan. 1951.

51   AGA, 1953, vol. 11, Arturo to José, Colorado, 23 March 1952.

52   AGA, 1950, vol. 4, Juan de Dios Arango to Governor, 5 Dec. 1951.

53   AGA, 1950, vol. 4, Conservative Committee to Governor, 5 Dec. 1951.

54   SGA, 1950, vol. 7, Administrador de Rentas, Zaragoza to Governor, 11 Nov. 1950.

55   AGA, 1950, vol. 4, Caucasia, José María Brand, registrador municipal to the Governor, Jan. 1951.

56   AGA, 1950, vol. 6, DiConsAnt to Governor, 5 March 1951.

57   AGA, 1950, vol. 6, BHM to Gonzálo Restrepo Jaramillo, Ministro de Relaciones Exteriores, Bogotá, 1 March 1951. In this and the following paragraph, all quotations refer to this letter.

58   The narrative that follows is based on the testimony provided by Angela Rosa Arango to the authorities in Medellín. The full transcript of her testimony may be found in SGA, 1953, vol. 7, "Declaración de Angela Rosa Arango," Departamento de Investigación Criminal, Medellín, 22 May 1953. Much of Angela Rosa's testimony is independently corroborated by archival sources and interviews with former guerrillas conducted by the author. Whenever a specific piece of information in her account can be verified by other sources, I include these in the notes to the text.

59   The hacienda "Nuevo Mundo" was located in Puerto Berrío and was the repeated target of guerrilla cattle rustling, see AGA 1953, vol. 8, Puerto Berrío, 6 June 1953. The mayor of Puerto Berrío reported that four policemen had been sent to the paraje "Nuevo Mundo" to capture the delinquent Manuel Mona who along with other men had attacked the police and killed one policeman. Mona was captured. See AGA, 1950, vol. 6, mayor of Puerto Berrío to Governor, 2 March 1951.

60   AGA, 1952, vol. 6, Yolombó, 9 June 1952. This is a report that the guerrillas were camped on a farm owned by Luis Segundo and Gabriel Alvarez and that they were linked to a Liberal leader from Yolombó and to a dentist and Liberal *jefe* from Yalí. The latter owned a *finca* called "La Sellada" thought to be part of a major supply route for guerrillas. On August 8, 1952, moreover, Pielroja's appearance in Maceo was reported by Liberal administrators of Conservative-owned haciendas in the area who reported that workers were called in by Pielroja and asked why the local Liberal leadership hadn't offered them material support. See AGA, 1952, vol. 5, 8 Aug. 1952.

61   Angela Rosa never mentioned how they supported themselves as they moved between one safe house and another through an area covering three municipalities. But we can infer from the mention in other parts of her testimony that the women were generally hired to provide domestic help and the men to clear and sow fields by the mayordomos or administrators left in charge of the large haciendas held by absentee landlords in the region.

62   AGA, 1952, vol. 3, 6 July 1952; Pielroja's presence is first reported along the haciendas of the railroad line.

63   LeGrand, *Frontier Expansion,* p. 265, defines a *corregimiento* as "the smallest administrative unit in the Colombian countryside, a subdivision of a municipality."

64   AGA, 1952, vol. 1, 28 Nov. 1952, corroborates Angela Rosa's version of this event.

65   AGA, 1952, vol. 1, 25 Nov. 1952; the army reported killing 26 guerrillas found with explosives near Virginias (on the railroad line) and on 26 Nov. 1952 reported killing 170 "revolutionaries" and capturing the guerrilla leader, Rangel. The last report proved to be false.

66   Captain Corneta admitted that his band stole indiscriminately from Liberal and Conservative haciendas alike. Captain Corneta (Francisco Montoya), interview with the author, Medellín, spring 1987.

67 Ibid.

68 Ibid. Indeed, Corneta reported that the majority of the men under his command were not Antioqueños but Santandereanos, so there was no reason for the women to have known them.

69 Ibid. This conforms to information given by Corneta who said that all his men, except for butchers and cooks, were armed.

70 Ibid. Corneta corroborated stealing uniforms from the police.

71 AGA, 1952, vol. 9, original message in code, but deciphered on the reverse, 4 Feb. 1952.

72 AGA, 1952, vol. 9, Yolombó, 9 Feb. 1952 and 27 Feb. 1952.

73 LeGrand, *Frontier Expansion,* p. 265, defines *caserio* as "a small rural village that has no administrative status." Regarding the attack, see AGA, 1952, vol. 1, Nechí, Caucasia, 27 Feb. 1952.

74 AGA, 1952, vol. 11, Governor to notary of Caucasia, 27 Feb. 1952.

75 AGA, 1952, vol. 1, police inspector, Puerto Nare, to Governor, 3 April 1952.

76 AGA, 1952, vol. 1, Sta Rita, Municipio de San Luis, 23 April 1952.

77 AGA, 1952, vol. 1, San Luis, 23 April 1952.

78 AGA, 1952, vol. 1, Puerto Nare, 30 April 1952.

79 AGA, 1952, vol. 11, 20 March 1952; AGA, 1952, vol. 8, Oficio no. 967, 24 March 1952.

80 AGA, 1952, vol. 10, Guarumo, Cáceres, 27 March 1952.

81 AGA, 1952, vol. 1, Segovia, 10 May 1952; AGA, 1952, vol. 1, Conservative Committee, Segovia to Governor, 10 May 1952.

82 SGA, 1952, vol. 3, Virginias, 20 May 1952.

83 AGA, 1952, vol. 3, 10 May 1952; SGA, 1952, vol. 3, Caracolí, 11 June 1952.

84 SGA, 1952, vol. 2, Puerto Berrío, 14 June 1952.

85 SGA, 1952, vol. 3, Cristalina, 22 June 1952; AGA, 1952, vol. 6, Remedios/Puerto Berrío, 23 June 1952.

86 SGA, 1952, vol. 3, Yalí/Yolombó, 25 June 1952.

87 AGA, 1952, vol. 6, El Jardín and Remedios, 28 June 1952; AGA, 1952, vol. 3, "La Alicia," Puerto Berrío, 6 July 1952; AGA, 1952, vol. 3, "El Delirio," Maceo, 7 July 1952; and AGA, 1952, vol. 2, Virginias, Puerto Berrío, and Maceo, 13 July 1952. AGA, 1952, vol. 3, Casabe, 19 July 1952; AGA, 1952, vol. 3, El Bagre, Zaragoza, 20 July 1952.

88 AGA, 1953, vol. 11, Luis Andrade, MinGob to Governor, 29 April 1952.

89 AGA, 1952, vol. 2, 7 April 1952.

90 AGA, 1952, vol. 1, Conservatives to Governor, 7 April 1952.

91 AGA, 1952, vol. 2, Governor to municipios, 7 April 1952.

92 San Roque, interview with Instituto de Estudios Regionales (hereafter, INER), Universidad de Antioquia, 4 Sept. 1988.

93 San Roque, interview with INER, 25 Aug. 1988.

94 San Carlos, interview with INER, 23 June 1988.

95 Ibid.

96   AGA, 1950, vol. 2, Directorio Liberal de Antioquia (hereafter, DiLib) to Governor, 12 Sept. 1951.

97   AGA, 1952, vol. 1, 30 April 1952.

98   AGA, 1952, vol. 11, various petitioners to Governor, 5 June 1952.

99   AGA, 1952, vol. 12, de Bedout to Colonel Luis Abadía, Commander of the Fourth Brigade, Medellín, 23 June 1952.

100 Ibid.

101 AGA, 1952, vol. 7, various signatories headed by Félix de Bedout to Governor, 23 June 1952.

102 SGA, 1948, vol. 9, Amalfi/Yolombó, "El Tigre," 29 Dec. 1947.

103 SGA, 1947, vol. 7, telegram no. 1230, EBG to President, Bogotá, July 1947.

104 SGA, 1948, vol. 9, Amalfi, personero to Governor, 12 Feb. 1948.

105 AGA, 1948, "O.P.," 5 June 1948.

106 AGA, 1948, "O.P.," telegram from Yolombó to Governor, 17 Aug. 1948.

107 AGA, 1952, vol. 12, Conservative Committee, El Tigre, Amalfi to Governor, 10 Nov. 1952.

108 AGA, 1952, vol. 3, El Tigre to Governor regarding Yolombó contrachusma attacks, 29 Dec. 1952.

109 AGA, 1952, vol. 12, priest to Governor, 23 Nov. 1952.

110 SGA, 1952, vol. 7, Caja de Credito Agrario to Governor, 23 Feb. 1953.

111 ANCB, v. 43 f. 235; v. 43 f. 507; v. 43 f. 445; v. 47 f. 65; v. 63 f. 387; v. 54 f. 604; v. 63. f. 360 (Puerto Berrío); v. 46 f. 317; v. 49 f. 211 (Remedios); v. 62 f. 299 (Yolombó); v. 74 f. 361 (Puerto Nare/San Luis); v. 69 f. 334 (San Roque); v. 74 f. 454 (Caracolí). See also LeGrand, *Frontier Expansion*. I am most grateful to Catherine LeGrand who generously shared with me her archival notes regarding *colono* disputes in Antioqueño towns.

112 Captain Corneta, interview with the author, Medellín, 1987.

113 SGA, 1953, vol. 11, San Roque, 1 Jan. 1953.

114 SGA, 1953, vol. 11, Puerto Berrío, 7 Jan. 1953.

115 SGA, 1953, vol. 12, Bedout to Governor, 4 Feb. 1953.

116 SGA, 1952, vol. 5, Inspector de Trabajo, Puerto Triunfo, 16 April 1952.

117 Ibid.

118 SGA, 1952, vol. 2, 14 June 1952.

119 Ibid.

120 AGA, 1952, vol. 5, priest, Yolombó to Governor, 1 Oct. 1952.

121 Granada, interview with INER, 16 June 1988; Alejandría, interview with INER, 29 Sept. 1988; and San Rafael, interview with INER, 16 June 1988.

122 For an explicit and detailed examination of the supposed racial and sexual threat posed by the overwhelmingly black and non-Antioqueño population that had settled the northeast and Magdalena Medio, see SGA, 1952, vol. 12, Antioquia, Secretaría de Obras Publicas, "Informe para el Sr. Gobernador de Antioquia," Medellín, 10 Nov. 1952. Female schoolteachers at the camp school were perceived to be endangered by the proximity of "the sort of class of racial types

such as Casabe's: the upper echelons of the hierarchy is in the hands of English-men, and 98 percent of Labor is made up of Caribbean coastal people [*costeños*] and people from Santander [*santandereanos*]. We would need to have lay female teachers who are awfully saintly to be able to resist the insinuations of this en-vironment."

123   SGA, 1952, vol. 2, Fuerzas Armadas, Puerto Berrío to Governor, 14 June 1952.

124   Ibid.

125   SGA, 1952, vol. 8, Maceo, 22 July 1952.

126   SGA, 1952, vol. 5, Maceo, 8 Aug. 1952.

127   AGA, 1952, vol. 6, Maceo, 16 Aug. 1952.

128   AGA, 1953, vol. 5, Colonel Gustavo Berrío, commander Fourth Brigade to DAF in a missive entitled, "Relaciones entre Comando Brigada y la Gobernación," 4 Jan. 1953; and AGA 1953, vol. 4, DAF to Colonel Gustavo Berrío, 15 January 1953.

129   AGA, 1952, vol. 3, Governor to municipal mayors, 20 Aug. 1952.

130   AGA, 1953, vol. 9, Fuerzas Armadas, circular marked "Reservado," 16 Sept. 1952.

131   AGA, 1952, vol. 4, Remedios to Governor, 29 Sept. 1952.

132   AGA, 1952, vol. 4, Caracolí to Governor, 5 Oct. 1952.

133   AGA, 1952, vol. 4, mayor, Yolombó to Governor, 7 Oct. 1952.

134   AGA, 1952, vol. 3, Remedios, Conservative committee to Governor, 14 Oct. 1952.

135   AGA, 1952, vol. 4, police inspector to Governor, 8 Oct. 1952.

136   SGA, 1953, vol. 8, Cisneros, 6 June 1953.

137   AGA, 1952, vol. 12, Colorado to Governor, 22 Nov. 1952.

138   Ibid.

139   Former president and Antioqueño native son, Maríano Ospina Pérez, and his moderate supporters, among them prominent Antioqueño Conservatives, were crucial to mobilizing the coup against Laureano Gómez. See Bushnell, *The Making of Modern Colombia,* p. 214.

140   AGA, 1952, vol. 3, Puerto Berrío, priest to Governor, 24 Dec. 1952.

141   AGA, 1953, vol. 9, "Informe sobre la acción del bandolerismo," 11 May 1953.

142   SGA, 1953, vol. 1, 28 Jan. 1953.

143   SGA, 1953, vol. 1, 11 Feb. 1953; SGA, 1953, vol. 1, 4 March 1953.

144   SGA, 1953, vol. 8, La Dorada, 12 May 1952.

145   SGA, 1953, vol. 8, priest, Amalfi to Governor, 9 June 1953; SGA, 1953, vol. 10, Conservative miner, Nús to Governor, 9 June 1953.

146   AGA, 1953, vol. 5, Yalí, 15 April 1953.

147   AGA, 1953, vol. 9, Remedios, 8 July 1953.

148   SGA, 1953, vol. 7, DiLibAnt to Governor Píoquinto Rengifo, 22 Aug. 1953.

149   AGA, 1953, vol. 8, Huila to Governor, 28 May 1953.

150   Sánchez, "La Violencia y sus efectos," p. 15.

151   San Roque, Alejandría, San Carlos, San Rafael, and Granada, various interviews with INER, 1988.

152   AGA, 1953, vol. 13, telegramas, San Roque, 14 Aug. 1953; Puerto Nare, 6 June

1953; Puerto Triunfo, 9 June 1953; Amalfi, 4 Aug. 1953 and 2 Sept. 1953; Puerto Perales, Sept. 1953; Yolombó, 13 Oct. 1953; Remedios, 28 Oct. 1953; and Cisneros, 1 Dec. 1953.

153   Captain Corneta (Francisco Montoya), interview with the author, Medellín, 1987.

154   SGA, 1953, vol. 12, former guerrillas in "El Tigre," Amalfi to DiLibAnt, 2 Sept. 1953.

3. Urabá and Western Antioquia

1   PEA, table 2.1.6, "Población por sexo, según municipios," pp. 77–81.

2   Ibid.

3   The following section draws heavily on material in my article, "Violencia, colonización y la geografía de la diferencia en Colombia," *Analísis Político* 35 (Sept.– Dec. 1998): 3–25. For an examination of the catalysts to violence in the area (currently part of the department of Córdoba) that bordered on Urabá and from which many of the armed groups operating during *la Violencia* in Antioquia came, see Mauricio Romero, "Tierra y violencia en Córdoba," *Revista Análisis* 4 (1990): 17–21, and *Rural Transformation and Political Violence in Colombia, 1953– 1990. A Comparative Study of Intra-Regional Change in a Non-Exporting Zone,* Center for Studies in Social Change (CSSC), New School for Social Research, Working Paper Series, Working Paper no. 183 (March 1994): 1–44.

4   Maria Teresa Uribe de H., *Urabá, Territorio o región?* (Medellín, 1992), pp. 95–96. LeGrand, *Frontier Expansion and Peasant Protest,* p. 29. Hermes Tovar Pinzón, *El movimiento campesino en Colombia,* p. 41; and Uribe de H., *Urabá, Territorio o región?,* p. 46 and pp. 95–96; Gloria Isabel Ocampo, "Entre la localidad y la Nación: Aspectos políticos de la construcción de identidades en un contexto regional," *Revista Colombiana de Antropología* 30, pp. 105–108, details diverse conceptions of identity and citizenship among inhabitants of different regions in Colombia.

5   AGA, 1948, "Telegramas," O.P., 9 April 1948. AGA, 1948, "Telegramas," O.P., 10 April 1948; and telegram, 26 April 1948.

6   AGA, 1948, "Telegramas," O.P., 14 April 1948.

7   AGA, 1948, Jorge Bejarano, Ministro de Higiene to Governor, 26 Aug. 1948.

8   AGA, 1948, "Telegramas," O.P., 29 Nov. 1948.

9   AGA, 1950, vol. 9, Departamento de Investigación Criminal to the Governor, 3 Nov. 1948, telegram regarding the behavior of the Colombian vice consul in Panama, Otila Salazar de Puerta, who allegedly used her diplomatic post to smuggle illicit arms to Liberal guerrillas in Urabá.

10   AGA, 1948, "ASPG," Turbo, 11 May 1949.

11   AGA, 1949, "MinGob," presidential delegates, Turbo to Governor, June 1949; AGA, 1949, "MinGob," Sopetran, 20 May 1949.

12   Aníbal Vallejo Alvarez, interview with the author, Medellín, spring 1987.

13   AGA, 1950, vol. 9, Colonel Eduardo Villamil, commander Cuarta Brigada, Medellín to EBG, 24 Nov. 1949.

14   AGA, 1949, "Telegramas," Turbo, Nov. 1949.

15   SGA, 1950, vol. 3, Dabeiba, Conservative committee to the Governor, 27 Feb. 1950.

16   The regional government had already bought and shipped a thousand revolvers to its supporters in January 1950.

17   SGA, 1950, vol. 1, Smith and Wesson representative, Cali to the Governor, 28 Feb. 1950.

18   SGA, 1950, vol. 9, Caicedo, 24 April 1950.

19   AGA, 1950, vol. 9, Jorge Salazar, Jefe Departamento de Investigación Criminal to Governor, 3 May 1950.

20   SGA, 1951, vol. 3, "Mapa de campamentos de bandoleros, Antadó."

21   SGA, 1951, vol. 8, "Asociación e Instigación para delinquir y demas delitos conexos. Autos de Detención," Ministerio de Justicia, Juzgado 82 de Instrucción Criminal, Oficio no. 0440, "A las autoridades de Policía de la República," 4 Feb. 1951.

22   SGA, 1951, vol. 2, oficio no. 61 regarding Frontino to Governor, May 18, 1951.

23   AGA, 1953, vol. 5, Camparusia/Dabeiba, 5 May 1952.

24   SGA, 1951, vol. 3, n.d.; SGA 1951, vol. 8, "Asociación e Instigación para delinquir y demas delitos conexos. Autos de Detención," Ministro de Justicia, Juzgado 82 de Instucción Criminal, oficio no. 0440, "A las autoridades de Policía de la República," 4 Feb. 1951.

25   SGA, 1951, vol. 8, José Parra Salazar, Visitador Administrativo Departamental to SecGob, Medellín, Oficio no. 1, 5 Dec. 1951.

26   Ibid.

27   Bernardo Ospina Román, interview with the author, Medellín, spring 1987. Ospina Román was a prominent regional *gaitanista* figure in Antioquia who helped the Liberal guerrillas and mediated between them and the party in Medellín.

28   AGA, 1950, vol. 9, Departamento de Investigación Criminal (hereafter, DIC) to Governor, 3 Nov. 1948; AGA, 1950, vol. 3, Tnte. Col. Hernandez Pardo, Secretario MinGuerra to Governor, 6 May 1950; AGA, 1950, vol. 1, police inspector to Governor, 21 June 1950; and AGA, 1950, vol. 1, police inspector to Governor, 22 June 1950.

29   AGA, 1950, vol. 3, police inspector, Frontino to Governor, 21 June 1950.

30   AGA, 1950, vol. 2, Luis Vásquez to Governor, 27 June 1950.

31   AGA, 1951, vol. 6, Gustavo Echavarría to Governor, "Memorandum sobre la situación de Orden Publico que se presenta en la región de Dabeiba a Chigorodó," 1 Feb. 1951.

32   AGA, 1949, "APSG," Quibdó (Chocó) to Governor, 3 July 1950; AGA, 1949, "APSG," Governor Valencia, Chocó to Governor, 3 July 1950.

33   SGA, 1952, vol. 8, Uramita, 8 April 1952.

34   AGA, 1950, vol. 9, Tucura/Dabeiba, BriCom-Cartagena to Governor, 16 July 1950.

35   AGA, 1950, vol. 9, Urrao, Father Zapata to Governor, 17 July 1950; AGA, 1949, "APSG," La Camara (Salgar), MinGob to Governor, 26 July 1950.

36   AGA, 1950, vol. 9, Colonel Villamil, Fourth Brigade, Medellín to Jorge Quintero, Subteniente, Dabeiba, Mutatá, Chigorodó, 26 July 1950.

37   AGA, 1950, vol. 9, Dabeiba, 31 July 1950.

38   AGA, 1949, "APSG," military commander, Caicedo to Governor, 2 Aug. 1950.

39   AGA, 1950, vol. 9, Colonel Villamil to the Governor, 3 Aug. 1950; AGA, 1949, "APSG," Jorge Salazar, Jefe DIC to Governor, 9 Aug. 1950.

40   AGA, 1949, "APSG," Caucasia, telegrapher to Governor, 9 Aug. 1950; SGA, 1950, vol. 7, Ituango, 10 Aug. 1950.

41   AGA, 1950, "APSG," Secretario General, DiConsAnt to Governor, 10 Aug. 1950.

42   AGA, 1950, "APSG," Domingo Saresty to Governor, 10 Aug. 1950.

43   AGA, 1953, vol. 9, "Informe sobre la acción del bandolerismo entre 1949 y mayo 10 de 1953," 11 May 1953.

44   AGA, 1949, "APSG," Urabá, 16 Aug. 1950; AGA, 1949, "APSG," 18 Aug. 1950; and AGA, 1949, "APSG," Rafael Posada, mayor to Governor, 22 Aug. 1950.

45   AGA, 1949–1950, oficio no. 86, José A. Echavarría, police inspector to Governor, 23 Aug. 1950.

46   AGA, 1952, vol. 8, Mayor Infantería Marina Luis Millán Vargas, Jefe Polinal División Antioquia, oficio no. 874 to Governor, 4 April 1952.

47   SGA, 1950, vol. 3, Conservative committee, Turbo to Governor, 24 Aug. 1950.

48   AGA, 1949, "APSG," Colonel Villamil to Governor, 29 Aug. 1950.

49   AGA, 1949, "APSG," EBG to Laureano Gómez, 18 Aug. 1950.

50   AGA, 1949, "APSG," BHM to Laureano Gómez, 24 Aug. 1950.

51   AGA, 1951, vol. 5, "Informe de Comisión Región Urabá," 16 Oct. 1950.

52   To assuage them, the colonel ordered five soldiers, an officer, and a light machine gun to complement the local police whose sole weapons were two used machetes.

53   LeGrand, *Frontier Expansion*, appendix D; and PEA, pp. 385–87.

54   AGA, 1951, vol. 5, "Informe de Comisión Región Urabá," 16 Oct. 1950.

55   Ibid.

56   AGA, 1950, "Papeles," telegram from mayor, San Juan de Urabá to Governor, 22 Aug. 1950; and "Papeles," 29 Aug. 1950.

57   AGA, 1951, vol. 5, "Informe de Comisión Región Urabá," 16 Oct. 1950.

58   At this time, the large concessions of land to transnational banana companies and to Colombian subcontractors had not yet begun. These would eventually accelerate and transform Urabá into one of Latin America's leading exporters of bananas and a site of considerable organized labor and leftist struggle after 1960, see Fernando Botero Herrera, *Urabá: Colonización, violencia, y crisis del*

estado (Medellín: Editorial Universidad de Antioquia, 1985); AGA, 1951, vol. 5, "Informe de Comisión Región Urabá," 16 Oct. 1950.

59   AGA, 1951, vol. 5, "Informe de Comisión Región Urabá," 16 Oct. 1950.

60   Ibid.

61   AGA, 1950, vol. 5, Turbo, 2 Nov. 1950; AGA, 1950, vol. 5, Puerto Abaldía, 12 Nov. 1950.

62   AGA, 1950, vol. 8, Governor to Secretaría de Hacienda, Chocó, 17 Nov. 1950; AGA, 1950, vol. 9, Cartagena to Governor, 12 Dec. 1950.

63   SGA, 1950, vol. 5, Urabá, 5 Dec. 1950; AGA, 1950, vol. 2, Nicolás Gaviria to MinGob, Bogotá, forwarded to Governor, 15 Dec. 1950.

64   AGA, 1950, vol. 3, Antonio Moreno Mosquera, governor of Chocó to Governor, 30 Nov. 1950.

65   AGA, 1950, vol. 3, Braulio Henao to Roberto Cavalier, governor of Bolívar, 10 Dec. 1950; AGA, 1950, vol. 6, Capt. Salcedo, Fourth Brigade, Medellín to the Governor, 27 Jan. 1951.

66   SGA, 1950, vol. 5, Nicolás Gaviria, Cañasgordas to Directorio Nacional Conservador and MinGob, 12 Dec. 1950.

67   SGA, 1951, vol. 1, Caja de Credito Agrario to Governor, 14 Dec. 1950.

68   Ibid.

69   Ibid.

70   AGA, 1950, vol. 4, Carlos Arrubla, subjefe seguridad to Governor, 27 Dec. 1950.

71   AGA, 1950, vol. 6, visitador ejecutivo to Governor, 8 Jan. 1951.

72   SGA, 1951, vol. 1, Caicedo to Governor, Jan. 1951.

73   Ibid.

74   AGA, 1950, vol. 6, Laureano Gómez to BHM (in code and deciphered on the back of the document), 25 Jan. 1951.

75   AGA, 1951, vol. 7, BHM to Gonzalo Restrepo Jaramillo, marked "confidential," 28 Feb. 1951.

76   AGA, 1951, vol. 7, detectives to Governor, 10 Jan. 1951.

77   AGA, 1951, vol. 5, Mutatá/Carepa, "Informe de Orden Publico," 2 Feb. 1951.

78   AGA, 1951, vol. 7, Inspector Nacional de Bosques to Governor, Jan. 1951.

79   AGA, 1951, vol. 4, "O.P.," 15 Dec. 1950.

80   PEA, p. 385.

81   See Roldán, "Violencia, colonización y geografía de la diferencia en Colombia," pp. 14–16.

82   SGA, 1951, vol. 7, Jefe de Seguridad to Governor, 29 March 1951; SGA, 1951, vol. 7, subjefe Seguridad to Governor, 5 April 1951.

83   AGA, 1951, vol. 7, mayor, Turbo to Governor, 24 Jan. 1951.

84   AGA, 1951, vol. 6, Colonel Luis Abadía to Governor, 12 Feb. 1951.

85   AGA, 1951, vol. 6, 16 Feb. 1951.

86   AGA, 1950, vol. 4, Major González to Governor, 17 Jan. 1951.

87 AGA, 1951, vol. 6, "Memorándum sobre la situatión de Orden Público," 1 Feb. 1951.

88 AGA, 1950, vol. 6, BHM to Laureano Gómez, rough draft of letter, n.d. 1951.

89 AGA, 1951, vol. 7, Conservative citizens, Abriaquí to Governor, 28 June 1951.

90 AGA, 1950, vol. 6, Anzá, 22 Jan. 1951; AGA, 1950, vol. 6, Colonel Abadía to Governor, 29 Jan. 1951.

91 AGA, 1951, vol. 6, "Memorándum sobre la situación de Orden Público," n.d. Jan. 1951.

92 AGA, 1950, vol. 6, Laureano Gómez to Governor (original in code, but deciphered on the reverse), 25 Jan. 1951; AGA, 1950, vol. 6, n.d. 1951.

93 AGA, 1951, vol. 7, BHM to Gonzalo Restrepo Jaramillo, 30 Jan. 1951.

94 SGA, 1951, vol. 1, "Plan de Orden Público #327," 3 Feb. 1951.

95 AGA, 1951, vol. 7, BHM to Gonzalo Restrepo Jaramillo, 28 Feb. 1951.

96 Ibid.

97 AGA, 1951, vol. 6, visitador administrativo to Governor, 28 Feb. 1951.

98 AGA, 1951, vol. 6, Governor to Fuerzas Armadas, 16 March 1951.

99 AGA, 1951, vol. 6, El Carmelo, 20 March 1951.

100 AGA, 1951, vol. 6, Turbo, 25 March 1951.

101 AGA, 1951, vol. 6, recolector de Hacienda, Chocó to Governor, 30 March 1951.

102 AGA, 1951, vol. 6, "Informe Orden Publico," Urabá, 30 March 1951.

103 AGA, 1951, vol. 6, 27 March 1951.

104 AGA, 1951, vol. 6, Dabeiba, 26 March 1951.

105 AGA, 1951, vol. 2, mayor, Frontino to Bogotá, 21 May 1951; AGA, 1951, vol. 3, Frontino, 26 June 1951.

106 AGA, 1951, vol. 7, Frontino, 3 July 1951.

107 AGA, 1951, vol. 2, Dabeiba, 9 Aug. 1951.

108 AGA, 1951, vol. 6, Tabacál, Buriticá, 16 Aug. 1951.

109 AGA, 1951, vol. 5, Caja de Credito, 26 Sept. 1951.

110 Ibid.

111 AGA, 1950, vol. 6, mayor, Ituango to Governor, 17 Jan. 1951.

112 SGA, 1950, vol. 1, DiConsAnt to Governor, 5 Sept. 1950.

113 AGA, 1951, vol. 2, Luis Andrade, Bishop of Santa Fé de Antioquia to Governor, 26 Feb. 1951.

114 AGA, 1951, vol. 2, Bishop of Santa Fé de Antioquia to Governor, 16 July 1951.

115 AGA, 1951, vol. 2, Bishop of Santa Fé de Antioquia to Governor, 26 Feb. 1951.

116 SGA, 1951, vol. 6, "Informe Confidencial," Medellín to Governor, 24 July 1951.

117 SGA, 1951, vol. 1, 14 March 1951.

118 AGA, 1951, vol. 2, Peque, 25 May 1951.

119 AGA, 1951, vol. 3, Anzá, 24 June 1951; AGA, 1951, vol. 2, Sabanalarga, 27 May 1951.

120 AGA, 1951, vol. 7, priest, Sabanalarga to Governor, 1 June 1951.

121 AGA, 1951, vol. 7, priest, Sabanalarga to Governor, 5 June 1951.

122 AGA, 1951, vol. 7, Colonel Abadía to Governor, 19 June 1951.

123 SGA, 1951, vol. 1, Fuerzas Armadas, marked "Reservado" to Governor, 5 July 1951.

124 AGA, 1951, vol. 2, Peque, 9 Aug. 1951.

125 SGA, 1951, vol. 7, "Encargado Telefonos," Jefe del Departamento de Seguridad to Governor, 10 Aug. 1951.

126 AGA, 1951, vol. 2, Peque, 10 Aug. 1951; AGA, 1951, vol. 6, Peque, 16 Aug. 1951.

127 AGA, 1951, vol. 1, Father Yepes, Sabanalarga to Governor, 27 Aug. 1951.

128 AGA, 1951, vol. 1, Carretera al Mar/Urabá, Fuerzas Armadas, oficio no. 07233 to Governor, 22 Aug. 1951.

129 AGA, 1951, vol. 5, FEDECAFE, Antioquia to Governor, 5 Sept. 1951.

130 AGA, 1951, vol. 2, Frontino/Salgar/Urrao, DiLibAnt, 20 Sept. 1951; AGA, 1951, vol. 9, Buriticá, 22 Sept. 1951; AGA, 1951, vol. 1, Dabeiba, 22 Sept. 1951; and AGA, 1951, vol. 5, Colonel Abadía regarding Juntas de Uramita to the Governor, 5 Oct. 1951.

131 AGA, 1951, vol. 5, lawyer for the Jefe de Orden Público, report on Frontino, 10 Oct. 1951.

132 SGA, 1951, vol. 2, FEDECAFE to the Governor regarding Cañasgordas, 21 Nov. 1951.

133 AGA, 1952, vol. 11, Father Hugo Helmar, Caicedo to Governor, 28 Feb. 1952.

134 AGA, 1952, vol. 12, Caicedo, 7 April 1952.

135 AGA, 1952, vol. 1, 7 April 1952.

136 SGA, 1952, vol. 10, priest, Ituango, letter forwarded to Director General de la Policía by Abogado Jefe de Orden Público, 6 May 1952.

137 SGA, 1952, vol. 2, Uramita, 12 May 1952.

138 SGA, 1952, vol. 3, Frontino, 24 July 1952.

139 AGA, 1952, vol. 5, Fuerzas Armadas, Fourth Brigade, Medellín to Governor, 10 June 1952.

140 AGA, 1951, vol. 9, Conservative committee, Toledo to DiConsAnt, 9 Sept. 1951.

141 AGA, 1951, vol. 5, Rioverde/Murrí, 8 Nov. 1951.

142 AGA, 1952, vol. 6, Polinal oficio no. 303, Girardota, 5 Feb. 1952.

143 AGA, 1952, vol. 8, Anzá, 5 March 1952; AGA, 1952, vol. 8, Buriticá, 12 March 1952; and AGA, 1952, vol. 12, Dabeiba, 14 March 1952.

144 AGA, 1952, vol. 12, Dabeiba, 18 March 1952.

145 SGA, 1952, vol. 3, Dabeiba, 30 June 1952.

146 SGA, 1952, vol. 6, Caja de Credito Agrario to Governor, 28 April 1952.

147 SGA, 1952, vol. 3, Camparusia (Dabeiba), 3 July 1952.

148 AGA, 1953, vol. 9, "Informe sobre la acción del bandolerismo," May 1953.

149 AGA, 1952, vol. 10, Abriaquí, 16 April 1952; AGA, 1952, vol. 10, Anocozca, Caicedo to Abriaquí, 23 April 1952.

150 Ibid.

151 SGA, 1952, vol. 5, mayor, Abriaquí to Nicolás Carmona Bernal, Aug. 1952.

152 AGA, 1953, vol. 9, "Informe sobre la acción del bandolerismo," 11 May 1953.

153   AGA, 1952, vol. 3, Governor to municipal mayors, 5 Sept. 1952.

154   AGA, 1952, vol. 4, mayor, Toledo to Governor, 1 Oct. 1952.

155   AGA, 1952, vol. 4, mayor, Toledo to Governor, 9 Oct. 1952.

156   AGA, 1952, vol. 4, Conservatives, Uramita/Cañasgordas to Governor, 9 Oct. 1952.

157   AGA, 1952, vol. 4, mayor, Cañasgordas to Governor, 14 Oct. 1952.

158   AGA, 1952, vol. 12, mayor, Dabeiba to Governor, 28 Dec. 1952.

159   SGA, 1953, vol. 8, mayor, Frontino to Governor, Jan. 1953.

160   SGA, 1953, vol. 7, Caja de Crédito Agrario regarding Frontino to Governor, 3 Feb. 1953.

161   SGA, 1953, vol. 8, Mario Javier Mesa, Visitador, "Informe correspondiente al conservatismo de Dabeiba," "Anexo," 17 Dec. 1952.

162   SGA, 1953, vol. 9, Jefe del Departamento Juridico to SecGobAnt, 12 March 1953; SGA, 1953, vol. 9, Caja de Crédito Agrario, El Carmen (Chocó), 23 March 1953.

163   AGA, 1953, vol. 5, Anzá, 24 March 1953; AGA, 1953, vol. 6, mayor, Riogrande/Turbo to Governor, 7 April 1953.

164   AGA, 1953, vol. 5, mayor, Caicedo to Governor, 15 April 1953.

165   SGA, 1953, vol. 3, Chigorodó, 14 April 1953.

166   AGA, 1953, vol. 3, military mayor, Chigorodó to Governor, 27 March 1953.

167   AGA, 1953, vol. 15, Gilberto Saldarriaga, Urabá to Governor, 18 April 1953.

168   SGA, 1953, vol. 9, Dimas Navarro Marín, Anzá to Governor, 2 May 1953.

169   SGA, 1953, vol. 8, Ramón Castaño, ex–municipal Conservative committee president, Dabeiba to Governor, 9 June 1953.

170   AGA, 1953, vol. 9, "Informe sobre el bandolerismo," 11 May 1953. AGA, 1953, Polinal, "Antioquia: Número de muertos desde agosto de 1952 hasta enero (11) de 1953," n.d. May 1953.

171   AGA, 1953, vol. 9, "Informe sobre la acción del bandolerismo," n.d. May 1953.

172   SGA, 1953, vol. 7, "Presos Políticos Liberales en la Carcel de "La Ladera" por orden de la Cuarta Brigada," 8 May 1953.

173   SGA, 1953, vol. 10, Father Blandón Berrío, Peque/Uramita to Governor, 27 June 1953.

174   AGA, 1953, vol. 8, mayor, Liborina to Governor, 14 May 1953.

175   SGA, 1953, vol. 10, FGM (owner of El Colombiano) to DAF, sent via private letter because the original article was censored from publication, 5 June 1953.

176   AGA, 1953, vol. 13, Governor orders all mayors to collect arms distributed under previous regime, 14 Aug. 1953.

177   SGA, 1953, vol. 7, Father Hugo Helmer, Caicedo to Governor, 19 July 1953.

178   SGA, 1953, vol. 12, mayor, San Jerónimo complains of abuses against workers on finca "Las Estancias," 30 July 1953.

179   SGA, 1953, vol. 7, DiLibAnt to Governor, 22 Aug. 1953.

180   AGA, 1953, vol. 4, Urama/Dabeiba to Governor, 25 Oct. 1953.

181   AGA, 1953, vol. 4, Caja de Credito Agrario regarding Uramita/Cañasgordas and Frontino to Governor, 13 Nov. 1953.

182 SGA, 1953, vol. 7, DiLibAnt to Governor, 27 Nov. 1953.

183 SGA, 1953, vol. 1, Polinal, Buriticá to Governor, 31 Dec. 1953.

184 Ibid.

185 SGA, 1953, vol. 5, Auditoría General del Departmento de Antioquia to Governor, 14 Oct. 1953.

186 SGA, 1953, vol. 7, DiLibAnt to Governor, 27 Nov. 1953.

187 This and all subsequent land-value figures were calculated from PEA, table 17.1.3.5, "Número y avalúo catastral de la propiedad gravada y no gravada, 1941–1958," pp. 638–39; and table 17.1.3.6, "Número y avalúo catastral de la propiedad gravada y no gravada 1961," pp. 640–41.

4. Urrao and the Southwest

1 Graciela Urrego, interview with the author, Urrao, 31 Aug. 1985.

2 Other southwestern towns such as Venecia and Andes also experienced violent incidents from 1950 to 1953, but these were episodic and primarily involved unionized workers employed by the railroad and public road construction and did not involve armed Liberal resistance against the state.

3 For an examination of the association between frontier and "barbarism" in other parts of Latin America, see Sarmiento, *Life in the Argentine Republic;* Silvio R. Duncan Baretta and John Markoff, "Civilization and Barbarism: Cattle Frontiers in Latin America," *Comparative Studies in Society and History* 20, no. 4 (1978): 587–620; and Slatta, *Gauchos and the Vanishing Frontier.*

4 Virginia Gutiérrez de Pineda, *Familia y Cultura en Colombia,* "Matrimonio Catolico y Union Libre 1951," p. 497, and "Ilegitimidad 1951," p. 509.

5 I am using the term here as Natalie Zemon Davis does in her essay "The Reasons of Misrule," in *Society and Culture in Early Modern France* (Stanford: Stanford University Press, 1975), pp. 97–123.

6 Joaquin Montoya Escobar, Liberal committee president and president of the municipal council during *la Violencia,* interview with the author, Urrao, 30 Aug. 1985.

7 AGA, 1948, "Telegramas," O.P., 11 April 1948.

8 AGA, 1949, "APSG," telegram, 18 Feb. 1949.

9 Joaquin Montoya Escobar, interview with the author, Urrao, 30 Aug. 1985.

10 AGA, 1949, "Telegramas," Valparaiso, 26 March 1949.

11 AGA, 1949, "MinGob," Jericó, 7 April 1949; AGA, 1949, "MinGob," Bolívar, 7 April 1949 and 8 April 1949.

12 Various individuals, informal interview with the author, Urrao, August 1985.

13 Joaquin Montoya Escobar, interview with the author, Urrao, 30 Aug. 1985; Josefina Montoya Montoya, interview with the author, Urrao, 30 Aug. 1985.

14 Alcaldía Municipal de Urrao, "Sumarios," 19 Dec. 1949.

15 For the use of drunkenness as a guise to resistance, see William Taylor, *Drinking, Homicide, and Resistance in Colonial Mexican Villages* (Stanford: Stanford University Press, 1979).

16   AGA, 1950, vol. 7, letter from Joaquin Montoya, Eugenio Arroyave, Pepe Arenas, Francisco Luis Guzman, and others, Urrao to Governor, 13 Oct. 1949.

17   AGA, 1950, vol. 7, Urrao, 14 Oct. 1949.

18   AGA, 1950, vol. 7, 27 Nov. 1949; Aníbal Vallejo Alvarez, interview with the author, Medellín, 1987; Joaquin Montoya Escobar, interview with the author, Urrao, 30 Aug. 1985.

19   It is not coincidental that in current dialogues with Marxist guerrilla organizations all warring factions have agreed that church officials should act as intermediaries in the resolution of conflict in Colombia.

20   Luis Andrade Valderrama, Obispo Santa Fé de Antioquia, *Cartas Pastorales*, (Medellín, n.d.).

21   AGA, 1950, no vol. no., anon. telegram to Governor, n.d.

22   AGA, 1950, vol. 6, letter from Colonel Eduardo Villamil to Governor, 24 Jan. 1951. Colonel Villamil made explicit his discomfort with the escalation of violence and confided that "the struggle there was tormenting me mentally."

23   Medianalga (Avelino Urrego), interview with the author, Urrao, 20 Aug. 1985. Army neutrality in Urrao is confirmed in confidential documents in the governor's archive in which members of the Conservative administration complained that the army aided the guerrillas and turned a blind eye to their activities in Urrao. See AGA 1952, vol. 2, "Declaración de José Nicanor Arboleda Rodriguez," Departamento de Seguridad, Identificación y Extranjeriá, Medellín, 4 April 1952.

24   Medianalga (Avelino Urrego), interview with the author, Urrao, 20 Aug. 1985.

25   Ibid.

26   Franco's letter to Pioquinto Rengifo was reproduced in the magazine *Cromos*, 9 May 1960, pp. 27–30. Froilan Montoya Mazo was the real author of Franco's letter to the governor. Froilan Montoya Mazo, interview with the author, Medellín, fall 1986.

27   Medianalga (Avelino Urrego), interview with the author, Urrao, 20 Aug. 1985.

28   AGA, 1950, vol. 3, Secretario General, Bogotá to Governor Braulio Henao Mejía, 3 Jan. 1951; AGA, 1950, vol. 6, Colonel Abadía to Governor Braulio Henao Mejía, 29 Jan. 1951.

29   AGA, 1951, vol. 8, telegram from José Gallego, mayor, Urrao to Governor, 19 Sept. 1950.

30   Medianalga (Avelino Urrego), interview with the author, Urrao, 20 Aug. 1985; Tarzán (Herlindo Montoya), interview with the author, Betulia, 25 Aug. 1985; and Graciela Urrego, interview with the author, Urrao, 31 Aug. 1985.

31   Tarzán (Herlindo Montoya), interview with the author, Betulia, 25 Aug. 1985.

32   By 1953, Franco was signing his missives to the government and other documents as "Major" Franco. The *plana mayor* was created some time after the initial organization of the guerrillas when some members of the group felt that Franco had become too dictatorial and that power should be shared. Tarzán (Herlindo Montoya), Betulia, 30 Aug. 1985.

33   AGA, 1952, vol. 2, Departamento de Seguridad, Identificación y Extrangería, Medellín, "Declaración de José Nicanor Arboleda Rodriguez," 4 April 1952; AGA, 1953, vol. 8, Alcaldía Municipal de Urrao, "Copia de la Declaración Rendida Por el Señor Argemiro Herrera Correa," 26 May 1953; Medianalga (Avelino Urrego), interview with the author, Urrao, 20 Aug. 1985; Tarzán (Herlindo Montoya), interview with the author, Betulia, 25 Aug. 1985; and Graciela Urrego, interview with the author, Urrao, 31 Aug. 1985.

34   Graciela Urrego, interview with the author, Urrao, 31 Aug. 1985.

35   The *trisagio* is a prayer to the Holy Trinity usually recited during the adoration of the Eucharist during Mass.

36   Medianalga (Avelino Urrego), interview with the author, Urrao, 20 Aug. 1985. On the day I interviewed Avelino Urrego, his wife and sister-in-law (Debora and Judith) were also present, and they contributed their memories of Franco's guerrillas, too.

37   Debora and Judith, interview with the author, Urrao, 20 Aug. 1985.

38   Medianalga (Avelino Urrego), interview with the author, Urrao, 20 Aug. 1985.

39   AGA, vol. 8, 1953, Alcaldía Municipal de Urrao, "Copia de la Declaración Rendida Por el Señor Argemiro Herrera Correa," 26 May 1953.

40   Graciela Urrego, interview with the author, Urrao, 31 Aug. 1985; AGA, 1952, vol. 7, Report of Colonel Luis Abadía, Comandante de la 4a Brigada to the Governor, 4 Aug. 1952; AGA, 1953, vol. 8, Alcaldía Municipal de Urrao, "Declaración del Señor Cruz Antonio Higuita Cossio," 26 May 1953.

41   Indeed, perhaps the closest parallel to Urrao's guerrilla forces would be the army of peasants organized by Zapata in Morelos during the Mexican Revolution.

42   AGA, vol. 8 (1953), judicial testimony, 11 May 1953.

43   Sara Ruddick has argued persuasively in "Toward a Feminist Peace Politics," *Gendering War Talk,* ed. Miriam Cooke and Angela Woollacott (Princeton: Princeton University Press, 1993), pp. 112–13, that "in most cultures, war's masculinity is constructed in tandem with a distinctively military femininity," which may include "masking or denying the sexual assaultiveness of 'our troops.'" Certainly Ruddick's assertion that the "loyal military female . . . eroticizes 'our' heroes" accurately describes the prevailing attitude of the female companions of the guerrillas in Urrao, but I would also suggest that because such women, in contrast to those of Ruddick's analysis, were at the battlefront with their men, they may have made the eroticized aggression that is generally so important an aspect of "assaultive masculinity" in times of war, less of a motivating factor in guerrilla warfare in Urrao. I am not arguing that women are inherently more moral, but rather that the circumstances of Urrao's guerrilla organization where war and domesticity were not mutually exclusive may have shaped a policy that repudiated sexual assault as a valid weapon of resistance among the guerrilla command.

44   There were no reports of sexual abduction, gang rape, or battles over control of concubines among Urrao's guerrillas. See also Germán Guzmán Campos,

Orlando Fals Borda, and Eduardo Umaña, *La Violencia en Colombia,* vol. 1, 9th ed. (Bogotá: Carlos Valencia Editores).

45   Medianalga (Avelino Urrego), interview with the author, Urrao, 20 Aug. 1985; Josefina Montoya Montoya, interview with the author, Urrao, 30 Aug. 1985.

46   It is interesting to note that until recently in Colombia even those who disagreed with the ideology and tactics of leftist guerrillas were wont to hope that if one of their loved ones were kidnapped it would be the guerrillas and not the army, right-wing paramilitary groups, or common delinquents who were responsible. It was widely believed that the guerrillas were likelier to treat their prisoners humanely than either the government or groups associated with the right would. See Herbert Braun, *Our Guerrillas, Our Sidewalks: A Journey into the Violence of Colombia* (Niwot, Colo.: University Press of Colorado, 1994); and Gabriel García Márquez, *News of a Kidnapping* (New York: Penguin Press, 1998).

47   Josefina Montoya, interview with the author, Urrao, 30 Aug. 1985.

48   Absalón Machado, interview with the author, Bogotá, fall 1986.

49   AGA, 1952, vol. 7, Colonel Luis Abadía A., commander, 4a Brigada to Governor, 4 Aug. 1952.

50   AGA, 1951, vol. 5, mayor, Urrao to Governor, 23 Oct. 1951.

51   AGA, 1949, "APSG," Ministro de Justicia to Governor, 1 Dec. 1949.

52   AGA, 1950, vol. 9, telegram from soldiers, Betulia to their superior, Medellín, 3 Dec. 1949.

53   AGA, 1949, "APSG," telegram, Ricardo Mejía, Administrador de Rentas and Ruben Vélez, Tesorero, Salgar accusing the army of "convivencia liberalismo" to Governor, 5 Dec. 1949.

54   AGA, 1949, "APSG," telegram, Colonel Villamil, Fourth Brigade to MinGob, 4 Jan. 1950.

55   AGA, 1949, "APSG," report of assassination of police inspector and mayor, Isleta, 3 March 1950.

56   SGA, 1950, vol. 1, 29 June 1950.

57   AGA, 1950, "Papeles," telegram, Directorio Conservador Medellín to MinGob, Bogotá, 29 July 1950.

58   AGA, 1950, vol. 1, administrator, Concordia to Francisco Ospina Pérez, 6 July 1950.

59   AGA, 1950, vol. 9, telegram, Colonel Villamil to Governor, 10 July 1950.

60   AGA, 1950, vol. 9, Father Zapata, Urrao to Governor, 17 July 1950; AGA, 1950, vol. 3, mayor, Salgar to Governor, 18 July 1950; and AGA, 1949, "APSG," message forwarded to Governor by MinGob, Bogotá, 26 July 1950.

61   AGA, 1950, vol. 3, Conservative committee, Salgar to Governor, 28 July 1950.

62   AGA, 1949, "APSG," Colonel Villamil to Governor, 1 Aug. 1950; AGA 1949, "APSG," "Informe de Orden Público, Urrao," 1 Aug. 1950.

63   AGA, 1950, "Papeles," telegram, Colonel Villamil to Governor, 1 Aug. 1950.

64   SGA, 1950, vol. 5, list of towns buying arms from the regional government: Támesis, Venecia, Titiribí, Anzá, Betania, and Pueblorrico, 31 July 1950.

65   The dates of guerrilla attacks in these different locales never differed by more than a couple of days although the objects of attack sometimes varied from area to area—more concentrated on the state, its offices, and representatives in places like Urabá, and more directed at individual Conservative families and their properties in places like Urrao, the Bajo Cauca, and western Antioquia. The coincidence of guerrilla attacks between 1950 and 1953 in different areas of Antioquia was too exact to have been mere chance; indeed, in several cases the guerrillas themselves, or those warning the government that an attack was imminent, indicated that these were coordinated. Whether the coordination was engineered in Medellín at Liberal party headquarters or in Bogotá is unclear, but that there was coordination is simply beyond doubt.

66   AGA, 1949, "APSG," Guasabra, Antioquia, 2 August 1950.

67   AGA, 1950, "Papeles," José Toro, Directorio Conservador Urrao to Secretario General del Presidente, 16 Aug. 1950.

68   AGA, 1949, "APSG," Jesús Arroyave, Urrao to Governor, 18 Aug. 1950.

69   SGA, 1950, vol. 7, "Informe," no. 5599, from Rafael Osorio, Director Departamento Jurídico to Governor, 8 Dec. 1950.

70   AGA, 1950, vol. 5, Urrao and Betulia, 4 Dec. 1950; AGA, 1950, vol. 5, Urrao, 14 Dec. 1950.

71   AGA, 1950, "Papeles," Directorio Conservador, Betulia to Governor, 24 Aug. 1950.

72   SGA, 1950, vol. 7, "Informe," no. 5599, from Rafael Osorio, Director Departamento Juridico to Governor, 28 Dec. 1950.

73   This runs contrary to what researchers such as Guzmán, Fals Borda, and Umaña argue regarding the barbaric quality of violence in Antioquia. I have no explanation for why I found so few explicit references to sexual mutilation and torture in the period from 1949 to 1953 (five among thousands of references). It is possible that such violence was more characteristic of the *pajaro* or contrachusma violence which emerged in particular areas of Antioquia after 1953 or that it was simply so commonplace as to not merit explicit mention in the reports or complaints filed with the authorities. See Guzmán, Fals Borda, and Umaña, *La Violencia en Colombia,* vol. 1, p. 90.

74   The dichotomization of troops into "us" and "them" and the attribution of barbarity to the enemy are commonly invoked and necessary tropes in the justification of war. Sara Ruddick notes, for instance, "typically, masculinities are also divided between the enemy and 'our troops.' 'We' are the just warrior-protectors. By contrast, a particularly malignant form of swaggering masculinity—a criminalized, sexualized aggression—is attributed to the enemy. When enemy males are racialized as predators from whom innocent countries or women and children need protection, they become killable killers ready to be

burned and buried in their trenches." See Ruddick, "Toward a Feminist Peace
Politics," p. 112.

75   SGA, 1950, vol. 7, "Informe," no. 5599, from Rafael Osorio, Director Departamento Jurídico to Governor, 28 Dec. 1950.

76   AGA, 1950, "Papeles," Directorio Conservador, Salgar to MinGob, Bogotá,
26 July 1950; AGA, 1950, "Papeles," police inspector, Buchadó, Chocó to Governor, 3 March 1950; AGA, 1950, "Papeles," Carmen, Chocó to Governor, 4 July
1950; AGA, 1950, vol. 1, telegram from Concordia to Governor, 6 July 1950; AGA,
1950, vol. 3, Conservative committee, Salgar, 28 July 1950 and 9 Aug. 1950.

77   Indeed, this author found amid the records of Urrao's municipal archive a form
letter sent out by Germán Saldarriaga (whose pseudonym was Testis Fidelis),
the author of *De Caín a Pilatos* (Medellín, 1952), a grisly account of Liberal barbarity executed between 1949 and 1951. Saldarriaga's letter explicitly solicited
"gruesome examples of guerrilla/Communist violence, the more hair-raising,
the better" for inclusion in a second edition to his book. Collected testimonial
literature such as *De Cain a Pilatos* resembled in content and propagandistic intent the Brazilian *literatura de cordel* recounting famous bandit exploits or Fox's
Book of Martyrs issued by Protestants during the reign of the Catholic English
queen, Mary Tudor, in the sixteenth century.

78   AGA, 1950, vol. 8, Colonel Villamil to Teniente Quintero, 26 July 1950.

79   AGA, 1951, vol. 7, Governor Braulio Henao Mejía to Laureano Gómez, 28 Feb.
1951.

80   SGA, 1951, vol. 2, telegram from Governor to president Conservative committee,
Urrao, 11 June 1951.

81   AGA, 1950, vol. 6, BHM to Laureano Gómez, undated rough draft of letter.

82   AGA, 1951, vol. 2, letter from Felipe Chica, engineer, Secretaría de Obras Publicas, Antioquia to Director General de Caminos, Concordia, 17 April 1951.

83   Ibid.

84   AGA, 1950, vol. 6, "Memorandum sobre la situación de Orden Público que se
presenta en la región de Dabeiba y Chigorodó," 1 Feb. 1951. Salgar reported an
attack of two hundred men on 28 July 1950, while Betulia reported that one
thousand guerrillas were stationed on a nearby hacienda, see AGA 1950, vol. 3,
telegram, Salgar, 9 Aug. 1950; and AGA, 1950, vol. 2, mayor, Betulia to the Governor, 4 Dec. and 14 Dec. 1950.

85   AGA, 1951, vol. 2, telegram, Governor to MinGob Urdaneta Arbelaez, 1 Aug.
1951.

86   AGA, 1951, vol. 7, Governor to Laureano Gómez, 13 April 1951.

87   AGA, 1952, vol. 2, "Declaración de José Nicanor Arboleda Rodríguez," Departamento de Seguridad, Identificación y Extrangería, Medellín, 4 April 1952.

88   Medianalga (Avelino Urrego) interview with the author, Urrao, 20 Aug. 1985.

89   AGA, 1951, vol. 7, Conservative committee, Urrao to Governor, 10 Aug. 1951.

90   AGA, 1951, vol. 3, Caja de Crédito Agrario to Governor, 30 Sept. 1951.

91   AGA, 1951, vol. 3, Colonel Abadía, 4a Brigada to Governor, 29 May 1951.

92   AGA, 1951, vol. 1, Bocas de Peque, 20 Sept. 1951.

93   AGA, 1951, vol. 5, Colonel Abadía, 4a Brigada to Governor, 5 Oct. 1951.

94   AGA, 1951, vol. 5, J. V. C. to Governor, 15 Nov. 1951.

95   Medianalga (Avelino Urrego), interview with the author, Urrao, 20 Aug. 1985.
     An ex-guerrilla confirmed Urrego's statement, see AGA 1952, vol. 2, "Declara-
     ción de José Nicanor Arboleda Rodríguez," Departamento de Seguridad, Iden-
     tificacion y Extrangería, Medellín, 4 April 1952.

96   Ibid.; and Tarzán (Herlindo Montoya), interview with the author, Betulia,
     25 Aug. 1985.

97   AGA, 1951, vol. 5, Urrao, 15 Nov. 1951.

98   AGA, 1951, vol. 2, Urrao, 5 Sept. 1951; AGA, 1951, vol. 1, Salgar, 7 Sept. 1951; AGA,
     1951, vol. 1, Salgar, 8 Sept. 1951.

99   AGA, 1952, vol. 10, Betulia, 23 Jan. 1952; AGA, 1952, vol. 9, Urrao, 14 Feb.
     1952; AGA, 1952, vol. 11, Concordia, 17 Feb. 1952; AGA, 1952, vol. 10, Conser-
     vative committee, Betulia to Governor, 18 Feb. 1952; AGA, 1952, vol. 8, Urrao,
     5 March 1952.

100 AGA, 1952, vol. 2, Conservative committee, Urrao to Governor, 14 Feb. 1952.

101 AGA, 1953, vol. 6, Emilio Botero, Cartagena, Bolívar to Governor, 23 Jan. 1952.

102 AGA, 1952, vol. 11, Conservative citizens, Concordia to Governor, 17 Feb. 1952.

103 AGA, 1952, vol. 10, Conservative committee, Betulia to Governor, 1 March 1952.

104 AGA, 1952, vol. 8, oficio no. 972, Betulia, 25 March 1952.

105 AGA, 1952, vol. 12, Conservative official, Titiribí to Governor, 7 April 1952.

106 AGA, 1952, vol. 1, Medellín, 7 April 1952.

107 AGA, 1952, vol. 3, Las Azules, 23 Oct. 1952.

108 SGA, 1953, vol. 10, Conservatives, Betulia to Governor, 18 May 1953.

109 While such records are clearly not exhaustive and probably severely underesti-
     mate the total number of dead, since many bodies were flung into rivers, dis-
     membered, or buried in unmarked graves before body counts could be done,
     they do provide a suggestive indication of the relative number of casualties
     among each of Antioquia's towns. AGA, 1953, vol. 9, "Informe sobre la acción
     del bandolerismo," May 1953.

110 Ibid.

111 No deaths were attributed to violence in parish ledgers for 1949, but this may
     simply be because Father Zapata made no distinction between violent and other
     deaths. In fact, his successor's (Father Ramirez) tendency to separate deaths due
     to violence from other deaths seems to have constituted a fairly isolated prac-
     tice in Antioquia. My research uncovered no other parish registries with similar
     notations.

112 Tarzán (Herlindo Montoya), interview with the author, Urrao, 25 Aug. 1985;
     Graciela Urrego, interview with the author, Urrao, 31 Aug. 1985.

113 AGA, 1952, vol. 7, Colonel Luis Abadía A., 4a Brigada to Governor, 4 Aug.

1952; AGA, 1952, vol. 4, telegram from mayor José Gómez, Urrao to Governor, 9 Oct. 1952.

114   Absalón Machado, interview with the author, Bogotá, fall 1986.

115   AGA, 1953, vol. 5, Caicedo, 16 Jan. 1953; AGA, 1953, vol. 5, Caicedo, 20 Jan. 1953; AGA, 1953, vol. 5, Caicedo, 23 Jan. 1953; and AGA, 1953, vol. 8, Urrao, 26 Jan. 1953.

116   AGA, 1953, vol. 5, Salgar, 6 March 1953; AGA, 1953, vol. 1, Montebello, Salgar, 7 March 1953; and AGA, 1953, vol. 5, La García, Caicedo, 22 March 1953.

117   AGA, 1953, vol. 2, Urrao, 26 Aug. 1953.

118   Criminal bands dedicated to the theft of coffee proliferated in towns to the south of Urrao in the later years of the 1950s, but it is not clear — with the exception of Jardín where a famous contrachusma band operated openly — to what degree these groups had any overt political affiliation or objectives after 1953.

119   Tarzán, interview with the author, Betulia, 25 Aug. 1985; Medianalga, interview with the author, Urrao, 20 Aug. 1985; and Graciela Urrego, interview with the author, Urrao, 31 Aug. 1985.

120   AGA, 1953, vol. 10, Governor to MinGob Andrade (in code but deciphered on the reverse), Urrao, 25 June 1952.

121   Ibid.

122   AGA, 1953, "Informe," Directorio Conservador, Medellín to Governor, July 1951.

123   AGA, 1953, vol. 9, Comité Conservador, Urrao to Governor, July 1951.

124   AGA, 1951, vol. 1, Comité Conservador, Urrao to Governor, 21 Aug. 1951.

125   AGA, 1951, vol. 9, Urrao, 9 Sept. 1951; AGA, 1951, vol. 5, Caja de Crédito Agrario to Governor, 30 Sept. 1951.

126   AGA, 1953, vol. 6, Salgar, 18 Feb. 1953.

127   AGA, 1952, vol. 2, Urrao, 3 April 3, 1952. Guerrillas were supposedly paid seventy to one hundred pesos per month plus bonuses (although Franco was alleged to have promised recruits a salary of six hundred pesos per month). See also, AGA, 1953, vol. 9, Capellán Fuerzas Armadas, Pereira to the Governor, 19 Jan. 1953, for accusations that the guerrillas received a salary.

128   AGA, 1952, vol. 6, Urrao forwarded to Governor, 21 May 1952.

129   AGA, 1952, vol. 10, Conservatives, Betulia to Governor, 1 March 1952.

130   AGA, 1952, vol. 6, Major Luis Millán, Director General, Polinal, Bogotá to Governor, 6 Feb. 1952. The major justified burning the entire area around the guerrilla camp of Camparusia in Dabeiba, arguing that despite the presence of twenty Conservative inhabitants, they were suspected of colluding with the guerrillas since "they freely travel without anyone bothering them."

131   SGA, 1953, vol. 10, Betulia, May 18, 1953.

132   SGA, 1953, vol. 1, report of mission to eradicate guerrillas in Betulia and Urrao undertaken by Arturo Velásquez to the Governor, 12 May 1953.

133   PEA, table 20.1.1.3, "Población ocupada, por ramas de actividad económica, Censos 1938–1973," p. 751.

134   Decree no. 53 issued by "The Revolutionary Forces of the West and the South-

west," General Guerrilla Headquarters, Pabón, Urrao, 24 July 1953, Froilan Montoya Mazo (Private Archive), Medellín.

135 "Decree no. 53 re: Public Order," signed Major Franco, Pabón, 24 July 1953, Froilan Montoya Mazo (Private Archive), Medellín. Froilan Montoya Mazo was a *gaitanista* Liberal leader who maintained close contact with Urrao's guerrillas throughout *la Violencia.*

136 Graciela Urrego, interview with the author, Urrao, 31 Aug. 1985; Medianalga (Avelino Urrego), interview with the author, 20 Aug. 1985; and Tarzán (Herlindo Montoya), Betulia, 25 Aug. 1985. In addition to repeatedly indicating that the Llanos guerrillas constituted Urrao's role model during *la Violencia,* Graciela Urrego insisted that the guerrillas had a communication system set up between Urrao and the Llanos made up of human relay runners who traveled from post to post from the west to the east to confer with their Llanos counterparts on strategy and orders.

137 *El Colombiano,* 16 July 1952.

138 *El Colombiano,* 18 April 1952.

139 *El Colombiano,* 19 May 1952.

140 Ibid.

141 *El Colombiano,* 25 May 1952.

142 *El Colombiano,* 16 May 1952.

143 AGA, 1953, vol. 9, Capellán Fuerzas Armadas, Pereira to Governor, 9 Jan. 1953.

144 AGA, 1953, vol. 19, "O.P.," "Algunas Notas Relativo [*sic*] a los Bandidos de Urrao," n.d. I am deducing that this was written by an English speaker because of the syntactical errors and literal translations scattered throughout the text and the obsession with Cold War ideology and the infiltration of Communism into the region.

145 Ibid., 1. These observations were delivered in the form of "bullets" numbered from 1 through 52. The above quote includes points 3 to 5 in the original report.

146 Ibid., points 11 through 15 under the heading "Situación Actual."

147 Ibid., point 18 under the heading "Las Resultas" [*sic*].

148 Ibid., point 19.

149 Ibid., points 20 and 21.

150 Ibid., point 22 under the heading "La Solución."

151 Ibid., point 32.

152 Ibid., point 35.

153 Guzmán, Fals Borda, and Umaña, in *La Violencia en Colombia,* estimated the number of active guerrillas in Antioquia at five thousand and many other researchers have reproduced this figure unquestioningly.

154 AGA, 1953, vol. 19, "Algunas notas," point 41 under the heading "Conclusiones: El bandolerismo en Colombia ahora no es lo que fuera a [*sic*] empezar."

155 Ibid., point 44 under the heading "Conclusiones."

156 Ibid., point 45.

157   Ibid., point 50.
158   Ibid., point 51.
159   Ibid., point 52.
160   The ensuing account is based on Graciela Urrego, interview with the author, Urrao, 31 Aug. 1985.

Epilogue

1   Greg Grandin discusses the findings and deliberations of the Guatemalan Truth Commission, particularly regarding the classification of violence in the Guatemalan case as genocide and highlights the historical antecedents that contributed to the state's targeting of particular groups of Mayan Indians during its counterinsurgency campaigns in an unpublished paper (2001), "Insoluble Acts and Historical Solutions: Law, History, and Latin American Cold War Terror." I am grateful to the author for bringing his paper to my attention. For interviews with military commanders during the Guatemalan civil war and an exploration of the logic behind their counterinsurgency campaign, see Jennifer Schirmer, *The Guatemalan Military Project.*

2   Steve J. Stern, ed., *Shining and Other Paths: War and Society in Peru, 1980–1995* (Durham, N.C.: Duke University Press, 1998), especially Nelson Manrique, "The War for the Central Sierra," pp. 193–223. The intersection of violence, race, and ethnicity in the Peruvian case is more explicitly developed in Manrique, "Political Violence, Ethnicity, and Racism in Peru in the Time of the War," *Journal of Latin American Studies* 4, no. 1; and, on this same theme, see also "Vietnam in the Andes: 'Pancho,'" in *The Peru Reader: History, Culture, Politics,* ed. Orin Starn, Carlos Iván DeGregori, and Robin Kirk (Durham, N.C.: Duke University Press, 1995), pp. 342–47.

3   Neil Harvey, *The Chiapas Rebellion: The Struggle for Land and Democracy* (Durham, N.C.: Duke University Press, 1998); John Womack Jr., ed., *Rebellion in Chiapas: A Historical Reader* (New York: New Press, 1999); *Shadows of Tender Fury: The Letters and Communiqués of Sub-Comandante Marcos and the Zapatista Army of National Liberation,* ed. Frank Bardacke, Leslie López, and the Watsonville, California, Human Rights Committee (New York: Monthly Review, 1995).

4   *New York Times,* "Crisis in Colombia as Civil Strife Uproots Peasants," 21 Oct. 1999.

5   The regional paper, *El Colombiano,* published a series of articles focusing on the problem of human displacement in Antioquia and Colombia and the large number of refugees from Urabá and the Magdalena Medio, among them "Campesinos rumbo al destierro: Pavarandó, el refugio," 31 Dec. 1997.

6   These fears are not baseless, see Carlos Castaño's warning that there would be many more massacres in towns perceived to be leftist supporters, in *El Tiempo,* "Va a haber muchos más mapiripanes," 28 Sept. 1997. For evidence that he has

made good on his promise, see *New York Times,* "Rightist Squads in Colombia Beating the Rebels," 5 Dec. 2000.

7   Alonso Salazar, *Born to Die in Medellín* (London: Verso, 1992).

8   Ibid.

9   Elaine Scarry, *The Body in Pain: The Making and Unmaking of the World* (New York: Oxford University Press, 1985) refers to this as the euphemistic and erroneous notion of the so-called indirect consequences of war.

10   *New York Times,* 21 Oct. 1999.

11   See the issues of the Colombian political magazine, *Alternativa,* devoted to Antioqueño Governor Alvaro Uribe Vélez's endorsement of a paramilitary solution to violence and the effects of this policy in Urabá in "Mano Dura? O Tenaza Militar?" in *Alternativa* 5 (15 Nov.– 15 Dec. 1996): 11–14; and the special issue devoted to analyzing the paramilitary phenomenon and the Colombian Supreme Court's debate regarding the constitutionality of privately financed armed groups with a special emphasis on the organization of *Convivirs* in Antioquia in "Retornan los pajáros," *Alternativa* 16 (15 Dec. 1997–1 Feb. 1998): 11–21.

12   "Se debe acabar con la mentira oficial," *Alternativa* 6 (15 Jan.–15 Feb. 1997): 10–17 (interview with ex–army colonel Carlos Alfonso Velásquez, former commander of Urabá, regarding the spread of paramilitary organizations and their collusion with the armed forces in Colombia); Cynthia Aronson and Robin Kirk, *State of War: Political Violence and Counterinsurgency in Colombia* (New York: Human Rights Watch/Americas, 1993); and Human Rights Watch/Americas–Arms Project, *Colombia's Killer Networks: The Military-Paramilitary Partnership and the United States* (New York: Human Rights Watch/Americas, 1996).

13   Manuel Enrique López B., "Implicaciones del conflicto armado en el modelo de economía cafetera. Aproximación al caso del suroeste antioqueño," in *Conflictos Regionales: La Crisis del Eje Cafetero,* ed. Gonzalo Sánchez G., Jorge Enrique Robledo Castillo, Absalón Machado C., Manuel E. López, and Christopher London (Bogotá: FESCOL and IEPRI, 1999), anexo 1 and 2, pp. 90–93.

14   During the 1980s and 1990s political dissent in these towns was expressed through support of the Unión Patriotica, a Communist affiliate, the majority of whose members have been assassinated.

15   The debate regarding the validity of "region" as an analytical category is one that has recently received a good deal of attention from Colombian scholars and is widely debated by scholars of Latin America in general. Among the relevant works for Colombia are Miguel Borja, *Estado, Sociedad y Ordenamiento Territorial en Colombia* (Bogotá: CEREC, 1996); and Fabio Zambrano Pantója, *Colombia, País de Regiones* (Bogotá: CINEP/Colciencias, 1998).

Bibliography

Archives and Manuscript Collections

Note on archival sources: There were 113 volumes of correspondence in the Archivo de la Gobernación de Antioquia for the period from 1947 to 1953. None of the material in the archive is indexed, nor were all of the volumes numbered. The absence of a volume number in the citations therefore is not an oversight. The material contained in the Archivo de la Gobernación, moreover, was not always in chronological order. Thus, it was possible for material from say, March 1947, to be included in different volumes of the 1947 correspondence or sometimes even in volumes for the correspondence of another year.

Archivo de la Secretaría de Gobierno de Antioquia, 1947–1953, 61 vols. (SGA)

Archivo Nacional de Colombia, Ministerio de Industrias, Correspodencia de Baldíos (ANCB)

Archivo Parroquial, Registro de funciones, 1948–1954, Urrao, Antioquia

Archivo Privado del Señor Gobernador de Antioquia, 1947–1953, 52 vols. (AGA)

Archivo Privado, Froilan Montoya Mazo, 1944–1954, Medellín

Archivo Privado, José Mejía y Mejía, Medellín

Centro Cultural Jorge Eliécer Gaitán, Correspondencia de Jorge Eliécer Gaitán, 1944–1948, Bogotá

Newspaper collection, library of the Universidad de Antioquia, Medellín

Newspapers and Magazines

Acción Católica Colombiana

Alternativa

El Colombiano

El Correo

Cromos

Crónica Municipal, Medellín

La Defensa

El Diario

New York Times

El 9 de Abril

El Obrero Católico

El Poder

El Pueblo

Revista de la Policía Nacional, Bogotá

Progreso

Revista del Estado Mayor
El Siglo
El Tiempo

Government Publications

Antioquia. Alcaldía de Medellín. 1989. *Convocatoria a la paz.* Medellín: Imprenta Municipal.

Antioquia. Departamento Administrativo de Planeación. 1963. *Distribución de los predios rurales en Antioquia según su tamaño 1962.* Medellín: Imprenta Departamental.

Antioquia. Dirección de Desarrollo. 1978. *Región Suroeste: Analísis de la situación actual. Informe Básico, Inventario y Carectización.* Medellín: Imprenta Departamental.

Colombia. Banco de la Repúbica. 1990. Memoria de Hacienda, Francisco de Paula Pérez, 1929, 1931, 1946. Bogotá.

Colombia. Camara de Representantes. 1981. *Laureano Gómez: Obras Selectas.* Part 1, vol. 15. Medellín: Editorial Bedout.

Colombia. Camara de Representantes. n.d. *Román Gómez: Obras selectas.* Bogotá: n.p.

Colombia. Departamento Administrativo Nacional de Estadística. 1978. *Censo nacional agropecuario, Antioquia.* Bogotá.

Colombia. Departamento Administrativo Nacional de Estadistíca. 1987. *Colombia Estadística.* Bogotá.

Colombia. 1949. *Decreto del Estado de Sitio.* Bogotá.

Colombia. Departamento Administrativo Nacional de Estadística. 1981. *Panorama estadístico de Antioquia.* Bogotá. (PEA)

Colombia. Departamento Administrativo Nacional de Estadística. *Estadística Electoral, 1947–1949.* Bogotá.

Colombia. Departamento de Antioquia. *Anales de la Asamblea de Antioquia.* Medellín: Imprenta Departamental.

Colombia. Departamento de Antioquia. *Anuario estadístico, años 1944, 1945, 1946.*

Colombia. Departamento de Antioquia. *Anuario estadístico, años 1947, 1948, 1949.*

Colombia. Departamento de Antioquia. *Anuario estadístico, años 1950–1952.*

Colombia. Ministerio de Gobierno, *Memorias 1939, 1940, 1941, 1942, 1943, 1944, 1945, 1946, 1947, 1948.* Bogotá.

Interviews

CONDUCTED BY THE AUTHOR

Manuel Mejía Vallejo, Medellín, Aug. 1985.

Medianalga [Avelino Urrego], Urrao, Antioquia, 20 Aug. 1985.

Judith and Debora, Urrao, 25 Aug. 1985.

Tarzán [Herlindo Montoya], Betulia, Antioquia, 25 Aug. 1985.

Joaquín Montoya Escobar, Urrao, Antioquia, 30 Aug. 1985.

Josefina Montoya, Urrao, Antioquia, 30 Aug. 1985.

Graciela Urrego, Urrao, Antioquia, 31 Aug. 1985.

Iván J. Cadavid (priest), Bogotá, fall 1986.

Absalón Machado, Bogotá, fall 1986.

Froilan Montoya Mazo, Medellín, fall 1986.

Emma Londoño de Mejía, Medellín, Oct. 1986.

Bernardo Ospina Román, Medellín, Nov. 1986.

Capitán Corneta [Francisco Montoya], Medellín, spring 1987.

Aníbal Vallejo Alvarez, Medellín, April 1987.

CONDUCTED BY RESEARCHERS AT THE INSTITUTO DE ESTUDIOS
REGIONALES (INER), UNIVERSIDAD DE ANTIOQUIA, MEDELLÍN
Alejandría, 29 Sept. 1988.

Granada, 16 June 1988.

San Carlos, 23 June 1988.

San Rafael, 16 June 1988.

San Roque, 2 June, 25 Aug., and 4 Sept. 1988.

Secondary Sources

Abel, Christopher. 1987. *Política, iglesia y partidos en Colombia*. Bogotá: FAES–
Universidad Nacional de Colombia.

Abella Rodríguez, Arturo. 2000. *Laureano Gómez*. Bogotá: Espara.

Abrams, Philip. 1988. "Notes on the Difficulty of Studying the State." *Journal of
Historical Sociology* 1 (1): 58–89.

Academia Antioqueña de Historia. 1986. *Un siglo de gobierno en Antioquia, 1886–
1986*. Medellín: Secretaría de Servicios Administrativos del Departamento de
Antioquia.

Alape, Arturo. 1983. *El Bogotazo: Memorias del olvido*. Bogotá: Editorial Pluma.
———. 1984. *Noche de Pájaros*. Bogotá: Planeta Colombiana Editorial, S.A.

Alexander, Robert. 1957. *Communism in Latin America*. New Brunswick, N.J.:
Rutgers University Press.

Alonso, Ana Maria. 1995. *Thread of Blood: Colonialism, Revolution, and Gender
on Mexico's Northern Frontier*. Tucson: University of Arizona Press.

Alvarez Gardeazábal, Gustavo. 1979. *Condores no entierran todos los días*. Bogotá:
Plaza y Janes Editores Colombia.

Anderson, Benedict. 1983. *Imagined Communities: Reflections on the Origin and
Spread of Nationalism*. London: Verso.

Andrade Valderrama, Luis. n.d. *Cartas Pastorales*. Medellín: n.p.

Appadurai, Arjun. 1998. "Dead Certainty: Ethnic Violence in the Era of Globalization." *Public Culture* 10 (2): 225–47.

Appelbaum, Nancy. 1997. "Remembering Riosucio: Region, Ethnicity, and Community in Western Antioquia, 1850–1920." Ph.D. diss. University of Wisconsin, Madison.

Arango, Mariano. 1981. *Café e industria, 1850–1930.* Bogotá: Carlos Valencia Editores.

———. 1982. *El café en Colombia, 1930–1958: Producción, circulación y política.* Bogotá: Carlos Valencia Editores.

Archila, Mauricio. 1990. "Paternalism and Social Relations in the Early Stages of Colombian Industrialization." Paper presented at the Latin American Labor History Conference, Yale University, 21 April 1990.

———. 1991. *Cultura e identidad obrera: Colombia, 1910–1945.* Bogotá: CINEP.

Arocha, Jaime. 1979. *La Violencia en el Quindío: Determinantes ecológicos y económicos del homicidio en un municipio caficultor.* Bogotá: n.p.

Aronson, Cynthia, and Robin Kirk. 1993. *State of War: Political Violence and Counterinsurgency in Colombia.* New York: Human Rights Watch/Americas.

Balibar, Etienne, and Immanuel Wallerstein. 1991. *Race, Nation, Class: Ambiguous Identities.* New York: Verso.

Bardecke, Frank, Leslie Lopez, and the Watsonville, California, Human Rights Committee. 1995. *Shadows of Tender Fury: The Letters and Communiqués of Sub-Comandante Marcos and the Zapatista Army of National Liberation.* New York: Monthly Review.

Baretta, Silvio R. Duncan, and John Markoff. 1978. "Civilization and Barbarism: Cattle Frontiers in Latin America." *Comparative Studies in Society and History* 20 (4): 587–620.

Bayer, Tulio. 1954. *Carretera al mar.* Medellín: n.p.

Bejarano, Jesús Antonio. 1982. "La economía." In *Manual de Historia de Colombia.* 2d ed. Ed. Jaime Jaramillo Uribe. Bogotá: Procultura S.A., Instituto Colombiano de Cultura.

———. 1985. *Economía y Poder.* Bogotá: Fondo Editorial CEREC.

———. 1987. *Ensayos de historia agraria colombiana.* Bogotá: CEREC.

Bell, P. L. 1921. *Colombia: A Commercial and Industrial Handbook.* U.S. Department of Commerce, Bureau of Foreign and Domestic Commerce. Special Agent Series no. 206. Washington, D.C.: Government Printing Office.

Bergquist, Charles W. 1978. *Coffee and Conflict in Colombia, 1886–1910.* Durham, N.C.: Duke University Press.

———. 1986. *Labor in Latin America: Comparative Essays on Chile, Argentina, Venezuela, and Colombia.* Stanford: Stanford University Press.

Bergquist, Charles, Ricardo Peñaranda, and Gonzalo Sánchez, eds. 1992. *Violence in Colombia: The Contemporary Crisis in Historical Perspective.* Wilmington, Del.: Scholarly Resources.

Berry, Albert R., and Ronald G. Hellman, ed. 1980. *Politics of Compromise: Coalition Government in Colombia.* New Brunswick, N.J.: Transaction Books.

Betancourt, Darío, and Martha L. García. 1990. *Matones y cuadrilleros: Origen y evolución de la Violencia en el occidente colombiano, 1946–1965.* Bogotá: Tercer Mundo Editores.

Bhabha, Homi K. 1990. "The Other Question: Difference, Discrimination, and the Discourse of Colonialism." In *Out There: Marginalization and Contemporary Cultures.* Eds. Russell Ferguson et al. Cambridge: MIT Press.

Borja, Miguel. 1996. *Estado, Sociedad y Ordenamiento Territorial en Colombia.* Bogotá: CEREC.

Botero Herrera, Fernando. 1990. *Urabá: Colonización, violencia, y crisis del estado.* Medellín: Editorial Universidad de Antioquia.

Bourdieu, Pierre. 1987. "What Makes a Social Class? On the Theoretical and Practical Existence of Groups." *Berkeley Journal of Sociology* 32: 1–17.

Braun, Herbert. 1985. *The Assassination of Gaitán: Public Life and Urban Violence in Colombia.* Madison: University of Wisconsin Press.

———. 1994. *Our Guerrillas, Our Sidewalks: A Journey into the Violence of Colombia.* Niwot, Colo.: University Press of Colorado.

Brew, Roger. 1971. "Aspects of Politics in Antioquia, 1850–1865." B.A. Phil. Thesis. Oxford University, St. Anthony's College.

———. 1977. *El desarrollo económico de Antioquia desde la independencia hasta 1920.* Bogotá: Banco de la República.

Buci-Glucksmann, Christine. 1980. *Gramsci and the State.* London: Lawrence and Wishart.

Builes, Miguel Angel. 1957. *Cartas Pastorales del Excelentisimo Señor Miguel Angel Builes Obispo de Santa Rosa de Osos.* 2 vols. Bogotá: Empresa Nacional de Publicaciones.

Buitrago Salazar, Evelio. 1977. *Zarpazo the Bandit: Memoirs of an Undercover Agent of the Colombian Army.* Mobile: University of Alabama Press.

Bushnell, David. 1967. *Eduardo Santos and the Good Neighbor Policy, 1938–1942.* Gainesville: University of Florida Press.

Bushnell, David, and Neill Macauley. 1988. *The Emergence of Latin America in the Nineteenth Century.* New York: Oxford University Press.

———. 1993. *The Making of Modern Colombia: A Nation in Spite of Itself.* Berkeley: University of California Press.

Campo, Urbano. 1980. *Urbanización y violencia en el Valle.* Bogotá: Ediciones Armadillo.

Canal Ramírez, Gonzalo. 1966. *Estámpas y testimonios de violencia.* Bogotá: n.p.

Cardona Grisales, Guillermo. 1989. *Para un estudio sobre la Violencia en Colombia.* Bogotá: CINEP.

Carmack, Robert M., ed. 1988. *Harvest of Violence: The Mayan Indian and the Guatemalan Crisis.* Norman: University of Oklahoma Press.

Casas Aguilar, Julio. 1986. *La Violencia en los Llanos Orientales.* Bogotá: ECOE Ediciones.

Casas, Ulises. 1987. *De la guerrilla liberal a la guerrilla comunista.* Bogotá: n.p.

Cepeda, Manuel José. 1986. *Cómo son las elecciones en Colombia: Guía de votante.* Bogotá: CEREC, FESCOL, CIDER.

Christie, Keith. 1978. "Antioqueño Colonization in Western Colombia: A Reappraisal." *Hispanic American Historical Review* 58 (May): 260–83.

———. 1986. *Oligarcas, campesinos, y política en Colombia.* Bogotá: Universidad Nacional de Colombia.

Colmenares, Germán. n.d. *Partidos políticos y clases sociales en Colombia.* Bogotá: n.p.

Colombia en cifras. 1946. Bogotá: El Mes Financiero y Económico.

Comaroff, Jean, and John Comaroff. 1992. *Ethnography and the Historical Imagination.* Boulder: Westview Press.

Comisión de estudios sobre la violencia. 1987. *Colombia: Violencia y democracia, Informe presentado al Ministerio de Gobierno.* Bogotá: Universidad Nacional de Colombia.

Conniff, Michael. 1982. *Latin American Populism in Comparative Perspective.* Albuquerque: University of New Mexico Press.

Cooper, Frederick, and Ann Laura Stoler. 1989. "Introduction: Tensions of Empire." *American Ethnologist* 16: 609–21.

Corrigan, Philip. 1994. "State Formation." In *Everyday Forms of State Formation.* Eds. Gilbert Joseph and Daniel Nugent. Durham, N.C.: Duke University Press.

da Cunha, Euclides. 1967. *Rebellion in the Backlands.* Trans. Samuel Putnam. Chicago: University of Chicago Press.

Davis, Natalie Zemon. 1975. *Society and Culture in Early Modern France.* Stanford: Stanford University Press.

Delgado, Carlos, ed. 1986. *El 9 de abril en fotos.* Bogotá: El Ancora Editores.

Delpar, Helen. 1981. *Red against Blue: The Liberal Party in Colombian Politics, 1863–1899.* Tuscaloosa: University of Alabama Press.

Derby, Robin L. H., and Richard Turits. 1990. "Histories of Terror and the Terrors of History: The 1937 Haitian Massacre in the Dominican Republic." Paper presented to the Committee on Latin American History at the annual meeting of the American Historical Association, New York, 29 December 1990.

Diacon, Todd A. 1991. *Millenarian Vision, Capitalist Reality: Brazil's Contestado Rebellion.* Durham, N.C.: Duke University Press.

Díaz Callejas, Apolinar. 1988. *El 9 de abríl 1948 en Barrancabermeja: Diez días de poder popular.* Bogotá: El Labrador.

Dix, Robert H. 1967. *Colombia: The Political Dimensions of Change.* New Haven: Yale University Press.

Duque Betancourt, Francisco. 1968. *Historia del Departamento de Antioquia.* 2d ed. Medellín: Editorial Albon Interprint.

Echavarría, Guillermo. 1979. *Camilo C. Restrepo.* Medellín: Semigráficos.

Echeverri Uruburu, Alvaro. 1987. *Elites y proceso político en Colombia, 1950–1978.* Bogotá: FUAC.

Fajardo, Darío. 1976. "La Violencia y las estructuras agrarias en tres muncipios cafeteros de Tolima: 1936–1970." In *El agro en el desarrollo histórico colombiano: Ensayos de economía.* Ed. Francisco Leal Buitrago et al. Bogotá: Punta de Lanza.

———. 1979. *Violencia y desarrollo: Transformaciones sociales en tres regiones cafetaleras del Tolima, 1936–1970.* Bogotá: Fondo Editorial Suramérica.

Fajardo, Luis H., n.d. *The Protestant Ethic of the Antioqueños?: Social Structure and Personality.* Cali: Ediciones Departamento de Sociología, Universidad del Valle.

Farnsworth-Alvear, Ann. 2000. *Dulcinea in the Factory: Myths, Morals, Men, and Women in Colombia's Industrial Experiment, 1905–1960.* Durham, N.C.: Duke University Press.

Feldman, Allen. 1991. *Formations of Violence: The Narrative of the Body and Political Terror in Northern Ireland.* Chicago: University of Chicago Press.

———. 1997. "Violence and Vision: The Prosthetics and Aesthetics of Terror." *Public Culture* 10 (1): 24–60.

Fidelis, Testis [pseud.]. 1952. *De Cain a Pilatos (Prologue by Juan Roca Lemus [Rubayata] and an endorsement by the Bishop of Santa Rosa de Osos, Miguel Angel Builes).* Medellín: n.p.

Flórez-Malagón, Alberto Guillermo. 1994. "Peasants, Landlords, and Political Culture in Colombia: The Ubaté Valley during 'La Violencia,' 1946–1958." Ph.D. diss. State University of New York at Stony Brook.

Fluharty, Vernon Lee. 1957. *Dance of the Millions: Military Rule and the Social Revolution in Colombia, 1930–1956.* Pittsburgh: University of Pittsburgh Press.

French, William E. 1994. "Progreso Forzado: Workers and the Inculcation of the Capitalist Work Ethic in the Parral Mining District." In *Rituals of Rule, Rituals of Resistance.* Eds. William Beezeley, Cheryl English Martin, and William E. French. Wilmington, Del.: Scholarly Resources.

Franco Isaza, Eduardo. 1976. *Las guerrillas del Llano.* 3d ed. Medellín: Ediciones Hombre Nuevo.

Gaitán de Valencia, Gloria. 1976. *Colombia: la lucha por la tierra en la década del treinta.* Bogotá: n.p.

Galvis, Silvia, and Alberto Donadio. 1986. *Colombia Nazi 1939–1945: Espionaje alemán, la cacería del FBI, Santos, López y los pactos secretos.* Bogotá: Planeta Colombiana Editorial.

———. 1988. *El Jefe Supremo: Rojas Pinilla en la violencia y en el poder.* Bogotá: Planeta.

García, Antonio. 1978. *Geografía económica de Caldas.* 2d ed. Bogotá: Banco de la República.

García Márquez, Gabriel. 1982. *La mala hora*. Bogotá: Editorial La Oveja Negra.

———. 1998. *News of a Kidnapping*. New York: Penguin Press.

Gilhodes, Pierre. 1970. "Agrarian Struggles in Colombia." In *Agrarian Problems and Peasant Movements in Latin America*. Ed. Rodolfo Stavenhagen. Garden City, N.Y.: Doubleday.

———. 1974. *La Question agraire en Colombie, 1958-71*. Paris: n.p.

Gilman, Sander L. 1985. *Difference and Pathology: Stereotypes of Sexuality, Race, and Madness*. Ithaca: Cornell University Press.

Gómez, Laureano. n.d. *El basilisco en acción*. Bogotá: n.p.

Gómez Martínez, Fernando. n.d. *Mordaza, diario secreto de un escritor público*. 2d ed. Medellín: Edición de El Colombiano.

González Arias, José Jairo, and Elsy Marulanda Alvarez. 1990. *Historias de frontera: Colonización y guerras en el Sumapaz*. Bogotá: CINEP.

Gónzalez Restrepo, Jorge. 1978. *Por los caminos de la muerte: Un recuento de La Violencia en Salgar*. MS, Fundación Antioqueña de Estudios Sociales, Medellín.

Gracian, Luis. n.d. *Laureano Gómez, un hombre, un partido, una nación*. Bogotá: Ediciones Nuevo Mundo.

Gramsci, Antonio. 1971. *Selections from the Prison Notebooks of Antonio Gramsci*. Eds. Quintin Hoare and Geoffrey Nowell Smith. New York: International Publishers.

Granados, Wilson. 1982. "La Violencia en Urrao, Antioquia, 1948-1953." Tesis de grado. Universidad de Antioquia.

Grandin, Greg. 2000. *The Blood of Guatemala: A History of Race and Nation*. Durham, N.C.: Duke University Press.

———. 2001. "Insoluble Acts and Historical Solutions: Law, History, and Latin American Cold War Terror." Unpublished manuscript.

Green, John W. 1996. " 'Vibrations of the Collective': The Popular Ideology of Gaitanismo on Colombia's Atlantic Coast, 1944-1948." *Hispanic American Historical Review* 76 (2): 283-311.

Guhl, Ernesto. 1975. *Colombia: Bosquejo de su geografía tropical*. 2 vols. Bogotá: Biblioteca Básica Colombiana.

Gutiérrez de Pineda, Virginia. 1975. *Familia y Cultura en Colombia*. Bogotá: Instituto Colombiano de Cultura, Departamento Administrativo Nacional de Estadística.

Guzmán Campos, Germán, Orlando Fals Borda, and Eduardo Umaña. 1980. *La Violencia en Colombia*. 2 vols. 9th ed. Bogotá: Carlos Valencia Editores.

Hagen, Everett E. 1962. *On the Theory of Social Change: How Economic Growth Begins*. Homewood, Ill.: Dorsey Press.

Hartlyn, Jonathan. 1981. "Consociational Politics in Colombia: Confrontation and Accomodation in Comparative Perspective." Ph.D. diss. Yale University.

———. 1985. "Producer Associations, the Political Regime, and Policy Processes in Contemporary Colombia." *Latin American Research Review* 20 (3): 111-38.

————. 1988. *The Politics of Coalition Rule in Colombia.* New York: Cambridge University Press.

Harvey, Neil. 1998. *The Chiapas Rebellion: The Struggle for Land and Democracy.* Durham, N.C.: Duke University Press.

Held, David. ed. 1983. *States and Societies.* New York: New York University Press.

Helg, Aline. 1987. *La educación en Colombia, 1918–1957: Una historia social, económica y política.* 2d ed. Bogotá: Fondo Editorial CEREC.

Henderson, James. 1985. *Las ideas de Laureano Gómez.* Bogotá: Tercer Mundo.

————. 1985. *When Colombia Bled: A History of the "Violencia" in Tolima.* Tuscaloosa: University of Alabama Press.

Hennessy, Alistair. 1978. *The Frontier in Latin American History.* Albuquerque: University of New Mexico Press.

Herrera, Ernesto León [Fidel Blandón Berrío]. 1954. *Lo que el cielo no perdona.* Bogotá: Editorial ARGRA.

Herrera Soto, Roberto. 1982. *Antología del pensamiento conservador en Colombia.* 2 vols. Bogotá: n.p.

Hobsbawm, Eric J. 1965. *Primitive Rebels: Studies in Archaic Forms of Social Movement in the Nineteenth and Twentieth Centuries.* New York: W. W. Norton.

————. 1981. *Bandits.* Rev. ed. New York: Pantheon Books.

Human Rights Watch/Americas–Arms Project. 1996. *Colombia's Killer Networks: The Military-Paramilitary Partnership and the United States.* New York: Human Rights Watch/Americas.

Jaramillo, Roberto Luis. 1984. "La otra cara de la colonización antioqueña hacia el sur." *Revista de Extensión Cultural* 18 (December).

Jaramillo Uribe, Jaime. 1982. *El pensamiento colombiano en el siglo xix.* Bogotá: Editorial Temis.

————. ed. 1982. *Manual de historia de Colombia.* 3 vols. 2d ed. Bogotá: Procultura S.A., Instituto Colombiano de Cultura.

Jiménez, Michael. 1986. "The Limits of Export Capitalism: Economic Structure, Class, and Politics in a Colombian Coffee Municipality, 1900–1930." Ph.D. diss., Harvard University.

Joseph, Gilbert M. 1990. "On the Trail of Latin American Bandits: A Reexamination of Peasant Resistance." *Latin American Research Review* 25 (2): 7–53.

Joseph, Gilbert M., and Daniel Nugent, eds. 1994. *Everyday Forms of State Formation: Revolution and the Negotiation of Rule in Modern Mexico.* Durham, N.C.: Duke University Press.

Kalmanowitz, Salomón. 1978. *Desarrollo de la agricultura en Colombia.* Bogotá: n.p.

————. 1986. *Economía y nación: Una breve historia de Colombia.* Bogotá: Siglo Veintiuno Editores, CINEP.

Knight, Alan. 1985. "The Mexican Revolution: Bourgeois? Nationalist? or Just a 'Great Rebellion'?" *Bulletin of Latin American Research* 4 (2): 1–37.

Koonings, Kee, and Dirk Kruijt, eds. 1999. *Societies of Fear: The Legacy of Civil War, Violence, and Terror in Latin America.* New York: St. Martin's Press.

Latorre, Emilio. 1986. *Transporte y crecimiento regional en Colombia.* Bogotá: Editorial Presencia.

Leal Buitrago, Francisco. 1984. *Estado y política en Colombia.* Bogotá: Siglo Veintiuno Editores de Colombia, CEREC.

LeGrand, Catherine. 1986. *Frontier Expansion and Peasant Protest in Colombia, 1830–1936.* Albuquerque: University of New Mexico Press.

———. 1997. "La política y la Violencia en Colombia, 1946–1965: Interpretaciones en la década de los ochenta." *Memoria y Sociedad* 2 (4): 79–109.

Lewin, Linda. 1979. "The Oligarchical Limitations of Social Banditry in Brazil: The Case of the 'Good' Thief Antonio Silvino." *Past and Present* 82: 116–46.

Lievano Aguirre, Indalecio. 1984. *Los grandes conflictos sociales y economicos de nuestra historia.* 2 vols. 10th ed. Bogotá: Tercer Mundo.

López, Alejandro. 1931. *Idearium liberal.* Paris: n.p.

———. 1976. *Escritos escogidos.* Bogotá: Biblioteca Básica Colombiana.

López B., Manuel Enrique. 1999. "Implicaciones del conflicto armado en el modelo de economiía cafetera. Aproximación al caso del suroeste antioqueño." In *Conflictos Regionales: La Crisis del Eje Cafetero,* ed. Gonzalo Sánchez G. et al. Bogota: FESCOL, IEPRI.

López C., Hugo. 1975. "La inflación en Colombia en la década de los veintes." *Cuadernos Colombianos* 5.

López de Mesa, Luis. 1970. *De cómo se ha formado la nación colombiana.* 2d ed. Medellín: n.p.

López Giraldo, Fermín. 1936. *El apostol desnudo: O dos años al lado de un mito.* Manizales: Editorial Zapata.

López Toro, Alvaro. 1979. *Migración y cambio social en Antioquia.* Medellín: Ediciones Hombre Nuevo.

Loveman, Brian, and Thomas M. Davies Jr., eds. 1997. *The Politics of Antipolitics: The Military in Latin America.* Rev. ed. Wilmington, Del.: Scholarly Resources Books.

Lynch, John. 1981. *Argentine Dictator: Juan Manuel Rosas, 1829–1852.* New York: Oxford University Press.

Machado, Absalón. 1977. *El café: De la aparcería al capitalismo.* Bogotá: Tercer Mundo Editores.

Malkki, Liisa H. 1995. *Purity and Exile, Violence, Memory, and National Cosmology among Hutu Refugees in Tanzania.* Chicago: University of Chicago Press.

Mallon, Florencia E. 1995. *Peasant and Nation: The Making of Postcolonial Mexico and Peru.* Berkeley: University of California Press.

Marcucci, Olindo. n.d. *La revolución agraria en Colombia: Partido social agrario nacionalista*. Bogotá: Editores Minerva.

Martz, John. 1962. *Colombia: A Contemporary Political Survey*. Chapel Hill: University of North Carolina Press.

Maullin, Richard. 1973. *Soldiers, Guerillas, and Politics in Colombia*. Lexington, Mass.: D. C. Heath.

Mayor Mora, Alberto. 1985. *Etica, trabajo y productividad*. 2d ed. Medellín: Ediciones Tercer Mundo.

McGreevey, William Paul. 1971. *An Economic History of Colombia, 1845–1930*. Cambridge: Cambridge University Press.

Medina, Medófilo. 1980. *Historia del Partido Comunista de Colombia*. Vol. 1. Bogotá: n.p.

———. 1984. *La protesta urbana en Colombia en el siglo veinte*. Bogotá: Ediciones Aurora.

Mejía Robledo, Alfonso, ed. 1951. *Vidas y empresas de Antioquia: Diccionario biográfico, bibliográfico y económico*. Medellín: Imprenta Departamental de Antioquia.

Mejía V., Gilberto. n.d. *El comunismo en Antioquia (María Cano): Memorias*. Medellín: Ediciones Pepe.

Mejía Vallejo, Manuel. 1964. *El día señalado*. Barcelona: Destino.

Melo, Jorge Orlando. 1988. "La política de 1904 a 1946." In *Historia de Antioquia*. Ed. Jorge Orlando Melo. Bogotá: Editorial Presencia y Suramericana de Seguros.

Molano, Alfredo. 1985. *Los años del tropel: Relatos de la Violencia*. Bogotá: Editorial Presencia.

Molina, Gerardo. 1970. *Las ideas liberales en Colombia, 1849–1914*. Bogotá: n.p.

———. 1974. *Las ideas liberales en Colombia, 1915–1934*. Bogotá: n.p.

Monografías de Antioquia. 1941. Medellín: n.p.

Mosse, George L. 1985. *Nationalism and Sexuality: Middle-Class Morality and Sexual Norms in Modern Europe*. Madison: University of Wisconsin Press.

———. 1991. *The Nationalization of the Masses: Political Symbolism and Mass Movements in Germany from the Napoleonic Wars through the Third Reich*. Ithaca: Cornell University Press [1975].

Murray, Pamela S. 1990. "Forging a Technocratic Elite in Colombia: A History of the Escuela Nacional de Minas of Medellín, 1887–1970." Ph.D. diss. Tulane University.

Nixon, Rob. 1993. "Of Balkans and Bantustans: 'Ethnic Cleansing' and the Crisis in National Legitimation." *Transition* 60: 4–26.

Ocampo, Gloria Isabel. 1986–1988. "Hacienda, parentesco y mentalidad: La colonización antioqueña en el Sinu." *Revista Colombiana de Antropología* 26: 8–39.

———. 1993. "Entre la localidad y la Nación: Aspectos políticos de la construcción de identidades en un contexto regional." *Revista Colombiana de Antropología* 30: 104–23.

Ocampo, José Antonio. 1984. *Colombia y la economía mundial, 1830–1910.* Mexico, D.F.: Siglo Veintiuno Editores.

———. 1989. "Los orígenes de la industria cafetera, 1830–1929." In *Nueva historia de Colombia.* Vol. 5. Ed. Jaime Jaramillo Uribe. Bogotá: Planeta.

Ocampo, José Antonio, and Santiago Montenegro, eds. 1984. *Crisis mundial, protección e industrialización.* Bogotá: Fondo Editorial CEREC.

Once Ensayos Sobre la Violencia. 1985. Bogotá: Fondo Editorial CEREC and Centrogaitán.

Oquist, Paul. 1980. *Violence, Conflict, and Politics in Colombia.* New York: Academic Press.

Ortiz Mesa, Luis Javier. 1988. "Antioquia bajo la regeneración, 1886–1904." In *Historia de Antioquia.* Ed. Jorge Orlando Melo. Bogotá: Editorial Presencia.

Ortiz Sarmiento, Carlos Miguel. 1984. "Fundadores y negociantes en la colonización del Quindío." *Lecturas de Economía* 13 (January–April): 105–39.

———. 1985. *Estado y subversión en Colombia: La Violencia en el Quindío, años 50.* Bogotá: Fondo Editorial CEREC.

———. 1986. "La Violencia y los negocios: Quindió años 50 y 60." In *Pasado y presente de la Violencia en Colombia.* Ed. Gonzalo Sánchez and Ricardo Peñaranda. Bogotá: Fondo Editorial CEREC.

———. 1990–1991. "Violencia política de los ochenta: Elementos para una reflexión historica." *Anuario Colombiano de Historia Social y de la Cultura* 18–19: 245–80.

Osorio, Iván Darío. n.d. *Historia del sindicalismo antioqueño, 1900–1986.* Medellín: Tipografía y Litografía Sigifredo.

Ospina, Tulio. 1930. *Protocolo Hispanoamericano de la urbanidad y el buen tono.* 3d ed. Medellín: Félix de Bedout e Hijos.

Ospina Vásquez, Luis. 1979. *Industria y protección en Colombia, 1810–1930.* 3d ed. Medellín: FAES, Editorial Lealon.

Palacios, Marco. 1983. *El café en Colombia, 1850–1970: Una historia económica, social y política.* 2d ed. Bogotá: Siglo Veintiuno Editores.

———. 1995. *Entre la legitimidad y la violencia: Colombia, 1875–1994.* Bogotá: Norma.

Pardo Pardo, Alberto. 1979. *Geografía económica y humana de Colombia.* 2d ed. Bogotá: Ediciones Tercer Mundo.

Park, James William. 1985. *Rafael Núñez and the Politics of Colombian Regionalism, 1863–1886.* Baton Rouge: Louisiana State University Press.

Parker, Andrew, et al. 1992. *Nationalisms and Sexualities.* London: Routledge.

Parsons, James. 1968. *Antioqueño Colonization in Western Colombia.* 2d ed. Berkeley: University of California Press.

———. 1979. *La colonización antioqueña en el occidente de Colombia.* 3d ed. Bogotá: Carlos Valencia Editores.

————. n.d. *Urabá, salida de Antioquia al mar.* Medellín: Corpourabá.

Partido Comunista de Colombia. n.d. *Treinta años de lucha del Partido Comunista de Colombia.* Bogotá: n.p.

Payne, Alexander. 1986. "Crecimiento y cambio social en Medellín, 1900–1930." *Estudios Sociales* 1 (1).

Payne, James L. 1968. *Patterns of Conflict in Colombia.* New Haven: Yale University Press.

Pécaut, Daniel. 1982. *Política y sindicalismo en Colombia.* 2d ed. Bogotá: Ediciones Culturales.

————. 1987. "Acerca de la Violencia de los años cincuenta." *Boletín Socioeconómico* 17.

————. 1987. *Orden y violencia: Colombia, 1930–1954.* 2 vols. Bogotá: Siglo Veintiuno Editores.

Pineda Giraldo, Roberto. 1960. *El impacto de la violencia en el tolima, el caso del Líbano.* Bogotá: Universidad Nacional de Colombia.

Pinzón, Martin Alonso. 1983. *Historia del conservatismo.* 2d ed. Bogotá: Tercer Mundo.

Posada, Francisco. 1969. *Colombia: Violencia y subdesarrollo.* Bogotá: n.p.

Ramsey, Russell W. 1973. "Critical Bibliography on La Violencia in Colombia." *Latin American Research Review* 8 (1): 3–44.

————. 1981. *Guerrilleros y soldados.* Bogotá: Editorial Tercer Mundo.

Reed, Nelson. 1964. *The Caste War of the Yucatan.* Stanford: Stanford University Press.

Restrepo Jaramillo, Gonzalo. 1936. *El pensamiento conservador.* Medellín: Tipografía Bedout.

Rippy, J. Fred. 1931. *The Capitalists and Colombia.* New York: n.p.

Rock, David, ed. 1994. *Latin America in the 1940s: War and Post-War Transitions.* Berkeley: University of California Press.

Rodríguez, Jaime O., ed. 1990. *The Revolutionary Process in Mexico: Essays on Political and Social Change, 1880–1940.* Los Angeles: Latin American Center, UCLA.

Roldán, Mary. 1988. "La política en Antioquia, 1946–1958." In *Historia de Antioquia.* Ed. Jorge Orlando Melo. Bogotá: Editorial Presencia.

————. 1989. "Guerrillas, contrachusmas y caudillos: La Violencia en Antioquia, 1946–1953." *Estudios Sociales* 4 (March): 55–85.

————. 1992. "Genesis and Evolution of La Violencia in Antioquia, Colombia, 1900–1953." Ph.D. diss. Harvard University.

————. 1998. "Violencia, colonización y la geografía de la diferencia en Colombia." *Análisis Político* 35 (Sept.–Dec.): 3–25.

Romero Aguirre, Alfonso. 1944. *El partido conservador ante la historia.* Bogotá: Librería America.

Romero, Mauricio. 1990. "Tierra y violencia en Córdoba." *Revista Análisis* 4: 17–21.

———. 1994. *Rural Transformation and Political Violence in Colombia, 1953–1990: A Comparative Study of Intra-Regional Change in a Non-Exporting Zone.* Center for Studies in Social Change, New School for Social Research, Working Paper no. 183.

Ruddick, Sara. 1993. "Toward a Feminist Peace Politics." In *Gendering War Talk.* Ed. Miriam Cooke and Angela Woollacott. Princeton: Princeton University Press.

Saénz Rovner, Eduardo. 1992. *La ofensiva empresarial: Industriales, políticos y violencia en los años cuarenta en Colombia.* Bogotá: Tercer Mundo.

Safford, Frank. 1965. "Significación de los antiqueños en el desarrollo económico colombiano: Un examen crítico de la tesis de Everett Hagen." *Anuario Colombiano de Historia Social y de la Cultura,* pp. 49–69.

———. 1976. *The Ideal of the Practical: Colombia's Struggle to Form a Technical Elite.* Austin: University of Texas Press.

———. 1991. "Race, Integration and Progress: Elite Attitudes and the Indian in Colombia, 1750–1870." *Hispanic American Historical Review* 71 (1): 1–33.

Sahlins, Peter. 1989. *Boundaries: The Making of France and Spain in the Pyrenees.* Berkeley: University of California Press.

Salazar, Alonso. 1992. *Born to Die in Medellín.* London: Verso.

Sánchez, Gonzalo. 1976. *Los "Bolsheviques del Líbano" (Tolima).* Bogotá: n.p.

———. 1976. "La Violencia y sus efectos en el sistema político colombiano." *Cuadernos Colombianos* 9 (Jan.–April): 1–44.

———. 1977. *Las ligas campesinas en Colombia.* Bogotá: Editorial Tiempo Presente.

———. 1983. *Los días de la revolucíon: Gaitanismo y 9 de abril en provincia.* Bogotá: Centro Gaitán.

———. 1985. "La Violencia in Colombia: New Research, New Questions." *Hispanic American Historical Review* 65 (4): 789–807.

———. 1986. "Los estudios sobre la Violencia: Balance y perspectivas." In *Pasado y presente de la Violencia en Colombia.* Ed. Gonzalo Sánchez and Ricardo Peñaranda. Bogotá: Fondo Editorial CEREC.

Sánchez, Gonzalo, and Donny Meertens. 1983. *Bandoleros, gamonales y campesinos: El caso de la Violencia en Colombia.* Bogotá: El Ancora.

Sanín Echeverri, Jaime. 1978. *Ospina supo esperar.* Medellín: Editorial Andes.

Sarmiento, Domingo. 1998. *Facundo, or, Civilization and Barbarism.* New York: Penguin.

Scarry, Elaine. 1985. *The Body in Pain: The Making and Unmaking of the World.* New York: Oxford University Press.

Schirmer, Jennifer. 1998. *The Guatemalan Military Project: A Violence Called Democracy.* Philadelphia: University of Pennsylvania Press.

Schmidt, Steffen W. 1974–1975. "La Violencia Revisited: The Clientelist Bases of Political Violence in Colombia." *Journal of Latin American Studies* 6–7 (May): 97–111.

————. 1977. "The Transformation of Clientelism in Rural Colombia." In *Friends, Followers, and Factions.* Ed. Steffen W. Schmidt et al. Berkeley: University of California Press.

Scott, James C. 1990. *Domination and the Art of Resistance: Hidden Transcripts.* New Haven: Yale University Press.

Sharpless, Richard E. 1978. *Gaitán of Colombia: A Political Biography.* Pittsburgh: University of Pittsburgh Press.

Silva, Renán. ed. 1994. *Territorios, Regiones, Sociedades.* Bogotá: CEREC.

Slatta, Richard W. 1983. *Gauchos and the Vanishing Frontier.* Lincoln: University of Nebraska Press.

————. 1987. *Bandidos: The Varieties of Latin American Banditry.* New York: Greenwood Press.

Socarras, José Francisco. 1942. *Laureano Gómez: Psicoanalisis de un resentido.* Bogotá: Ediciones Librería Siglo XX.

Sommer, Doris. 1991. *Foundational Fictions: The National Romances of Latin America.* Berkeley: University of California Press.

Stallybrass, Peter, and Allon White. 1986. *The Politics and Poetics of Transgression.* Ithaca: Cornell University Press.

Starn, Orin, Carlos Iván DeGregori, and Robin Kirk. 1995. *The Peru Reader: History, Culture, Politics.* Durham, N.C.: Duke University Press.

Stern, Steve J., ed. 1998. *Shining and Other Paths: War and Society in Peru, 1980–1995.* Durham, N.C.: Duke University Press.

Stoler, Ann Laura. 1989. "Making Empire Respectable: The Politics of Race and Sexual Morality in Twentieth-Century Colonial Cultures." *American Ethnologist* 16: 634–60.

————. 1992. "Sexual Affronts and Racial Frontiers: European Identities and the Cultural Politics of Exclusion in Colonial Southeast Asia." *Comparative Studies in Society and History* 34 (3): 514–51.

Stoler, Richard. 1995. "Alfonso López Pumarejo and Liberal Radicalism in 1930s Colombia." *Journal of Latin American Studies* 27 (2): 367–97.

Taussig, Michael. 1989. "Terror as Usual: Walter Benjamin's Theory of History as a State of Siege." *Social Text* 23 (fall/winter): 3–20.

Taylor, William. 1979. *Drinking, Homicide, and Resistance in Colonial Mexican Villages.* Stanford: Stanford University Press.

Thomas, Nicholas. 1994. *Colonialism's Culture, Anthropology, Travel, and Government.* Princeton: Princeton University Press.

Tirado Mejía, Alvaro. 1976. *Aspectos sociales de las guerras civiles en Colombia.* Instituto Colombiano de la Cultura. Bogotá: Editorial Andes.

————. 1981. *Aspectos políticos del primer gobierno de Alfonso López Pumarejo, 1934–1938.* Instituto Colombiano de la Cultura. Bogotá: Gráfica Cabrera e Hijos.

————. 1983. *Descentralización y centralismo en Colombia.* Bogotá: Editorial

Oveja Negra Serie Monográfica de Ciencias Sociales y Política de la Fundación Friedrich Naumann.

Torres Giraldo, Ignacio. 1967. *La huelga general en Medellín.* Medellín: Editores Bedout.

———. n.d. *Los inconformes.* Bogotá: Cooperativa Editores.

Tovar Pinzón, Hermes. 1975. *El movimiento campesino en Colombia durante los siglos xix y xx.* Bogotá: n.p.

Uribe Angel, Manuel. 1886. *Geografía general del estado de Antioquia.* Paris: n.p.

Uribe de H., Maria Teresa. 1992. *Urabá, Región o Territorio? Un análisis en el contexto de la política, la historia y la etnicidad.* Medellín: n.p.

Uribe de Hincapié, María Teresa, and Jesús María Alvarez. 1987. *Poderes y regiones: Problemas en la constitución de la nación colombiana, 1810–1850.* Medellín: Centro de Investigaciones de las Ciencias Sociales, Universidad de Antioquia.

Uribe, Maria Victoria. 1990. *Matar, rematar y contramatar: Las masacres de la Violencia en el Tolima, 1948–1964.* Bogotá: CINEP.

Urrutia, Miguel. 1969. *The Development of the Colombian Labor Movement.* New Haven: Yale University Press.

———. 1978. *Historia del sindicalismo en Colombia.* 3d ed. Medellín: Editorial Lealon.

Vanderwood, Paul J. 1992. *Disorder and Progress: Bandits, Police, and Mexican Development.* Wilmington, Del.: Scholarly Resources Books.

Vargas Velásquez, Alejo. 1992. *Colonización y Conflicto Armado.* Bogotá: CINEP.

Varones ilustres de Antioquia: Biografías de los academicos de números fallecidos. 1978. Medellín: Editorial Universo.

Vega Cantor, Renan. 1988. *Crisis y caída de la República Liberal, 1942–1946.* Bogotá: Editorial Mohan.

Wade, Peter. 1985. "Race and Class: The Case of South American Blacks." *Ethnic and Racial Studies* 8 (2): 233–49.

———. 1993. *Blackness and Race Mixture: The Dynamics of Racial Identity in Colombia.* Baltimore: Johns Hopkins University Press.

Waller, Altina L. 1988. *Feud: Hatfields, McCoys, and Social Change in Appalachia, 1860–1900.* Chapel Hill: University of North Carolina Press.

Walton, John. 1984. *Reluctant Rebels: Comparative Studies of Revolution and Underdevelopment.* New York: Columbia University Press.

Weinert, Richard. 1966. "Violence in Pre-Modern Societies: Rural Colombia." *American Political Science Review* 60 (June): 340–47.

West, Robert C. 1957. *The Pacific Lowlands of Colombia: A Negroid Area in the American Tropics.* Baton Rouge: Louisiana State University Press.

Wickham-Crowley, Timothy P. 1992. *Guerrillas and Revolution in Latin America: A Comparative Study of Insurgents and Regimes since 1956.* Princeton: Princeton University Press.

Williams, Raymond. 1976. *Keywords: A Vocabulary of Culture and Society.*
   Oxford: Oxford University Press.

Williamson, Robert. 1965. "Toward a Theory of Political Violence: The Case of
   Rural Colombia." *Western Political Quarterly* 18 (March).

Womack, John Jr. 1968. *Zapata and the Mexican Revolution.* New York: Vintage.

————, ed. 1999. *Rebellion in Chiapas: A Historical Reader.* New York: New
   Press.

Zambrano Pantója, Fabio. 1998. *Colombia, País de Regiones.* Bogotá: CINEP,
   Colciencias.

Zamosc, Leon. 1986. *The Agrarian Question and the Peasant Movement in Colombia, 1967–81.* New York: Cambridge University Press.

Zapata Restrepo, Miguel. 1973. *La mitra azul, Miguel Angel Builes: el hombre, el
   obispo, el caudillo.* Medellín: Editorial Beta.

————. 1978. *El obispo tropezó 3 veces.* Medellín: Editorial Bedout.

Index

Mary Roldán is Associate Professor of Latin
American History at Cornell University.

Library of Congress Cataloging-in-Publication Data
Roldán, Mary
Blood and fire : *La Violencia* in Antioquia,
Colombia, 1946–1953 / Mary Roldán.
p. cm.   Includes bibliographical references and index.
ISBN 0-8223-2903-4 (cloth : alk. paper)
ISBN 0-8223-2918-2 (pbk. : alk. paper)
1. Violence—Colombia—Antioquia (Dept.)
2. Colombia—Politics and government—1946–1974.
3. Political violence—Colombia—Antioquia
(Dept.)—History.   I. Title.
HN310.A5 R64 2000   986.1′260632—dc21   2001007184